Pathways to Democracy:

The Political Economy of Democratic Transitions

James F. Hollifield and Calvin Jillson, Editors

Routledge • New York • London

Published in 2000 by
Routledge
29 West 35th Street
New York, NY 10001

Published in Great Britain by
Routledge
11 New Fetter Lane
London EC4P 4EE

10 9 8 7 6 5 4 3 2 1

Library of Congress Cataloging-in-Publication Data

Hollifield, James Frank, 1954-
    Pathways to democracy : the political economy of democratic transitions / James F. Hollifield and Calvin Jillson, editors.
        p. cm.
    Includes bibliographical references and index.
    ISBN 0-415-92433-2 (hb.) - ISBN 0-415-92434-0 (pb.)
    1. Democracy. 2. Democratization. I. Jillson, Calvin C., 1949- II Title

JC421 .H65 1999
320.9049-dc21

99-035009

Contents

Preface   *vii*

PART I

Introduction: The Democratic Transformations—Lessons
and Prospects   *3*

PART II The Political Economy of Democratic Transitions

1. Democracy and Its Enemies
   Lucian W. Pye   21

2. On Markets and Democracy
   William Glade   37

3. Transitions to What? The Social Foundations of the
   Democratic Citizenship
   Stephen Macedo   53

PART III The End of Authoritarianism in South and Central America

4. Transition Pathways: Institutional Legacies, the Military,
   and Democracy in South America
   Felipe Agüero   73

5. The Transformation of Labor-Based One-Partyism at the End
   of the Twentieth Century: The Case of Mexico
   Ruth Berins Collier   93

6. External Actors in the Transitions to Democracy in Latin America
   Arturo Valenzuela   116

PART IV The Successes and Failures of the Developmental State in Asia

7. Democracy and Civil Society in Korea
   Bruce Cumings   133

8. From Confrontation to Conciliation: The Philippine Path toward Democratic Consolidation
   Gretchen Casper   *147*

9. Modernization, Democracy, and the Developmental State in Asia: A Virtuous Cycle or Unraveling Strands?
   Cal Clark   *160*

10. Democratic Inauguration and Transition in East Asia
    Steve Chan   *178*

PART V The Challenge of Consolidation in Russia and Eastern Europe

11. Regime Transition and Democratic Consolidation: Federalism and Party Development in Russia
    Thomas F. Remington   *195*

12. The Longest Transition
    Joseph S. Berliner   *213*

13. International Influences on Democratization in Postcommunist Europe
    J. C. Sharman and Roger E. Kanet   *226*

PART VI The Colonial Legacy and Sponsored Transitions in Africa

14. Understanding Ambiguity during Democratization in Africa
    Jeffrey Herbst   *245*

15. A Virtuous Circle? Democratization and Economic Reform in Africa
    Peter M. Lewis   *259*

PART VII Conclusion

16. Democratization, International Relations, and U.S. Foreign Policy
    Ben Hunt   *275*

About the Contributors   *290*
Notes   *294*
Bibliography   *301*
Index   *322*

Preface

MARIAN TOWER AND her father, former senator John Goodwin Tower (R—TX), were killed in a plane crash near New Brunswick, Georgia, on April 5, 1991. In the wake of that tragedy, Senator Tower's friends and family established the John G. Tower Center for Political Studies at Southern Methodist University (SMU) in Dallas, Texas. Senator Tower's two remaining daughters and their families, Mr. and Mrs. Berry Cox and Dr. and Mrs. David Cook, established the Marian Tower International Conference Series within the Tower Center.

The first Marian Tower International Conference was held at SMU on April 4 and 5, 1997. The title of the conference and of this volume, *Pathways to Democracy: The Political Economy of Democratic Transitions*, invites attention to the fact that within the worldwide shift toward democratic politics and free markets that occurred after 1979, different countries and regions of the world followed different paths from authoritarianism to some sort of more open or democratic society. Some began from military dictatorship, some from communism, and some from other types of authoritarian regimes. Most seem to have ended up with a more-or-less secure hold on democracy.

The question that motivates this volume is: What effect do both the starting point and the path taken from authoritarianism to democracy have on the character, shape, and feel of the democracy that results? Leading scholars and practitioners draw on their expertise and experience to address these questions in regard to Latin America, Africa, Asia, Eastern Europe, and Russia. What results is a fascinating study of the political, economic, and foreign policy opportunities and difficulties that confront nations attempting the difficult transition from authoritarianism to democracy.

A great many people contributed to the creation of this volume. We would like to thank the Board of Directors of the John G. Tower Center for Political Studies for their generous support of the Center faculty's scholarly activities. We would also like to thank the contributors to this volume for their cheerful and timely responses to our request. The staff of the Tower Center, the Political Science Department, and the International Studies program, especially Noëlle McAlpine and Jane Sterling, were tireless in their preparation for and conduct of the conference and the manuscript preparation that followed. The professional staff of Routledge, directed by Acquisitions Editor Amy Shipper, were a pleasure to work with and have produced an excellent volume. Finally, we would like to thank several anonymous reviewers for their helpful comments and constructive criticism.

Part I

Introduction

Introduction:

The Democratic Transformations—Lessons

and Prospects

IN THE LATE twentieth century, people are freer to govern themselves and to seek their own economic interests than ever before. Communism has collapsed and authoritarian regimes are on the defensive. With the occasional glaring exceptions, the world is at peace—a liberal and democratic peace based not so much on the balance of power as upon the dual dynamic of markets and rights, supported by an interdependent system of liberal states and a variety of international organizations and institutions. Markets have expanded both domestically and internationally, stimulated by the revolution in information technologies and supported by a highly integrated system of international trade and finance. Exchange of goods, services, capital, people, and ideas has increased across the board, and the wealth of nations is more than ever tied to capital and to a complex international division of labor. Yet many worry that economic tribulations in Asia, Russia, and Latin America might weaken or even threaten these nascent democracies.

As we approach the end of the millennium, trends in world politics and economics give us cause for optimism and concern. While the latter half of the twentieth century has surely been characterized by impressive gains for democratic politics and free markets around the world, these gains are insecure. To get beyond broad generalizations about the triumph of markets and democracy (here defined as the ability of people to choose or change their government)[1] and the end of history, we have set two objectives for this book. First we seek to describe and compare the pathways to democracy taken in different regions of the world (Latin America, Asia, East Central Europe, and

Africa). Among the questions we ask within this comparative framework are: How did the transitions to democracy begin? What were the necessary pre-conditions? And to what extent were the transitions influenced by domestic or international forces? Our second objective is to look generally at what can be done to stabilize and consolidate the new democracies, and more specifically at what established democracies and the international community can do actively to promote and invest in democratization.[2]

Even though recent transitions to democracy have had a profound impact on world politics, this is not the first democratic transformation, and hopefully it will not be the last. In some sense, the recent transitions are but the latest chapter in the history of the Enlightenment; and we can see many of the themes of the eighteenth and nineteenth centuries (rationalism, liberalism, and humanitarianism) repeating themselves. To discover what is different about the most recent democratic transformation, we must look back at earlier episodes of democratization with an eye to understanding how our thinking about political and economic development has changed. We must also compare and explore the pathways to democracy taken by the newly democratic states.

We assume that the latest democratic transformation, like earlier ones, has its origins primarily in politics (changing relations of authority) and economics (changing relations of exchange). The common features of this transformation emerge clearly from the case studies in this volume. They are (1) a renewed emphasis on the rights of individuals, which find their most basic expression in free and fair elections; (2) free markets, which require competition, the rule of law, and a free flow of information; and (3) the resurgence of civil society (a dynamic realm of associations and groups that are autonomous from the state) in various parts of the globe.[3] But if we look back in time, we see two failures of modernization in the 1930s and 1960s, which led to the breakdown of democracies. Here we review the first two waves of democratization to glean some lessons from earlier failures of modernization and to gain a better understanding of the current transformation.

Modernization and the First End of History

The end of the nineteenth century saw the completion of a dual revolution in politics and economics. The liberal ideals of popular government and self-regulating markets had taken root in Europe and America, spurred on by the forces of political revolution in America (1776) and France (1789), and by the Industrial Revolution, which began in England and spread rapidly around the globe.[4] The Jacksonian reforms of the 1820s and 1830s in the United States, together with the Reform Acts of 1832 and 1867 in England, vastly increased suffrage for men. The triumph of the North in the American Civil War

(1865) put an end to slavery in the American South, and with it, a whole social and economic system based on exploitation and human bondage collapsed. In Britain, the power of landed elites and the crown was further reduced by the Parliament Act of 1911, which drastically reduced the power of the House of Lords. The vindication of Captain Dreyfus in Third Republic France (1906) marked an important turning point in the consolidation of liberal and republican principles of government, such as the rule of law, due process, and equal protection. A little over two decades later, women were enfranchised in the United States (1920) and in Britain (1928).

Also by the end of the nineteenth century, capitalism appeared triumphant in Europe, North America, and (thanks to the Meiji reforms that began in 1868) Japan. The Industrial Revolution transformed the old feudal and agricultural societies of Western Europe. Per capita income soared, and factories and towns sprang up virtually overnight. Scientific and technological change unleashed forces of invention and production on a scale unseen before in human history. Prometheus was truly unbound,[5] and the predictions of Parson Malthus a century earlier (1798) that poverty and starvation were unavoidable—because the means of subsistence could never keep pace with population increases—seemed almost laughable. The Scottish political economist, Adam Smith, who advanced the theory of the self-regulating market and gave us in *The Wealth of Nations* (1776) the doctrine of laissez-faire, seemed a much better philosopher for *la belle époque* and the age of capital.

What Samuel Huntington has called the first wave of democracy,[6] which lasted roughly from the 1820s to 1914, established a close historical correlation between economic and political development. The West European experience spawned the modernization theory of development. In this perspective, economic development will lead to an increasingly complex, that is modern, division of labor, including a separation of the public from the private sphere and of the church from the state, rising levels of income and education, and a new democratic or civic culture with rule of law and the requisite institutions of popular government, especially political parties that compete for votes in fair and open elections.[7]

Just as the Prussian philosopher G. W. F. Hegel, saw the end of history in the modern state, as it was developing in Prussia and the Europe of his day (1770–1831), so the American political theorist Francis Fukuyama has discerned a new end of history in the triumph of liberal and capitalist democracy over communism and authoritarianism at the end of the twentieth century.[8] But the "great transformation" of the nineteenth century, which brought with it radical individualism and new forms of alienation, also provoked what Karl Polanyi called a "self-protective reaction" from society, leading to new forms of regulation and collectivism, which would find their fullest expression in nationalism and socialism.[9] One of the principal lessons of the first experience of modernization is that the progress of democracy and markets is not smooth, and there is always a risk of nationalist and xenophobic reactions when the economy goes bad. Recent events in Russia and Asia remind us that progress is more commonly the ungainly advance of two steps forward, one back, rather than a steady upward ascent.

Nationalism and the First Failure of Modernization

In the early 1900s, a powerful critique of liberalism and modernization had coalesced around the works of Karl Marx, specifically *Das Kapital* (1867), in which he advanced the theory of dialectical materialism. Like the English liberals—John Locke, Adam Smith, and John Stuart Mill—Marx was heavily influenced by Enlightenment thought. Marx also perceived an end to history. But unlike the liberals, who saw history proceeding in a more-or-less linear fashion, he believed that history advanced dialectically, driven by technological and economic change. Rather than ever-increasing wealth, a peaceful and cooperative civil society, and political democracy, he predicted that economic modernization would lead to class struggle, pitting workers against the owners of capital, leading to greater poverty, conflict, the breakdown of civil society, revolution, and eventually the emergence of a classless, communist society.

The Russian philosopher and revolutionary V. I. Lenin later (1916–1917) extended Marx's argument to include an analysis of the world economy and international system, especially imperialism, which Lenin saw as the highest stage of capitalism because of its ability to project a fundamentally European system of social and economic organization into the four corners of the globe, thereby solving some of the fundamental crises and contradictions of capitalism. Lenin argued that imperialism, by opening new markets and new outlets for productive investment, would provide only a temporary reprieve from revolution. In his view, it was just a matter of time before a strongly organized and disciplined communist party, backed by military force, would lead the working class in its worldwide struggle against capitalism.

But neither Marx nor the English liberals were able to foresee that nationalism would become the most powerful form of politics in the twentieth century. It was nationalism and the Great War (1914–1918), not class struggle, which put an end to the first wave of democratization and opened the way in 1917 for Lenin and the Bolshevik Party to seize power in Russia. World War I, the October Revolution, and the rise of fascism in Italy and Germany set the stage for a protracted struggle between what Barrington Moore called the three routes to modernity: (1) capitalist and parliamentary democracy, or the *liberal route*, growing out of the "bourgeois revolutions" in England, France, and the United States; (2) the capitalist and *fascist route*, accompanied by nationalist and militarist "revolutions from above," orchestrated initially by semifeudal elites in Germany and Japan; and (3) the *communist route*, having its "main but not exclusive origins among peasants" in Russia and China.[10] In this formulation, Moore amended the Marxist theory of class struggle to take account of twentieth-century realities: he kept the importance of the bourgeoisie as a force for the development of capitalist democracy, but added "lord and peasant" as equally powerful forces in shaping political outcomes, specifically dictatorship and democracy.

Moore's theory seems to account well for what happened in the first half of the twentieth century. In countries with a strong bourgeoisie or middle class (like England and the United States), capitalist democracy survived and flourished, with the obvious exception of the Great Depression; whereas in countries that were late to develop, where traditional elites maintained their grip on power and the middle class was politically and economically weak (like Germany and Japan), the outcome was militaristic nationalism and fascist dictatorship.[11] Finally, in predominantly peasant societies (like Russia and China), which experienced a forced march to modernization, politics evolved rapidly and brutally into communist dictatorships.

But Moore's theory of revolution and his typology of regime types have a number of obvious weaknesses that make them less useful for understanding what has happened in the second half of the twentieth century, especially during the second (1950s and 1960s) and third (1970s to 1990s) waves of democratization. Chief among these weaknesses, as Theda Skocpol has noted, are the failure to account for the importance of changing international contexts and the lack of serious attention given to the state (and institutions more generally) as an autonomous force for change.[12] To this list let us add two more: no attention is given to the importance of civil (or political) society as a force for continuity and change, and class-based or structural theories of social change have difficulty explaining the widely different patterns of legitimacy that emerge from specific historical and cultural circumstances in the non-Western world. The theories of Marx, Lenin, and Moore are profoundly Eurocentric.[13]

The Second Wave: Decolonization and the Second Failure of Modernization

The second wave of democratization began in the aftermath of World War II with decolonization and the extension of democratic forms of government into cultures and societies that, in most cases, had weak civil societies and no previous history of popular government or market economics. Nevertheless, it seemed that in 1945 the victors would win the war *and* the peace, avoiding the mistakes of 1919, having a chance to fulfill Woodrow Wilson's dream of making the world "safe for democracy," and with fewer illusions about what this would take in terms of self-sacrifice and a willingness to project American power.[14]

However, within a few short years after the end of World War II, the international system shifted from a multilateral system based on Great Power Politics—where each of the European powers competed for territory and markets in Africa, Asia, and the Americas—to a bipolar system, based on a nuclear balance of terror, with only two superpowers (the United States and the Soviet Union) competing for influence and dominance, each within its own sphere of influence.[15] During the Cold War, all regions of the globe, including Europe, became a field of competition between the superpowers, and many former colonies (would-be democracies) in Africa and Asia literally became battlefields.

In retrospect, the second wave of democratization had a much less auspicious beginning than the first. Democracies established in the eighteenth and nineteenth centuries had the benefit of the Enlightenment and two to three centuries of economic and social development. They had time, from a position of strength in the global economy, to find their democratic feet. By contrast, the newly democratizing states of Africa, Asia, and Latin America during the 1950s and 1960s were sucked into the maelstrom of the Cold War and caught in a situation of *"dependencia."*[16] The economic fate and the legitimacy of many developing states seemed to be in the hands of American or European powers (bankers, multinational corporations, and the like) or their proxies—the World Bank and the International Monetary Fund (IMF). These international institutions had been created after World War II to help stabilize the international political economy by providing loans for economic development (in the case of the World Bank) and liquidity for economic adjustment and balance of payments problems (in the case of the IMF). By the same token, the Soviet Union had its client states in East Central Europe, Asia, Africa, and the Americas. These states, especially in Central Europe, would become totally dependent on the USSR for their political and economic survival.

In many developing states, democracy quickly became a sham, as corrupt rulers siphoned wealth—including loans from the World Bank and the IMF—out of their countries and into unnumbered, offshore bank accounts. The economies of developing states deteriorated and collapsed, usually accompanied by balance of payments crises and hyperinflation. More often than not, the military (re)asserted itself as the only semilegitimate force for order in these changing societies.[17] The watchwords of political development and underdevelopment during the 1960s and 1970s were *dependencia*, the breakdown of democracy, and a new authoritarianism. Marxist and structural analysis was suddenly back in fashion, as scholars sought an explanation for the widespread failure of democracy.[18]

For the second time in this century—the first being the collapse of Weimar and the descent of much of Western Europe into fascism, militarism, and totalitarianism—modernization theory was seen as a failure. Dependency and world systems theory—which stressed the inherently unequal relations of exchange between the core capitalist states of Western Europe and North America, on the one hand, and the underdeveloped, largely agrarian societies of the Latin American, African, and Asian periphery, on the other—seemed to offer a more powerful explanation of social, economic, and political development in the late twentieth century.[19] Lest we forget, the situation of Soviet client states was equally precarious, and—as the revolutions of 1989 and 1990 in Eastern Europe would demonstrate—the legitimacy of these states rested almost entirely on Soviet military power. Democracy there was prohibited.

While democracy was secure in much of Western Europe, the United States, and the former British Dominions of Canada, Australia, and New Zealand, many analysts assumed that it would have a difficult time expanding elsewhere. Modernization theorists attributed these failures to low levels of economic development, a weak middle class, high levels of illiteracy, the lack of social pluralism, and the absence of market-based economies; whereas dependency theorists stressed that less developed countries (LDCs) needed to prepare themselves for the leap to democracy through an extended period of state-led industrial development focusing on import substitution.[20]

Because of the oil shocks of the 1970s and the worldwide recessions that followed, many LDCs became heavily indebted, leading some, like Mexico (in 1982), to default on their loans. The debt crisis forced the majority of states in Latin America and Africa to turn to the IMF—the international lender of last resort—which imposed stringent conditions (devaluation and fiscal restrictions) on the granting of these loans. All in all, the situation in the developing world was so bleak that dependency theorists seemed to have been vindicated. The great lesson in the second wave was that economic stringency and mismanagement starve new democracies.

But, somewhat unexpectedly, a new series of democratic transitions began, first in Southern Europe in the 1970s, then in Latin America and South Africa in the 1980s, and finally in East Central Europe and the former Soviet Union in the late 1980s and early 1990s. With respect to the third wave, we ask the following questions: (1) How did the transition in a particular region/country begin? (2) Were these transitions influenced primarily by domestic or international factors? (3) What can be done to consolidate and invest in the new democracies? (4) What role can established democracies and the international community play in the democratization process? For each region (Latin America, Asia, Africa, and Eastern Europe), we have chapters by three types of scholars: an area specialist, a political economist, and a foreign policy analyst. This gives us three distinct perspectives from which to view the problems of democratization. But before we turn to the regional/country studies, let us look briefly at the "pathways to democracy" in the third wave, especially the thorny issue of consolidation.

The Third Wave: The Integrating Effects of an International Political Economy

One way to understand the process of democratization in the third wave is to look at the pathways to democracy taken by societies in different regions of the globe. We can conceive of three pathways, each of which conforms to a rather classical (liberal-democratic) model of political development. In the third wave of democratization, the *first* path to more open regimes began from rule by the military, especially in Southern Europe (for example, Greece, Spain, and Portugal) and Latin America (for example, Brazil, Argentina, and Chile). The *second* set of transitions grew out of authoritarian regimes ruled by a single dominant party, as was the case in Asia (for example, Taiwan and the Philippines) and South Africa. The *third* and final set of transitions began in regimes dominated by a communist oligarchy, as in East Central Europe and the former Soviet Union.

In each case the starting point (authoritarianism) is the same. These were regimes—many with long histories—which had solved the basic Hobbesian problem of political order and in some cases had established at least rudimentary forms of civil society, with traditional institutions such as the family, the clan, the tribe, or the church playing a role in providing order.[21] The crucial first step from authoritarianism (the initial Hobbesian contract revolving around political order) to representative government (the Lockean contract revolving around trust and liberty) is a central concern of this book. What factors determine the speed and ease with which societies make this transition? And what are the next steps in the process of consolidation of democracy?

These are exceedingly difficult questions to answer, but three factors seem to stand out. First is the strength of civil society at the moment of transition, because not only must a society be strong enough to weather the transition without a complete breakdown of political order, it must also be capable of providing alternative sources of rule and leadership. The second factor that heavily influences the speed and ease of the transition is the economic performance of the new regime; economic reform provides a way for new democratic regimes to rebuild and reinforce civil society. The third factor that seems to determine whether or not a society can move to the final phase of consolidation and the establishment of political democracy is the emergence of a civic culture based on rule of law and competitive elections.

If democracies are to have a chance to consolidate themselves, society must develop apart from the state. A rich associational life will foster pluralism, and assuming that groups and individuals are predisposed to democratic forms of politics and have the basic values and cultural orientations necessary to sustain democracy, then the regime will have a fighting chance to consolidate itself and establish its legitimacy.[22]

Looking at the third wave, two things are clear and should be kept in mind in reading the country studies in this volume. The latest transitions to democracy have occurred with dizzying speed, giving the societies involved little time to prepare for the leap to representative government, much less the nurturing of a civic culture. Whereas democracies in Western Europe, the United States, and the former British Dominions had a gestation period of one or two centuries, in the third wave, democratization has come virtually overnight. This has led to a great deal of improvisation and many setbacks. The second major difference between the first and the third wave of democratization is the heightened importance of international or external factors in spurring regime change. Although it is something of a truism, globalization of economies has placed enormous pressures and constraints on almost every society. Few countries can escape the reach of international trade, finance, and migration, and autarky seems no longer to be an option for states in the international system. All the authors in this volume are attentive to the importance of external or international factors in the transitions to democracy.

If societies are able to overcome the three most fundamental problems of development—(1) establishing order and creating civil society, (2) organizing production and promoting the growth of free markets, and (3) building and nurturing a civic culture—they have a good chance of consolidating democratic gains. Consolidation entails a reduction of venality and corruption, the building of a public bureaucracy (with a sense of public service), extension of the franchise, the development of political parties and a party system (replete with crosscutting cleavages),[23] and some degree of decentralization of political power. Not surprisingly, democratic theorists now concern themselves less with the prerequisites to democracy and the difficulty of achieving them than they do with how to stabilize and consolidate new democracies.[24] However, economists and political scientists often differ in their recommendations on how best to consolidate the new democracies. Many economists wish to move aggressively to market solutions, while political scientists and sociologists often warn of the negative social and political consequences that rapid reforms are likely to produce.[25] This debate has been given new energy by the clear threat that economic decline has posed to democratic stability in Russia, Asia, and beyond

Structure and Summary of the Book

The book is divided into seven parts: (I) this introduction, which serves as a historical and theoretical overview; sections on (II) the political economy of democratic transitions, (III) the end of authoritarianism in South and Central America, (IV) the successes and failures of the developmental state in Asia, (V) the challenge of consolidation in Russia and Eastern Europe, and (VI) the colonial legacy and sponsored transitions in Africa; and (VII) a concluding chapter on foreign policy and the relationship between democratization and international relations.

The three chapters in Part II explore the political, economic, and social underpinnings of democratization and market liberalization. Each of the authors notes that the broader society must provide structural (pluralism) and intellectual (civic culture, political ideology, public opinion) supports for democratic politics and open markets. Neither democratic politics nor free markets can work in the absence of social pluralism, the rule of law, and elite and mass opinion that supports openness, competition, and respect for the rights of individuals.

Lucian Pye, in a chapter entitled "Democracy and Its Enemies," argues that modern democracies rest most securely on pluralist societies in which both elites and masses accept universal suffrage and respect for individual rights. Pye argues that the best checklist of the institutional requisites to democratic politics is provided by Robert Dahl, and includes free speech, association, and assembly, universal suffrage, free and fair elections, competing parties and sources of information, and government policies that reflect electoral outcomes. These institutional routines and guarantees create space for the growth and maturation of more fully developed civil societies.

William Glade, in a chapter entitled "On Markets and Democracy," challenges the widespread assumption that political and economic pluralism—that is, democratization and open markets—are interrelated foundations for social development. In fact, he argues that through most of the 1950s, 1960s, and 1970s state-managed development was common in Asia, Latin America, the communist world, and even the nations of Northern Europe. Some argued, particularly in regard to Asia and Latin America, that economic restructuring should be secured before democratization. The 1980s and 1990s present a somewhat different case. While political and economic liberalization appear simultaneously in many parts of the world, Glade still finds a causal connection difficult to show.

Stephen Macedo, in a chapter entitled "Transitions to What? The Social Foundations of the Democratic Citizenship," argues that meaningful democracy depends as much, perhaps even more, on the nature and shape of civil society than on formal rules and institutions. New democracies and their international sponsors must seek to foster a democratic way of life, a broad social ideal of inclusion, participation, equity, and fairness that can cushion and support the practice and performance of democratic politics and free markets. New democracies face the complicated task of delivering effective government and economic growth while allowing and even fostering a broad array of individual freedoms.

Pye, Glade, and Macedo agree that democracy stands the best chance to thrive and grow in a society that enjoys social differentiation or pluralism, universal suffrage and respect for individual rights, and economic growth. They also note, however, that these desirable circumstances almost never exist in regions of the world where new democracies are struggling to be born. In regions and nations where circumstances are mixed, even if not wholly unfavorable, prospects for political and economic reform must be uncertain.

Part III explores the transition from authoritarian to democratic regimes in Latin America. Felipe Agüero asks how important the transition regime is, particularly as it defines the way the military will be treated by the future democratic regime, to the quality and character of that regime. Ruth Collier asks what effect the presence of a dominant labor-based party, the PRI, had on the development of democratic institutions and processes in Mexico. Arturo Valenzuela asks what effect external actors such as international financial institutions, regional security groups, and regional and global superpowers such as the United States have had and can have on the emergence and consolidation of democracy in Latin America.

Agüero explores the transition legacies of military regimes in Latin America. What military prerogatives remained after the transition, and how did these influence the nature of the new democracy and its consolidation? He concludes that "transitions produce outcomes which are landmarks in setting the context, the opportunities, and constraints for subsequent democratic processes." Military regimes that begin the transition to democracy from positions of strength generally maintain the prerogatives that they set aside for themselves. Regimes that begin from a position of weakness are forced to bargain and compromise with their opponents and generally see their prerogatives fade once they are out of power and the democratic regime is in place.

Ruth Collier studies the case of regime change in Mexico. Looking at structure and agency, she demonstrates how the labor-based, one-party political system struggled to cope with the effects of external economic crises. She breaks the Mexican story into "three rounds" of change and three actors. The first round is provoked by the debt crisis of 1982, which leads the major players to seek a change in the dominant-party regime in order to break up the state-labor coalition and take economic policy out of the hands of populist politicians. The second round begins with the elections of 1988 and the Salinas project for restructuring the Mexican economy along neoliberal lines. In this round, the PRI loses its populist labor base, setting the stage for round three, in which the Zedillo government must cope with the effects of liberalization of the economy. The upshot, according to Collier, is that labor-based, one-party regimes like Mexico will be forced to seek a new basis for their legitimacy, with wholly new patterns of conflict and cooperation, a more competitive party system, and a breakup of state-labor alliances.

Arturo Valenzuela explores the relative weight of domestic and international factors, especially the role of the United States, in the recent wave of democratizations in Latin America. He concludes that while the US inhibited democracy in earlier periods, it played a relatively minor role in the transitions to democracy in the 1980s and 1990s. Valenzuela contends that most transitions to democracy result from choices made by local elites in the face of inconclusive or stalemated struggles for control and advantage. Countries with some historical experience with elections and legislative assemblies have an easier time stabilizing and consolidating democracy.

In Part IV, we learn that Asian nations have not followed the classic development model. The "virtuous cycle" of the development model, in which economic progress leads to political reform, which encourages social change and a politics of ever-broader inclusion, is rarely evident. Rather, both Cal Clark and Steve Chan describe developmental patterns that consciously sought economic development before, and in Singapore and China even in lieu of, political reform. Does this argue for a distinctive Asian model of political and economic development? Clark and Chan are inclined to say yes. Bruce Cumings, on the other hand, sees a civil society in South Korea that is much more vibrantly democratic than its state, and Gretchen Casper describes in the Philippines a rare case of an authoritarian government being overthrown and replaced by an increasingly successful democracy.

Cal Clark notes that Asia has been offered as the prime example of Francis Fukuyama's "end of history" argument—that democratic capitalism distinctively produces economic plenty, political freedom, and social change generated by industrialization and modernization. Yet Clark notes, on the economic side, Asian states are predominantly developmental states in which state bureaucracy rather than the free market guides investment and allocation decisions, while, on the political side, Asian values place a higher priority on order and the collective good than on liberty, individual choice, and competition. Clark concludes that, while much progress has been made, most states in Asia cannot be considered stable or consolidated democracies.

Bruce Cumings looks closely at the depth and audacity of the South Korean transition from authoritarianism to democracy, and compares it quite favorably, in terms of breadth and depth, with the United States and other Western democracies. He notes the exuberant political dialogue, high turnout rates, and vibrant civil society in South Korea. Cumings points particularly to the active and constructive role of student and worker protest in moving the Korean democracy forward and protecting it once in place.

Gretchen Casper notes that most authoritarian regimes are overthrown and replaced by other authoritarians or negotiate their exit while they still have enough leverage to strike a deal. Casper argues that the transition from Marcos to Aquino in the Philippines was a rare case of an authoritarian regime being overthrown and replaced by a democracy when "people power" held back a military junta ready to take power. While the stability of the new democratic regime was threatened repeatedly during its first decade, "the Philippines has been moving slowly from confrontation to conciliation, and from restoration toward reform."

Chan explores the origins of democracy in East Asia and the role played by outside forces, especially the United States, in its establishment and consolidation. Chan notes that Asian culture places a higher value on group conformity and collective well-being, as well as expecting that the government should serve as the custodian of the public interest, than is the case in the West. These attitudes and values shape the nature and performance of democracy in Asia. They suggest, for example, that "order and growth should precede participation and distribution," and, not surprisingly, they have. They also shape the extent to which outsiders, including the United States, can affect political and economic choices and developments in the region. Chan raises the disturbing prospect that, while established democracies seldom go to war against each other, new democracies face domestic and international uncertainties that make them unstable and unpredictable.

Part V looks at the challenge of consolidation in East Central Europe. The formerly communist world is undergoing the double disruption of simultaneous transformations in both the political and economic realms. Such a prospect was definitely not envisioned when Mikhail Gorbachev was selected to lead the Soviet Union in 1985. The political transition is hard enough, but the difficulty of creating a market economy—with the pricing structures, property and financial regimes, and so much more—where none previously existed is massive.

Joseph Berliner concludes that what Russia and the other transition states most need from the international community, and from the United States in particular, is private investment and the access to human capital and expertise that comes with it. Private investment gives westerners a powerful incentive to deliver to their Russian and East European partners the expertise and experience to deal effectively in national and international markets with which they have previously had little experience.

Thomas Remington argues that two elements of the Russian political and constitutional structure are critical to the consolidation of democracy there. One is the development of "a working competitive system of political parties," and the other is "a healthy balance of central, regional, and local political power." What makes the democratic transition in Russia particularly doubt-ful is that the preceding communist regime so thoroughly demolished the group structure of the society, which was not very strong to begin with. Currently, parties are highly fragmented and voter identification with them is low and weak. Federalism, wherein real political power is delegated to subna-tional units, is wholly new to Russia. Whether federalism will develop into a working distribution of authority in Russia and the party system will bind the levels of the system together remain to be seen.

Given the dramatic character of events in Russia and Eastern Europe since 1989, much attention has been focused upon what the West can do to help strengthen and consolidate these new democracies. J. C. Sharman and Roger Kanet contend that Western attempts to provide assistance have been con-fused by a failure to recognize that it is often difficult to promote market reforms and political stability simultaneously. The West must be aware of trade-offs between economic reform and political stability and be willing to set priorities between them at particular points in time. Finally, the West must recognize that its efforts can have only a modest effect on democratic consol-idation in Russia and Eastern Europe. Success depends upon the slow growth of local ideas and institutions that both embody and further strengthen social pluralism, democratic politics, and competitive, open markets.

Part VI deals with democratization in Africa, which presents distinctive problems. The nations of Africa are very poor, averaging only $460 per capi-ta per annum, and most have little experience with democracy. If pluralism in the former Soviet Union and Eastern Europe must take root in the thin soil of their pulverized societies, in Africa, democracy and markets must be born in the desiccated fields of grinding poverty and ethnic division.

Jeffrey Herbst argues that the democratization process may take decades and will almost certainly be characterized by a mix of success and failure. Herbst analyzes the 46 nations of sub-Saharan Africa along both political and human rights dimensions and classifies them by stages of democratization. He concludes that the nations that move toward a more liberal polity, allow-ing such rights as free press and assembly, may have a better chance at demo-cratic stability than those that had the earliest transition from authoritarian-ism or the first elections.

Peter Lewis points out that many African nations, like most of the nations of Eastern Europe, face the dual tasks of political and economic liberaliza-tion. Moreover, they do so from a more impoverished base of wealth and democratic experience. Lewis explores the relationship between economic and political reform in Africa. Are they mutually reinforcing, mutually dis-ruptive, or largely unrelated? Lewis concludes that the strongest linkage is the destructive one between economic stagnation and political instability. Progress will be limited by the lack of economic infrastructure and the effect of ethnic and tribal ties on the development of social pluralism and political flexibility. Nonetheless, given the demands of international investors and institutions, African states have little choice but to continue both political and economic liberalization, and most are, if only haltingly.

In the concluding chapter, which forms Part VII, Ben Hunt asks what the United States, or any other international actor or institution, can do to foster consolidation in the newly democratic or democratizing nations of the world. He notes that each nation takes a somewhat distinctive path to democracy, reflecting its particular history, culture, and place in the international system. Thus foreign assistance, to be appropriate, has to vary case by case. But it is still possible to think systematically about the kinds of actions and policy choices the established democracies should reward and what kind of backsliding they should systematically discourage or punish. Hunt argues that United States officials should keep the task of supporting democracy clear and simple, both so that they can be consistent and so that political leaders in developing nations know what the United States will and will not support. Hunt argues that the basic decision-rule should be that the United States will support regimes that hold multiparty elections and withhold support from those who do not.

By the standards of the already vast literature on political and economic development, the theoretical ambitions of this volume are relatively modest. We have not set out to test any of the grand propositions arising from the development literature, which generally fall into one of two theoretical categories: modernization or dependency.[26] Rather, we have opted for a more comparative, historical, and monographic approach to answering basic questions about the course of democratic transitions in the third wave.

What we have found is that each region of the globe (if not individual states within regions) has taken a rather specific pathway to democracy, depending upon preexisting social, political, and economic conditions. The set of structures and constraints associated with the old communist regimes in Eastern Europe, for example, is very different from those associated with bureaucratic authoritarianism and military regimes in Latin America, the developmental state in Asia, or the colonial legacy in Africa. What each of these pathways have in common, however, is the necessity of quickly restoring economic stability and some measure of growth in order to respond to the needs of their own people and to the constraints imposed by the international political economy. One of the distinguishing features of the third wave is just how little (economic) room for maneuver the new democracies have. International financial institutions (both public and private) can quickly and severely punish any regime that does not move with dispatch to get its fiscal and monetary house in order. These economic constraints tend to drive the types of political coalitions that form in the aftermath of transition and the types of institutions that will be built during the phase of consolidation. This is especially true for political parties and the party system.

But one factor, more than any other, seems to stand out as a crucial indicator of the success or failure of democratization, and that is the strength or weakness of civil society. Almost every contributor to this volume points to civil society (and state-society relations) as centrally important in the transition and consolidation. Civil society must be strong and autonomous enough to weather the initial transition, then it must be nurtured by the state, new institutions, political parties, and the like during the consolidation phase. Extreme care must be taken not to damage or destroy associational life with radical market reforms. So democratizing states are constantly engaged in a balancing act, trying to encourage participation and build legitimacy for the new regime while at the same time reforming and restructuring the economy to meet the stringent demands of international investors. How do they do it? What role do established democracies, international organizations, and the international community play in helping them to meet the challenges of democratization? For answers to these and other questions, we must now turn to the case studies themselves.

Part II

The Political Economy of

Democratic Transitions

1

Democracy and Its Enemies

Lucian W. Pye

LET US START by stating the self-evident: few ideas have as universal and as deep an appeal as the concept of democracy. Irrespective of cultural differences, people worldwide are instinctively attracted to the vision of democratic government. The most basic concepts of justice include the idea that people should have some say in the way they are governed. Even its greatest enemies, authoritarian governments, pay it the compliment of cynically labeling themselves as democracies, some as "people's democracies" and others as "democratic republics." This fact is proof that in the modern world the legitimacy of governments depends upon an acknowledgment of the superior virtues of democracy. Indeed, this is the fundamental fact to come out of the end of the Cold War. Just as the United States is the sole remaining superpower, so the idea of democracy is the only competitor as the universal ideal for the goal of history.[1]

Yet, in spite of this near universal appeal of the ideal, there is considerable confusion as to what the essential elements of a democracy are. Different people have tended to emphasize different key characteristics in their definition of democracy. There has been great variety in the practice of democracy, and thus there is no single model of what a democracy is or should be. As Plato wrote in *The Republic*, "Democracy is a charming form of government, full of variety and disorder, and dispensing a sort of equality to equals and unequals alike." Historically democracies have embraced different combinations and priorities of ideals, and they have operated with a variety of institutional forms.

Thus in the contemporary world the general ideal of democracy has gained increasing popularity even though variations in practices have grown. Indeed, since Samuel P. Huntington identified in 1991 the "third wave" of democratization, the pace of transformation has continued, especially with the various component parts of the collapsed Soviet Union all turning to democracy. Democracy gained even in Africa, where in 1996 relatively free elections were held in Ghana, Benin, Sierra Leone, and Uganda, and more questionable ones in Chad, Niger, and Gambia. According to Huntington, the first wave was a long one, lasting from the mid-nineteenth century to the 1920s, and it ended with the rise of fascism and communism. The second wave came after World War II with the many attempts at democracy by the newly independent states that emerged with the end of European colonialism. This second wave was short-lived and died out with a drift toward one-party dictatorships, especially in Africa and parts of Asia, and a series of military coups, such as in Greece, Turkey, South Korea, Pakistan, and many Latin American countries. The third wave started in 1974 with the Portuguese and Spanish breaks from dictatorships and the successes of democracy in Latin America and East Asia (Huntington 1991). In contrast to Francis Fukuyama's optimistic "end of history" forecast, Huntington believes that there is a dialectical process in history, so that with each of the waves there has come a counterdrift, and therefore he is not prepared to say that the "third wave" will be decisive in history (Fukuyama 1992).[2]

The events of more recent years suggest that while there have been no alternative visions of regime types to compete with democracy, the achievement of sustainable and genuinely liberal democracy has been difficult. The rhetoric of democracy has been easier to master than the practice. There have also been differences in the vision of what standards need to be met in arriving at the condition of democracy. Indeed, over time the concept of democracy has evolved as the nature of human society has changed. It is conventional to think of democracy as having been first established in the city-state of Athens. The early Greek thinkers helped to define the essential qualities of a democracy as a system based on direct citizen participation in government. Thus democracy began with the ideal of all qualified citizens being directly involved in collective decision-making. The idea of representative democracy emerged out of the experiences of the British in their clashes between crown and Parliament, and then it achieved its modern form with the French and American revolutions. The concepts basic to liberal, representative democracy were refined through the writings of such theorists as Rousseau and his doctrine of the social contract, Locke and his theories of law and private property rights, and the Founding Fathers of the United

States with their analyses of how to organize the checks and balances of a continent-sized state.

With the rise of modern political science, a transition occurred in theorizing about democracy. Whereas the classical writers focused on the vision inherent in the democratic ideal, modern political scientists sought to explain the practical workings of ongoing democracies. To understand democracy came to mean understanding the functions performed by ward heelers, urban party machines, electoral behavior, and interest group activities. Thus our understanding of the practical elements of democracy was greatly enriched by the empirical contributions of Pendelton Herring, David Truman, E. E. Schattschneider, Harold Lasswell, Charles Merriam, David Easton, Gabriel Almond, and many others. It is impossible here to summarize their findings and insights about the practical requirements for effective democratic government. For our purposes of establishing a baseline for analyzing the general obstacles to true democracy, we can, however, turn to Robert Dahl, the foremost authority on polyarchy as the theoretical essence of democracy who has brilliantly integrated our empirical knowledge and summarized it in general theoretical form, thereby significantly advancing the theory of democracy. Dahl has identified eight essential guarantees which have to have solid institutional protection if the people's preferences are to be identified and organized into policy programs.

First, there must be the guarantee of freedom to form and join organizations that are outside the state's control. The organizations that seek to advance the people's interests must be totally autonomous and in no way under the influence of the government. Second, there must be freedom of expression so that the people can publicly articulate their preferences. Americans do see this principle of freedom of speech as absolutely basic to democracy. The third guarantee is the right to vote without intimidation or inhibition.

Closely related is the fourth guarantee, which is that the elections will be conducted in a free and fair manner. The actual voting must be in secret, and the counting of the ballots must be openly checked by nongovernment people. Fifth is the right of political leaders to compete for support. The state cannot limit who gets to compete. A sixth requirement is that there must be alternative sources of information so that the people can hear different views. The state cannot monopolize the mass media or control the press. Seventh, there must be institutional guarantees that there are fair rules of eligibility for holding office. The government cannot screen who can or cannot be candidates for office. Finally, the processes for making government policies must depend upon the votes of the people's representatives. The legislature or congress must be free to establish the laws and public policies and not be a rubber stamp for the government.

It should also be noted that liberal democracy cannot operate without a system of rule by law because there has to be strong legal support for these essential guarantees. There must also be effective enforcement of the laws that the people's representatives have enacted. The will of the people cannot truly rule if the laws they have passed are not respected.

Dahl's eight requirements are a succinct summary of the standards Americans generally associate with a liberal democracy. Moreover, Americans tend to use these same requirements as a way of judging whether a country is democratic. Countries that aspire to become democratic may uphold some of the requirements, and by checking the list it is possible to identify what still needs to be achieved for the country to become fully democratic. Some countries that are marginally democratic may, for example, hold elections but the government may indirectly control the press or make it difficult for opposition parties effectively to organize public support. In other countries there may be reasonably fair elections but the government officials responsible for conducting official policies may ignore the will of those elected.

Liberal democracies, however, need more than just these institutional requirements. They also require that the people share certain attitudes and values that are consistent with democracy, and that can be summarized as a civic culture. Key elements of the civic culture include a population with a reasonable degree of knowledge about how the government and the political system operate, and who have positive attitudes toward government and a sense of civic pride. More generally there must be genuine tolerance for the political views of others, a reasonable degree of trust in other people, genuine respect for the rights of others, and a willingness to cooperate with others to achieve collective goals. Democracy calls for compromise, not fierce partisanship even in support of democracy; for, as the British philosopher Bertrand Russell wrote, "A fanatical belief in democracy makes democratic institutions impossible."

Basic to the concept of a civic culture is a very special kind of individualism that Americans in particular believe to be essential for democracy. It is not a self-centered and selfish form of individualism, but it is a balanced form of individualism which respects both the dignity of the self and the individual worth of all people. By respecting others as truly distinctive and unique beings, one automatically sets limits for advancing one's own interests so as not to infringe on the rights of others. There is thus a reciprocal pattern of respecting the preferences of others and of expecting others to respect one's own preferences. Everyone should thus be able to feel free and comfortable in expressing his or her ideas and preferences.

Unfortunately, given the forces of history and the cussedness of man, the glowing vision of democracy we have just outlined has been hard to realize in its full glory even in modern times. The collapse of the Soviet Union has revealed how difficult it is to make the transition from a centrally planned system to a liberal democracy.

The obstacles to the advancement of democracy in the developing world are of course more complex and intractable. They range from the limited parochial perspectives of marginally educated populations to long-established traditions of autocratic leadership. The key problems in most cases can be subsumed under the label of modernization difficulties, the most fundamental of which is the achievement of an acceptable balance between the country's traditional cultural legacies and the imperatives of the modern world culture; that is, a blending of parochial and universal values. The process is made more complex by the challenges of economic development and of fitting into the world economy. The fundamental question raised about the merits of democracy in many such countries is whether democracy is the best form of government for achieving rapid economic growth. The idea of checks and balances that can bring political paralysis to even established democracies—and hence a cause of alienation there—may have little appeal for impatient emerging nations. Winston Churchill's dictum, "Democracy is the worst form of government, except for all the others," is hardly an inspiring rallying cry for Third World people.

In order to get a better grip on studying the problems for democracy in both the developed and the developing areas, it is useful to simplify the task by turning for guidance to what theory can tell us about required changes inherent in the process of transitions to democracy.

Regime Changes: Transitions to and from Democracy

Starting as early as with Aristotle's typology of political systems and his theories of transitions from one category to another, there have been many theories about regime change and the conditions necessary for the establishment of a liberal democracy. From the time of the Greeks it has been widely assumed that democracy requires a strong middle class, and hence democracy was inappropriate until a society had reached a significant level of economic development. This was the argument used by colonial authorities to justify their continued rule in Asia and Africa; and it is still used by autocratic governments to resist any movement toward democracy. The relationship between democracy and economic development is, however, complex, as we shall shortly note.

Contemporary theories about transitions to democracy, and the conditions essential for its maintenance, fall generally into three main categories. First, there is the approach that stresses the social, structural, and economic conditions which favor successful democratic development. Many studies have followed Seymour Martin Lipset's pioneering lead in examining levels of economic growth as the key independent variable for democracy (Lipset 1960).

The underlying assumption is that economic growth and general well-being will automatically and inevitably facilitate transitions to democracy. It has been this faith in a linkage between economic growth and democracy that inspired America's foreign aid program, particularly during the Kennedy administration. The doctrine was that once a country achieved self-sustaining economic growth, it would move on to become democratic and hence a peace-loving member of the international community. It is this same belief in the powers of economic growth to produce democracy that President Clinton appealed to in his 1997 State of the Union address, when he held out the vision of China's continued economic achievements bringing about the ultimate triumph of democracy there.

A second approach focuses on political considerations and, in particular, elite decision-making. This more dynamic approach was pioneered by Dankwart A. Rustow (1970, pp. 37 ff). Instead of stressing impersonal and nonpolitical forces, this approach focuses upon the purposeful acts of leadership groups. The key questions thus become the degree of commitment of the leadership to good governance and their willingness to risk competitive politics. Change comes when autocratic rulers find out that the cost of continued repression is greater than the risk of democracy.

The third approach stresses the cultural orientations and basic values of both the leaders and the population as a whole. This approach was significantly advanced by Gabriel Almond and Sidney Verba in their classic work, *The Civic Culture*, with its case studies of five political cultures (Almond and Verba, 1963). This third approach can involve more than just public attitudes and opinions, for it also includes the organization of civil society and the ways in which public actions can influence the political process. The key to democratic development is the existence of voluntary associations which can mobilize political power by articulating and aggregating the interests of major elements of society. The civil society includes the role of the mass media and the free play of opinion-makers. The ultimate test is the ability of society to place political checks on the government and thereby compel the ruler to respect the interests of the people. Most recent studies of transitions and regime transformations have generally involved a combination of these three approaches (O'Donnell and Schmitter 1986; Diamond, Linz, and Lipset 1988–89). Thus, in examining in greater detail what each approach can tell us about the problems for democracy in the current era, we shall blur somewhat the lines between the approaches.

Hard Economic Facts Dictate Soft Democratic Conclusions

The relationship between levels of economic development and stable democracy is more complex than the popular assumptions of policy-makers would suggest. It is easy to point to striking exceptions to the rule that economic growth dictates the realization of democracy. At the one extreme there is India, which supports the point that low per capita GNP does not need to be an obstacle to democracy. At the other extreme there is Singapore, where rising general prosperity has not brought democracy. Yet there are also the supporting examples of South Korea, Taiwan, and the fact that all rich countries are democracies.

As we just noted, many studies have taken up the challenge of testing Lipset's theory about this relationship (Diamond 1992). Most recently Adam Przeworski and Fernando Limongi tested hypotheses about the relationship of per capita GNP and the rise of democracies (or the death of dictatorships) in 135 countries from 1950 to 1990, which meant observing 224 regimes in all, 101 democratic and 123 authoritarian (Przeworski and Limongi 1992). Although in gross terms Lipset's theory seems to have been borne out, they still concluded that it was flawed by the existence of such "anomalies" as Argentina and Uruguay in Latin America, the Southern European cases of Greece, Spain, and Portugal, and Poland and Czechoslovakia under communism. In their desire to achieve a level of pristine rigor, they kept their analysis to just the naked facts of economic conditions and tolerated no extraneous considerations, such as the presence of fascism and communism, and other commonsense qualifications.

If we grant that, with the help of some intervening considerations, Lipset's theory is tolerably correct, there are still further questions about the relationship of economics to development. For example, there is the matter of whether rapid economic growth is better facilitated by authoritarian or democratic governments. The standard argument, first advanced by Gerschenkron, is that late-developing countries need the discipline of an authoritarian state (1962). Economists such as Walter Galenson and Karl de Schweinitz and political scientist Samuel Huntington have argued that democracy encourages the diversion of resources from investment to consumption and that political participation can divert energies from the main task of economic growth (Galenson 1959; de Schweinitz, 1959; Huntington and Nelson 1976; Przeworski and Limongi 1992). The evidence for what once seemed self-evident is less conclusive as development theory has shifted toward greater respect for markets than for planning. India's relatively poor record through the 1970s may have had less to do with its democracy and more to do with its commitment to massive government intervention and state planning. In the case of China we now know that there was little growth under Mao, and only with liberalization under Deng has there been significant growth. Similarly, a case can be made that both South Korea and Taiwan might have had economic successes earlier if democracy had come sooner. What makes the difference may be less regime type and more the quality of the leadership, which brings in a more detailed look at the second major approach to transition to democracy.

Leadership and the Importance of Good Governance

It is impossible to overstate the importance of leadership in establishing democratic systems, but it is extremely difficult to talk about leadership in analytical terms. So much about it seems accidental, undefinable, and just idiosyncratic. We simply cannot explain America's successful experiment with democracy without taking into account the Founding Fathers; or India's remarkable adherence to secular democracy without appreciating the importance of Nehru and Gandhi; or the role of Sukarno in exterminating competitive party politics in Indonesia, and of Marcos's near-extermination of Philippine democracy. It is not just that leadership calls for skill in upholding the vision of a democratic society; it also requires the practical skills and intuitions to make the right day-to-day political decisions which will substantially advance democracy. Thus, while appropriate leadership may be hard to define or analyze in general terms, it is easy to recognize.

In the process of transition from autocratic rule to democracy, a major challenge to leadership is the problem of what to do with the former autocratic rulers, particularly if they are military men with continuing ties to the services. The problem is compounded because of the contradictory values of justice, which may call for punishments, and reconciliation, which may require forgiveness. A delicate arrangement had to be worked out with General Augusto Pinochet to get him to give up the presidency of Chile and return to the barracks. In Argentina, when the military rulers lost public respect because of their military defeat after trying to take the Falklands from Britain, the first civilian government tried to punish several generals for crimes they committed during the junta's rule; but then the second civilian president, Carlos Menem, pardoned the military in order to put the bad period behind the country. Possibly the most dramatic example of setting aside shocking political and governmental crimes in order to get on with advancing democracy is the South African case after the end of apartheid, in which a Truth Commission under Bishop Desmond Tutu was established so that all former officials who publicly confessed to crimes could be pardoned.

The sense of alienation and frustration with government in the established democracies is often articulated by the lament about the paucity of good leaders. Technocratic knowledge about policy matters and administration has grown exponentially in recent decades, but confidence about government's abilities has shrunk even faster. The result is an ominous swelling of the antidemocratic view that government is at best irrelevant and at worst a part of the problem.

The test of good governance is even more critical for any transitions to democracy in the developing world. The Asian Development Bank, in a significant recent study of the lesson to be learned from the successfully developing East Asian economies, concluded that the key was not regime type, whether democratic or autocratic, but rather the quality of governance (Root 1996). According to the study, good governance is not synonymous with good institutional design but rather calls for a clear understanding of appropriate policy goals, an awareness of political feasibility, a strong but limited state, a high degree of sensitivity to equity questions, and transparency in decision-making—in short, a combination of technocratic skills, adequate power, and the "vision thing." Government needs to be seen as providing predictability, which has to be grounded in institutions.

Whereas successful democracy calls for good governance, it does not follow that good governance alone will produce democracy. There is that awkward example of Singapore, a country obviously blessed with good governance in any technical sense of that word, but which is not democratic—except in the sense of being democratic according to its odd definition of "Asian values," which we will address shortly.

Thus, while not all democratic regimes have provided good governance, the burden of history is that nondemocratic governments have been even less capable of doing so. Even when the presumed goal is limited to furthering economic growth, the record shows that autocratic regimes have only rarely been successful. Throughout history most poor countries have had autocratic governments. In democracies the presumption is that if the people do not like what their government is doing, they can bring about a change in leadership.

There is, however, the argument most recently advanced by Anthony King that American politicians cannot provide good government because they are engaged in a continuous process of election, fund-raising, and campaigning (King 1996). Instead of the public merely selecting their representatives and then leaving them free to manage the government, America has a massive industry of pollsters, consultants, speech-writers, lobbyists, and fund-raisers who encourage a populist approach to government and who keep the public constantly checking on politicians, who in turn have to remain more sensitive to election considerations than what is demanded for good governance.

This problem of leadership and the behavior of mass publics brings us to the third approach to the problems of democracy, that of the values and attitudes of the people as reflected in their political culture and in the relative strength of the country's civil society.

Civil Society and the Articulation of Interests

For the effective operation of a democracy, there has to be a stable balance of power and authority between state and society, between the government and the citizens. To achieve such a balance, the citizens have to have their own structures and organizations, which must be independent of the state. For society to perform this balancing role in a democracy, the people have to have what has been called a "civil society." This term refers to the presence within the society of a substantial body of autonomous, nongovernmental institutions and power centers that are strong enough to stand up to the state and serve as a counterbalance to the authority of the government. For the people to be able to voice their desires and to assert their preferences, they have to have access to independent power bases which can command the attention and respect of the authorities.

When the French political philosopher Alexis de Tocqueville visited the United States in 1831, he was impressed with the fact that everywhere he went he found all manner of voluntary associations which made it possible for Americans to look after most of their community affairs without the state having to take an active role. He concluded that America was a nation of "joiners," as everyone seemed to belong to one or more such associations. He went on to speculate that this characteristic gave America a strong basis for its democracy. What Tocqueville had observed was the vitality of America's civic society.

Recently Robert Putnam has stirred considerable debate by suggesting that Americans are no longer the joiners they once were, but now live more in their separate private worlds; instead of bowling as teams they choose to bowl alone and not in organized group (Putnam 1995, 1996; Schudson, Skocpol, and Valelly 1997).[3] Unquestionably television has changed social, patterns and made staying at home less lonely. But there are also other changes in society that may not have actually reduced the importance of belonging to groups but only altered the nature of the groups.

The question of the proper balance between respect for individual rights and deference to society's needs has become an increasingly debated matter even in established democracies. In recent years there has been considerable concern in America that the balance has gone too far in favor of stark individualism with inadequate concerns for society as a whole. Thus parallel to Putman's "bowling alone" argument has been the rise of communitarianism. President Clinton in his second inaugural address declared, "Our greatest responsibility is to embrace a new spirit of community for a new century." Amitai Etzioni, the intellectual leader of the communitarian movement, has called for a new Golden Rule: "Respect and uphold society's moral order as you would have society respect and uphold your autonomy" (Etzioni 1997).

Democracy thus requires a balance between the individual's rights and collective responsibility. In dynamic democratic systems there is a constant process of shifting and adjusting as the balance goes too far in one direction and then the other (Ehrenhalt 1995). Stability in the balance is best achieved when there is a well-developed civil society that can give a basis for protecting the interests of both the individual and the collectivity.

In modern industrial democracies the institutions and power centers that make up the civil society cover a wide range of organizations, from trade unions and business associations to corporations and universities. The civil society of modernized countries also includes professional societies, farmers' federations, veterans' organizations, churches and religious institutions, philanthropic foundations, and perhaps politically most important of all, independent newspapers, radio, television, journals, and a book publishing industry. These associations and citizens' institutions, interacting with each other, act as a powerful counterforce to state power, and they thereby ensure that the authorities will have to respect the interests of the people. They are indeed the creative and dynamic expressions of the people's interests. They give structure and weight to the society so that the people cannot be easily intimidated by government.

The state also needs a civil society if there is to be democracy. This is because the state needs to know the active interests of the people, the state of public opinion, and, more particularly, how much support various specific interests can command with respect to different policy options. For the government to carry out rational policies according to the logic of a government of the people, for the people, and by the people, it must be able to judge what would be the society's responses to different policy trade-offs and mixes of options.

Possibly the most important reason why historically countries have failed in their attempts to establish democracies is that they lacked the essential elements of a civil society. It is not enough for the people to want to have a democracy and for the leaders to genuinely desire to build a democracy; there must also be a structural basis for a civil society. Preparing the ground for the planting of the seeds of democracy therefore calls for more than just educating the people about civic virtues and responsibilities. There must also be in place the institutions that constitute a civil society so that the people will have their autonomous power bases and the state will have valid indicators of the popular will.

In the modern world the strength of a country depends not on the power of its government but on the vitality of its civil society. It is the civil society that creates wealth, advances knowledge, ensures nearly all forms of progress. When the state seeks national stability by repressing the growth of civil society, it can only weaken the country. In contrast, when the state liberalizes and allows the civil society to become stronger, the country as a whole will also become stronger and more stable.

Thus the expansion of civil society is fundamental not only for the development of democracy but also for the making of national strength and wealth. Economic development, cultural progress, intellectual advancement, and national well-being all depend more on the civil society than on the state. Indeed, the contrasting story of how civil society emerged in the West and failed to do so in much of the developing world helps to explain the different histories with respect to both democratic development and the formation of modern nation-states.

The history of the development of democracy in the West is, indeed, largely the story of state-society relations in terms of the growth of modern civil societies. Initially there were the dual and balancing authorities of church and state. The division of temporal and spiritual authority in Europe established early the need of each for the other; kings needed the blessing of the pope, and the pope needed the secular power of kings and emperors. But each also needed to be separate and independent of the other. This division of authority vividly established the distinction between state and society.

The state-society division was then reinforced by the basic institutions of European feudalism, and in particular the divided powers of the kings and the landed aristocracy. The nobles with their estates were autonomous power centers who owed allegiance to the crown but who also could challenge the authority of the king if he violated the existing division of authorities. The institutions of feudalism thus established early the tradition of plural authorities and competing power centers, which in time paved the way for the establishment of competitive democracies. With progress towards modernization, the European monarchies became the state and the nobles became an establishment that gave authority to society and thereby served as a check on the state.

This process was greatly accelerated with the growth of commerce and the rise of cities with their emerging merchant classes. The merchants and a rising middle class in the cities expanded the power base of the European civil society by compelling the rulers to respect their interests, particularly by insisting that the rulers had to adhere to the rule of law, a principle that was essential for the orderly development of commerce and industry.

Historically the Japanese state and society evolved in ways comparable to what happened in Europe. Japanese feudalism produced the divisions of real power between the *daimyos* or lords with their estates and castles, the *shogun* or supreme temporal authority, the emperor as a semireligious figure, and the *chonin* or urban merchant class. The feudal institutions of Europe and Japan established traditions of divided and competing authorities that most other major cultures did not have.

The other great civilization that produced limited prerequisites for democracy is, of course, the Confucian or Sinic world, which idealized monolithic authority and not competing power centers. In China the tradition was that of a bureaucratic state composed of scholar-officials and an emperor who, with the Mandate of Heaven, monopolized all legitimate political authority. China did not have the powerful class of nobles with their large, independent estates that Europe and Japan had. In Chinese architecture all the grand buildings were those of the state, whether the Forbidden City in Beijing or the government buildings in the provinces, and there are none of the great houses or castles that dot the landscape of Europe and Japan. The Chinese gentry class in the countryside did have great local power, but as a class it did not seek to challenge openly the authority of the bureaucracy. Instead they tended quietly to seek out understandings with the local magistrates as to the best way for protecting their interests. In the cities the merchants were organized into guilds, as in Europe, but the Chinese guilds did not seek directly and openly to challenge the political authorities but rather operated indirectly to try to make sure that the state policies were not applied in ways that might hurt their interests. That is to say, the private sector in China did not develop the tradition of pressure group politics as a way of advancing their own interests and shaping governmental policies. Instead in China, when private parties did organize for group actions, it was largely as protective associations that sought special considerations for their members in the application of the imperial laws and regulations. The decrees of the emperor were not to be questioned, but rather it was more prudent to ask for exceptions when it came to their application in one's own particular case.

Instead of the clear division of state and society of Europe and Japan, the Chinese tended toward a three-way division of state *(guan)*, public *(gong)*, and private *(si)*. The state sphere was that of the mandarin bureaucracy, from the emperor at the top to the local magistrate at his *yamen* at the bottom. It monopolized all legitimate political authority. The private sphere was that of the family and the individual, and it was not supposed to be assertive as far as the other spheres were concerned. Indeed, there was always something slightly negative about the concept of the private realm because in Chinese culture selfishness has always been considered to be a gross social evil—the ultimate sin.

In between these two realms there was a fairly clearly defined third, public sphere that consisted of the collective actions of the gentry in the countryside and the merchants in the cities. Actions within this sphere help to explain why the Chinese failed to develop early a civic culture but did have a strong sense of civic virtue and of public-spiritedness. The merchants and gentry did have their societies *(hui)* and more particularly their benevolent societies *(tongshan hui)*, which were often active in establishing schools, foundling homes, and community temples. Local elites could thus contribute to education, water control, welfare, famine relief, and the building of roads, ferries, bridges, temples, and shrines. Indeed, they often assumed the most basic of governmental functions by providing public security by organizing a local militia. Significantly, the public role of these local institutions became more active when the dynasties were in decline and the state was weak, as happened during the late Ming.

The key point was that in China there was cooperation between local elites and the government, with the local leaders seeing that state responsibilities were carried out, often by supplementing limited government funds. The public sphere of action thus operated on behalf of the state even though it was not an agent of the state. The local elites thus complemented the state, and did not, as in Europe and Japan, challenge the state with a different agenda of interests and concerns.

With the ending of the imperial era and the establishment of the republic, there was a growth in the number of institutions that could have become the basis for a stronger civil society. Thus in the industrial cities significant number of labor unions were organized, and a wide variety of independent newspapers and publishing houses sprang up, along with many kinds of business and professional associations. Under the communists, however, all these institutions were taken over by the state and the Party, so that they lost any potential for being the independent voices of society. Instead there has been a reversion to the tradition of a monolithic government upholding a moral order and repressing any sign of an autonomous civil society. The tradition of seeing any assertion of private interests as being a shameful expression of selfishness and greed is still strong in China. The traditional Chinese faith that a benevolent government should be able to take care of all the legitimate interests of the people without any prompting from society remains strong. This might have been possible when China was a predominately agricultural society, but now that China is becoming increasingly modernized and industrialized it is also becoming more diversified, and therefore there is bound to be a dramatic expansion in the diversity of competing and conflicting legitimate interests in the society. If these interests are not openly acknowledged and allowed to make public their cases for policy support, they will have to operate in dishonorable ways, using the "back door," exploiting the power of *guanxi*, or personal relationships, and practicing outright corruption.

The example of Taiwan or South Korea suggests, however, that Confucianism is not an absolute hindrance to democracy. Hence there is widespread hope in the West that with continued economic successes, China too may move toward democracy. Unfortunately for such an optimistic vision, there is the example of Singapore, where spectacular economic successes have not produced democratic politics. Instead Singapore has become the champion of the idea of "Asian values," which holds that Asian culture rejects the individualism that is basic to Western democracy and instead adheres to community values. Society's rights are greater than the individual's, and the citizen has obligations and duties that supersede personal preferences. The theory of Asian values resonates in many ways with the ideas behind the communitarian movement in America, but with important differences. The Western communitarian movement still has room for a high degree of respect for the individual's rights, while the Asian values argument identifies the community with the state and state power. Indeed, the Asian values case rests upon some faulty understanding of historic Asian social and political arrangements. At one time in most Asian cultures the individual did find his identity in terms of a group, usually the family, class, village, or caste. What former prime minister and now senior minister Lee Kwan Yew has done is to claim that the "community" now should be the state. The "state" however is a modern invention and not the same community as was once the basis for individual identity. Historically the Chinese did not personally identify themselves with the imperial structure of government. Many analysts now argue that Lee's notion of "Asian values," which has been picked up by Mahathir of Malaysia and many Chinese leaders and academics, is really an argument in justification of autocratic government and the repression of democracy.

Lee Kwan Yew has combined his argument about Asian values with the idea that programs for welcoming direct foreign investment by multinational corporations can produce both rapid economic growth and also political stability. At a time when many American academics were taken up with dependency theories about the evils of multinational corporations, which turned out to be a prescription for economic stagnation, Lee was convinced that the opposite policy of courting multinationals could rapidly raise living standards. He also concluded that foreign multinationals would prefer the political stability and predictability of autocratic, one-party rule to liberal democratic politics. He carried his message to Beijing, where he told Chinese leaders that they could easily combine a policy of opening up to foreign investments with continued political repression. He insisted that American businessmen, for example, who had investments in China trade would become strong allies in countering pressures on human rights, and thus they would make sure that Washington did not cause trouble about Chinese human rights practices. He argued that both Taiwan and South Korea made the mistake of keeping out direct foreign investment, hence their indigenous businessmen and industrialists eventually came to demand a voice in government, and hence those countries moved to democracy.

Summary: The Ideal and the Reality of Democracy in the Contemporary World

We are thus brought to a contradictory conclusion. On the one hand, the appeal of democracy is more universal than ever before for there are no competing visions of an alternative nature. On the other hand, from our review of the problems of democracy it is apparent that the strain between the ideal and the reality of democracy is as great if not greater now than at any time in history. The drama of the students in Tiananmen Square in 1989 is testimony to how quickly and easily a people who have long been isolated from publicly thinking about democracy can grasp the vision. The repression that followed is also grim testimony of how strong the enemies of democracy can be, even in this age of instant communications.

With the end of the Cold War, the goal of promoting democracy is certain to become a major element in American foreign policy and that of Western governments as a whole. The rationale for such actions should be the universal appeal of democracy. Such a policy is also supported by the shibboleth that this is the road to a more peaceful world because democracies do not fight each other. Unfortunately that is only a half-truth: established democracies do not make war with each other, but countries in transition to democracy are prone to war (Mansfield and Snyder 1995). The problem, of course, is that people's passions can be easily stirred up in the process of arriving at a new sense of national identity, and leaders in search of a new basis of legitimacy will maximize the perception of foreign threats.

Democracies' advantages may lie more in the longer run of history. The vast majority of the elements that make up modern life favor the expansion of democracy. It is true that some developments in the contemporary world, as we have noted, have their negative effects, but the balance of social, economic, and political forces lies on the side of democracy.

This, however, does not mean that the trend will be toward homogeneity and uniformity in ideals and practices. As more non-Western countries become established democracies, we will have a world with greater diversity in the form and practices of democracy.

2

On Markets and Democracy

William Glade

Introduction: The Marriage of Political and Economic Liberalization

The ambiguities of history notwithstanding, it is patent that a radically new vision today pervades the policy communities of countries in many parts of the world. The basic tenet of this new conviction holds that political and economic pluralism—the former achieved through democratization and the latter through a liberalizing reform of economic policy—are interrelated foundations for successful development.[1] True, the relationship seems more assumed or asserted than demonstrated. Nevertheless, the development strategies that have come into favor of late contain, paradoxically, what amounts to a revival of some of the goals that once informed the Marshall Plan and, later, the Alliance for Progress. Although both of these regional efforts enshrined a version of economic planning, for reconstruction in one case and development in the other, both also related the possibilities for sustaining (in Europe) or installing (in Latin America) democracy to a set of economic policies that would build growth momentum, encourage national capital accumulation and regional economic cooperation, and strengthen export capability.

Neither program was a blueprint for economic liberalization in its present form, but each plainly eschewed the autarkic policies that went before and envisaged more vibrant links with the world economy—and in that sense represented a halfway house on the road to more comprehensive restructuring. Such, for instance, was inherent in the European Coal and Steel Community. Further, the multilateralism explicit in each effort, especially in Europe, in effect tilted the balance of public/private sector relations in the direction of marketized decisional processes, though this was perhaps an unwitting by-product rather than an intended aim.

In addition, the Alliance for Progress, which was launched in an institutional environment quite different from that of Western Europe, not only incorporated, at least gesturally, a variety of structural reforms (in land tenure, the fiscal system, educational and health delivery systems, housing, and so on) but it also embraced a variety of associated undertakings: for instance, the Peace Corps, the American Institute for Free Labor Development, the Inter-American Foundation, and a host of nongovernmental citizen initiatives. All of these were predicated on aspirations for a more participatory form of development that would enhance democracy, and were designed to build into national programs the ligaments of what has come to be called civil society.

This ambitious linking of political and economic objectives was not unprecedented. Just before the Marshall Plan was launched to encourage European economic cooperation came the first effort to meld economic restructuring with democratization. Right on the heels of World War II, occupation authorities from the Western Allies instituted sweeping political reforms to foster democratic organization while dismantling the tight economic planning the Nazis had used to mobilize resources for waging war. A compliant German Federal Republic acquiesced to both remarkably successful restructurings and within a few years introduced a touch of its own, the social market economy, to forge a consensus on strategies for rebuilding the country's devastated production system (Smyser 1993, pp. 14–24; Giersch et al. 1994, pp. 16–44).

A recovery of export capacity was, correctly, judged to be pivotal in reconstruction. Thus decisions taken about resource allocation within the economy had to be compatible with the structure of signals in the external market, and there was little room for policy-induced distortions (Giersch et al. 1994, pp. 88–124).[2] Although a number of major companies were state-owned, by the federal government in some instances and by *Länder* governments in more, the export-driven context that constrained decisions throughout the German economy meant that they, too, had to meet performance criteria not too different from those that guided the private conglomerates. Unlike British Labor's commitment to national planning or the French fascination with indicative planning, postwar German governments, the Hitlerian legacy fresh in mind, eschewed any form of centralized guidance of the economic system—with results that came to be called the German Miracle.[3]

Meanwhile, the corporatist economic controls employed by fascist Italy were also abandoned in the postwar program of political liberalization. Although extensive bureaucratic involvement in the economy continued through the IRI holding company and other entities in a decentralized kind of state capitalism, and although clientelism provided a way of consolidating ties between political and economic elites, no centralized planning was employed, and the general environment gave birth to a dynamic private sector (Holland 1972, pp. 5–55). As in Germany, this was partly due to force of circumstances, for Italy likewise had to earn its way back to economic health by exporting. Thus it, too, necessarily opted for a development path that was, relatively speaking, market-constrained.

Soon thereafter, continental Western European nations, including both West Germany and Italy, embarked on the grand scheme to build a Common Market, a project designed to avert future conflicts by cementing economic ties among its members. Implicitly, the actions of those who signed the Treaty of Rome aimed also at strengthening the material and institutional underpinnings of democracy, thereby fulfilling the generous vision of Monnet, Adenauer, and others. As it happened, the substantial economic opening instituted by the regional integration scheme, especially when extended in the Single European Act of 1986, tended to accentuate a policy imperative already present in the general need to export. Unintentionally, therefore, regional integration limited the room for maneuver in national policy formation and the efficacy of state planning (Jenny 1995, pp. 70–95). Eventually, as the experience with the European Monetary Union shows, the accumulating requirements of the regional association reduced the scope for national discretion in fiscal and monetary policy, to say nothing of other policy arenas.

Ever so subtly, the norms of managerial professionalism and the exigencies of cross-border competition in a widening multinational common market impelled the state-owned enterprises that loomed large on the continent to act rather more like their private-sector counterparts even when their controlling shareholder, the state, persisted in setting political limits on both decisional scope and outcomes (Mazzolini 1979; Aharoni 1986; Marklew, 1995).[4] This is not to say that the stable of Western European state-owned enterprises did not include a number of firms, some of them quite large, that required either continuing or intermittent transfers from treasury to stay afloat. (The Crédit Lyonnais mess constitutes the most recent conspicuous reminder.) But compared with equivalent companies in Latin America, they tended to operate much closer to the norms of the private sector, and in Germany there were even complaints from Social Democrats that they were *too* much like private corporations.

To be sure, no direct link was explicitly postulated in Western Europe between the diminution of intervention and a consolidation of democratic political systems, but the outcome nevertheless worked to further both—and not just among the original members. A strikingly effective restructuring was, for example, introduced in Spain as that country prepared for admission to the Common Market, whose political prerequisites called for liberalizing the Spanish system of governance (Baklanoff 1976). Portuguese struggles to democratize following the end of the Salazar regime similarly joined political with economic liberalization, and for the same end: namely, to ready the country for admission to the European Economic Community, wherein would-be adherents confronted political as well as economic conditionality. Hence Western European cases in general argue for at least a loose functional association between democracy and economic liberalism.

Economic and Political Liberalization in Asian Restructurings

In the Far East, the scenarios of the last half of this century have been more complex and correlations between economic restructuring and democratization more ambiguous. While efforts to install democratic rule in postwar Japan were being made, at least a limited economic restructuring was undertaken through agrarian reform and breaking up of the *zaibatsu* structure that had dominated prewar Japanese industry and collaborated unstintingly with military aggression. Whether the democratization instigated by the American government of occupation was achieved may be open to debate, though the country took on at least the costume of democracy. On the other hand, there has been a notable lack of transparency in the decisional processes of the public sector as well as in the large conglomerates of the private sector. The collusion between the two, the latter now organized as *keiretsu* that look like reborn *zaibatsu*, has been shrouded in confidentiality, if not secrecy. Indeed, the importance of bureaucratic politics and bureaucratic guidance in shaping the national project raises troubling issues of accountability, the issue that provides the ultimate grounding for any version of democracy (Johnson 1982, pp. 305–24; Hart 1992, pp. 84–86).

The combined bureaucratic leadership in the entente joining the public and private sectors seems to have laid the foundations for a predatory form of Japanese capitalism behind the myriad barriers that have been erected against either competition in the home market from imports or foreign direct investment. "Japan, Inc." captures the essence of the techno-mercantilism that was adopted to steer the national economic machine and control economic interaction with the rest of the world. Scholarly interpreters have differed in their readings of this phenomenon, but seldom if ever has the Japanese style of systemic management been confused with laissez-faire and economic liberalism.

Elsewhere in Asia, the connection between the market-friendly policies of restructuring and the process of democratization has been no less tenuous, as

Chan and Cumings indicate elsewhere in this volume. Indeed, experience in the postwar period has led some to postulate that economic restructuring and other policies to accelerate growth can more easily be undertaken when democratization is put on the back burner. The Oriental combination of state control and export-driven economic policies that was pioneered by Japan was, with variations, eventually adopted by Korea, Taiwan, Hong Kong, and Singapore—in each instance in a political context of authoritarian rule. Though the last two, as historic trading emporiums with a limited resource base of their own, probably had no real alternative to export-led growth, they seem, for different reasons, to have organized their political regimes with a very circumscribed popular participation.

The two larger of the Four Little Tigers, Korea and Taiwan, began the postwar era with import-substituting industrialization programs not unlike those tried in Latin America, Turkey, India, and elsewhere. But the governments, cognizant of internal resource limitations, soon switched to a more advantageous strategy built on export expansion and diversification (World Bank, 1993).[5] In time Thailand and Malaysia—and more recently Indonesia —followed suit, but in none was there a positive correlation between economic and political liberalization. As Wade and others have pointed out, the recasting of Japanese development strategy that took place in these success stories bears little resemblance to any plausible model of economic liberalism (Wade, 1990, pp. 297–342). In no instance, moreover, did the economic success that was achieved seem to involve a classical form of marketization.

The most recent large-scale Asian experiment with limited economic liberalization, in the People's Republic of China, simply drives the point home. Despite two decades of policy innovation that gradually expanded the area for market-based decisions, political repression continues to be practiced on a grotesque scale and to a horrifying degree. True, what has happened in the aftermath of Tiananmen Square has been obscured by the full-scale retreat of the United States government—bedazzled by the lure of huge business profits and influenced by who-knows-what payments—from its erstwhile concern with human rights. Yet behind all the jockeying for pecuniary advantage in Chinese labor and product markets lies a tale that delinks in a compelling way the processes of liberalization and democratization.

Even regional integration, popular in both Europe and Latin America as a way station on the road to globalization, has been different in Asia. The contrast between the vagueness of ASEAN and APEC economic cooperation schemes and the procedural and substantive specificity of the EEC, for example, illustrates a considerable difference between the regions in their willingness to embrace external constraints, including those connected with the merging of national markets, on internal policy choices. True, the first round of regional integration in Latin America, in the 1960s, eventually ground to a standstill because of national reluctance to make serious policy conces-sions, but at least a notional version of regional integration survived—in the Latin American Integration Association and the Latin American Economic System—to be dusted off again when democracy and restructuring spread throughout the region in the 1980s. And just as European regional integra-tion was intimately linked with the preservation of democracy, the first round of Latin American integration, like the later inception of the Southern Common Market or MERCOSUR, was clearly predicated on a return to demo-cratic governance. In contrast to these cases, none of the Asian agreements, revealingly, paid much heed to political preconditions for association or even took democratization for granted.

Delinking Economic and Political Liberalization in Latin America

It is worth recalling that the first and second instances of a liberalizing radi-cal structural adjustment on this side of the Pacific also cast doubt on the con-nection between economic liberalization and democratization. In the first, as Fuentes Irurozqui (1952) recounts, a military takeover of Peru by General Manuel Odría inaugurated an early attempt to dismantle the populist eco-nomic regulations that had been promulgated in the 1940s. His set of reforms bore a strong family resemblance to those introduced in more recent times: for example, diversification of exports, attraction of foreign capital, lowered inflation, and a raised investment rate. Until undermined in the 1960s, these policies gave Peru one of the highest export-led growth rates in Latin America, but even so, no other countries were inspired to replicate the Peruvian example.

The second case, that of Chile, has in fact been used by some to propose that structural adjustment and democratization may even be incompatible (Sheahan 1980; Petras 1986).[6] According to this interpretation, Chile was able to carry out its program successfully, complete with midcourse correc-tions when policy mistakes transpired, precisely because its authoritarian gov-ernment could afford to take a long view and weather the short-term costs of adjustment in hopes of reaching eventually the long-term restructuring gains (Valdés 1995). Further, authoritarian continuity meant that the regime could harvest the fruits of social learning and make midcourse corrections in policy without having to accommodate the myriad political interests that had, dur-ing the 1960s and earlier, enfeebled the economy and, ironically, the polity, bringing the country to economic ruin and unprecedented political disorder during the government of Allende in the early 1970s.

For that matter, the problematic relationship between democracy and eco-nomic organization and performance goes back even further in modern Latin American history. On the one hand, democratic Uruguay, once called the

Switzerland of South America, was eventually mired in economic stagnation, thanks to the populist policies its democracy produced. What is more, the military regime that ousted the democrats proved no more capable than its civilian predecessors in generating prosperity. On the other hand, Brazil experienced impressive state-led economic growth under an authoritarian military regime that came to power in 1964, rivaling the long-term performance of Mexico to 1982, where a ruling party took control of government in the late 1920s and remains in office still. The Argentine economy, in contrast, performed woefully for decades during an era when a variety of authoritarian regimes, with interspersed episodes of civilian rule, beset the country. When the generals were finally booted out, the first elected civilian government in over half a century to be succeeded by another elected civilian government paid lip service, at most, to restructuring and was notable mainly for generating hyperinflation.

A review of the 1932 to 1982 period shows that regimes both authoritarian and relatively democratic, those run by civilians and those run by the military, customarily made ample use of the interventionary powers of the state to guide their economic destinies. Sometimes interventionism worked for a considerable period of time, as in Brazil and Mexico; more often it succeeded only sporadically. And sometimes it didn't work at all. Eventually, what Dornbusch and Edwards (1991) have baptized macroeconomic populism led, throughout the region (even in democratically governed countries), to a variety of increasingly serious economic ailments, of which undue reliance on the market was not one. Peruvian populism, for instance, brought to heel—first under military and later under civilian auspices—what had previously been a high-growth economy (Schydlowsky and Wicht 1979; Webb 1977). But even here the picture was mixed, for populism in Mexico, one of the best performers, constituted the very fabric of the political regime that was born in the throes of revolution, and political organization resembled a kind of non-Leninist democratic centralism.

During the high tide of interventionism, when developed as well as underdeveloped countries were caught up in the zeitgeist of the omnicompetent state, Milton Friedman and Friedrich von Hayek, among others, argued that political and economic freedoms were positively related to each other (Friedman 1962; Hayek 1960). Yet, throughout the world, the social trends that prevailed were, at the very least, inconclusive on this point. If anything, before the debt crisis hit the developing world with great severity in the 1980s, the preference for open-economy policies in less-developed countries looked to be mainly associated with authoritarian regimes—if to the Asian cases were added those of Odría's Peru, Pinochet's Chile, and the fitful flirtations with economic orthodoxy (of sorts) that the Argentine military carried on (Mallon and Sourrouille 1975).

Understandably, market-oriented reform was suspect, if not outright distasteful, to many in the intersection of the policy and intellectual communities through the 1970s, especially given the widespread belief, consolidated by the work of the UN Economic Commission for Latin America, that interventionism was the sine qua non of Latin America's growth. To many, including many with democratic political preferences, the state was uncritically regarded as the paladin of national sovereignty and development aspirations. Prevailing analysis acknowledged the sundry forms of market failure but overlooked almost entirely the emerging research and theorizing on government or public-sector failure.[7] Market-centered policies advocated by the World Bank and the United States had yet to make their mark in the region, and monetarism, the name bestowed on the orthodox corrective programs of the 1970s, came in for bitter criticism (Foxley 1983; Ramos 1986).

The legacy of these conflicted times lingers on today in a somewhat muted antipathy toward IMF-inspired adjustment policies and a suspicion that the business sector, the clearest beneficiary of interventionism in most cases (until it produced economic crisis), is somehow poised to take advantage of austerity and adjustment programs in promoting its own somewhat exclusionary version of the national project (Conaghan 1992; Bartell and Payne 1995). At the very least, the actively mobilized constituencies on behalf of structural adjustment are few and far between (Maxfield and Schneider 1997), centered mainly among techno-bureaucrats and some portions of the business community, whose acceptance of the seeming inevitability of reform is generally grudging.

In short, the explicit connection between political and economic liberalization that was fashioned into public policy in postwar Germany and Italy found few if any parallels in other parts of the world before the 1980s. Even in Europe the connection was not always in fashion. British Labor and social democrats in Sweden, Denmark, Norway, the Low Countries, and Austria all proclaimed their devotion to a welfare state and a system of macroeconomic management that, in their view, made Eurocapitalism, with a characteristically large state sector, the very avatar of humane development—even while regional integration was undercutting the leading role ascribed the state in most versions of Eurocapitalism (Vernon 1974). Until scarcely a decade and a half ago, in other words, the canon of development policy for both Europe and the developing world envisioned state-managed development as the key to economic democracy, the logical counterpart to and completion of political democracy.

Economic Restructuring and Democratization in Latin America

In certain respects, the "growth with equity" theme that surfaced in the 1970s anticipated part of today's thinking in positing normative connections between political and economic organization. As the first Decade of Development, the name given by the UN to the 1960s, had done little to even out economic disparities within countries, the Second Development Decade, the 1970s, brought a further rethinking of program design, mainly in the direction of policy-created links between economic and sociopolitical objectives. There was as yet, however, no general backpedaling from interventionism in either the so-called basic needs strategy or the other redistributionist approaches that circulated in this period (Griffin 1989). The groping toward more equitable patterns of development was, in any event, soon swamped by the need for policies to cope with the oil shocks of the 1970s and by the manifest political irresponsibility that became epidemic when growing reserves of petrodollars and rising global inflation triggered a borrowing binge that lasted until 1982.

In that year, the debt crisis struck Latin America and selected countries elsewhere. Mexico led the way into default, bringing into the open the results of several years of overborrowing and runaway interventionism. More or less concurrently with this denouement, there was growing public exasperation with the dictatorships that seized office in the 1960s and 1970s—and even a new impatience with the durable authoritarianism of the Mexican regime after the incautious populism of the 1970s had discredited the government's claim to sagacity in economic management. Both circumstances prompted a search for alternative, more attractive options, as Collier explains elsewhere in this volume in her examination of Mexican political changes.

Thereupon, while countries were unseating their authoritarian overlords, what the Inter-American Development Bank has aptly described as a silent revolution in economic policy set in, and thinking about relationships between economic and political variables was altered profoundly (Balassa et al. 1986). Not the least surprising aspect of this turnabout has been the newfound favor of market-based growth policies (Williamson 1990) and the priority now being given to programs that strengthen civil society.

Doubtless this revisionism reflects some borrowing from contemporary European notions of subsidiarity—along with a healthy interest in the installation of institutional arrangements to reduce the risk of a return to bureaucratic authoritarianism, as the last interval of dictatorial rule had been labeled. No doubt, too, part of the explanation lies in the political-ideological legitimation provided market reforms by the socialist government of Felipe Gonzalez in Spain, a much admired figure in Latin American democratic circles, who pushed even closer to market criteria the restructuring that began under Franco. Moreover, before a decade of experience with the new policies had passed, the dramatic events on which the 1980s ended in Europe provided external reinforcement for Latin American revisionism when Central European and post-Soviet "economies in transition" began, as

Sharman and Kanet, as well as Remington and Berliner, show in their analyses elsewhere in this volume, a somewhat similar quest for new combinations of economic and social policy to fit an evolving polity (Solimano et al., 1994).

One other factor seems to have contributed to a shift in the dominant policy paradigm. As the "lost decade of development" unfolded, there was a spreading awareness in Latin American policy circles that another newly industrializing region, Asia, had largely escaped the economic turmoil that gripped Latin America. Although some of the Asian economies had run up external debt and had to adjust to oil shocks and the prolonged OECD recession, they generally fared much better than Latin America, where only one major country, Colombia, went through the debt-crisis decade largely unscathed. Further, whereas in 1965 the average real per capita income in Latin America and the Caribbean was nearly twice as high as it was in what are now called the newly industrialized Asian economies, today the Asian Tiger level is about two and a half times that of Latin America (IMF, 1997). The conspicuous contrast between the two regions spurred on a searching reassessment of the policy path Latin America had followed into the troubled 1980s.

Special sections on poverty, social security, the environment, investments in health, workers and globalization, human resources, and fiscal decentralization in the annual analytical reports of the World Bank and the Inter-American Development Bank have profiled the evolution of new concerns— or, perhaps more accurately, the revived interest in some old concerns dressed up in different clothing. What is new about the items now on the agenda is the basis on which they are now being addressed: that is, on the fundamental presumption, stemming from the massive policy failure that put an end to import-substituting industrialization and state-led development, that the most serviceable general framework for public policy today derives from allocative signals anchored in market relationships.

It remains difficult, however, to find a causal association between economic restructuring and democratization. Almost all of the countries of the hemisphere, save Cuba, have opted for democracy in one guise or another, though in Nicaragua it exists under internal siege, thanks to the armed squads of Sandinistas. But they are by no means all the same in the progress they have made in realigning their economies. Chile, Mexico, and Bolivia were first on board, with Costa Rica close on their heels. The first three have enacted reforms across a broad front of policy domains: fiscal reform, trade reform, financial market reform, privatization, and, much more unevenly, labor market reform. Argentina and Peru came into the process somewhat later but made up for lost time by pressing ahead vigorously in their reform programs in the 1990s. And though democratic governance has clearly increased in Chile, Argentina, and Bolivia, "democracy" still rides in quotation marks in Mexico[8] and Peru,[9] albeit for different reasons.

The Argentine case is of special interest, for it was there that a restored democratic government, that of Alfonsín, proved remarkably ineffective in carrying out economic reforms and simply worsened the macroeconomic instability inherited from a discredited military regime. It was left to the Peronists, of all people, to introduce a serious program of restructuring and marketization. Inasmuch as many of the problems the current economic renovation is intended to correct had been implanted decades earlier (in one of the richest economies in the world) by the first Peronists, the historical script for Argentine economic reconstruction seems almost to have been written by Borges.

Meanwhile Venezuela has gone back and forth (it seems forth at present) and with exquisite historical irony has come up with a proponent of liberalization who reassures Wall Street, despite his past as a Marxist guerrilla leader and a founder of the Movement Toward Socialism. Brazil, where politics has sometimes resembled one of the country's famous *telenovelas*, has lagged notably behind in key fields, though presidential rhetoric has repeatedly reaffirmed a broad commitment to structural adjustment, and some major advances, in trade liberalization and privatization, have been made. Uruguay instituted financial market reform in the (probably vain) hope of reemerging as a regional financial center but has fallen behind in almost everything else. Ecuador, for its part, has yet to make any serious effort and, though it temporarily hired the architect of the Argentine restructuring plan, remains trapped in a stew made up of equal portions of populism and indecision.

Around the region, in other words, the retreat of the state from its posture of formal interventionism has taken place in contexts too varied to permit unequivocal conclusions to be drawn. Further, there is a growing appreciation that democracy itself is a variable concept and that there is no single template that fits all the cases. It would be exaggerating to say that each country is *sui generis*, but idiosyncracies abound, and it may well be that all of the current manifestations are, in some sense, provisional and incomplete (Whitehead 1992). At the very least, recent experience suggests that there is nothing linear about the way democratization, and its relation to policy reform, has evolved in the region.

That Mexico was the second major Latin American economy to embark on market-oriented restructuring highlights the problematic relationship between markets and democracy. There, a "neoliberal" model was imposed on the populace following a period of populist-engineered economic disintegration, albeit one not as chaotic as the Chilean version. And while the Mexican government differs significantly from the Chilean restructuring regimes, either during or after Pinochet, its flirtation with democratization has been, at the very least, exceedingly coy. To complicate the picture, the Mexican reform, which began around 1984 and deepened when Mexico entered the GATT, was accompanied by an unaccustomed macroeconomic instability (Aspe 1993; Lustig 1992) and growing restiveness in the political system. As the benefits of restructuring have made themselves felt only gradually, there was a general tendency for critics to skirt past the policy excesses of the 1970 to 1982 period that engendered the crisis in order to stir up public antipathy to the restructuring program. Thus, when Salinas was faced with the strongest electoral challenge any PRI candidate for the presidency had ever encountered, the vote for political pluralism was not, in large measure, a vote for liberalized restructuring.

The Mexican quandary illustrates the *inquietudes* that can abound when the prospects for democratization are beclouded by economic uncertainty. The collapse of the country's economy in 1982 after 50 years of positive aggregate growth, a record unmatched anywhere else, destroyed the enviable policy credibility of government, eroded confidence in official institutions generally, and ended, when it proved difficult to get the economy back on track, by undercutting the legitimacy of the ruling party. Thus even the timid beginnings of democratization under de la Madrid, amidst shaky economic circumstances, quickly, considering the longevity of the PRI hegemony, produced a questionable electoral victory for Salinas. The speed with which so much political capital evaporated helps explain why elected governments elsewhere have entered the process of structural adjustment with such trepidation.

The fact of the matter is that one cannot find a single Latin American case in which market-friendly restructuring was instituted by popular demand in a democratic setting—or even where it has drawn popular acclaim once under way. The most that can be said is that it has generally met with an agnostic and somewhat grumbling acquiescence from an electorate benumbed by economic catastrophe. Rather than representing a voluntary political choice democratically arrived at, restructuring has more often resembled the product of a force majeure, something adopted in extremis in hopes that economic salvation might lie beyond the purgatory of adjustment.

Economic Restructuring as a Support for Democratization

Although the ultimate vindication of restructuring will come from sustained growth, there are nevertheless some spin-offs that may, in the longer run, favor an opening of the political system to pluralistic competition. By reviewing what has emerged out of the experience of the 1980s and 1990s, it might be possible to see how economic liberalization and political democratization fit together in a world where economic choices are increasingly constrained by the exigencies of globalization. In almost all cases, though, the outcome of the tension between economic and political liberalization results from a waiting game: accepting the fact that many of the short-term adjustment costs fall due well before a restructured economy has time to yield its longer term pay-offs. Understandably, it is a gamble that risk-averse politicians may be loath to take.

The first contribution of restructuring to democratization derives from the fact that government is generally, by its nature, inefficient, and much more coercive than people generally realize, particularly when the political system is inaccessible to many citizens and there is wide latitude for regulatory interpretation and application by the bureaucracy. As multiple layers of bureaucracy accumulated over the decades and executive and legislative oversight grew weaker, the principal/agent problem thus emerged with a vengeance in most of Latin America. The fiscal and regulatory systems became a playing field for bureaucratic politics, clientelism, and corruption, and filled with rent-seeking opportunities. Decisional processes in the public sector were lost to public view as transparency diminished, and accountability, not very great to begin with, suffered enormously. So, too, did responsibility and responsiveness.

Admittedly, we do not as yet have reliable empirical research to support the contention. Yet there are a priori reasons to believe that this system, which increasingly operated to serve a self-aggrandizing bureaucracy or state bourgeoisie and its favored private-sector interests, the concessionary capitalists,[10] not only produced the fiscal crisis of the state but also skewed the distribution of income and wealth (and access to the opportunity structure) to a degree that Latin America became notorious for the lopsidedness of these patterns.

By all accounts, a system in which only its inequity is transparent has bred widespread mistrust of government and public policy (Camp 1996)—breeding a corrosive cynicism that, as Elliot Richardson has argued in his recent *Reflections of a Radical Moderate* (1996), deprives democracy of the only foundation on which it can ultimately rest: mutual trust. Hence downsizing and simplifying a dysfunctionally complex administrative system, reducing the scope of bureaucratic authority over resource allocation, should eventually do much to rebuild citizen trust, enhance the standing of the legislative branch of government, and bring more decisions under open scrutiny.

By building a more reliable and predictable transactional framework and lowering transaction costs, the changes that come from both structural adjustment and democratic reform should help build what, in a somewhat different context, John R. Commons called "industrial goodwill": that is, a presumption that the rules of the game, transparent in themselves, can promote growth by improving the circumstances within which decisions are taken and the polity organizes for collective effort (Commons 1919). Just as Commons recognized this to be an intangible asset of immense value in labor-management relations (and hence to both microlevel and systemic productivity), the same kind of mutual trust and expectational reliability, combined with socially acceptable levels of access, is conducive to the formation of social capital and the social capability that nourishes both the political system and the regime of production (Koo and Perkins 1995).

What the trimming of the public budget, trade liberalization, privatization, deregulation, and the imposition of fiscal and monetary rectitude promise, therefore, is exposing the allocational system to the play of markets near and far, as well as to the scrutiny of the electorate, so that both can override behind-the-scenes political maneuvering.[11] It may be too much to hope that market competition can squeeze out the cost overburden of corruption that has become pervasive in Latin America, but if the opportunities for rent-seeking can be reduced, so, too, can the trade in rent-conferring favors that channels resources in directions different from either the market or the presumptive patterns of democratic governance.

Trimming back bureaucracy and its discretionary powers also reduces the crowding-out effects that have produced an overextended administrative machinery on the one hand and undernourished social and economic programs on the other, including public investment programs that reach beyond the favored inner circles of the state-managed economy. In principle, too, the divestiture of revenue-absorbing public enterprises should free up resources for social investment programs that can finally begin to attend to the needs of those whom national development plans and economic growth have heretofore bypassed.

Not least of the political advantages of state retrenchment is that with the state's patronage powers reduced, there are greater opportunities for contested elections to result in upsets and greater opportunities for firms and households—and the press—to escape the sanctions the state has been able to apply to dissenting voices: for example, the withholding of state-owned enterprises' advertising budgets from critical periodicals, the use of fiscal centralization to choke off funds to areas where political opposition develops, to say nothing of the distribution of patronage, regulatory, and fiscal favors to coopt the leadership of such subsidiary organizations as labor unions, peasant organizations, trade associations, and teachers unions. All in all, reducing the armamentarium of politically deployed favors and coercive measures can only provide more social space for the flowering of civil society.

Fiscal decentralization has a particularly critical function in reassembling the economy in ways more conducive to social as well as economic efficiency. Increasingly it has come to be recognized, for example, that the social-investment priorities defined at the peak of government diverge considerably from those perceived at the grass roots where the voters actual live, especially in regions distant from the capital city and its influence market. Moreover, there is often a substantial information problem in communicating resource

scarcities and returns on alternative public investment options from less-influential regions to the political center of the national fiscal structure. In addition, there are generally such ineffective implementing and monitoring mechanisms for public investment programs that their geographical reach often tends to be limited, leaving significant segments of the population little touched thereby.

For these reasons, there is a mounting interest in redesigning systems of public finance to place more resources and the authority over their allocation in the hands of subnational levels of government where public supervision can be more direct and the pattern of allocation can be more responsive to locally and regionally defined priorities. Fiscal decentralization carries with it, therefore, a potential for fiscal democratization and consensus-building.

One should not, however, expect economic restructuring to work miracles in cleaning up the institutional detritus of more than five decades of interventionism in Latin America—and centuries of systematic stifling of human and social capital at the grass roots. It is perfectly plain that the playing field inherited from the prerestructuring days is far from level and that ample opportunity still exists for an informal economy in which political favor is demanded and supplied. If public disclosure and investigative journalism have not been able to close down an unlicensed hotel operation on Pennsylvania Avenue in Washington or prevent the conversion of foreign policy into an export industry with paying customers, there is still less reason to think that economic restructuring can quickly shore up the institutional basis for democracy in Latin America.

A final note, to return to what might be learned from postwar history; while the restructuring undertaken by occupying authorities reestablished a market economy on the ruins of Hitler's war machine, the democratization that was introduced alongside economic reforms converted the market economy into a *social* market economy, one in which market-produced imbalances were partially redressed by collective (not necessarily state) effort. By generating positive shared expectations, the policies in effect generated an implicit incomes policy that was conducive to both high rates of capital formation and, as a reflection of industrial goodwill, a high level of labor exertion. Further, the pattern of social investment in technical education and training and in health and housing was conducive to the accumulation of human capital and rapid advances in worker productivity.

Interestingly, although the limited restructuring undertaken by the successful Asian economies came unaccompanied by democratization, it was accompanied by land tenure reforms and a distribution of public investment and other policies that kept much of the population in touch with the opportunity structure and with income far less unequally distributed than in Latin America. Additionally, a significant investment in human capital formation distributed productive assets, of which human capital is one of the most important, much more widely than was generally the case in Latin America, so that South Korea and Taiwan were making far more effective use of their human resources than were the Latin American countries whose policy proclivities let these resources lie fallow or even caused their deterioration.

In short, a close reading of the postwar economic history of different regions leads one to conclude provisionally that economic and political liberalization may need to be conjoined with social policies that widen active participation if the economic growth that nourishes democratization is to be sustainable. Institutional sustainability, in other words, is as much a part of the growth equation today as is environmental sustainability.

3

Transitions to What?
The Social Foundations of the Democratic
Citizenship

Stephen Macedo

Introduction

Experts from "advanced" democratic countries are increasingly being called upon to offer advice to emerging democracies, but one wonders whether they are really in a position to supply it. Mature democratic systems seem, after all, to be in the throes of their own crisis of democratic citizenship. "Crisis" may be too strong a word, for while many older and newer democracies are plagued by citizen distrust and lack of confidence in major institutions, along with low levels of participation and an increasingly rampant privatism, these pathologies do not yet threaten the foundations of mature democracies.

Observers of the older democracies are in the process of relearning lessons that newer democrats should also heed: the foundations of democracy lie as much in civil society as in formal political institutions. The conviction that motivates this chapter is that we should think about liberal democracy as the pursuit of a broad social ideal. Constituting a healthy democracy means constituting not simply a set of formal political institutions, the rule of law, and effective governance, important as those may be; we must also nurture a democratic way of life. I want, in particular, to emphasize just how deeply rooted is the thought that in modern mass commercial societies, the civic capabilities of citizens are nurtured by civil society: in the welter of associations, institutions, and social networks intermediate between families and individuals, on the one side, and the state on the other.

Whether we are citizens of newer or older democracies, we are all still (and seem destined to remain) aspiring democrats. These reflections are, therefore, directed as much to fellow citizens of fairly stable but imperfect democracies as to those who hope to become—in certain respects at least— more like us.

Markets and the Foundations of Free Societies

The billionaire and international philanthropist George Soros has recently caused something of a stir—putting his mouth where his money is—by arguing that the greatest threat to the emergent open societies of the postcommunist world is the free market ideology itself (Soros 1997). Echoing not only Hegel (whose *Philosophy of History* Soros cites) but also Thucydides, Plato, and Aristotle, Soros warns that political systems should beware "the morbid intensification of their own first principles." The first principle of modern commercial democracies is the free pursuit of individual self-interest: the equal right of individuals to define and pursue their own interests. Soros is far from eccentric in warning that free societies can be threatened not only by state tyranny, but by an excess of a certain kind of narrowly privatistic individualism.

Soros directs his worries at the course being pursued by postcommunist democracies, but milder versions of these concerns are widely voiced with respect to advanced liberal democracies. Rising levels of citizen distrust and declining levels of social cooperation and political participation seem to be nearly universal concerns. The eminent political scientist Robert Lane goes so far as to argue that all modern Western societies are characterized by increasing levels of dysphoria and distrust. Clinical depression has increased by three times in the last two generations, and is increasing fastest in the United States. Distrust of major institutions, and of other people, is rising in all modern Western countries. Participation in informal social networks also appears to have declined, but since family breakup is more common, these networks are increasingly called upon in times of trouble. Adult suicides are not up, but attempted suicides are up (further proof that citizens are both more depressed and less competent!) (Lane 1994; Putnam 1995). Civic malaise must be of concern wherever it appears, but it is most worrisome where it conspires with economic hardship and shallow democratic roots to threaten the very survival of political freedom.

We would all do well at this juncture to ask ourselves certain fundamental political questions: How adequate is our understanding of the foundations of a free society? Have we, in our relatively well-off and stable democracies of the West, forgotten what it takes to sustain free societies? Do we focus too single-mindedly on free markets and formal political institutions while neglecting the social supports of citizenship, and are we passing along these faulty understandings to nascent democracies?

A chorus of critics of liberal democratic political thinking will answer these questions with a resounding "yes!" The critics, I want to argue, are right to be concerned about the civic dimension of our lives, but wrong to suggest that we must go outside the liberal democratic tradition to recover the right sorts of civic resources.

Liberal Democracy and Its Critics

Modern liberal democracy emerges from the conviction that human beings are born free and equal: their political and moral obligations are chosen, not inherited from their forebears, foisted upon them by their communities, or somehow knit into the fabric of the universe into which they are born. The political philosopher Thomas Hobbes is rightly seen as a progenitor of modern liberal democracy because of his conviction that legitimate political authority is created by a social contract among the people themselves. Hobbes was also a skeptic, who denied the existence of shared understandings of justice or rights discoverable by reason, and who believed that people would pursue power without limit. For these reasons Hobbes argued that nothing short of a near-absolute political sovereign could succeed in keeping political order, and so he was at most a protoliberal democrat (1981).

Subsequent liberal democratic thinking accepts the Hobbesian starting point of natural freedom and equality, but then takes upon itself the urgent problem of justifying limits on political power. The founders of American democracy, for example, while drawing on a multiplicity of intellectual sources, adopted the language and the logic of the liberal social contract theory of John Locke (1963). The Declaration of Independence famously insisted that individuals are endowed with certain "unalienable" rights, to life, liberty, and the pursuit of happiness. These rights were further elaborated in the first ten amendments to the U.S. Constitution.

The most politically astute of the American founders did not view the enumeration of rights as the most important means of keeping government power limited and regular. More important to Alexander Hamilton, James Madison, and John Jay (the authors of the *Federalist Papers*) were the structure and allocation of political power. Separating and sharing powers among distinct branches of government, legislative bicameralism, and federalism were viewed as more important and more reliable than the "parchment barriers" of a bill of rights. Structures like the separation of powers could be relied upon, it has often been said, because they do not depend on uncertain expectation of virtuous self-restraint, but merely on the self-interest of officeholders: power would be limited by pitting ambition against ambition (Hamilton et al. 1961, no. 48, 51).

It is sometimes said that the framers of the U.S. Constitution believed that their devices for limiting and directing political power were so finely wrought that the whole could be thought of as a "machine that would go of itself" (Kammen 1986). The new system would be powered by the ambitions of officeholders and the self-interest of citizens, at least once this self-interest is rendered tame and manageable by being spread out over a vast and diverse "extended republic" (Madison, *Federalist* no. 10, in Hamilton et al. 1961). Thanks to the insights of the new political science, modern constitutionalism could do without the civic virtue on which the ancient constitutions of Athens and Rome had depended so heavily.

In important respects, the sort of picture I have begun to sketch is an inadequate and misleading guide for the citizens and political leaders of emerging democracies. It is one thing to say that modern constitutional democracies economize on civic virtue and public-spiritedness, another to say that they do without it altogether. True enough, the institutional mechanisms and procedures of modern constitutionalism will help channel and refine the application of political power. They in no way immunize a polity from breakdown, however, if leaders and citizens are motivated by narrow and short-term interests. The system will not work as it should without a modicum of virtue in political leaders and the citizens themselves. And so Hamilton, surely the most hardheaded of the founders, near the close of his extended defense of the Constitution, asked:

> What is the liberty of the press? Who can give it any definition which would not leave the utmost latitude for evasion? I hold it to be impracticable; and from this I infer that its security, whatever fine declarations may be inserted in any constitution respecting it, must altogether depend on public opinion, and on the general spirit of the people and of the government. And here, after all, ... must we seek for the only solid basis of all our rights. (Hamilton, *Federalist* no. 84, in Hamilton et al. 1961)

Both the Lockean social contract and the American founding documents focus on two elements: fundamental principles of justice, at the core of which are liberty and equality, and the elaboration of formal institutional structures that, it is hoped, will help keep political power limited and directed toward its proper ends. The most influential and prestigious political thinking about liberal democracy over the last few decades has followed a similar pattern:

political theorists wrestle over how to justify one conception or another of liberty and equality, individual rights and justice, while the main agenda of political scientists has been with the study of formal institutions and their interactions, along with voting behavior and interest-group politics.

What is missing from the political science of the Founders, and of their more recent successors, is a fully developed account of where citizen virtue comes from. What is often missing from our thinking about "liberal democracy" is a view of the political and social institutions needed to sustain a citizenry capable of and willing to support actively and extend liberal principles of justice. This has left liberal democracy vulnerable to a variety of critics who charge that the theory and practice of the modern democracies are impoverished and deeply flawed.

Communitarian critics argue that the preoccupation with individual rights tends to neglect the importance of communal ties, social solidarity, and citizen virtue. Modern liberal democratic political thinking—with its emphasis on abstract, universalistic individualism—neglects the shared projects and goals that, according to communitarians, would make citizens more than self-interested "atoms" (Taylor 1985, esp. chs. 7 and 8; MacIntyre 1981, esp. ch. 8, and 1988, esp. chs. 1 and 20; Sandel 1982; and for a response, Macedo 1992).

Civic republican critics focus more specifically on the relative neglect of political community in liberal democratic theory and statecraft. Some republicans charge that bourgeois society, with its emphasis on social goods such as material security and well-being, no longer has a place for the political activity that was prized by the ancients (Arendt 1958; Walzer 1981, 1983). Others worry that liberal freedom and equality have turned into a sweeping moral nonjudgmentalism that leaves no room for public moral judgments about good citizenship. In America and increasingly elsewhere, the critics charge, this morally thin liberalism has supplanted an older civic republican tradition that emphasized the importance of maintaining social and economic conditions in which the capacity for citizen virtue would be nurtured (Sandel 1996).

Debunking the Skeptics

How should citizens of advanced and nascent democracies react to these sorts of criticisms? Has the liberal democratic tradition run out of moral and civic steam? Is our understanding of what it means to create and to sustain a liberal democracy impoverished? One possible response is to dismiss the critics' concerns out of hand. Perhaps not all the consequences of individual freedom and choice are positive, the skeptic might argue, but the dangers of misguided government intervention are worse. If we concede that government has a legitimate role in promoting civic virtue and the "good society," what articulable limits on government power will be left? Better to confine governments to narrower concerns—internal and external security, the enforcement of rules of property and contract, the provision of a social safety net—and to leave the promotion of the "good society" to private action: to churches and voluntary groups.

More to the point of this volume, if our concern is with the stability of transitions to democracy, it can be argued that the crucial thing is indeed the level of economic development. The leaders of the emergent democracies need to focus on the speedy transition to efficient market institutions, to create a rising living standard as soon as possible, and then all this talk of civic malaise will melt away.

The faith that economic development leads to democratization, articulated by Seymour Martin Lipset in 1959 and widely debated ever since, is appealing, but it does not seem to be true in any simple sense (Lipset 1959). Recent evidence shows that Lipset was right to think that richer countries are more likely to sustain democracy, but according to Adam Przeworski and Fernando Limongi, it also seems to be the case that dictatorships that generate economic development and wealth also become quite stable (Przeworski and Limongi 1997). Economic development does not, in and of itself, seem to promote the overthrow of dictatorships and the emergence of democracy. If we want to promote democracy, according to Przeworski and Limongi, we must promote democracy.

Alternatively, one might argue that of course the citizens of postcommunist societies are distrustful, dissatisfied, and disillusioned: many postcommunist governments, perhaps especially in Russia, are in the throes of a "crisis of governability" (Holmes 1995). The reason, Stephen Holmes has recently argued, is that many postcommunist governments are failing to deliver the most basic public services: stable and effectively enforced rules of property, contract, and torts, internal security, upright and efficient public administration, reliable supplies of electricity, water, food, and housing, a stable currency, a social safety net, and a growing economy. Weak states are plagued by corruption, banditism, insecurity, declining living standards, scarce and uncertain supplies of basic goods, irregular law enforcement, administrative incompetence, and pervasively short time horizons. Under such conditions it makes no sense to attribute distrust and disillusionment to cultural legacies, Holmes argues: these attitudes are a perfectly reasonable responses to institutional weakness and basic government incompetence. Free markets cannot work in the absence of an effective legal system or without the basic institutions of effective governance. Before the Lockean solution looks attractive, Holmes says, the Hobbesian problem has got to be solved. So one might say that before citizens of emerging democracies start worrying about the decline of associations, social networks, and civic participation, they need to settle the

Hobbesian and Lockean agendas: public safety, the rule of law, and effective basic political institutions.

These are very fair observations, but we want to be careful how we respond to them. For if we focus solely on the lack of security, basic administrative competence, declining living standards, and the like, we might conclude that the old system was not after all so bad. The old system at least solved the Hobbesian problem of personal security: most citizens of communist tyranny were safe and secure.

We should not simply dismiss out of hand the widely felt civic malaise that I described in the beginning. Political stability, personal security, and regular law enforcement, along with a reasonable level of material prosperity, may be of basic importance, but they are not all-important. When we talk about our hopes for "transitions to democracy" we typically have in mind more than mere stability, security, and regime legitimacy. Regime stability and wealth creation are not all that citizens care about. The quality of civic life also matters to people across the globe. The important question with respect to democratic transitions is: How can we combine effective governance with a broad array of individual freedoms and a democratic civil society? To answer that question, we cannot ignore the problem of trying to discern how to foster an engaged and active citizenry capable of self-governance.

The die-hard skeptic might still reply that all this talk about the health of civil society is nothing more than Western analysts projecting their own anomie and disconnection onto the emerging democracies. So let us ask: Do these worries about the state of the civic culture and the health of associations and memberships really apply beyond the familiar contexts of Western Europe and North America?

The importance of rejuvenating—or just juvenating—civil society institutions and an active, self-confident citizenry in the nations of the former Soviet Empire are widely discussed. Communist rule was built on preventing the development of institutions and associations autonomous of the party apparatus. There is a widespread sense that one legacy of communism is pervasive distrust, disengagement, and an atrophy of cooperativeness and the tendency to associate freely (Di Palma 1991; Rose 1994).

Some scholars hope that the collapse of communist rule signals a "revolution of citizenship." Under the old system, legitimacy flowed from the top: from a party claiming possession of political truth. Now legitimacy will flow up from the bottom, or at least, it will if citizens take advantage of participatory channels. Without downplaying the basic importance of "peace, security, and justice," many observers of Central Europe urge Western funding agencies to focus more on "the indigenous capacity of a country's population—as individuals acting alone or in association with one another" to "call leaders to account and ensure the tenets of democracy" (Nelson 1996, pp. 360–63). On the other hand, some worry that forms of solidarity, mutual assistance, and intellectual mobilization nurtured in opposition to communist rule in Central Europe are waning now that formal institutions are more democratic and now that activists formerly united by their opposition to communism are increasingly divided by the normal democratic disagreements over politics and public policy (Di Palma 1991; Isaac 1996).

Analyst Michael Shifter discerns across Latin America a growing concern with representation, participation, and accountability, noting that many of those who would pursue these democratic values more vigorously understand that doing so may mean trading off some measure of economic growth and political efficiency. Among the signs of a renewed determination to deepen democratic institutions are the rise of independent citizens groups concerned with combating official corruption, greater representation and political activity among women and indigenous people, the establishment of ombudsman's offices to receive citizen's complaints, promote public education, and protect human rights, and a more active and independent press (Shifter 1997, pp. 118–20).

Asia is one region of the world where some say that human rights, multiparty democracy, and free and open political contestation are Western ideals at odds with a distinct set of "Asian values" (Chan, this volume). Is Asia the continent where the concern with civil society and active citizenship founders on the shoals of cultural relativism?

It seems to me perilous to draw conclusions about what the people of Asian countries really want from their political systems if those people have not had the sort of robust and open debate that can only be had in conditions of broad intellectual freedom. Free democratic deliberation must be a prerequisite to any sound claim about what the people of Asia, or any other continent, really want. That free deliberation requires an absence of censorship or the threat of censorship, autonomous universities where professors are not punished for opposing or simply refusing to cooperate with the government, a free press, broad freedoms of association, the freedom to organize political parties and to criticize the government. It is simply not possible to say that the citizens of any country value these freedoms less than cleanliness, order, personal security, and material prosperity, unless those citizens have already experienced these freedoms.

And so it is not surprising that many scholars regard the emergence of civil society institutions as crucial to democratization in China, Korea, and elsewhere in Asia. Student dissident movements and associations of industrial workers have long been politically active in South Korea and elsewhere in Asia. Bruce Cumings argues that the calls for reform issued by student groups in Korea have echoed through the wider Korean public thanks to that public's eagerness to read newspapers and gather in ubiquitous neighborhood tearooms to talk politics (Cumings, this volume). Since 1987, a plethora of social movements has blossomed in Korea, thanks to concessions made by the regime to political liberalization. The new movements include groups concerned with women's issues, the environment, social justice, consumer protection, and antinuclear and peace issues (Lee 1993).

In China, too, while the post-Tiananmen era is hardly characterized by a blossoming of civil society, scholars continue to insist that a nascent civil society is discernible, especially in urban areas, and that the attitudes of "critical citizenship" that might be associated with a vibrant civil society are apparent among important sectors of the population, especially the young (Chan and Nesbitt-Larking 1995).

Admittedly, here, as elsewhere, we should expect civil society institutions, patterns of political conflict, and the process of democratization not simply to mimic Western norms, but to assume a hybrid character reflecting the distinctive history and character of the region (Ling and Shih 1998). But of course, the very categories of "Western norms" and "Asian values" encompass societies with very different economic, social, political, and cultural traditions. While we should not be surprised to see a diversity of political styles and institutions both across and within these vast regions, it is hard to see what special local justification there is for denying the importance to Asian democracy of a free press, freedom of association and political organization, and free and fair multiparty elections.

Large parts of Africa, finally, are characterized by intense levels of poverty along with political instability and institutional underdevelopment. Here the concern with civil society may indeed seem premature or beside the point: stable governance and basic material security have yet to be established. Nevertheless, there seems little doubt for many scholars that progress toward greater democratization will depend on the development of civil society, on broader social solidarities capable of confronting the state, and on interests that cut across affinities based on kinship and local and ethnic affinities. Large parts of sub-Saharan Africa may lack the rudiments of civil society and an active public sphere, but the path to democracy seems, here as elsewhere, to proceed toward these familiar democratic landmarks (Lewis 1996; Bienen and Herbst 1996).

Worries about the health of civil society do indeed seem to have wide resonance, certainly to all the areas of the world covered by this volume.

Toward a Civic Liberalism

The critics of recent liberal democratic theory and practice are right to worry about the civic consequences of greater individual freedom and economic development. Where they go wrong and, I believe, where they would lead the nascent democracies astray, is in thinking that concern about the state of our civic lives—the health of communities, the capacity of citizens, the prevalence of social trust and cooperation—means we must abandon the liberal democratic tradition. The fact is that the liberal democratic tradition contains a more powerful civic dimension than is often noted. Contrary to the rather caricaturish picture I presented at the beginning of this section, the dependence on citizen virtue is somewhat in the background of modern constitutional thinking, but it is not altogether absent: civic virtue is a muted but vital theme of liberal democratic constitutionalism. Moving that civic dimension closer to the foreground of our political thinking would offer improved models for those who seek either to set out on the liberal democratic path or to continue on it.

Taking up the civic question does not require that we write off the liberal democratic tradition. There is much in this great tradition that suggests that the free self-governing society is about more than individual choice and the size and the distribution of the GNP. The critics I have mentioned offer a false choice between a political order in which individual liberty is central, and one in which we care about citizenship, community, and the quality of our civic lives. Newer and older democracies should strive for a political order in which the protection of individual freedom is a central and basic aim without being all-important.

The liberal tradition makes the protection of equal rights and individual freedom its central aim, and it is not as demanding with respect to civic virtue as some other forms of government, such as the republican ideals described by Plato (1968) and Rousseau (1983). Nevertheless, sensible liberal democrats will allow that freedom and equality may be constrained in various ways to help promote certain civic goods, such as a reasonably active and engaged citizenry who are prepared to take initiatives and act on their own to solve problems without constantly looking to government for assistance. A liberal democracy prizes freedom, of course (this is the liberal element), but also self-government, both as a means to protect liberty and prevent tyranny, and as a distinctive and valuable way of exercising our rational capacities. Sensible liberal democrats, in newer or older democracies, should want not simply to maximize individual choice and equality but to gently encourage the development of certain civic virtues: tolerance and, indeed, respect for one's fellow citizens, cooperativeness, a decent level of concern for and willingness to contribute to public things, a capacity to accept short-term sacrifices for long-term gains, an ability to weigh competing reasons and evidence, and so on.

Civic education is not undertaken only in the most direct and obvious ways—through schools, civics curricula, and direct political pedagogy—and it should not be confused with the coercive imposition of a particular conception of the good life. People are educated indirectly in a host of ways: our social and political lives are themselves educative, not only for children but for adults as well. Institutional and public policy choices of all sorts shape our social and political lives and will thereby often have important educative dimensions; these behavior- and character-shaping dimensions of public policy are inevitable, and should be attended to as means of gaining leverage over the problem of promoting a healthy civic life. Indeed, liberal citizens can be encouraged to use their freedom—including their freedom to associate and cooperate—to contribute indirectly to the task of liberal civic education.

Why is civic education important? One thing that the shapers of emerging democracies should remember is that the mere fact that a nation has thrown off dictatorship does not mean that it has permanently cast aside all of the pathologies we would associate with dictatorship. Individual citizens of democratic states may have a tendency—not unlike the subjects of a dictatorship—to look constantly to the central government to satisfy every need. Both a dictatorship and a democracy can guarantee individual equality and both can make appeals to individuals based on opposition to social privileges and inequalities that thrive at the local level. "The natural tendency of a democratic people [is] to centralize the business of government," de Tocqueville famously warned, and this must be resisted if liberty is to be preserved (1861, p. 243).

Liberty, the ability of citizens to freely pursue their own interests, can be threatened most dramatically by political tyranny. It can also, however, slowly slip through the fingers of citizens who cede too much responsibility to a government. The problem, for civic liberals such as de Tocqueville, is not an active government per se, but the political and wider civic passivity that can result if remote agencies of government relieve individuals, local governments, and voluntary associations of too much responsibility (de Tocqueville 1969).

There is every reason to think that the problem of civic life is endemic to modern commercial democracies, new and old. This is not, as the critics of liberalism sometimes allege, because these modern societies have suffered a moral decline when compared with ancient societies such as Athens or Sparta. As Benjamin Constant pointed out long ago, political participation is far less attractive in modern mass societies primarily on account of their vast scale: the individual citizen of a modern democracy is one voice among millions, less capable of being heard than were citizens of the small polis of old. Citizens of the ancient polis also enjoyed the leisure provided by ownership of slaves (Constant 1988).

Though a defender of the modern emphasis on private liberty as opposed to public participation, Constant argued for the need to supplement private pursuits, to temper the inherent privatism of mass commercial societies with a measure of civic-spiritedness. The mass scale and commercial nature of modern societies may lessen the relative benefits to individuals of political and civic activity. And modern political institutions such as representative government, separation of powers, and other constitutional devices may lessen our dependence on civic virtue. Nevertheless, modern democracies continue to depend on some measure of civic-spiritedness. This requires not that we supplant but rather that we temper and supplement the core principles—the privatism and self-interest—of modern commercial democracy.

The concern with civic virtue and community life within the liberal tradition is in important part an account of the importance of resisting the push toward centralization and the disappearance of small communities. Tocqueville's version of this story is well known and it has recently found support in the work of Robert Putnam and others (Putnam 1994, 1995). I want here to focus on another, less well known version of this story, one that will perhaps make especially clear that emerging democracies do not need to look to the critics of modern liberal democracy to recognize the importance of attending to the health of associations and civic life. We can look, rather, to the father of the modern economy himself, Adam Smith.

Smith certainly regarded the new commercial order as a monumental advance over previous social forms, but it was a flawed advance: economic development could, he thought, undermine the social bases of many forms of civic competence and personal well-being. For Smith, capitalism's advance depended on an ever-more-developed division of labor, ever-more-extensive markets composed of vast networks of people whose relations are fragmentary, indirect, and often quite distant. Modern commercial society is a society of strangers: an anonymous society of people with distant and fragmentary relations.

The Great Society is anonymous and liberating in part because people's conduct simply becomes so much harder to monitor as people uproot themselves and settle in expanding urban centers. While important forms of freedom become possible only in the Great Society—not to mention the division of labor and, along with it, unheard-of advances in productivity—this new freedom is also dangerous: liberation from the thick texture of small-scale communities and social networks of traditional village life could prove demoralizing.

Smith did not take a laissez-faire attitude toward the deleterious consequences of the commercial order for citizen character and competence. He worried that the social structure of an increasingly urban, mass society would undermine moral character, and so he sought to promote and shape substitutes for the small-scale communities of the old regime. It was for this reason that Smith arrestingly described religious "sects" or churches as "Institutions for the Instruction of People of all Ages" (Smith 1979, p. 788). Religious communities were effective moral educators because they did more than preach morality: the very nature of the small, face-to-face community was itself a crucial means for actually securing responsible conduct.

Popular religious communities provided peer groups that notice and care about the conduct of ordinary people, thereby giving them an incentive to attend to their own conduct, think about and plan for the future, and behave responsibly. Membership in these face-to-face communities gave ordinary people a public character or reputation to lose, and thereby a social incentive to display prudent, responsible conduct.

The *economic* benefits of personal responsibility were obvious to Smith—the great mass of poor people was doomed to horrible poverty in the absence of economic growth—but Smith also stressed the intrinsic importance of intellectual and moral development. Communal memberships would help make people not simply more frugal, but more self-respecting and confident, more open to fellow feeling and sympathy.

Smith also offered a political plan to blunt the potentially sharp edges of the austere moral system animating religious sects: he sought, in other words, indirectly to shape these communities toward civic aims. He recommends that free rein be given to all who would undertake gay "publick diversions," since these will help "dissipate the melancholy and gloom" of religious austerity. And Smith sought to promote science—"the great antidote to the poison of enthusiasm and superstition"—by making the study of science a precondition for admittance to prestigious professions. He believed that these educational requirements for professionals would have cultural "trickle-down" effects for society as a whole, especially once the attraction of a career in the church declined (Smith 1979, pp. 795–96).

Most important for those who would promote the health of newer commercial democracies, Smith saw no contradiction in both praising the great advantages of a commercial society while recommending gentle, unobtrusive measures to combat the potentially demoralizing anonymity of a mass society. Smith rightly recognizes that the promotion of free self-government must be about more than merely limiting public authority in the name of individual freedom and about more than simply unleashing the power of markets to create wealth. More fundamentally, modern liberal democratic statecraft must be about constituting a social and political order that—in both its public and private spheres—promotes a decent and orderly, active and self-controlled citizenry. The lesson for citizens and leaders of democracies, new or old, is that we can respect freedom without neglecting to take care over the realm of associations: the freedom to associate may do most of the needed work, but gentle public interventions may also help ensure that associations promote civic education and the public good.

The Pluralist Ideal

The big question for newer democracies as much as the older ones is to discern how to foster a pattern of associative life that supports the liberal democratic political project. The goal seems clear enough: pluralism is essential. Much social science after Smith reaffirms the importance of fostering an overlapping, pluralistic pattern of group memberships and communal allegiances.

Pluralism is important because groups can be oppressive. Groups that totally absorb the allegiances of their members destroy the possibility of individual liberty. Freedom and tolerance are fostered by multiple group memberships; being pulled in a multiplicity of directions is the best way of maintaining a critical distance from the demands and expectations of any particular source of identity or allegiance. Also useful, of course, are the clashes among particular group-based allegiances and the more inclusive shared identity created by our status as citizens. It is the state, as Emile Durkheim observed, that protects individual rights and, by so doing, guards the possibility of escape from group oppression. The state must:

> permeate all those secondary groups of family, trade and professional association, Church, regional areas and so on . . . which tend . . . to absorb the personality of their members. It must do this in order to prevent this absorption and free these individuals, and so to remind these partial societies that they are not alone and that there is a right that stands above their own rights. (Durkheim 1957, p. 65.)

While groups prevent social atomization and individual demoralization in the face of a distant centralized state and a modern mass society, the state safeguards individuals against the domination of particular groups. A tolerant, self-critical individuality is fostered by this tension among the conflicting partial allegiances of groups and the more inclusive role of citizen. The leaders of totalitarian states have recognized all of this and so they strive precisely to maintain mass society conditions: to keep individuals isolated and to prevent the emergence of rival sources of loyalty and power, all of which helps sustain the isolation, distrust, and passivity that are the opposite of democratic citizenship but the essence of dictatorial control (Durkheim 1957, p. 62; Kornhauser 1959).

The lesson is that tolerant and freedom-promoting social orders are *pluralistic*: societies of partial allegiances in which groups endlessly compete with each other and with the state for the allegiances of individuals, and in which individuals' loyalties are divided among a variety of "crosscutting" (or only partially overlapping) memberships and affiliations. The free society needs community life, therefore, and it needs community life to be constituted in a certain way. Pluralism is, as Gabriel A. Almond and Sidney Verba note, the key: "pluralism, even if not explicitly political pluralism, may indeed be one of the most important foundations of political democracy" (Almond and Verba 1963, pp. 319–20)

Fostering pluralism is especially important today. Religious, racial, ethnic, and national identities have reasserted themselves in many places with a vigor that is often frightening. And yet modern societies are increasingly diverse. Such societies are ill served by totalizing identities that wholly capture the allegiances of citizens (Kornhauser 1959, pp. 32, 30–62).

The healthy structures of group life are characterized by rich networks of broad and relatively weak group ties. Particular groups will foster cooperativeness among members, but when individuals belong to networks of partially overlapping groups, this should help foster a more generalized attitude of cooperativeness and reciprocity. Then particular groups achieve the benefits of cooperation among members, without foreclosing the possibility of new and wider forms of cooperation across group lines.

The right sort of associational life appears not simply to provide the psychic benefits of combating anomie and alienation; we can also identify economic and moral benefits. On the economic side, membership in associations provides ordinary individuals with a public character, as Smith predicted, a form of credit: a substitute for the more personalized reputations possessed by outstanding individuals.

In societies with dense, overlapping networks of associations, trust can be lent: as Putnam observes, "Social networks allow trust to become transitive and spread: I trust you, because I trust her and she assures me that she trusts you" (Putnam 1994, p. 169). Individuals in cooperative schemes witness the gains of cooperation and acquire the reputation that make them eligible for more such endeavors. Individuals have an incentive to preserve this eligibility: the experience of successful cooperation provides both incentives to and collective resources for further cooperation. Putnam's work suggests that the quality of our civic lives—the health of our communities and associations—in turn promotes the health of the economy (Putnam 1994). A society with the right structure of associational life is a society in which collective action problems can be solved without constant resort to centralized political intervention.

The healthy structure of group life that I have described may also have important moral benefits for newer and older democracies: it may well help foster character traits that are conducive to the realization of a just society. The picture of civil society that I have sketched seems to allow us to at least partially bridge the gulf separating the hardheaded expectations of economists and the more moralistic hopes of those who promote liberal ideals of justice.

A natural response to the theory of justice of John Rawls—which emphasizes the inviolability of basic liberties and the need to strive for principles of fairness and distributive justice—is to think that the goal of a just society is admirable but probably unattainable, especially, perhaps, in a capitalist society in which self-interest plays such a large role. It is often thought, therefore, that a great gap lies between the hopes of a political moralist such as Rawls and the more hardheaded expectations of economists and others who assume that people act on the basis of self-interest.

The civil society story we have told shows, we can now see, that there is a whole set of "cooperative virtues" that occupy a crucial position intermediate between the noblest forms of self-sacrifice and the narrowest forms of self-interest. Indeed, Rawls himself suggests that approximating liberal justice in practice may not depend on getting individuals to adopt an utterly selfless moral point of view but, rather, may build on the cooperativeness and reciprocity exhibited in group life.

Rawls describes the "cooperative virtues" as "the virtue of reasonableness and a sense of fairness, a spirit of compromise and a readiness to meet others halfway, all of which are connected with the willingness to cooperate with others on political terms that everyone can publicly accept." The core citizen virtue in Rawls's scheme is reasonableness. Reasonable people are not altruists (or, from a different viewpoint, "suckers") moved by impartially defined principles irrespective of how others behave, and they are not, at the other extreme, mere pursuers of rational self-interest. Reasonable people are willing to "propose principles and standards as fair terms of cooperation and to abide by them willingly, given the assurance that others will likewise do so." They seek "a social world in which they can cooperate with others on terms all can accept as free and equal. They insist that reciprocity should hold within that world so that each benefits along with the others" (Rawls 1993, pp. 163, 49–50; Rawls 1971, p. 494). The reciprocity and cooperativeness fostered by networks of groups and associations should, therefore, help promote a sense of fairness that is conducive to the realization of a wider social justice.

Those who would shape nascent democracies with an eye to civic-spiritedness, economic well-being, and the pursuit of social justice have reason to attend to the health and the structure of civil society. Those who practice reciprocity in their ordinary dealings are the natural supporters of fair principles of cooperation. The moral education of citizens, as Rawls describes it, does not consist primarily of moral suasion or philosophical argument. Rather, a crucial educative role is played by the experience of cooperation in face-to-face associations, for here the ties of friendship and mutual trust are especially intense and here too, feelings of anger, resentment, and guilt are most likely to be visited upon or felt by those who shirk their duties (Rawls 1971, pp. 475, 470). The lesson is that a healthy structure of group life appears capable of helping to bridge the gap between the narrower forms of self-interest and the wider cooperativeness on which healthy societies depend.

What Is to Be Done?

No claim in political science is unassailable, and surely we have much more to learn about the nature and role of democratic civil society. Nevertheless, there is evidence enough, I believe, to say that there is a lesson here that emerging democracies will ignore at their peril: liberal democratic transitions should be conceived of in broad rather than narrow terms. The critics of liberalism help identify dimensions of the free society that members of established liberal democracies sometimes neglect. Modern liberal democracy is a project of free self-government. To secure the conditions of self-government—governance of one's own life and the participation in collective self-government—requires that we attend to the educative resources of communities and associations. We have reason, therefore, to worry about the state of civil society institutions in emergent democracies. The remaining question may be the most difficult: What is to be done?

It is doubtful that there is a "magic bullet" for promoting or restoring a vibrant civil society. In the United States there has been considerable debate about the causes of the falling rates of participation in voluntary groups and declining levels of trust. The causes are not easy to identify (possible causes include greater mobility, too much TV, increased political centralization, increasing economic dislocation, greater family instability, more time spent working, and, relatedly, the entry of women into the workforce). If the causes of our civic malaise are multiple, it seems likely that the requisite responses will be as well.

Even if the causes were apparent, it could be difficult to say what is to be done. Turning back the clock to a bygone era may be attractive to some, but this will often be unjustified and, in any case, impossible. It seems likely, for example, that some erosion of civic participation has been brought about by the entry of women into the workforce. Nevertheless, basic principles of equality argue for economic opportunities for women, and it is, in any event, well-nigh impossible to imagine that we will return to the family structure of old. Here as elsewhere, not all the consequences of greater freedom and equality are good, and just how we should respond to the negative consequences of changing family structures is by no means easy to say. Suggested remedies are liable to be of questionable effectiveness and to involve difficult trade-offs, and both the efficacy and the trade-offs will be gauged differently in different contexts.

The story I have told yields no simple blueprint for the future. A good deal of work will have to be done to devise what Michael Ignatieff has called "a civil society strategy" for the emerging democracies. Such a strategy would mean:

> funding independent media; maintaining ties not simply with governments and regimes but with their oppositions; providing aid and assistance to

strengthen the key institutions of civil society, the courts, judiciary, and police; developing charitable and voluntary associations so that the population ceases to look to the state and begins to look to its own strengths; developing non-governmental channels for delivery of Western technical aid and assistance, and educational and cultural exchanges. (1995)

I agree with all this, including its implicit message that civic agendas will need to be devised in particular contexts by many agencies.

Conclusion

A civic agenda will have to proceed along a variety of fronts, doing many small things in the hope that they add up and make a difference. This is not, then, an exciting or simple recommendation, but it is hard to see that any other is warranted. There is no substitute for the resolve to pay closer attention to the civic consequences of major public policies and of international aid. What is needed is a kind of "civic cost benefit analysis": a determination to take seriously the impact (insofar as it can be discerned) of major public policies and aid programs on the health of associations, nongovernmental institutions, public spaces, and civic activity.

The citizens of older and newer democracies also need to recognize that it may be that there are incompatibilities and trade-offs among some of the elements of the free, self-governing, commercial republics for which we strive. "Negative" freedom from government interference and the pursuit of economic efficiency may be among the central features of life in a modern democracy, but they alone will not sustain a social order capable of nurturing the interest in and capacity for self-government.

Part III

The End of

Authoritarianism in South

and Central America

4

Transition Pathways: Institutional Legacies, the Military, and Democracy in South America

Felipe Agüero

STUDIES OF POSTAUTHORITARIAN regimes now focus mostly on "the democratic or nondemocratic quality of political processes and outcomes" (Comisso 1995, p. 202; Lowenthal and Domínguez 1996). Appraisals that stem from this focus are often quite critical of these regimes.[1] A recent review of democratic regimes in Latin America, for instance, concluded that "effective democratic governance is still incipient, inchoate, fragile, highly uneven, incomplete. . . ." (Lowenthal and Domínguez 1996, p. 7). Supporting this assessment is the extended presence of problems of participation and representation (Hagopian 1995), accountability (O'Donnell 1994; Stokes 1997), rule of law (Holston and Caldeira, 1995), economic constraints and inequality (Mainwaring 1995), and civilian control (Zaverucha 1993).

The literature on new democracies, however, is inconclusive about the source of those problems. Some studies find the source in the more or less distant past: a long tradition lacking in pluralism or rule of law, the ill-fated consequences of the preceding authoritarian regimes, or the mode of transition to postauthoritarian regimes. Another body of literature places the source of difficulties in posttransition arrangements, institutions, and dynamics. Yet another finds that perverse influences from the past are being countered with new institutional arrangements.

This chapter assesses the impact of the past, particularly transition legacies, by focusing on one important aspect affecting the quality of democracy: military prerogatives.[2] Expanded military prerogatives lessen the prospects of affirming civilian control, "a necessary condition for polyarchy" (Dahl, 1989, p. 250). A postauthoritarian regime may display all the institutions necessary for the regular practice of competitive elections, but high levels of military prerogatives will severely curtail its democratic nature. Thus, along with the institutions and guarantees for political competition, limits on military prerogatives are indispensable for effective democratic governance (Karl 1990, p. 2).

Given the significance that military institutions have had in their history and the military nature of their authoritarian regimes, a focus on the civil-military aspect of democratization in Argentina, Brazil, Chile, Peru, and Uruguay allows for a useful exploration of the impact of modes of transition upon the quality of these new democracies. To what extent have predictions about democratic outcomes based on transition mode held true? Does the present state of military influence in new democracies carry the imprint of the transitions? Or have transitions' institutional traces been wiped away? By contrasting the expectations born out of the transitions with the current state of military power and constraints on new democracies, we can gain insight into the impact of transitions on the quality of democratic governance in the new regimes.

This chapter proceeds first with a review of the literature on the effect of the past on "the democratic or nondemocratic quality" of postauthoritarian regimes. Although the focus is on South American countries, the debate is presented as it has appeared in the democratization literature more generally. Then, with a focus on the military, the chapter presents the factors that influenced different transition modes in these countries in order to highlight the expectations that they generated about the quality of successor democracies and particularly the constraints that the military would present for them. Those expectations are then contrasted with the current state of military prerogatives. This contrast leads to the conclusion that, although some of these cases have challenged those expectations, most have actually remained consistent with them.

Transition modes have been decisive in shaping the current state of military prerogatives and constraints on democracy. This conclusion contradicts the trend to minimize the impact of transitions relative to older legacies or new, posttransition institutional designs. Furthermore, this study shows that the military's ability to sustain prerogatives acquired under authoritarianism has been strongly influenced by the legal-institutional factors with which the armed forces entered the transition.

In Chile, where the military sustains comparatively the highest level of prerogatives, the constitutional factor—an authoritarian constitution— proved decisive in the transition. In cases where military prerogatives have been significantly reduced, such as Argentina and Uruguay, this factor—the absence of an authoritarian constitution—was decisive as well. From the examination of cases where the current state of military prerogatives did not fully match the expectations raised from the transition, this study concludes that those expectations must be reassessed to include the impact of formal legal-institutional factors in the transition.

Blaming a Recent or Not-So-Recent Past

The problems of new democracies are often considered to be a legacy of the past. In the case of Eastern Europe and the former Soviet Union, the legacy of the past looms especially heavily as a result of protracted authoritarian or posttotalitarian experience. The Leninist legacy is charged with creating obstacles to democratic governance (Jowitt 1992); however, constraints on democracy also are traced to pre-Leninist times, where the existence of a nonpluralist cultural tradition added its own perverse influence.

This view of a nondemocratic past haunting present democracies is also applied to Latin America. Scholars have concluded that democracy is challenged by numerous obstacles: a cyclical pattern "alternating democratic and authoritarian 'moments'" (Malloy 1987, p. 236); clientelistic features, from the recent as well as the distant past, that pervade political institutions (O'Donnel, 1996); a profound crisis of the state compounded with recent economic crises (O'Donnell 1993); or a historically omnipresent "constitution of tyranny" (Loveman 1993). The military-authoritarian regimes that formed the latest authoritarian wave also left numerous imprints on their successors, hindering effective democratic governance (O'Donnell 1992; Agüero 1995a; Hagopian, 1996).

The mode of the transition, too, has been said to add its own thick layer to the legacy impacting a new democracy. It has been argued that the transition "is a founding moment the legacy of which helps to shape the new democratic regime for years" (Friedheim 1993, p. 482). The manner in which the transition is carried out, the character of the main forces pushing for it and leading it, their relative strengths, and the pace of the transition are factors specific to the transition that have been said to affect democratic governance in successor regimes (O'Donnell and Schmitter 1986; Stepan, 1986; Karl, 1990; Karl and Schmitter 1991; Valenzuela 1992; Bruszt and Stark, 1992; Mainwaring 1992; McGuire 1995). Linz and Stepan (1996) have recently argued that the tasks and chances of democratic consolidation are strongly influenced by the prior regime type and its leadership structure as well as by who initiates and controls the transition. Shain and Linz (1995) have further emphasized the importance of the transition by making the case that "the type of interim administration is crucial in determining the subsequent regime" (p. 4).

In sum, among those who view democracies as negatively affected by their past, disagreement exists regarding which element of their past is the most determinant. For some it is the manner of transition and/or the nature of the immediately preceding authoritarian regime. Others have explicitly rejected the predictive power of features of the authoritarian regimes or the transition. For instance, revising his previous work, O'Donnell argues that problems in new democracies reveal instead the resurgence of an old "schizophrenia" that predates authoritarianism, on which newer problems are superimposed (1993, pp. 1356, 1359–60).

However, many others posit that the problems of new democracies are based in posttransition arrangements, such as the newly created institutions. For instance, the powers granted the presidency in Poland or the resumption of presidentialism in Latin America are regarded as problematic for demo cratic governance (Gross 1992; Linz 1994; Valenzuela 1994). Institutional responses, including policies, policy-making styles, and strategies to face economic crises or pursue economic reform, have also been viewed as troublesome for democracy (Przeworski 1993, p. 175; Smith and Acuña 1994).

Other scholars' focus on new institutions is associated, however, with an acknowldgement of their endurance and ability to erode the perverse influence of legacies even in the face of enormous challenges (Remmer 1995). Geddes (1995), for instance, maintains that new democratic institutions "create a set of compelling incentives that structure the behavior of political elites" (p. 270) in ways that lead to the erosion of negative cultural legacies. Along similar lines Hunter (1997) argues, with a focus on Brazil, "that electoral competition creates incentives for politicians to reduce the interference of a politically powerful and active military" (p. 8) that otherwise had been expected to operate as a hard constraining legacy. Also with a focus on the Latin American military, Pion-Berlin (1995) has argued against an emphasis on factors of continuity with the past, favoring a focus on civilian leaders' strategies and "sequence of intelligent moves" (p. 161) that may better capture actual successes in democratization.

An emphasis on new institutions leads to the view that institutional traces from the past exhibited by new democracies may be rendered less and less relevant: they "can be gradually wiped away" (Przeworski 1991, p. 98). Thus the debate becomes quite inconclusive. In their analysis of the postcommunist regimes in Eastern Europe, Crawford and Lijphart (1995) conclude that "distinction between the two approaches [old legacies and new institutions] is not as sharp as their proponents would claim" (p. 176). But this inconclusiveness is best captured in Przeworski's statement about new democracies: "where one is going matters as much as where one is coming from" (1991, p. 99).

This chapter reclaims and highlights the importance of "where one is coming from" by arguing that transitions have decisively influenced the varying extent of military prerogatives in the current state of successor democracies under study. The analysis proceeds by contrasting the present state of civil-military relations and its adequacy to democratic norms and practices against the predictions based on the modes of transition that these countries underwent.

Militarization, Institutionalization, and Modes of Transition

Compared with most other regions touched by democratization's "third wave," South America stood out because of the military nature of the authoritarian regimes that sprang up in the 1960s and 1970s (Agüero 1995b). The military nature of these regimes was clearly marked by their origin: coups staged by the armed forces led by hierarchical chiefs of the armed services. The governments they installed were led by military men and were, in different ways, accountable to the military, which decided on the major orientations of the regime, legislation, and the constitution, and on the individual who was to occupy the chief executive post.

Militarization had several consequences for the South American regimes. The transition from authoritarianism involved military extrication from government and, consequently, a large military role in the transition. In addition, the military was praised for regime successes or accomplishments and blamed for its failures and crimes. When blamed for the latter, the military found added incentive to influence the transition to secure protection from retribution for itself and its members prior to exiting.

Beyond their shared military nature, these regimes differed, however, in regard to their institutionalization. Institutionalization in a military-authoritarian regime is the establishment of formal rules that regulate the power structure within the regime and the assignment of government functions to nonrepresentative or semirepresentative bodies, including the armed forces. A good expression of institutionalization the adoption of a new constitution, as was the case in Brazil in 1967 to 1969 and Chile in 1980.

One important consequence of institutionalization was that it helped provide for stability in the military leadership. Leadership succession, a critical problem for nondemocratic regimes, became more predictable as a minimum set of rules governing intramilitary relations and relations between the military and government evolved (Linz 1973). Usually this involved attaining some degree of separation between the military as institution and government. Stability in regime and military leadership—that is, the ability to maintain an unchallenged hierarchical structure and cohesion—strengthened a military's position during the transition.

In Uruguay, Peru, and especially Argentina, the absence of a separation between the military as institution and government led to relatively more internal bickering and, hence, instability at the top. Leadership of the military and the regime was thus more uncertain than in Brazil and Chile, weakening the military's position when faced with regime transitions. Another perhaps more important consequence of institutionalization was that constitutions provided a framework from which to face demands from the opposition without having to resort to improvised responses. This was the case in Brazil and Chile, and clearly not in Argentina, Peru, and Uruguay, which failed to attain institutionalization. In these three cases, the military was forced to devise a plan for extrication that included reaching out to the opposition.

An important distinction in transition modes is the degree of strength with which the ruling military entered the transition.[3] This determines whether the military may proceed without compromise, imposing its own terms, or must reach out to the opposition to compromise on the execution of the transition. In Chile and Brazil, the military faced the transition from a comparatively greater position of strength. It did not need to compromise with the opposition; rather, the opposition was forced to submit itself to the terms dictated by the outgoing authoritarian regime.[4] The military could remain confident about well-entrenched regulations and mechanisms to secure guarantees for itself and its interests into the future. These factors were not present in Uruguay, Peru, and Argentina, where the military faced the transition from a comparatively weaker position. The military could not arrange a transition according to its own terms and needed to reach out to the opposition in an attempt to retain part of its power after extrication from government (Mainwaring 1992). Uruguay and Peru are cases of compromise, while Argentina is a special case of attempted, but failed, compromise.

In the cases of weaker militaries, the opposition obtained most of what it desired for the transition: free elections (except in Uruguay, where the military kept the most popular politician from running in the first election) and either a new, democratically approved constitution or the resumption of the previous democratic constitution. In Brazil and Chile, stronger militaries executed transitions without compromise. The opposition could not obtain the democratic process it desired, and submitted itself to the authoritarian constitutions.

Expectations Raised from the Transitions

What expectations did these modes of transition create in terms of the military's capacity to constrain successor democracies? Clearly, expectations of military restrictions to democracy were greater in the cases of Brazil and Chile. In Brazil, these expectations were confirmed after the lamentable circumstances of Sarney's assumption of the presidency, which frustrated the opposition's hopes of a sharper break with military rule.[5] Democracy in these countries recommenced with ugly "birth defects" (Karl 1990, p. 14; Hagopian 1990, p. 149), which were expected to place high constraints on the successor regime.

The military would constitute an obstacle to a full resumption of democracy in the other cases as well, but the manner in which they sought extrication was expected to prevent them from imposing weighty restrictions on democratic government. Still, the fact that in Uruguay a pact had formally been reached in which the military had made demands for specific action by the successor government made democracy look constrained as well. In Peru, the military exited with a few guarantees for itself that gave it autonomy in specific circumstances and with the expectation that military matters would be dealt with carefully and in consensus with its leadership. As insurgency flourished during successor civilian democratic administrations, the legislation that the military passed right before its exit proved to be critical in allowing it to operate in complete autonomy in areas declared a state of emergency. In Argentina, the military exited with no guarantees other than those it granted itself, which the successor government promised not to honor. Argentina was the only case in which the military exited with no standing legislation or agreement with successor forces to protect it. In sum, transitions led to expectations of weighty restrictions on democracy in Chile and Brazil, moderate restrictions in Uruguay and Peru, and unfettered democracy in Argentina.

However, the issue of treatment of human rights violations by the military presented an element of extreme uncertainty in the transitions most affected by it: those of Argentina, Chile, and Uruguay. In the first two cases, the military had granted amnesty for crimes committed during the military-authoritarian period, and attempts to undo amnesty would create unpredictable tensions with the military. General Pinochet had at one point stated that he was staying on as army chief "so that my men are not touched." In Uruguay, the appointment of the last junta chief (General Medina) as defense minister in the successor democratic administration clearly signified a warning that his men were not to be touched either.

The Transitions and the Present

Argentina, Chile, and Peru remained in positions that are consistent with the expectations that arose from the transition. Argentina, fifteen years later, and Chile, eight years later, are at opposite positions in terms of the constraints that the military impose on democracy: a high level of constraints in Chile and a low one in Argentina. Eighteen years later in Peru, constraints are not as strong as in Chile, but they are consistent with the expectation of moderate restrictions. On the other hand, they are lower than initially expected in Uruguay, fourteen years since redemocratization, and in Brazil, thirteen years since the election of a civilian president. The following sections review each country from the angle of the constraints that the military imposes on democracy. This review follows Stepan's well-known proposed focus on the dimensions of "articulated military contestation" and "military institutional prerogatives" (1988, p. 68).

Chile

The strong initial tensions regarding civilian-military accommodation under the democratic regime inaugurated in 1990 had been toned down by the mid-1990s. A modus vivendi developed between civilian authorities and the military, allowing for the handling of the numerous crises that surfaced, without the fear of an outright authoritarian regression. These crises arose from military intolerance to measures taken by civilian officials regarding human rights issues, the pursuit of investigations of irregularities and corruption among army generals, and the imprisonment of Pinochet's initial chief intelligence/repression officer for the assassination of an opposition leader in Washington, D.C., in 1976. These crises gave way to turbulent episodes of military contestation orchestrated by Pinochet or senior officers, involving the mobilization and deployment of troops in flagrant disobedience of civilian authority. These mobilizations were not intended as coup threats but rather as blunt displays of the military's specific power capability (Anderson 1967) aimed at strong-arming the government for concessions in subsequent negotiation. Every time the army attained its goal: stopping a government initiative; forcing the government to do something it had not contemplated to appease the military; or obtaining compensatory responses. The second democratic administration, inaugurated in 1994, was for the most part spared the staging of these military demonstrations, although military chiefs have remained outspoken on political issues, contesting government or other civilian parties' views. And tensions resumed as a result of the arrest of General Pinochet in London in October 1998 on the request of Spanish courts charging him with human right crimes.

What the successor democracy in Chile has not been spared, however, is the constraints resulting from clauses in the 1980 constitution and specific organic laws that maintain enhanced military prerogatives. Despite repeated reform attempts by the first and second democratic administrations since 1990, these laws and clauses remain fully in place. These constraints prevent the president from exercising powers assigned his office in the previous constitution, such as removing and freely appointing the commanding general officers in each of the armed services. The president could not, for instance, remove General Pinochet from the post of commander-in-chief of the army, which he held for almost twenty-six years until March 1998, and cannot remove the other service chiefs once they are appointed for fixed four-year terms. The president is dependent on these chiefs' proposals for the promotion and assignment of general officers, and has no say on promotions and assignments at lower levels. In addition, the president and three other civilian officials sit on equal terms with the heads of the three armed services and carabineros in the National Security Council (NSC), which the military has the power to convene for the debate of issues it deems relevant for national security. The council also appoints four senators and designates two members of the Constitutional Court. Up until very recently, officials serving on appointment by the NSC had been designated before the transfer of power to the first democratic administration and were thus appointed directly by the military. As the tenure of those appointed officials has begun to end, the NSC has had to appoint new members, for instance, to the Constitutional Court, placing the president and the military chiefs in opposite positions. Through the NSC, the military exerted strong pressure on the government regarding measures to contest Pinochet's detention.

The military maintains much budgetary autonomy, as a substantial part of its budget is constitutionally mandated not to drop under a certain level, and another part comes as a fixed percent of copper exports, the state's largest source of foreign revenue. Many of these constraints could disappear or be softened with constitutional reform or new bills, but reform attempts have been obstructed by nonelected senators as well as elected representatives in the opposition. The constitution inherited from the military sets high minimum vote requirements for such reforms, thus enabling the obstructive stance by the opposition.

There certainly has been progress during the tenure of democratic administrations, which have attempted to contest military prerogatives. For instance, early during President Aylwin's term (1990 to 1994), the Constitutional Court supported the president's interpretation that he could refrain from promoting a general proposed by the army chief. Also, the government managed to create a civilian-led agency for information-gathering and coordination on terrorist activities that surfaced during Aylwin's term, and to suppress them with the police, led from the interior ministry, rather than the army. Much progress had been made in diminishing distrust between the military and former opposition leaders and parties now in government, especially as they collaborated on efforts at military modernization, but much of this progress receded as a result of conflicting views adopted on Pinochet's detention. The magnitude of the constitutionally enshrined prerogatives of the military and its ability to contest some government decisions make this case clearly consistent with the predictions made from the transition.

Argentina

After failure in governance and military defeat at the Malvinas/Falkland Islands, the armed forces were in no position to threaten the new democracy. However, the amnesty that the military had granted itself immediate prior to the transfer of power and the successor government's commitment to retribution augured conflict of unpredictable proportions. The military's ability to react to what it perceived as threats to the institution as a whole had been underestimated. Indeed, the pursuit of cases of human rights violations were the basis of the well-known military mutinies that took place in 1987, 1988, and 1990 (Norden 1996), which severely harmed civilian government and its attempt to pursue justice. But in 1989, Menem's government, the second democratic administration, pardoned nearly 200 officers charged during the previous administration with human rights abuses or mutiny. Attempting to appease the military, the pardon included members of the former military junta, unprecedentedly sentenced for human rights crimes. In 1990, Menem faced and firmly defeated yet another rebellion, this time a bloody coup attempt by a group of NCOs and junior officers. The crushing of the mutiny helped strengthen military hierarchy and put an end to rebellious behavior. No new episodes of military contestation took place in Argentina, thus inaugurating a period of uncontested military cooperation, however disgruntled, with government reform plans aimed at downsizing and reprofessionalizing the forces. In stark contrast to Chile, where the military reacted strongly to the arrest of General Pinochet in London, the Argentine military did not oppose detention in 1998 of former army chiefs, some of whom had benefited from President Menem's pardon, on charges of kidnapping children during the "dirty war."

In the area of military prerogatives, the situation is simpler and more straightforward. With the military's exit, democracy resumed with the previous constitution unaltered. Dating from 1853, the constitution did not expand much on civilian-military powers beyond the assignment of supremacy to the president. But President Alfonsín further empowered himself during his term with a battery of decrees and bills that introduced substantial changes. Military leadership was purged and significantly reduced in size. The command structures of the armed services were reorganized and incorporated into the structure of the Ministry of Defense, directly under the supervision of the minister. A new Defense Law was passed in 1988 that, for the first time in history, ended the assignment of internal roles for the military. The forces were veritably reduced, as was their budget. However, political tension from the trials on human rights and the succession of mutinies led to government concessions in this area and to a lull in military reform.

After the presidential pardons and the end to rebellions at the beginning of Menem's administration, military reform resumed with greater vigor. The constitutional reform of 1993 reaffirmed presidential powers over the military: the president is the commander-in-chief, decides on posts and promotions with the consent of the Senate, and determines its organization and deployment. Budget and personnel rationalization was intensified, leading to further reductions. The number of civilians in the Ministry of Defense was expanded: the minister, two secretaries of state, and four undersecretaries. Defense industries and some agencies were privatized and the military removed from participation in agencies not strictly related to military roles. In a move that took the military by surprise, Menem decreed in 1994 the substitution of a volunteer format for the draft, and women have been incorporated in the military career. Plans for deployment of military force in the territory have been advanced in order to rationalize and reduce it. Instruction, education, and norms for promotion have been reformed accordingly. The actual implementation of many of these reforms, however, was much slower than desired. The reasons were budgetary constraints and foot-dragging by the services, reluctant, for instance, to substitute simpler joint structures for overlapping bureaus and agencies.

Military reform in Argentina has been accompanied and encouraged by a number of defense-related initiatives in foreign policy that have helped promote the ascendancy of civilian officials. These initiatives include the termination of a missile development program, the opening of nuclear facilities to international inspection, the promotion of military cooperation and joint activities with Brazil, and the resolution of many border disputes with Chile. Also very important in terms of mission reorientation has been the large participation of Argentine contingents in international peacekeeping, which has become a critical component of reprofessionalization. The army views international peacekeeping as contributing to one of Argentina's central international interests, and has thus joined in making it a central concern of its reform process. In sum, from the angle of both contestation and prerogatives, the military in Argentina placed no restrictions on democracy, in stark contrast with the case of Chile.

Peru

The military exited in 1980, making sure it would retain autonomy in the handling of its affairs and prerogatives in the area of internal security. The military's exit coincided with the dramatic surge of subversion staged by two powerful clandestine organizations: Shining Path and the Tupac Amaru revolutionary movement (MRTA). Much of the dynamics in civilian-military relations has since been influenced by this challenge. Belaunde's (1980 to 1985) incompetent policy in this area resulted in simply turning the whole issue over to the armed forces, which saw their budget grow and their involvement in repression amplified. With the government's acquiescence and with little or no civilian oversight, the military simply made use of the prerogatives in the area of internal security that it had granted itself in 1980. As a consequence, what had been mostly a feature of military-authoritarian regimes in neighboring countries—gross human rights violations—became a feature of military activity under Peru's successor democracy. Occasional and feeble attempts to bring accountability to the military's handling of repression have been the main motive for military contestation since 1980. The military has systematically refused to accept responsibility for human rights violations. The clearest expression of this was provided by the army's commander-general Nicolás de Bari Hermoza, who responded to an invitation from Congress's Human Rights Committee with a sudden and defiant display of tank maneuvers in the streets of Lima in May 1993 (Basombrío 1997).

The APRA government of Alan García (1985 to 1990) tried to use its initially large popular backing to carry out measures to bring the military under government control and to promote accountability. He created a ministry of defense to replace separate agencies for each service and to facilitate government control. This initiative was bitterly resisted by the air force, whose chief also expressed his repudiation with ominous maneuvers, this time of fighter planes over the skies of Lima. The president prevailed, but only formally: the ministry has always remained in the charge of an active-duty army general. Instead of becoming an instrument of government control, it became a military agency. Furthermore, with the escalation in the struggle with subversion, the military was in direct control of areas declared in state of emergency, about a third of the national territory. In these areas, the military exercised full military and political control under no oversight authority (Degregori and Rivera 1994). This expansion of military roles went along with an extreme deterioration of political institutions and a veritable decline in the president's popularity in the context of profound economic crisis. With no political controls, military autonomy grew, and violations of human rights turned into outright massacres in the countryside and in prisons around the country.

The ascent of Alberto Fujimori to the presidency in 1990 brought about an expansion of the military's legal prerogatives to put them on a par with its actual prerogatives (Degregori and Rivera 1994). Through a series of presidential decrees allowed by Congress, the role of the armed forces in internal control and repression was greatly expanded. Congress later reconsidered and rolled back many of those decrees, but the president, tightly allied with the top military leadership, closed Congress and began rule as a dictator. Under international pressure, principally from the Organization of American States, elections were held for a constituent assembly, and a new constitution was passed in 1993. The constitution, however, validated Fujimori's personal powers in the presidency (and allowed for his reelection) and restored all of those decrees that Congress had attempted to roll back.[6] Fujimori had established a tight alliance with the military hierarchy, particularly with the army chief he appointed in 1990 and who, by presidential approval, remains in charge as of this writing. While the president supports (and protects) through his formal-legal powers the military clique he appointed in 1990, the top military chiefs have given unconditional support to his policies in all areas (Mauceri 1995). The politicization of the military hierarchy has resulted in serious divisions, reflected in the spectacular desertion of renowned army generals denouncing corruption and complicity in human rights crimes by the top military leadership. This, in turn, has led the president to rely ever more strongly on the national intelligence system to suppress dissent in the ranks. The system that has resulted is thus one of expanded autonomy for the top military leadership in alliance with the president. The president appoints and dismisses army chiefs, according to the constitution, but the military performs its internal functions with no outside controls. The present position of the armed forces and their capacity to obstruct accountability to representative institutions is consistent with predictions raised from the transition.

Brazil

Brazil and Uruguay, in turn, did not fully match predictions. In both cases military influence amounted to less than had initially been anticipated. After the transition in Brazil, there has never been military contestation of the kind that took place in Argentina during Alfonsín's term (mutiny), or in Chile (emergency billeting of the forces or mobilization). Contestation took the form of overtly voiced concerns by groups in the military and, occasionally, by its top chiefs, especially over the salary situation. The armed forces have resented the discriminatory treatment given them by Congress compared to the rest of the public bureaucracy. President Itamar Franco had to appease the military by promising major raises and by appointing up to nine active duty officers to the Cabinet in 1994. Complaints have sometimes been expressed about developments in culture and society that groups of officers oppose, and which reflect the cultural distance of the military from demo cratic cultural orientations (Hunter 1997, p. 144).

Instead of contestation, the military participated amply in the political process. There was much continuity after Sarney's assumption of the presidency in 1985. During his term, the military held six positions in the Cabinet, moved with autonomy to repress labor mobilization or strikes, and intervened in a wide array of policy areas, including development projects in the Amazon, nuclear energy, and national intelligence. When the Congress elected in 1986 initiated deliberations for a new constitution, the military successfully lobbied to obstruct the substitution of parliamentarism for presidentialism, the shortening of President Sarney's term, and the creation of a ministry of defense (Mesquita 1995). The 1988 constitution did not innovate much in regard to the role of the armed forces, which continued to include the protection of law and order. In previous constitutions, however, this internal mission was dependent on the authority of the president, with the military constitutionally empowered to interpret the legality of that authority (Stepan 1971). Now the internal mission could be called upon by any of the constitutional powers (the Executive, the Congress, or the Judiciary), giving the military room to maneuver between them. It did, however, significantly eliminate the clause that allowed for military discretion in interpreting the president's authority (Oliveira 1987).[7] Furthermore, in 1991 President Collor passed a law specifying that the military's internal role may be invoked exclusively by the president; Congress and the Judiciary may only petition the president to do so (Zaverucha 1994, p. 228). Formally, these changes represent an important curtailment of military prerogatives.

Fernando Collor, who took over in 1990 after the first direct presidential elections since military rule, vigorously delivered on his campaign promise to reduce military power. The number of military officers in the cabinet was reduced from six to only the three service ministers. A civilian was appointed to head the newly created Secretariat for Strategic Affairs to replace the old military-led National Information Service. Collor disciplined officers who verbally challenged his authority, and took other steps that would have been unthinkable a few years earlier: he dismantled a military program aimed at testing nuclear explosives (Mesquita 1995, p. 222), worked with Argentina to set up a system of international safeguards, and created a reserve in the Amazon for imperiled Yanomami Indians, all of which the military opposed. Furthermore, during the protracted political turbulence that led to Collor's removal by Congress in October 1992 and his subsequent impeachment on corruption charges, the military, breaking with a long tradition of intervention in crises of this nature, stayed on the sidelines and supported the full observance of legal procedures.

The weakening of the presidency resulting from Collor's impeachment led to a reassertion of military influence during the administration of Itamar Franco (1992 to 1995), the vice president in Collor's administration, who assumed the presidency to finish his term. The military was often put in situations of public disagreement with civilian authorities on issues of corruption and salaries. Franco resorted to military officials to fill numerous Cabinet positions and to run government agencies and public-sector companies.

Contestation and Cabinet participation were again rolled back, however, after the assumption of President Cardoso in 1995. During his presidency, the military budget has continued to decline and important initiatives have been taken to affirm the leading role of the executive on defense matters. However, despite the "erosion of military influence" (Hunter 1997), the military continued muscling influence in government agencies, and controlled areas as important as national intelligence and drug interdiction from central government positions (Zaverucha 1998). But this level of influence is substantially less than what was anticipated from the transition in 1985.

Uruguay

The transition augured military constraints on democracy because of demands expressed by the military in the transition pact. But the military's expectation that the National Security Council would be approved and incorporated in the constitution by Congress never actually materialized. The expectation that top military chiefs would be selected by the president in accordance with the services foundered when President Lacalle (1990 to 1995) appointed chiefs who were not to the liking of the top brass. The military concentrated instead on its priority concern: avoiding prosecution for human rights crimes. The transition pact had not included any specific reference to the mode of treatment of this issue, but the military always made clear, before and after the pact, that it would not tolerate prosecution. During the first postmilitary administration, former army chief and former president General Medina, appointed defense minister by the successor democratic president, made sure that no military officers showed up in court when summoned. This untenable situation forced the government to submit a special expiry law *(ley de caducidad)* that would prevent prosecution of military officers. But when this bill was passed by Congress, an enraged citizenry mobilized to make use of the constitutional provision that allows for a referendum if requested by one fourth of the electorate. After a contentious campaign, over half a million Uruguayans petitioned for a referendum to invalidate the *ley de caducidad*. However, out of fear of military retaliation, voters rejected the referendum proposal in April 1989.

All human-rights-related unrest in the military subsided after the referendum. Military obstacles to full democratization disappeared, and remaining areas of difficulty were restricted to internal disputes in the military over issues of modernization and reorganization, and budgetary constraints (Rial 1996, p. 139). Civil-military tensions over the human rights question were expected in Uruguay following the transition. Less expected was the frustration of some of the other military demands. The current state of military prerogatives is thus better, from the angle of democratic governance, than anticipated from the transition.

Legacies of Transitions and Legal-Institutional Factors

The legacy of military rule is visible in all these cases. First, all of them faced severe restraints from the military in the human rights area. Even the cases that appear today as the most successful in terms of lesser military restrictions on democracy have been unable to punish criminals and dispense justice. For instance, Menem's pardons in Argentina were instrumental in securing the end of contestation, but the fate of the disappeared—the location of the bodies and an account of the causes of death—remains undisclosed. The weight of the military legacy in this area is also felt in the overwhelming desire by government officials to reassure the military that human rights questions that keep surfacing will not affect it (except in the cases of kidnapping of children, which were not covered in the previous amnesties). Also, in Uruguay, where military officers could not be prosecuted, the inevitable surfacing of human rights problems from the past has led government officials to reassure the military. In Chile, only a handful of military officers were imprisoned for crimes not covered in the amnesty, and the fate of those who disappeared remains unknown (Garretón 1994; Ensalaco, 1995; de Brito 1997).

Second, the military legacy is visible in that, despite success in limiting the military's restraints on democracy, the full assertion of civilian control is still a distant goal. Again, even in the most successful cases—Argentina and Uruguay—there are areas where civilian officials have no access, such as military education, or where the jurisdiction of civilian courts is restricted, while jurisdiction for military justice remains broad. Also, military reform and modernization programs have for the most part been conceived and carried out by the military exclusively (Pion-Berlin 1997). And where they are in control, civilians are often guided by a desire to reassure the military and not to conflict with its goals and interests.

However, there are differences in the extent to which the military restricts democratic governance. In these differences, the impact of the transition appears most clearly and decisively in the cases in which there is correspondence between expectations and the situation found at present. Chile and Argentina reveal a break with historic patterns in the involvement of the military in politics, highlighting the impact of the transition. Argentina has broken with the historic pattern of military intervention in politics that took hold during most of this century. Chile has broken with the pattern of no military intervention or participation in politics established in the democratic period between 1932 and 1973. In both cases, this break is the result of the mode of transition.

Transitions produce outcomes that are landmarks in setting the context, the opportunities and constraints for subsequent democratic processes. The first postauthoritarian arrangement is an institutional setting that differentially empowers the military and civilian officials for the ensuing process. In this process, however, many other elements may come into play, but they are subsumed in the transition's institutional outcome. In Argentina, for instance, the transition outcome allowed for an assertive civilian attempt on the human rights issue and the initiation of military reforms. The military was put on the defensive. However, the very attempts at retribution and reform ignited a reaction in the military that allowed it to reassert itself, rebelling repeatedly in pursuit of its goals.

Military contestation ended in Argentina because the government appeased the military with amnesties and pardons, and because of the failure of the last rebellious attempt, which made it possible to rid the army of rebellious leaders. Further weakening of the military's political clout was aided by the imperatives of economic and fiscal reform. In this sense, Argentina's has been a "de facto [budget-driven] demilitarization" (Franko 1994, p. 37). This, however, would have been impossible without the institutional outcome of the transition, which returned unrestricted constitutional powers to civilian government facing a weakened military.

In Chile, on the other hand, the transition produced a postauthoritarian arrangement based on the authoritarian constitution, which assigned large prerogatives to the military. The burden of initiating reform to remove the military from positions of influence fell on the successor government. Reform attempts were tried repeatedly, but failed because of the rigidities imposed by the constitution itself. Constitutional restrictions on the successor government inherited from the military regime have found renewed sustenance in the power of parties of the right in Congress. Former allies of the military in the authoritarian regime, representatives of these parties have, jointly with the nonelected senators, denied the votes necessary for reforms. The power of the right is, in part, due to the electoral system and the constitution's clause on nonelected senators, both imposed by the military.

In Peru, the transition left the military with a significant level of autonomy, especially in its capacity to intervene against subversion. Trying not to antagonize the military, the first successor government respected its autonomy and, by inaction, contributed in practice to expanding it. Since the transition, the military nurtured this autonomy and substantially expanded its capacity. This was aided by the dramatic surge of subversive violence and the virtual freedom of action that civilian authorities have given the military, with the exception of the few attempts to the contrary during part of García's administration. So much did this autonomy develop that, as Degregori and Rivera (1994, p. 14) have shown convincingly, Fujimori's decrees on military role expansion did no more than bring actual roles and prerogatives to match. The current state of affairs regarding military prerogatives may be traced back to the transition. It is perfectly conceivable, however, that military prerogatives could have been reduced had there been assertive action on the part of civilian adminis-trations, lessening the impact of the transition. This lack of assertive action, however, can be traced back to the transition, as it was based on the view that civilian rule could best be stabilized by leaving the military alone.

Why couldn't the military in Uruguay sustain their aspirations on prerog-atives way into the successor regime? The answer highlights the importance of legal-formal factors: unlike in Chile, the Uruguayan military failed to insti-tutionalize an extrication from direct rule with an authoritarian constitution. In lieu of that, the military attempted to retain some of those aspirations in a transition pact. Other than the restoration of elections and the previous con-stitution, this pact did not produce a binding agreement, in part because there was no written document. Institutional Act 19, which followed the pact, established the continuation of the National Security Council for a limited time. Only Congress could have, as the military had desired, reformed the constitution to incorporate it permanently. In addition to the lack of a bind-ing agreement or legal legacy, the military, in the successor regime, had to face up to the fact that during its rule it had antagonized all political parties, both the left and the two traditional parties. Therefore, other than on the issue of the *ley de caducidad*, the military, unlike in Chile, had no allies among political parties—nobody willing to defend and promote its legacy. Expectations from the transition could have been satisfied had the latter expressed military demands in formal-legal, binding terms. The successor parties could have then tried to suppress those demands, but it would have been costlier for them, since they would have had to assume the burden of changing a formalized agreement or law. Had the military succeeded in the constitutional referendum in 1980, as it did in Chile, a transition would most likely have taken a very different course.

Along with Chile, Brazil entered the transition with an authoritarian con-stitution and with a strong military that could afford to reject the opposition's campaign for a new constitution or direct elections. Why then did military influence erode? Why did expectations from the transition not materialize as they have in Chile? Again, the answer lies with legal-institutional factors, and demands a closer look at the authoritarian constitution of 1967 to 1969. The constitution comprised several institutional acts passed by the military since 1964, and highlighted national security functions for the military. But it established the primacy of the president over the armed forces, and contained "liberal" elements such as the existence of a Congress, political parties, and opposition. Military rule thus relied on the primacy of the executive and its ability to secure a majority for its supporting party in Congress. For this, the president empowered himself with an additional resource—Institutional Act No. 5 (IA5)—which allowed him to dictate emergency measures at his discre-tion. When the military decided to start a process of liberalization, it dropped

IA5 and relied instead on specific decrees that could help it contain the rising electoral power of the opposition and its representation in Congress. We know that the government ultimately failed in the attempt to control the forces unleashed by its own liberalization process that resulted in the 1985 election of a civilian president.

Without the control of the presidency, the military could no longer resort to emergency decrees to secure its interests. Now it could rely only on the constitution. But even if it highlighted national security roles for the armed forces, the constitution did not specify any special guarantees for a military out of government. In addition, no constitutional clause stood in the way of reform or the drafting of a new constitution. Therefore nothing impeded the new president from submitting in 1985 a constitutional amendment to enable the Congress elected in 1986 to produce a new constitution. A constituent assembly thus offered an open-ended process that could substantially alter the legal-institutional basis of military power. This is a major difference from the case of Chile, where the constitution made sure that military powers remained enhanced even if the military no longer controlled the executive. The Chilean constitution established high requirements for reform and specific military prerogatives in the NSC, and was accompanied by organic laws of constitutional status that restricted presidential powers over the military.

The new centrality that the constituent process gave Congress in Brazil led the military to organize several ways of influencing its deliberations. While military influence in a constituent process obviously goes against the sovereignty of elected representation, it did at least signal that the military was willing to abide by its decisions. The constitution approved in 1988 reflected the military's influence on a number of issues but it also denied some of the military aspirations.

In sum, Brazilian civilian elites were freer to transform the military legacy than they have been in Chile. The military tried to maintain core elements of its power by influencing elected officials and negotiating with them, instead of imposing a rigid legal-institutional legacy. This is what accounts for the lessened prerogatives of the Brazilian military relative to expectations from the transition. Certainly, peculiar features of Brazil's political system and parties facilitated the military's strategy of systematic lobbying of civilian officials: the weakness of political parties and the absence of party discipline (Lamounier 1996).

Conclusion

Differences in the manner in and extent to which military power constrains new democracies in South America are strongly influenced by the mode of transition from authoritarian rule. In neither Argentina, Brazil, Chile, Peru, nor Uruguay were the patterns of previous periods of democratic rule simply reproduced in the new democracies. Chile and Argentina represent a stark break with previous patterns. In the other cases, the military's influence or form of participation has acquired new traits.

The expectations raised from the transition of the level of restriction that the military would impose in new democracies were clearly matched in Argentina, Chile, and Peru. In Brazil and Uruguay, where military influence turned out to be lower than expected, the major factors were also related to the transition. This study has highlighted the importance of formal legal-institutional factors in the transition and the type of institutionalization attained by military-authoritarian regimes. A military will not be able to sustain in the postauthoritarian regime the power and influence with which it enters the transition if this power is not backed with formal-legal arrangements. These arrangements unevenly raise the cost of actions for contending actors in the process ensuing after the end of the transition. Clearly, it has been harder for Chilean authorities to curtail military power, because this is backed by an authoritarian constitution, than it has been for Uruguayan or Argentinian authorities not constrained by such arrangements.

It might seem somewhat of a paradox that formal-legal factors may play such a role in a region not known for exemplary rule of law. But despite different traditions, a legalistic approach seems to have been shared by all. Besides, while these factors may not pervade all spheres of politics and society, they certainly take added importance in the regulation of power between state institutions.

Certainly, the impact of factors specific to the transition on the extent and manner of military influence in the new democracies ought not to obscure the role of other factors beyond the transition. Factors such as the economy and its effect on budgets, political parties and their ties to the military, and subversion have affected the transition legacy, strengthening or weakening it. Neither should factors from an older past and tradition be ignored. Reality is more complex than the emphasis on singular dimensions tolerates.

But in the array of factors influencing differences in the state of military power in the new democracies, this study has highlighted the specific impact of transition factors, and this has practical implications. "Deliberate effort and crafting" to overcome problems of democracy that will not be mitigated by the simple impact of competitive institutions (Lamounier 1996, p. 187) require a focus on the specific target. Identifying the specific transition factors influencing the present should help better appraise the kind of strategy, pace, and institutional design needed to overcome their influence.

5

The Transformation of Labor-Based One-Partyism at the End of the Twentieth Century: The Case of Mexico

Ruth Berins Collier

THIS ESSAY EXPLORES the process of regime change in Mexico. At the same time that Mexico in many ways represents a unique case, it stands at the intersection of two more general processes at the end of the twentieth century. The first is the wave of democratization that has swept over countries beyond those where democracy has been long institutionalized. Mexico represents a particular path of democratization—one that embarks from a one-party regime. Indeed, it is a case of the democratization of the world's longest-lived dominant-party regime. The second concerns the challenges and tensions faced by governing or majoritarian labor-based parties (LBPs), that is, parties with a core support base in the labor movement. Regimes characterized by majoritarian or (pre)dominant LBPs face serious challenges in the current economic environment, challenges that exert pressures on both of their two central features: the (pre)dominance of a single party and the support base of the party—indeed of the state—in the labor movement. In Mexico, these two processes have been closely connected, and the challenges facing governing

LBPs have been a central part of the ongoing process of democratization, which has taken the form of the gradual transformation of the dominant-LBP regime.

The politics of regime change should be understood in terms of both a structural story about the common challenges or crises confronting governing LBPs and an actor-based story about political strategies and political struggle. The structural factors are the transformations in the world economy that change the preferences of key groups and actors. Structures constrain, enable, or facilitate, but the outcome is also a product of political struggle. Put another way, regime change is an outcome of 1) a changing set of preferences affected by the opportunities and constraints of the new economic conditions, 2) existing political institutions that afford certain kinds of capacities and possibilities, 3) conjunctural factors, including external shocks, and 4) the strategic calculations of the main actors.

Labor-Based One-Partyism in the Twentieth Century

The structural argument refers to the changing economic conditions that gave rise to, supported, and later challenged LBPs in many countries throughout the world. LBPs were formed with the emergence of the new class structure that arose with an urban, commercial, and industrial economy, most obviously with the formation of a proletarianized working class and the organization of labor unions. These LBPs were able to achieve majoritarian or (pre)dominant status in the context of a world economy in which the dynamism and the major economic models were based on the creation of national industrial capacity and national markets (models that variously took the form of Keynesianism, ISI, or central planning). These economic models were consistent with class settlements or class compromises, which could simultaneously address the problem of sustained production and protect workers from an untrammeled labor market. They could thus potentially provide the material base for majoritarian political coalitions that included the labor movement as a core constituency. The political success and even dominance of different LBPs, then, was due to their ability to oversee different sorts of class settlements.

The economic conditions that facilitated a proliferation of governing LBPs began to change in the 1970s, with a fundamental reordering of the world economy that took place on several levels—the global division of labor, the location of production, and the internationalization of markets, production, and finance, as well as firm restructuring involving new patterns of subcontracting, production technologies, and labor processes. If the old pattern of national industrialization was based on fixed, dependable patterns of production, the new model, oriented toward internationally competitive production, saw flexibilization of, rather than rigidities in, the labor market as compatible with increasing production. The policy basis for class settlements was severely challenged, if not eliminated, and the material base for governing LBPs was substantially reduced. These changed conditions have produced various political challenges to the governing LBP. Many LBPs have, in one way or another, been forced into the opposition for the first time after decades in which they held power—as seen most dramatically in the Communist bloc, but also, to a lesser extent, for example, in Scandinavian countries. Those that have managed to retain or regain power have often been under substantial internal tension.

The new structural conditions have produced dilemmas and strategic questions for both LBPs and labor movements. Governing LBPs are often torn between policies of economic restructuring and their labor constituencies, which oppose those policies. Similarly, party-affiliated labor movements face the dilemma of deciding whether to remain loyal to the party and retain access to power or to risk political opposition and marginalization. Both parties and union movements have tended to be internally divided in confronting the new situation. In some cases the labor movement has factionalized as it has struggled to devise a strategic response to the new economic orientation, where one has been adopted. Demand-side economic models, such as ISI and Keynesianism, homogenized labor and provided the logic for national and centralized labor confederations as a relatively unitary political actor and coalition partner. Supply-side and more market-based economic models fragment and heterogenize labor according to market power, undermining the logic of national and centralized labor organizations.[1] Thus part of the story about the national labor movement is, to different degrees, its disarticulation as a unitary actor.

The Mexican Dominant-LBP Regime

In Mexico, the dominant party virtually monopolized political office for six decades after its founding in 1929. Though nondemocratic practices were sometimes employed, an electoral majority was sustained largely by consent, achieved through continual negotiation, exchanges, distribution, and co-optation, as well as an ideological appeal based on the Mexican Revolution. The core labor constituency was cemented during the presidency of Lázaro Cárdenas (1936 to 1940), who mobilized labor support through a radical appeal that included support for unions as organizations and for workers in terms of their wage demands and conflict with capital, as well as collective landholding in the countryside and, under some conditions, worker ownership and management. The party was organized by "sectors" based on collective membership through unions: the labor sector—unions primarily of blue-collar workers; the popular sector—unions primarily of public-service workers as well as various professional and occupational groups; and the peasant sector—unions of peasants. Union leaders held positions in the party and often ran as party candidates.

A conservative reaction to the radical populism of Cárdenas followed, leading to a reordering of the alliance on terms less favorable to labor but nevertheless maintaining union support and effecting a kind of class compromise. The party (now called the PRI) conservatized and expanded the class base of its support to achieve something approaching a coalition of the whole, including most sectors of capital. This multiclass coalition, which continued to include most of the labor movement as a core constituency, formed the basis for a well-institutionalized dominant-party regime. On this basis, the government had the political resources to defeat both dissident union movements and any electoral opposition.[2]

In addition to these political and organizational resources, the inclusionary, multiclass coalition of the whole was underwritten by the import-substitution industrialization model of economic growth, which relied on the domestic market as the outlet for nationally produced industrial goods. As the wage level is a central factor in determining the size of a domestic market, this model provided the conditions for a class compromise between labor and management: profits and production were enhanced by union and government activity, which would solve the collective-action problem of competing workers and competing firms, allowing both to forego the bidding down of wages and instead to achieve rising real wages (and hence an expanding market) in line with productivity gains. Indeed, after a plunge in real wages that occurred with the conservative reaction to radical populism in the immediate post-Cárdenas years, real wages rose steadily from the beginning of the 1950s to the mid-1970s, during which time a relatively sustained and robust pattern of growth led many analysts to refer to the "Mexican Miracle."

In emphasizing these points, I do not want to belittle the degree to which the dominant LBP regime in Mexico was a mechanism of control over the working class. The populist LBP in Mexico institutionalized a support base in the labor movement that secured legitimacy for the one-party regime and provided a mechanism for achieving labor cooperation and industrial peace. Furthermore, coercion was employed to maintain control when corporatist resources were insufficient. From the point of view of labor, the PRI was an ambiguous or double-edged affiliation. It meant both that organized labor was "cut in" with respect to the governing coalition and that it was a subordinated coalition partner that had lost its autonomy of action. These are important factors in the preferences of factions within both the PRI and the labor movement to retain or oppose the dominant-LBP regime in Mexico.

In the 1980s, Mexico dramatically reoriented its economic policy. For a number of reasons—including its large debt (Mexico's insolvency initiated the world debt crisis in 1982), the asymmetrical balance of power between capital and labor, and the unusual political capacity afforded the state by the dominant-LBP regime itself—the PRI government turned abruptly from a highly protectionist, interventionist ISI model to a liberal economic model based on market rather than state coordination, free trade, and international competitiveness. Starting in response to the 1982 crisis as a short-term stabilization program under IMF conditionality, by 1985 the model became a long-term commitment to fundamental economic restructuring.

The new set of economic policies, first undertaken during De la Madrid's term of office (1982 to 1988) and pursued by a technocratic team surrounding the president, clashed with labor interests along lines now quite familiar. Wages were held down both as a stabilization measure and as a way to boost international competitiveness. After decades of nearly constant growth, the six years of the De la Madrid presidency saw average real manufacturing wages reduced by almost 40 percent.[3] The working class also felt the employment effects of the worst recession since at least the Great Depression and the brunt of fiscal austerity, which directly affected social spending. Finally, the government reduced subsidies on the prices of many wage goods that were important components of workers' consumption basket, and it embarked on an extensive privatization campaign, restructuring and downsizing important industrial sectors and annulling labor contracts.

The new economic context undermined the dominant-LBP regime from both within and without. From without it produced opposition from the right and the left. On the right, marketizers within the private sector sought a more competitive regime as a way to institutionalize political access and ensure a more consistent neoliberal economic policy without reversions to "populist excesses." The left similarly sought to mobilize influence through more democratic political channels in order to exert pressure on economic policy, but in the opposite direction: to slow down and moderate economic liberalization. From within, the new economic context led to tensions and contradictions within the LBP, the dominant faction of which tried to reformulate or restructure its constituency relations—to look for new bases of popular support and to refashion its relationship with its long-standing labor constituency. It also led to pressures on the labor movement to defect from the PRI.

We can analyze the process of regime change in terms of a game of strategic interactions of four main actors across three rounds, each round roughly corresponding to a presidential term, but more importantly, each initiated by a crisis that affected strategic calculations of key actors. The actors consist of three party/electoral actors (LBP, right, and left) and the labor movement.

Though the former are riven by factions and divided over strategies, one can treat them as unitary actors in terms of a party position actually adopted. The labor movement, which cannot be seen as a faction within the PRI since some unions have remained autonomous from the party, cannot be treated similarly as a unitary actor. Indeed one of the points of this analysis will be to demonstrate the increasing factionalization of the labor movement as it has struggled to devise a response to the changing regime and the new economic orientation.

The different rounds of the regime-change game reflect the changing strengths of actors brought about by "external" crises as well as by the way the regime-change game was played and the particular successes of or contradictions in the strategies. The first round is characterized by the emergence of three projects for regime change. Multiple lines of cleavage and cooperation make the game a complex one. Two of these projects were adopted by economic liberalizers and one by resisters. In a crosscutting cleavage, one project was adopted by the "ins" (or the governing party) and the others by the "outs" (or opposition forces). The result is a fluid and multifaceted pattern of alternative cleavages and alliances, heightened by divisions over strategy within all four actors.

Round One: Three New Projects

The first round was ushered in by the debt crisis of 1982 and the dramatic bank nationalization of the same year. In the reverberations, three projects for regime change were launched. Two of these projects were adopted by advocates of the change to neoliberal economic policies: private-sector groups in alliance with and working through the Partido Acción Nacional (PAN), and the dominant faction within the PRI, allied with the president. The third, adopted after 1982 by defectors from the PRI and the left opposition parties, was part of a reaction against the neoliberal policies.

The Right
The first project for political liberalization was adopted by the PAN, the only major opposition party in Mexico at the time, and a newly politicized private sector. Though its oppositional weight had been minimal, for four decades the PAN represented an alternative on the political right of the PRI, opposing the PRI's "collectivist," corporatist, and populist orientation and appealing to a middle-class constituency under a banner of liberalism—both economic and political. It was thus an obvious political vehicle for private-sector opposition when state-business relations began to fray in the 1970s. During that decade, the state sector grew enormously at the same time as, in line with the emerging new global economy, the export-processing sector on

the US border was also becoming a center of economic dynamism, creating a new group of northern industrialists oriented toward free markets and international integration. While these businessmen were particularly irked by the populist rhetoric and policies of the 1970s, the coup de grâce came with the 1982 bank nationalization, which in their eyes finally delegitimated a government based on a populist coalition.[4]

With the influx of businessmen as new party militants (called *neopanistas*), the PAN was transformed from a loyal and compliant to an assertive opposition party. The PAN and its business supporters criticized the government as beholden to labor, and mobilized to bring about a regime that would afford greater access to and influence over policy-making by the private sector. Such a regime had two requirements: first, the dissolution of the state-labor coalition; and second, a more competitive regime with room for a party that would represent business interests and had a possibility of winning elections. The PAN began to achieve some electoral success, particularly in the north, in the 1980s.

The LBP

The second project for regime change was adopted after 1985 by the dominant PRI faction in control of the presidency. Like the businessmen in the PAN, the government recognized that a marketizing economic project was inconsistent with the labor support base of the state. The government no longer wanted to win or reproduce workers' and peasants' support with concessions that would protect them from the market. Rather, it wanted to impose market discipline on these sectors. Further, in the context of unpopular economic policies, the dominant-LBP regime was declining in its ability to perform its main function: providing legitimacy. The economic shock treatment had induced a deep recession, which generated substantial discontent and political opposition. And even though the PRI was still the majority party, the PAN's electoral inroads seemed to undermine its legitimacy.

The solution was to change the legitimacy claim of the regime. The old claim had been to revolutionary legitimacy. The dominant-party system was based on a broad inclusionary coalition of the "revolutionary classes," and its most powerful ideological symbols had continued to make reference to the Mexican Revolution. In the 1980s, however, these symbols were no longer readily available to the government, and the "revolutionary classes" were no longer a convenient base of support. The new claim to legitimacy would be a democratic claim.

The project for regime change involved two different shifts. First, a democratic claim to legitimacy necessitated a shift from a dominant-party regime to a more competitive regime. What was envisioned was not that the PRI would actually lose power, but that it would win it through more competitive elections and share it somewhat more. The new government project was for an unequal two-plus (or one-and-a-half-plus) party system based on a majoritarian PRI, a challenging PAN that basically shared the PRI's economic orientation and which for the first time could actually win—and be allowed to win—local, state, and congressional elections, and a number of small, leftist parties that had long been a manageable feature of Mexican political life. This project was reflected in the electoral law of 1986. The law not only increased the representation of opposition parties, guaranteeing them a minimum of 30 percent of the seats in the House of Deputies, but it no longer discriminated against the emergence of a second strong party, as had previous reforms. It did, however, include as a PRI safeguard a "governability clause," which guaranteed a bare congressional majority to the largest party.[5]

The second shift was in the constituency of the PRI. Corresponding to the new direction of economic policy was a need to establish greater state autonomy from those sectors the state had been protecting through populist policies. The PRI's project envisioned that the terms of the state-labor alliance would be substantially restructured and the party would make more of an effort to be more centrally based in the growing urban middle classes. This shift in the core constituency of the PRI was premised on the party's ability to retain the support of the popular sectors as a captive voting block: with no viable alternative, the popular sectors would continue to vote PRI. On the other hand, the party would, have to redouble its efforts to compete with the newly challenging PAN for middle-class votes.

Needless to say, not everyone in the party fell in line behind the new project. In particular, three groups opposed the new direction. The first of these were the traditional party bosses, whose power was not based on popular electoral support but was embedded in the web of clientelistic relationships that had constituted the conciliating, negotiating basis of the coalition of the whole. They also resisted aspects of economic reform insofar as these might undercut the material base of these clientelistic relationships. The traditional sectors of the PRI, particularly the labor sector, also opposed the economic and political project (see below). While these first two groups of dissenters stayed within the party, the third ended up leaving the party, reflecting the way in which economic liberalization splintered coalitions and produced the basis for multiparty politics. These dissidents were a central part of the third project for political reform.

The Left
The third project for regime change emerged later, just before the 1988 elections. It was pursued by those opposed to the new economic policies— particularly to the adverse social consequences of their relatively rapid

implementation. The main groups behind this project were a combination of the traditional left and a new group of dissenters who split from the PRI. The latter was led by Cuauhtémoc Cárdenas, who ran as an opposition candidate in 1988.

Sharing with the PAN an oppositionist stance, the new splinter group joined minority parties primarily on the left in opposing one-partyism and became champions of free and fair electoral competition. The Cárdenas forces also sought to loosen the state-labor alliance effected through the PRI. More than the PAN, they saw workers as a potential constituency, on the basis that their opposition to the government's economic policies would better serve workers' interests than loyalty to a party that had abandoned them with its new economic direction. The political project was thus similar to that of the PAN, but the economic connection was different: they favored regime change to increase the political access of market resisters rather than of marketeers.

At the last minute, the Cárdenas campaign had surprising success in the 1988 elections, outpolling the inveterate PAN, coming in a strong second in official returns, and claiming fraud and outright victory.

The Labor Movement

How did the labor movement position itself with respect to these projects for regime change? The labor movement confronted its own dilemma. A victim of neoliberalism, the union movement generally opposed the new economic policies but was hesitant to break with the PRI politically. Since no opposition party had ever won, opting for political opposition ran a high risk of political marginalization and even retaliation. Under the leadership of its venerable leader Fidel Velázquez, the dominant faction in the labor movement rejected all of the projects, opposing both a more competitive regime and an alteration of the state-labor alliance. Instead it fought a rear-guard action to preserve the old regime.

This position was the mirror image of the PRI project, as most of the labor movement opposed regime change for the same reason that the "modernizers" within the PRI found it attractive: the party-affiliated labor movement derived its position through negotiation within the PRI; political competition and reform could weaken its position. In explaining this opposition, one must take due account of the Michelsian role of a leadership oligarchy, of corruption and co-optation, and of state control both through corporatist political resources and through overt coercion, in short, of what has come to be known in Mexico as *charrismo*. However, one must also recognize that the alternative to negotiation was not simply greater labor autonomy from state control, but also the concomitant lack of existing levels of state protection. With weak market power and relatively weak electoral power due both to the

size of the organized working class and to the difficulty of effective oppositional politics, particularly the weaker sectors of the labor movement had
relied on their ability—albeit limited—to negotiate from a position of being
formally cut in on the governing coalition.

The *fidelista* position of fighting to preserve the state-labor coalition was
the dominant but not the only position within the labor movement. A small
number of unions had a history of political independence and even opposition, and some, including the powerful and newly defecting petroleum workers, supported Cárdenas. Thus divisions within the labor movement were
beginning to widen, but the *fidelistas* were the largest faction and retained
dominance within the movement and the leadership of the CTM, the largest
union confederation, and of the CT, the national labor central.

In sum, all three projects for regime change had two central concerns.
First, all wanted to move away from the traditional dominant-party regime,
though the PRI's enthusiasm was contingent on its continued capacity to
retain an electoral majority. Each project also envisioned altering or aban-
doning the state-labor coalition, the PAN and the dominant PRI faction in
order to eliminate populist exchanges and flexibilize the labor market, the left
opposition in order to remove a mechanism of control over the labor movement. As long as electoral alternatives in the left remained weak, the labor
movement had a collective action problem regarding the option of going into
overt opposition to the government, given the risk of political marginalization and perhaps retaliation. This dilemma helps explain why the dominant
faction (which included many economically weak and vulnerable unions)
opposed regime change and continued its commitment to the old pattern of
LBP dominance.

Round Two: The 1988 Elections and Alternative Cleavages

The reorienting event that ushered in the second round and triggered a
change in strategic calculations was the 1988 national elections and the unanticipated strength of the left. According to official returns, the PRI, accustomed to winning at least three quarters of the popular vote, claimed only the
barest of majorities: 50.4 percent. The PAN got 17 percent, up only slightly
from its previous 16 percent in 1982, prior to the real onset of the economic
crisis or the change in policy. An astounding 31 percent was officially recognized as the vote for the Cárdenas forces. Blatant fraud left no question that
the PRI failed to win a majority of votes and left at least credible the claim
that Cárdenas actually won a plurality. This strong showing by the parties in
the electoral front that had backed Cárdenas created an impetus for founding
a new opposition party on the left, the PRD.

The 1988 elections, then, seemed to mark the emergence of a viable electoral force to the left of the PRI. Furthermore, despite the formal endorsement of most unions, the election results revealed a significant erosion of support among the PRI's traditional working-class base. This development had important strategic implications for both the PRI and the PAN. Before the elections, neither had thought that a left opposition party would move successfully into a more competitive electoral arena; rather, each in different ways had seen itself as the beneficiary. These calculations were clearly called into question. In the new context, a competing line of cleavage was presented as an alternative to the axis of opposition versus government that was salient before the elections: an axis on which the PRI and PAN might cooperate not only on economic policy but also on limited political reform to stop the PRD, whose victory would be the worst alternative for either the PRI or the PAN.

The Left
With its unexpected success, the PRD faced fewer strategic contradictions than the other forces yet was singularly unable to forge ahead as a united opposition. After 1988, the left was encouraged in its oppositional stance. The PRD became a strong voice for a regime-change project, as it now seemed that voters would in fact be willing to defect from their habitual voting patterns, and victory seemed within reach. It took a hard line against cooperating with the PRI, instead pushing for electoral reform to ensure free and fair elections, from which it expected to be the major beneficiary. With a presence in the lower chamber, the PRD, along with a more divided PAN, became a substantial force in the politics around a new reform law. At issue was the elimination of electoral fraud in all its many forms, from initial registration procedures, final counts, and electoral oversight to the campaign advantages that accrued to the PRI as the incumbent and "official" party: privileged access to and control over the media, access to financial resources, including state funds, and so forth. The attack on the PRI became more fundamental: a competitive regime could not be realized short of an opposition victory; and this was sometimes seen as requiring the elimination of a basically unreformable PRI.

The position opposing the state-labor alliance was also further elaborated. Like the PAN, the PRD saw an unfair electoral advantage given to the PRI by its relationship with labor in terms of both the informal interpenetration of party and union leadership and the collective form of party membership by which workers belonging to most unions were automatically members of the PRI by virtue of the union's membership in the party. Unlike the PAN, the PRD also opposed the state-labor alliance as a mechanism of control, which deprived many organized workers of political autonomy through which they could pursue their own interests effectively and take independent policy positions.

All in all, the PRD did not emerge from this round in good shape. Despite the relative success of the Cárdenas opposition in 1988, the new PRD fared poorly in elections held during the next presidential term. In part this outcome reflected government harassment (see below). In part it reflected its own inability to forge a coherently organized party out of the electoral front that had supported the Cárdenas candidacy— not all the parties joined the PRD, and among those that did, divisions remained. Beyond that, it proved difficult to establish links with a mass base and institutionalize a capacity for electoral mobilization. In addition, the economy was recovering, and Salinas managed to convince lower-class voters that anti-inflationary measures and his brand of "social liberalism" would benefit them. By the end of the next presidential term, the PRD had been reduced from a formidable challenger to a distant third electoral force, unable to capture power at the level of a single state.

The Right
The PAN's strategic situation was more complicated. The 1988 election seemed to indicate that, contrary to what it had anticipated, it was not the PAN that would be the main beneficiary of a more competitive regime, but the PRD, a party whose economic policies the PAN regarded as much more objectionable than those of the newly neoliberal PRI. The outcome of the 1988 election thus seemed to pose a contradiction between a more competitive regime on the one hand and both PAN electoral success and neoliberalism on the other. The strategic choice, therefore, was whether to cooperate with the PRI as neoliberal partners in perhaps limited political opening and reform, or to cooperate with the PRD as opposition partners in pushing for more radical regime change. During the course of the second round, despite splits within the party over this issue, the PAN opted for cooperation with the PRI, not only on economic policy but also on issues like electoral reform and negotiated outcomes of disputed elections.

The PAN fared considerably better than the PRD during the second round, both in its organizational activities and in the corresponding electoral results. In some states where it had traditional strength, the PAN's victories effectively eliminated the dominant-party regime and effectuated a two-party system on this subnational level.

The LBP
For the PRI, the unexpected rise of the PRD exposed the contradictions of its project of pursuing neoliberalism via greater party competition. The PRD challenged both the new policy direction and the PRI's electoral support base. It seemed that the PRI could no longer rely on a captive mass support

base now that a surprisingly viable, potentially victorious alternative existed that could attract the lower classes in a way the PAN could not. In fact, there had been substantial defection of workers in the 1988 elections.

Despite resulting pressure to moderate the hard-line approach to the economy, particularly from sizable and powerful party factions that favored such a move, the dominant Salinas faction ensured that the policy orientation remained unchanged. What, then, was the response of the PRI with respect to the twin issues of party competitiveness and the state-labor alliance?

With respect to the former, the PRI did four things in the first years of the new Salinas government. First, it tried to recreate the strategic environment in which the old project made sense through a series of moves to ensure that the PAN and not the PRD would be the main opposition faced by the PRI. These included manipulation of electoral machinery to recognize PAN electoral victories but reject PRD victories, and harassment of the PRD, the scope of which is suggested by the large number of unsolved murders of PRD activists.

Second, from a position of still-substantial strength, the PRI negotiated yet another electoral law. Its logic revealed that the PRI was continuing its strategy toward a more competitive regime while simultaneously maximizing the possibilities of continued control of the government. This time, however, the electoral framework would have to respond to the new form of electoral challenge. If the 1986 law supported a change in the status of the PRI from a dominant to a majoritarian party, the new law protected the PRI's governing position by attempting to accommodate its possible decline to only a plurality party.[6]

Third, as it had in the past, the PRI undertook yet another attempt at internal party reform to renovate the party, to make it more competitive and advance the shift in its support base. The labor sector was once again successful in defeating any attempt to decorporatize the party by moving from sectoral organization and collective membership to territorial organization and individual membership, although a reorganization of the party downgraded the position of the sectors. More generally, the reforms actually implemented fell far short of the rhetoric of party democratization. Nevertheless, the renewal process had some results, with the selection of more attractive candidates and a set of surprising electoral turnarounds in off-term elections during the Salinas term.

Fourth, in the face of the PRD challenge, the PRI government attempted to secure or recapture its support among the unorganized lower classes, often in the informal sector—a particularly important group not only because of its size, but also because its interests were not in conflict with economic restructuring in the same way as those of unionized workers and peasants. In part as an end run around the traditional forces within the party, the government launched PRONASOL, a major community development program that counteracted some of the effects of neoliberalism on poor communities and which was often targeted at communities where the presidential party faction wanted to increase the PRI's electoral support.

Party strategy toward the state-labor alliance had to navigate carefully between the new economic policy and the newly heightened concern with retaining labor support. Despite initial speculation that, as a weak president lacking legitimacy, Salinas would actively court the traditional PRI constituencies, barely a month after occupying the presidency Salinas began a series of dramatic moves against traditional labor bosses—including one of the most powerful of them, the longtime head of the petroleum workers' union—when they ran afoul of government plans for industrial restructuring or privatization. The old constituency in its traditional form would not be preserved.

Yet political support was of central importance for the PRI. Out of this concern came an attempt to redefine a new relationship between the party and its labor base that was called the New Unionism. The goal of the New Unionism was to replace the old corporatist basis of labor support with a new framework for preserving or renewing that support while simultaneously reducing the influence of organized labor in national politics and advancing economic restructuring. Unions were to be more internally representative and, as such, better interlocutors for generating working-class support than the traditional, often oligarchic unions. A companion component was the idea of the "participatory firm" that would emphasize cooperative labor relations and worker input to improve productivity. The model was a "new union" that was oriented toward firm-level issues of production and away from national-level negotiations over state concessions and protection.[7]

The strategy of the PRI during this round was partially successful. First, aided by the end of the economic crisis, Salinas became a popular president, and by 1991 the PRI seemed to have recovered from the 1988 debacle, winning a landslide victory in midterm elections. Second, with the decline in the popularity of the PRD, the PRI's project for a one-and-a-half-plus or two-plus party regime, in which the PRI faced an electoral challenge primarily from the PAN (a party with which it had basic economic agreement), seemed back on track. On the other hand, internal party reform had been limited, and the New Unionism was fraught with contradictions that would render it unable to constitute an appropriate framework for a reconfigured labor constituency: union democracy had the obvious potential of producing a more militant unionism that might challenge firm restructuring, confront the state's neoliberal policies, and politically oppose the PRI.

The Labor Movement

The labor movement was deeply divided by the differential effect of market logic on workers in different economic sectors. The majority and minority factions of the first round were reinforced in round two, and a third faction got outlined more distinctively. This last, constituted by a small number of unions, fell in behind the New Unionism, which in many ways grew out of the model already in place in one of these unions—the Telephone Workers' Union (STRM) under Francisco Hernández Juárez. These workers were in an unusual position in Mexico. They were not fundamentally threatened by industrial restructuring but able to adapt to it and even benefit from any resulting revitalization of the sector. Furthermore, the union was already internally democratic and had already opted out of the corporatist ties to the party, though the leadership individually supported the government and demonstrated a capacity to perform the desired interlocutory function with the rank and file. Few unions, however, were in this position, and Hernández Juárez was unable to extend his leadership over the larger union movement on the basis of this new model.[8]

Another group of unions confronted their firms and the government over economic restructuring and ended up (or remained) in political opposition to the PRI government. Both democratic unions and bureaucratized, oligarchic, boss-led unions were in this confrontational category. Several of these unions were attacked by the state, quite literally when the military invaded the personal compound of the leader of the petroleum workers' union. Together, the actions of the government, firms, and traditional labor leaders severely limited the space available for confrontation.

The third response was retrenchment: a continuation of the strategy to preserve the state-labor alliance and the political position of organized labor within the PRI. This position was most associated with the traditional leaders of the national federations that integrated the smaller, weaker unions in less dynamic or modern sectors. These labor centrals had most depended on the political connections of the old alliance, and these leaders had most benefited from that alliance through their personal position within the PRI. Attempting to demonstrate their political indispensability to the PRI government by acceding to the main outlines of economic policy, supporting the government on firm restructuring, and even entering into a series of annual tripartite pacts that helped to stabilize the economy, the dominant PRI-affiliated faction managed to force something of a compromise to the extent it blocked plans to abolish the "sectoral" organization of the party or change the labor law in a direction of great labor market flexibility.

In sum, at the end of the Salinas presidency, with the partial success of its project, the PRI looked poised to do well in the upcoming elections, especially as it had overseen something of an economic recovery and had chosen an attractive presidential candidate.[9] The vulnerability of the project was that, despite its apparent renewed popularity, the party had hardly been successful in consolidating a middle-class or an informal-sector constituency and it had failed to reconfigure a new basis for attracting labor support; indeed, for the important, annually negotiated, tripartite economic pacts, the government continued to rely on cooperation with traditional labor bosses—those who most directly embodied the old pattern of labor support and exchange that the new project sought to supersede.

Round Three: Multiple Crises and Shifting Alignments

The current round three, which roughly corresponds to the Zedillo presidency, began with a multiplicity of crises in quick succession. This round is characterized by continual uncertainty and constant change, with both advances and reversals of the positions of the actors on many fronts. Despite these uncertain and haphazard conditions, the overall trend is toward a greater political openness that is indicative of the unraveling of the old system. Although it is impossible to predict, it may also be indicative of the emergence of an ongoing competitive party system that will continue to have the fluidity and unpredictability that are expected of more competitive regimes.

Three crises marked the onset of round three and affected the strategies of the major players in three distinct ways. The first was the economic crisis and collapse following the December 1994 currency devaluation, which simultaneously got Zedillo's presidency off to a devastating start, as it was virtually his first policy move, and discredited Salinas, whose economic policies were also implicated. In 1995, according to a government report, the gross domestic product declined by nearly 7 percent, purchasing power dropped 15 to 20 percent, unemployment more than doubled, and 5 million more Mexicans joined those classified as living in extreme poverty, bringing the figure to nearly a quarter of the population.[10] The second was the legitimacy crisis of the PRI regime, which not only had failed economically but had to endure nearly daily revelations of major scandals, including unsolved political murders (the most notable of which were the PRI's presidential candidate and secretary general), high-level corruption that included Salinas's brother, and the encroaching power and influence within state agencies of drug traffickers.

Third, in reaction to the consequences of the new economic model, new left-wing opposition social movements appeared and took the offensive in more dramatic and challenging ways. Most important was the rise of two novel movements: the Zapatistas, a peasant-based armed guerrilla movement (EZLN), and El Barzón, a largely middle-class debtors movement—as well as the subsequent appearance of the EPR, a more radical guerrilla group. The Zapatistas' goals of full democracy in Mexico, an end to the government's neoliberal economic policies, and land and freedom for the indigenous peoples, combined with their skillful use of the Internet and the personal appeal of Subcomandante Marcos, initially generated an enormous amount of sympathy both domestically and internationally. El Barzón, founded by farmers in 1993, rapidly spread to urban small producers and consumer credit card debtors. This organization of small debtors unable to repay their loans because of the high interest rates sustained by Mexican economic policy claimed over a million members in all of Mexico's states.

These social movements further challenged the legitimacy of the government, its policies, and even its ability to maintain order. With world media coverage and widespread international sympathy, they also challenged the government to respond in a nonrepressive mode that did not violate human rights—a challenge the government failed to meet. At the same time, the eruption of this new opposition seemed to indicate an underlying discontent that the PRD could potentially tap and, by the same token, the limits of the popularity of an economic policy orientation also advocated by the PAN.

The LBP

The PRI has continued to be unable to resolve the set of dilemmas it faced all along: how to retain popular support in the face of greater electoral competition while pursuing an unpopular and crisis-prone economic model. It has remained divided over strategy and indeed saw an unusual eruption of internal opposition. Its prospects during this round have fluctuated.

The party began the round severely weakened. Far from winning the anticipated landslide in the 1994 elections, the PRI managed only to repeat its official 1988 performance, winning about half the votes. This time, the election results were not highly contested, but the party faced a serious legitimacy crisis as it began to sink ever deeper into a web of scandal and drug associations, the economic crisis took its toll, and the Zapatistas hit a responsive chord in the country at large. In response, Zedillo deepened the PRI strategy of attempting to offset an unyielding commitment to neoliberal economic policy by identifying, beyond Salinas, with the project of furthering political reform and multipartyism. However, he often faced intransigence from within the PRI, and his own democratic conduct has been inconsistent. With cross-pressures and with the party deeply divided, political reform has seen both advances and stalls.

Zedillo has pursued reform at three levels: in the party; in the relationships among the party, the state, and the presidency; and in the electoral arena. Within the party, he vowed to end the *dedazo* (presidential choice), indicating he will not choose party candidates for political office, including his successor, and his administration took steps to correct abuses by some of the reform-resistant local parties. He also stated a commitment to alter the balance of power between the president and legislature, proposing congressional approval of major judicial appointments and congressional oversight of government spending through a new auditing agency.[11] Finally, Zedillo took credit for the electoral reform that the parties finally agreed upon in August 1996, including some important measures—a directly elected mayor for Mexico City, better electoral oversight, and somewhat more equitable distribution of financial and media resources among the parties. The latter measures were later reversed to some degree by the PRI's congressional majority but have nevertheless altered the ability of the opposition to mount an electoral campaign.

The PRI move to reform has continued to be marked by ambivalence. The record on the ground has not conformed to the president's reformist statements and has included ongoing incidents of electoral fraud, particularly at state and local levels, and repression of opposition movements. The moves back and forth reflect both divisions within the party and the changing strategic situation that follows the party's shifting electoral fortunes. After poor PRI showings in a string of state elections in 1995, Zedillo seemed to be eager to regain the support of the hard-line factions within the party.[12] Even more dramatically, in the 1997 off-term national elections, the PRI lost for the first time both their majority in the Chamber of Deputies and control of the Mexico City mayoralty, home of one fifth of Mexico's population. In 1998, however, presumably in response to some more open and successful nomination procedures, the PRI recovered some of this lost electoral ground, making the current balance difficult to assess.

Despite the apparent payoff, the rhythm of internal party reform has mirrored divisions within the party. Once again, groups within the party defeated an effort to diminish the influence of the sectoral organizations. In a more surprising assertion of independence from the leadership, those opposed to reform also demonstrated their power by making previous party experience and prior electoral success prerequisites for presidential candidacy, requirements that would have disqualified the recent technocratic presidents.

As the fight over party reform indicates, the dilemma has continued regarding the party's relationship to labor in the face of the government's neoliberal policies. The president has again been trying to reconfigure the relationship with labor, but a new formula remains elusive. The new attempt —dubbed the "New Labor Culture"—seems even more vague than the New Unionism, and many unions have rejected it. At the same time, the government has made some approach to the more traditional labor sectors and continues rhetorically to claim a commitment to the historic state-labor alliance, though it has not displayed any willingness to come forward with substantial corresponding economic concessions.[13]

The Right
The PAN's basic dilemma has continued to be maneuvering between two alternatives: cooperating with the PRD to further challenge the political

position of the PRI and its institutional bases of power or cooperating on economic policy issues with the PRI, to which it is often closer. The party's strategy from the earlier round—fighting hard to contest elections while simultaneously negotiating the outcome of several of those elections with the PRI—paid off. The PAN started this round much stronger than it did the previous round, having moved from a disappointing third-place outcome in the 1988 election to a significant second-place showing in 1994. In the course of this round, the PAN has often been seen as a viable challenger to the PRI.

The PAN, then, has met substantial electoral success. Of the five gubernatorial races in 1995, the party won by large margins in three states and lost narrowly in the other two. In municipal elections the PAN has also performed well, winning several state capitals and well over half of Mexico's twenty largest cities. Areas of the country are now seen as essentially having local two-party regimes, and the PAN claims to rule a third of the Mexican population at the local level. With these successes, internal party divisions seem to have become less intense, though tensions remain between pro-market forces and those that want to make a broader appeal, because of either commitment or a strategic choice to move toward the center.

The Left

Round three marked dramatic fluctuations for the PRD. If it entered the previous round unexpectedly strong and ended weak, in round three its fortunes were just the reverse. By 1994, the PRD's electoral support had substantially declined, and it was being outflanked on the left by the new social movements, which presented a more dramatic and nonelectoral opposition. Under these circumstances, the strategy of drawing closer to and making common cause with these groups seemed attractive. Some cooperation indeed began between the PRD and left social movements, though in most instances at the initiative of the EZLN rather than the PRD. In July 1996, the EZLN held a conference on state reform that gathered delegates from the PRD, Coordinadora Intersindical (see below), El Barzón, and other organizations. Following the conference, the EZLN announced the establishment of "formal ties" for some type of cooperation with the PRD in the 1997 midterm elections to prevent the electoral domination of the right. In addition, the PRD created a new secretariat for union affairs and cooperated with dissident unions.

This strategy, however, shifted with the 1997 election. At that time the PRD made a stunning recovery, not only in winning the mayoralty of Mexico City but also in tying the PAN in winning the opposition vote. The PRD's successes in the 1997 election's mainstream constituencies have substantially countered the leftward pull of the EZLN and El Barzón, as the party has shifted its strategy from mass demonstrations to the ballot box. Along with this shift has come the strategy of appealing to the center rather than radical-izing and allying with these new social movements.

The Labor Movement

In round three, divisions within the labor movement have become more insti-tutionalized, but at the same time labor opposition has become more marked. Under the leadership of Hernández Juárez, the "New Unions" were trans-formed and reorganized as the Foro in 1995. The Foro, representing more than two million workers from both independent unions and those affiliated with umbrella Congreso de Trabajo (CT), has moved to distance labor from the government, seeking the democratization of the labor movement, auton-omy from the PRI, and a new economic policy that defends jobs and salaries. It has engaged in several large-scale acts of defiance against the PRI and "offi-cial" unionism, including a massive protest against a bill to reform the social security system, a reform that had the support of the CT, the CTM, and the PRI's labor-sector deputies; an independent May Day march despite threats of expulsion from the CT when Velázquez canceled the traditional parade for the second year in a row; and abstention from the CT's internal elections.

The death of Fidel Velázquez, Mexico's major national labor leader since 1941, added greater uncertainty and perhaps fluidity to the picture. A minor-ity of the Foro unions left the CT and formed the UNT, aspiring to be a more autonomous rival national labor central. At the same time, the Foro unions that remained in the CT reinforced its internal divisions as that orga-nization, with its dominant member, the CTM, under new leadership for the first time in nearly six decades, felt its way forward.[14]

While the picture remains one of flux, the trend points in the direction of breakdown of the old system of a labor movement affiliated with the governing party, cooperating with the government, and supportive of its policies. Opposition parties oppose the old corporatist pattern. The PRI has remained ambivalent about the terms on which it relates to a labor constituency, and the government has moved away from tripartite wage-price agreements. The labor movement is divided over the alternatives of the old corporatist pattern versus greater autonomy combined with a more aggressive posture in demand making. The UNT seems open to negotiating a reform of the federal labor law, which was successfully resisted by Velázquez and the CT. Any such change would fur-ther undermine the historical form of labor movement institutionalization.[15]

Conclusion

The current era is a difficult one for governing labor-based parties and especially for labor-based-party-dominant regimes. Changes in the world economy—and, in countries like Mexico, pressures deriving from the debt crisis—altered the interests and preferences of many state and social actors and thereby produced incentives to change the economic model, one that had been compatible with a form of compromise or settlement between capital and labor. These changes may have two major consequences for labor-based-party-dominant regimes. First, they may challenge the regime's base of support in the labor movement, which was consistent with the old economic model, but finds little scope in the new neoliberal model. Indeed, economic liberalization and the flexibilization of labor markets have contributed to the fragmentation of the labor movement and its declining influence as a political actor. The simultaneous move to political competition and marketization creates a tension between the LBP's continuing reliance on labor votes and simultaneous desire to distance itself from its traditional policies. On the labor side, some groups, given the weakening market position, continue to rely on their political relationship to the LBP, though they may be increasingly tempted to defect to the PRD given the PRI's unstable electoral performance.

Second, by removing the material base for class compromise, economic pressures may reduce the space for consensus and give rise to political opposition, thereby undermining one-partyism and producing more open political contestation. Thus, structural factors have challenged both the labor base of the state and party dominance.

Over the last decade, both of these effects have been playing out in Mexico, where the dominant-LBP regime is being undermined from within as well as without. From without, economic pressures have given rise to opposition from both the right and the left. From within, they have led to tensions and contradictions within the LBP, which has tried to reformulate or restructure its constituency—to look for new bases of electoral support and to refashion its relationship with its labor base. Thus structural changes have led to a process of regime change—an alteration in both the pattern of contestation and the support base of the state and of the regime—but the process and outcome of regime change must be seen in terms of the strategic interaction of the major actors as they respond to the new economic conditions and engage in political struggle over both economic policy and political reform.

The above discussion analyzed this political struggle as a "regime-change game" played by four key actors that took positions on these salient economic and political issues as each sought to change or retain the status quo with respect to economic policy (to radicalize or resist marketization) and the nature of the regime (LBP dominance, encompassing the twin issues of [1]the labor movement's political position—its coalitional and party affiliation and its status as a support base for the state—and [2] party competition and the degree of political contestation). Simplifying and dichotomizing the two dimensions produces four distinct combinations occupied by the different players while at the same time showing the possibility of different alliances, lines of cooperation, or coinciding strategies with the changing salience of the two issues. The actors and their positions on economic and political change are summarized in Figure 1.

Figure 1.
Actor's Positions on Reform

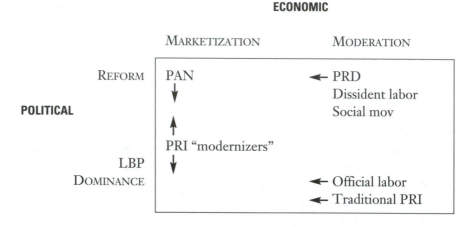

Each of three rounds of play began with a crisis—an exogenously or endogenously derived shock—that altered the resources and strategic calculations of the actors. As a result, fluctuating cleavages and patterns of cooperation emerged across the rounds. In round one there was some tendency toward a horizontal line of cleavage along political differences, a cleavage that emphasized the newly emerging opposition of both the PAN and what would become the PRD, while the governing PRI, divided on economic policy, was only beginning to move, hesitantly and with enormous ambivalence, toward a position of political reform. In round two, the alternate line of cleavage became more prominent in light of the PRD "threat" commonly felt by both the PRI and PAN, which moved toward cooperation on political reform. Having started this round as a strong electoral challenger, the PRD remained firm and contentious on political reform but tended toward economic moderation to maximize what had appeared to be its promising electoral base. Patterns of cleavage and cooperation became even more fluid in round three. The prominence of new social movements spawned by the adverse consequences of the changed economic policy potentially strengthened the position previously occupied primarily by the PRD and a minority dissident current within the labor movement. They have produced a dynamic for the growth and revitalization of that pole. At the same time, all three parties have cooperated in furthering political reform, though a newly assertive posture by the traditional forces within the PRI displayed a capacity to obstruct the plans of the reformers.

Over the rounds of the regime-change game, then, different patterns of cooperation and conflict emerged, with some movement in certain directions in response to changes in the strategic environment as well as internal divisions: (1) PAN: vertical movement down somewhat, as the party backs away from political reform to prevent a PRD victory; (2) PRI: vertical movement alternately toward and away from political reform, in response to a legitimacy crisis, impending electoral adversity, and the party's internal distribution of power; (3) PRD: horizontal movement on the axis of economic reform as the party is presented with the possibilities of appealing to a larger electoral constituency in the center versus capitalizing on the vigor of social movements on the left; (4) official labor and traditional PRI: horizontal movement in the trade-off between retaining the state-labor alliance at the cost of accepting market reforms and the alternative of more overt and autonomous opposition to government policy; in addition, the official labor movement has shown still-incipient vertical movement upward under the post-Velázquez leadership.

The course of regime change, then, has been characterized by uncertainty and strategic fluctuations as actors respond to crises that initiate each new round and alter their calculations. At the same time, a secular trend of regime change has been evident across the rounds. With respect to economic policy, of course, the resisters have been unable to deflect what has generally been a consistent, unidirectional move toward marketization. Similarly, and partly in response to this economic path, one can observe rather gradual but steady movement toward regime change. First, during the course of the decade-and-a-half analyzed here, party competition and political contestation have increased. The PRI has not yet lost the presidency, but for the first time such an eventuality is being contemplated as a possible or even likely outcome in 2000. Second, the traditional state-labor alliance and the labor base of the state is being altered, if not superseded. Step by step, the long-standing LBP-dominant regime in Mexico is drawing to an end.

Acknowledgments

With a few changes, this chapter was previously published in *The Awkward Embrace: One-Party Domination and Democracy*, edited by Hermann Giliomee and Charles Simkins, Harwood Academic Publishers, 1999. I would like to acknowledge the research and editorial assistance of Benjamin Goldfrank, and thank Max Cameron, Paul Dosh, Kenneth Greene, Timothy Kessler, and James Samstad for their many valuable suggestions.

6

External Actors in the Transitions to Democracy in Latin America

Arturo Valenzuela

ALMOST TWO HUNDRED years ago, the colonies of the Spanish crown in the New World achieved independence and sought to emulate their counterparts in the United States of America by adopting republican forms of government inspired by the ideals of the Enlightenment. One hundred years later, Brazil jettisoned monarchical rule and followed the example of the former Spanish colonies by also adopting a constitutional framework closely patterned after the document crafted in Philadelphia in 1789. It is not until this final decade of the twentieth century that nearly all of the nations of the hemisphere are being simultaneously governed by leaders who attained office following constitutional precepts based on the doctrine of popular sovereignty; Cuba remains the sole exception.

The experience with constitutional government in Ibero-America has varied widely from country to country and over time (Hartlyn and Valenzuela 1994). During the nineteenth century, Chile stood out as the country that most successfully established constitutional continuity, forging relatively strong republican institutions that permitted alternation in power and the gradual expansion of suffrage. By the second decade of the twentieth century, fourteen of nineteen countries in the region, including Argentina, Brazil, Chile, Colombia, Costa Rica, Peru, and Uruguay, could be characterized as "oligarchical democracies"; that is, democracies that adhered to constitutional requirements and held regular presidential and congressional elections, albeit with restricted electorates.

Those governments were not too dissimilar to those in much of Europe at the time, also dominated by upper-class political leaders relying on reduced suffrage, competing in often questionable elections. And, as Epstein reminds us, in Europe "political power was often not effectively transferred from hereditary rulers to representative assemblies, no matter how narrow their electorates, until late in the nineteenth century" (Epstein 1967, p. 192).

As in Europe, the economic crisis brought on by World War I and the Great Depression, the declining prestige of politicians and parliaments, and the growing popularity of fascist and Marxist critiques of capitalism and bourgeois democracy contributed to a wave of regime breakdowns. Ten coups in the period from 1930 to 1933 led to a reversal of constitutional government in all but five countries of Ibero-America. Military establishments generally viewed their role as referees of the political process, imposing order or blocking the aspirations of politicians, such as Peron in Argentina or Haya de la Torre in Peru, with populist appeals. In two separate swings of the pendulum, at the end of World War II and again in the late 1950s, military governments gave way to civilian rule in most of the region.

Democratic experiments suffered sharp setbacks in the 1960s, with eight military takeovers between 1962 and 1964 alone. The nature of the military regimes that came to power also changed significantly. With the Brazilian coup of 1964, the military government abandoned the traditional role of moderator and sought to implement far-reaching transformations with no set time frame (Stepan 1971). Military coups in Argentina, Peru, Chile, and Uruguay also ushered in variants of the bureaucratic authoritarian state, each seeking to recast the socioeconomic and institutional order in response to threats from the left or in attempts to preempt that threat (O'Donnell 1973). During the 1970s, between twelve and sixteen authoritarian regimes governed in Latin America, excluding from power not only the politicians but the citizenry as well. The advent of bureaucratic authoritarian regimes and the breakdown of democracy in countries such as Uruguay and Chile were related to the growing perception among middle and upper-middle-class sectors, business elites, and the armed forces that the popular sectors and the left were tangible threats to their basic interests. Particularly after the triumph of the Cuban Revolution in the early sixties, they viewed weak democratic governments and practices as playing directly into the hands of the enemy. The United States, locked in the East-West conflict with Soviet power, was also determined not to permit another Cuba from emerging in the Western hemisphere, often siding with those forces who sought refuge in authoritarian solutions (Bethell 1991).

It was in the 1980s, in the throes of the worst economic crisis since the 1930s, that the most dramatic political reversal since the Great Depression took place. Throughout the continent, dictatorships gradually gave way to elected governments. This democratic tide included countries with strong democratic histories, such as Uruguay and Chile, as well as countries where democracy had not fared well in the past, such as those of Central America. Although it is likely that there will be democratic reversals in the region, there is reason to be optimistic that the pendulum will not swing back as far as it has in the past. For some countries in the region, the prospects of democratic consolidation appear to be relatively good.

The objective of this paper is to review the recent process of democratic transition in Latin America, exploring the relative weight of domestic and international factors, particularly the role of the United States. The paper argues that the United States, while inhibiting the democratization process in earlier periods, played a fairly minor role in the transitions of the late 1980s. The paper concludes with a discussion of the conditions for consolidation of stable democracies in the region and the role the United States and the international community can play in the democratization process.

Understanding the Transitions to Democracy in Latin America

The starting point for any discussion of democratization and transitions to democracy is to stress that no set of economic or cultural determinants appears to explain in a satisfactory manner the origin and evolution of the democratic experience. Certain socioeconomic and cultural factors may be helpful in fostering the conditions for democracy; none appears to be necessary in promoting a democratic outcome (Hartlyn and Valenzuela 1994, p. 102).

Chile was as conservative religiously and culturally as other Spanish colonies, and yet its elites were able to make democratic institutions work from an early date. Argentina was one of the wealthiest countries in the world in the first decades of this century, but it failed to consolidate democratic institutions after the crisis of the 1930s. Uruguay, culturally similar to Argentina with a strikingly similar immigrant population, developed one of the most exemplary democratic regimes of the century.

In Central America, Costa Rica overcame decades of civil strife to establish a successful democracy after a civil war in 1948. Venezuela, one of countries with the poorest record of democratic performance until the 1950s, managed, with Colombia and Costa Rica, to avoid the pattern of military rule of the 1970s. And although democracy was generally illusive in Latin America in this difficult century, it is important to underscore that in the period from 1930 to 1990, the eight largest countries in the region, with the bulk of the continent's population, were governed by elected constitutional governments 64 percent of the time.

The origins and evolution of democratic institutions, procedures, and practices and the transition to democratic governance result more from the choices made by key political elites seeking to maximize their interests within the framework of specific structural and political parameters than from cultural or economic factors. More often than not, these choices may stem from an inconclusive struggle for power, a situation of stalemate where there are no clear winners or losers. It may also result from the successful challenge of groups and interests outside of elite circles.

As such, democracy can be understood as resulting from a set of accommodations and compromises—even second preference choices—in which the concurrence of nondemocrats may be as important as the support of democrats. Once democratic practices are accepted, they provide the key rules of the game for determining power in society, and defining the parameters for action and the strategies to be pursued by relevant actors. Democracy will become consolidated provided that it continues to give guarantees to relevant players and remains the preferred or only option in seeking political power. In time, democratic rules may come to be accepted as the only proper rules for political conduct, adding a powerful legitimizing factor to democratic practices and procedures (Valenzuela 1989, p. 182).

It is important to stress that the process of democratic transition does not lead to a uniform outcome. Some countries, such as Chile and Uruguay, and to a lesser degree Brazil and Argentina, are going through a process of redemocratization. They can draw on long-term experiences with democratic institutions and practices, including functioning legislatures, state and local governments, political parties, and judicial institutions, in consolidating democracy. Other countries, such as Paraguay, Ecuador, Bolivia, Mexico, and most of the countries of Central America, are only now embarking on the process of democratization with a shallow legacy of democratic institutions and practices to inform their work. It stands to reason that the success of democratic consolidation is far less assured in the latter cases (Hartlyn 1997).

The modalities of regime transition in the most recent wave also varied widely. In some cases the transitions resulted from tacit or explicit pacts entered into by military regimes with their civilian opponents, as in the cases of Uruguay and Brazil. In Argentina, the transition to civilian rule came through a rupture of the military regime following its devastating defeat at the hands of the British in the Falklands War. In Bolivia, the military regime imploded as a result of its own widespread corruption and abuse of power. In Chile, the transition took place within the constitutional framework of the military regime, although the opposition succeeded in defeating the military in a plebiscite designed to prolong authoritarian rule.

In Central America the transition process was influenced by the United States, which initially pressed for regime liberalization as a condition for continued support against domestic insurgencies, and the Central American peace accords that provided the broader blueprint for regional peace and democratic elections. In Paraguay and Haiti, transitions occurred following the overthrow of longtime dictatorships and the subsequent liberalization of the political systems by military rulers.

It is not clear that the particular path followed by a given nation during the transition process will have a more or less positive effect in the consolidation of democracy. Far more important than the modality of regime transition is the longer historic experience of a particular country with democratic institutions and practices. Countries with generations of democratic practice and well-developed democratic institutions, such as political parties and legislative assemblies, will have a far easier time in consolidating democracies than those countries with no tradition of elections and weak democratic institutions. It is true that transitions may affect democratic consolidation in the short term by leaving in place certain authoritarian enclaves or by leaving unresolved difficult issues such as the resolution of human rights violations. However, over the long haul, democratic consolidation will be more dependent on the prior experience a country has with democracy or a given country's ability to forge legitimate mechanisms and institutions of representation that are fully accountable to the citizenry.

Three factors are important in understanding the transitions to democracy in the 1980s in Latin America: the historic legitimacy of democratic practices, the failure of authoritarian regimes, and the decline of the left. The enduring nature of democracy as an ideal and as a set of institutions and practices cannot be dismissed lightly in analyzing the recent transitions to democracy in Latin America. For generations, Latin American countries have experimented with elections, elected assemblies, local governments, and political parties of varying ideological persuasions. Although constitutions have often been violated, most countries have highly legalistic traditions and take constitutional precepts seriously.

By contrast with other regions of the world, the legitimacy of democracy as the most appropriate institutional arrangement for governing a country and resolving conflicts peacefully has been an enduring part of the political culture, even as liberal democracy has been challenged by other political ideologies. Democracy has retained a permanence on the continent—as an aspiration, as an option, and as a set of more or less institutionalized procedures and practices. Military regimes or de facto governments were almost always viewed as aberrations, as tyrannies that should give way to a normalization of the political process.

Although the direct causes of regime transition vary, they generally stemmed from the significant failure of authoritarian regimes to govern adequately or, in countries with civil conflicts, establish a lasting peace. Military regimes were severely undermined by internal conflicts and disagreements over policy and political succession. With the exception of the Chilean military government, few were able to implement necessary reforms, particularly those aimed at addressing the devastating economic crisis of the early eighties. That failure, combined with widespread criticism of human rights abuses, abuse of power, and corruption, led to a dramatic decline in the prestige of military establishments. Several began to negotiate a return to the barracks after efforts to legitimize their own rule through plebiscites, elections, or constitutional plebiscites were decisively defeated by a disenchanted citizenry. These negotiations often began with splits among the ruling elites in response to challenges from outside—splits that led moderates in the regime to reach out to moderates in the opposition to begin to forge a transition (O'Donnell, Schmitter, and Whitehead 1986).

Although the Mexican regime was very different from the military regimes of the rest of the continent, by the 1980s Mexico's one-party state had also lost considerable legitimacy. The significant erosion of the corporatist pillars of the ruling party resulting from widespread structural changes in Mexican society, combined with the severe economic downturn following the debt crisis, led to a dramatic decline in support for the PRI in the 1988 presidential election. After the election, marred by allegations of fraud, pressure increased on the regime to liberalize and institute fair electoral rules and procedures. President Salinas, however, chose to push for economic reforms, including a dramatic opening of the economy to international trade, while downplaying political reforms. Following the 1994 electoral contest, won by the PRI, significant electoral reforms were concluded after extensive interparty bargaining. The 1995 peso crisis, combined with increasing deterioration of the ruling party, led to dramatic gains for the opposition that portend an end to the Mexican one-party state (Valenzuela 1997; Bailey and Valenzuela 1997).

The deterioration of military and authoritarian governments in the Americas came at a time when the challenge of the left as a radical force in the region declined significantly, undermining the raison d'être of regimes that claimed that their continued existence was necessary to guarantee the social order. In Brazil, Argentina, and Uruguay, credible leftist threats were crushed by the military in the early years of military rule. In Chile, ironically, the radical left was undermined more by the growing success of the democratic opposition, including socialists who had abandoned radical options, than by the strong-arm tactics of the regime. Prior to the collapse of the Soviet bloc and disintegration of the Soviet Union, much of the left in South America had abandoned Marxist-Leninist formulae, adopting instead discourse of "socialist renewal" that highlighted the value of democratic institutions and the politics of compromise and accommodation in their own right, and not simply as a mechanism to attain power (Castañeda 1993; Walker 1990).

The victory of the Sandinistas in Nicaragua and the continued insurrectionary capability of guerrilla forces in Salvador and Guatemala kept the challenge of the radical left alive longer in Central America. The Reagan administration waged a determined effort to defeat the Sandinista government and sought to support the anti-insurgency activities of military regimes in Salvador and Guatemala while turning to Costa Rica and Honduras as bases for regional military activities (Carothers 1991). However, the dramatic foreign-policy reorientation of the Soviet Union after 1985 led to a retreat of Soviet support for the Nicaraguan government and rebel forces in other countries and a sharp curtailment of support for Cuba. By the end of the decade, Soviet officials were pressing both Cuba and Nicaragua to end their support for insurgency movements in the region and collaborating with the United States in support of the UN-sponsored peace process. While the end of direct support undermined leftist insurgencies, the collapse of socialism in Eastern and Central Europe dealt an even more significant blow to the left, as it lost much of the power of its ideological discourse as well as the tangible support it received from its international supporters. The end of the Cold War helped spur the progress of the peace process in Central America, spearheaded by Costa Rican president Oscar Arias, and contributed to the trend toward democratization.

The Role of the United States and International Actors in the Democratic Transitions

The United States has historically had shifting and at times contradictory policies toward the promotion of human rights and democracy in the Americas.[1] In the twenties, Woodrow Wilson intervened militarily in several Central American and Caribbean states in failed attempts to promote democratic institutions. Under Franklin Delano Roosevelt, the United States forged a new era of cooperation in the hemisphere based on support for the doctrine of nonintervention, pressed on the United States by Latin American governments wary of U.S. designs in the region. For FDR, the nature of a particular regime was less important than its willingness to cooperate with the United States, particularly as the war in Europe became a reality (Bethell, 1991).

Although the war's end saw the emergence of many new democracies in the hemisphere, the United States, preoccupied with the growing Soviet threat elsewhere, paid little attention to a hemisphere that was viewed as secure. Latin America received only 2 percent of foreign aid aimed at bolstering the developing policy of communist containment, and when democratic governments were overthrown in Peru and Venezuela in 1948, the United States responded by giving early recognition to the military governments. By 1954, United States concern over communist inroads in the Americas led

American officials to seek the forceful overthrow of the elected government of Jacobo Arbenz in Guatemala after it attempted to institute far-reaching agrarian reform policies. U.S. aid to the region, however, did not increase substantially, and Latin America continued on the back burner of U.S. foreign policy priorities (Valenzuela, 1985).

The success of the Cuban Revolution encouraged a significant shift in US policy. The new Kennedy administration argued that Latin America was central to U.S. interests and a battleground that the United States could not lose to the Soviets. The administration also argued that stability, and thus containment, could be attained only with reform and democratization. Dictatorships, by providing the fertile ground on which communism grew, were thus fundamental threats to U.S. national interests.

With enthusiastic support in Latin America, the administration pressed for the creation of the Alliance for Progress to encourage reform, development, and stable governments (Levinson and Onis 1970). However, when military forces overthrew weak democratic regimes in a rash of military coups, Kennedy quickly, if reluctantly, acquiesced. Security imperatives overrode the original concern for reform. President Johnson signaled once again a shift in policy when, in 1965, he sent U.S. troops to oppose reformist army officers in the Dominican Republic intent on restoring the deposed constitutional president. The first direct U.S. military intervention in the region in 30 years stemmed directly from fear that communists were playing a prominent role in the rebel movement.

The overriding concern for potential Soviet expansionism in the Americas led the Nixon administration to covert measures to prevent the elected leftist government of Salvador Allende from coming to office, and to support attempts to undermine his government after he came to power. As Nelson Rockefeller noted in his report to Nixon on the hemisphere, security considerations were paramount in the region and the United States should not be concerned about dealing with modernizing military establishments in a region that was not ready for democracy (Rockefeller 1969).

Widespread condemnation of human rights abuses by Latin American dictatorships and the role played by the United States in the overthrow of the Allende government led to a backlash against U.S. policy. The U.S. Congress and the new Carter administration reversed course and pressed once again for human rights and democratic openings. The administration played a positive role in pressing for democratization in the Dominican Republic. However, the cutoff of U.S. military aid and public criticism of military governments by the United States had little direct effect on the process of regime liberalization.

The pendulum in U.S. policy swung once again in the early years of the Reagan administration. The Sandinista victory in Nicaragua in 1979 and the continued leftist insurrections in El Salvador and Guatemala led the administration to focus on Central America as a primary threat to U.S. security interests in the world (Pastor 1987). At the same time, the new government sought to improve relationships with the military regimes of the Southern Cone, particularly Brazil, Chile, and Argentina. The promotion of democracy and human rights would take a back seat to ensuring the viability of anticommunist regimes in the region. Ironically, this shift in US policy came at a time when the military regimes of the Southern Cone were weakening and the transition to democracy was under way.

The Reagan administration's policy toward the region evolved, however, into a more complex mix, one that was accentuated during Reagan's second term. Congressional opposition to the administration's support for the Contras and concern over human rights abuses led the administration to push for liberalization in El Salvador, Guatemala, and Honduras. At the same time, the administration pressed for democratic change in Chile, the only country in South America save Paraguay that remained under military rule after 1985.

In Central America the democratic transition was closely linked to the overall peace process begun by the Contadora group of countries in 1983 (Colombia, Mexico, Panama,and Venezuela) and culminating with the stunning 1987 Esquipulas peace accords forged by the five Central American presidents. Following the leadership of Oscar Arias of Costa Rica, and despite U.S. opposition, they agreed to recognize the legitimacy of all governments in the region, support pluralist representative democracy and fair elections, seek an end to extraregional support for insurrectionary movements, and provide a framework for the resolution of internal conflicts through negotiations. With the U.S. administration hampered in pursuing a military solution after the revelations of the Iran-Contra scandal, the prospects of a negotiated outcome improved.

The rapid deterioration of the Soviet bloc and the collapse of the Soviet Union, combined with declining popular support, in turn persuaded the left that a negotiated outcome was also in their best interests. As John Booth notes, the Esquipulas Accord "ultimately prevailed because it offered Central Americans of all ideologies vehicles for seeking an end to dangerous regional tensions and bloody but stagnated civil wars" (Booth 1995, p. 203). Beginning in 1988, the Bush administration, in a significant shift away from the bellicose strategy of the Reagan administration, made a concerted effort to work with the parties in Central American to implement the accords.

This account of the role of the United States in the recent wave of democratic transitions in the region suggests that the United States did not play a significant role in the transition process, and far from a determinative one. US policy varied from administration to administration, and the sharp disagreements between Republican administrations and Democratic Congresses on policy with respect to human rights and democracy sent decidedly mixed signals to key actors in the region. The primary factors that led to the transition to democracy in Latin America were largely domestic, related to the deterioration of authoritarian regimes and the mobilization of internal opposition pressing for a constitutional outcome at a time of diminishing insurrectionary threats (Carothers 1991).

This does not mean that international elements played no role in the democratic transitions. External pressure from nongovernmental organizations, international organizations, and governments, demanding respect for human rights and questioning the fundamental legitimacy of governments by force, contributed to eroding the internal legitimacy and confidence of military governments. Support from international foundations, both public and private, in Europe, Canada, and the United States was often critical to the survival of democratic activists, opposition think tanks, and alternative media outlets. And the movement of military governments toward democracy had a powerful demonstrative effect, particularly as the ranks of constitutional regimes increased. In Central America, the concerted role of other Latin American states with strong European support, initially opposed by the United States, provided critical support for the peace process and democratization.

Democratic Consolidation and U.S. Foreign Policy in the Post–Cold War Era

With the end of the Cold War, the United States has sought to redefine its foreign policy in the Western hemisphere. The overriding concern for preventing the establishment of a Soviet presence in the Americas has given way to a multiplicity of concerns—from trade, to immigration, to narcotics trafficking, to the environment. At the same time, the United States has stressed the promotion and consolidation of democracy as a primary objective. In so doing, the United States is drawing on a long tradition of stressing core domestic values in formulating foreign policy priorities. But the emphasis on democracy not only responds to normative considerations; it also stems from the belief that the legitimacy of democratic governments contributes to more stable and less conflictive societies better able to respect fundamental human rights while addressing pressing national problems. Democratic governments are also viewed as far more reliable international partners in an increasingly interdependent world. As such, fundamental U.S. national interests are better safeguarded in a world of democratic states than in one with less stable authoritarian regimes or quasi-democracies.

In the Western hemisphere, U.S. policy coincides with a new hemispheric consensus in favor of democratic consolidation and a willingness to take collective action in defense of democratic continuity. With the end of the Cold War and the fear that the United States would press for collective action to advance its own definition of hemispheric security, the American nations have moved away from their own overriding concern with nonintervention to an acceptance of the legitimacy of external noncoercive action in the defense of democracy. Many of the over 50 national elections held in the region since the democratic wave began in the 1980s have been monitored by international observers, both official and nongovernmental, in an effort to ensure the legitimacy of the electoral process.

Through the Organization of American States (OAS), the governments of the Americas went a step further, adopting, in June 1991, the Santiago Commitment to Democracy and the Renewal of the Inter-American System. According to Resolution 1080, interruption of the constitutional order in a member state could lead to an immediate convening of the hemispheric foreign ministers to take appropriate action. The Washington Protocol, adopted two years later, provided for the suspension of a member state from the regional organization with the interruption of the constitutional order (Acevedo and Grossman 1996).

Resolution 1080 was invoked following the overthrow of President Aristide in Haiti and the constitutional crises in Ecuador, Guatemala, Paraguay, and Peru. In the case of Haiti, the OAS refused to recognize the de facto government in Port-au-Prince, and imposed an unprecedented trade embargo to force the restoration of democratic government. Although the organization did not sanction the use of force, member states did not openly criticize the United States when, with UN support, the United States engineered a multilateral force to restore democracy to the island.

In instances of direct threats to democratic continuity, the decisive response of the hemisphere, through both collective action and the entreaties of individual states, helped to prevent a serious reversal of the constitutional order. In Peru, President Fujimori agreed to hold new congressional elections after dissolving the Congress. In Guatemala and Ecuador, the legislatures elected new presidents after serious confrontations between executive and legislative authority led to presidential resignations. In Paraguay, the strong support of the international community, including the MERCOSUR countries acting as a group, was critical in bolstering President Wasmosy's resolve in standing up to military insurrection (Valenzuela 1997).

In other cases of more subtle challenges to democratic progress in the region, external actors also played important roles. After serious concerns over the 1994 elections in the Dominican Republic were voiced by opposition elements, the United States and other countries pressed strongly for a solution that would prevent violent unrest. After considerable hesitation the Balaguer government agreed to shorten its term in office to two years and call new elections. In Mexico, concerns over the legitimacy of the electoral process were voiced by U.S. and other officials, contributing with UN support to holding the fairest presidential elections in modern Mexico in 1994. Never before in history have disruptions or threats to the constitutional order received such strong and concerted international attention. By their actions, the nations of the hemisphere substantially increased the costs for those seeking extraconstitutional mechanisms in pressing their interests.

The constitutional crises described above, however, are also evidence that the process of democratic consolidation is fragile and incomplete. Democratic institutions remain weak as elected governments face the daunting problems of massive inequalities, corruption, street crime, and widespread disenchantment with public authority. As in many other regions of the world, Latin American democracies face, in varying degrees, serious crises of representation, accountability, and efficacy (Valenzuela 1997). The crisis of representation refers to the difficulties of translating the will of the citizenry into public policy. The failures of electoral mechanisms to provide adequate representation and the weakness of political parties as mechanisms for the aggregation and articulation of interests make representative democracy alien to many citizens. The distance between the world of politics and the trials of daily life requires that democracy be brought closer to the people, that representative democracy not be thought of only as a system where elections every so many years send politicians to do the people's business in faraway places. Strengthening the participatory aspects of democracy at the local and community level must be an important priority throughout the Americas.

At the same time, elected officials are often not able to secure the public trust. Problems of accountability stem not only from widespread corruption, but also from the weakness of institutions such as legislatures and local governments and the lack of democratic responsibility of privileged sectors, including fairly autonomous military establishments. Finally, many countries don't have the resources or institutional capacity to address many of the problems of society. Large states often hide weak states unable to implement taxation mechanisms or regulatory procedures that are critical even in an era of smaller governments and free markets.

Although the consolidation of democratic institutions will ultimately depend on the choices made by the citizens of individual countries, the United States can play a continuing leadership role in the process of democratic consolidation. It is critical for the United States to continue to work with hemispheric nations to make clear that any interruption of the constitutional order will be extremely costly for de facto governments. In a far more interdependent world, where international trade and cooperation have become essential ingredients for national development, the isolation of a particular state by its peers can have serious repercussions. This message is increasingly understood by elements of the business community and privileged sections of society that often in the past turned to the barracks to ensure support.

Reaction to constitutional crises after they have occurred, however, is not enough. The experience of the inter-American system in responding to interruptions in the constitutional order has been mixed. The invocation of Resolution 1080 signaled the hemisphere's displeasure with the course of events in a particular country after the crisis was well under way. In most cases there were ample warning signals of impending difficulties, but neither individual countries nor the OAS assembled systematic information on the problem or set in motion efforts to address it before matters came to a head. The secretary general of the OAS, through a special office in the Unit for the Promotion of Democracy of the organization, needs to be provided with timely information and analysis of impending difficulties and should establish a concerted mechanism, working with relevant countries in the region, to address problems before they reach crisis proportions. International missions to Peru, Guatemala, and Ecuador aimed at addressing the serious impasse that occurred in those countries between executive and legislative authorities might have contributed to relaxing tensions and promoting a search for alternative outcomes. Multilateral responses, however, cannot substitute for decisive actions by key states. The mechanism of assembling a set of "friends" or "guarantors," invited by the government in question, as an aid to the peaceful resolution of internal or international conflicts, is an important mechanism in the post–Cold War era.

Crisis prevention is critical because the problems of democracy must be resolved within the framework of democratic rules and procedures. Too often in the past, extraconstitutional formulae, mostly in the guise of a military coup, were used to restore order or resolve political deadlock, only to weaken further the institutions of democracy that need to find solutions to national problems through compromise and accommodation within constitutional frameworks.

But crisis prevention is only part of the challenge. The consolidation of democracy in new and weak democratic systems requires a concerted hemispheric effort to address the underlying problems that contribute to the crisis of representation, accountability, and efficacy on the continent. Working with the OAS and with the support of the Inter-American Development Bank, the United States should join other countries in pressing for a stronger international advisory role for the OAS Unit for Democracy. Canada and Brazil, the responsible coordinators for the implementation of the democracy and human rights sections of the Summit of the Americas, have made valuable suggestions for a more active role for the unit.

The unit, however, requires more resources to help coordinate hemispheric efforts to address institutional shortcomings in electoral systems and political parties and the functioning of legislative institutions in the region. At the same time, the United States should strengthen its own bilateral aid efforts in these areas, not only in Central America, where the bulk of U.S. money is spent, but in other areas of the hemisphere where efforts at political and governmental reform are under way.

The crisis of accountability, and particularly the problem of corruption that so directly affects accountability in the region, must continue to be addressed through hemispheric cooperation. The Working Group on Honesty and Public Ethics of the Summit of the Americas and the recently signed Inter-American Convention against Corruption are very important steps in that direction. These efforts signal a willingness to press for international cooperation in law enforcement and to encourage national reforms aimed at establishing more ethical governance. Reform efforts are under way in such areas as campaign finance, illicit enrichment, and regulatory and administrative law as well as in efforts to enhance the capacity of the courts and prosecution systems. Support for the implementation of integrated financial management and comprehensive audit systems is also encouraging. While many changes can be achieved through legislation and constitutional reform, more international resources should be made available to complement local efforts in weaker democracies to build stronger institutions.

Ultimately, however, the forging of stronger democratic institutions that are more responsible, accountable, and effective can come only through the open and competitive process of a free society. The genius of democracy is that it provides for peaceful mechanisms to change the nation's leadership—for "throwing the rascals out"—based on the verdict of the electorate. It is no accident that the countries in Latin America with the fewest problems of corruption and the strongest states are those countries with the longest trajectory of democratic practices. Democracy itself is not designed to solve particular policy problems or address deep-seated societal needs. That is the responsibility of individual governments. It is the competitiveness of democracy, the oversight of legislative institutions, and the accountability of leaders to the verdict of the electorate that forge stronger democratic institutions and help make individual governments more accountable.

Latin America stands at an important crossroads. For the first time in this century the continent has an opportunity to build on its historic commitment to representative government to fashion viable democratic institutions. The United States, which has spent countless billions in this century fighting ideologies that were inimical to democratic institutions and freedoms, should not retreat inward but should commit resources to work with its hemispheric partners to help consolidate democratic institutions on a continent that promises a better future for its 800 million citizens.

Part IV

The Successes and Failures of the

Developmental State in Asia

7

Democracy and Civil Society in Korea

Bruce Cumings

IN THIS PAPER I take up the problematic of civil society and democracy in the United States and in East Asia (but primarily South Korea). In the first section I examine the work of people who theorize about civil society, including Harvard theorists Robert Putnam and Michael Sandel, and the strengths and weaknesses of their work, including the Western bias and essentialism of their accounts. I then take up the question of Korean democracy: the popular struggles and elite responses that brought about a particular, Schumpeterian form of democratic system in 1993; the current crisis of transition from authoritarianism to democracy, unmatched in the world for its depth and audacity (a crisis that threatens but may also transform the 1993 system); and the remaining agenda of democratization in Korea. The final section addresses the question: What is democracy? in the light of the American and Korean experience.

Civil Society in Search of Itself

In the United States in the mid-1990s, the political spectrum from right to left is suffused with deeply conflicted concerns about American civil society. All commentators point to the same symptoms: the pathologies and dangers of the public space (that is, cities), high rates of crime amid a more general breakdown of morality, the disintegration of nuclear families, citizen apathy and disinterest in voting, cynicism about the political system, the debasement of public debate (particularly on television, the primary medium for delivering this debate), and an absence of political and national leadership.

According to a Gallup Poll published in February 1994, 80 percent of the American people do not believe that government can be trusted to do what is right; 75 percent are dissatisfied with the way the political process works; about the same number of people believe that government benefits a few big interests rather than the interests of all. In 1992, 1994, and 1996, protest politicians (Ross Perot, Newt Gingrich, and Patrick Buchanan) have again sought to mobilize voters on the basis of these many grievances, usually citing the 1950s as a golden age when everything was fine with America (Gingrich has recommended the year 1955 as the apogee of the American system).

Simultaneously, contemporary writers of great influence argue that civil society is inherently a Western concept, and that it is absent in the remaining communist countries, the thing most in need of creation in postcommunist countries, and the thing mostly absent in East Asia—whether in authoritarian Singapore, democratic Japan, or the "NICS" (newly industrialized countries) of South Korea and Taiwan. Samuel Huntington of Harvard University made this view notorious in his essay "The Clash of Civilizations," which sought to fashion a new paradigm for post–Cold War global politics (Huntington 1993). But perhaps Karel van Wolferen's *Enigma of Japanese Power* (1989) is the best recent example of the argument that East Asia industrialized without civil society and without an Enlightenment. This book would merit no more than a footnote were it not so influential in American circles: at one point in late 1993 van Wolferen performed the feat of having articles published simultaneously in the *New Left Review*, *Foreign Affairs*, and the *National Interest*, thereby blanketing the spectrum of intellectual opinion from left to right. The editors of the *New York Times* not only have opened their op-ed page to him several times, but have written editorials based on his work—which they think located a "third system" after capitalism and communism, namely, the East Asian System.

For van Wolferen, "the West" connotes a site of "independent, universal truths or immutable religious beliefs, transcending the worldly reality of social dictates and the decrees of power-holders"; Japan, however, is a place where people adjust their beliefs to situations, in "a political culture that does not recognize the possibility of transcendental truths." As in nineteenth-century accounts of "the Orient," Japan for van Wolferen is an enigma, opaque, led by a mysterious "System," and "single-mindedly pursuing some obscure aim of its own." The System "systematically suppresses individualism," he writes, and the Japanese do not accept Western logic or metaphysics going all the way back to "the Greeks." The "crucial factor" that proves these generalizations is "the near absence [in Japan] of any idea that there can be truths, rules, principles or morals that always apply, no matter what the circumstances" (1989, pp. 1–10, 23–24). Koreans might think the same thing of Japan, but van Wolferen does not like any of the East Asian political systems: "The Japanese, Korean and Taiwanese experiences show that a third category of political economy can exist, beside the Western and communist types." These states represent "a largely uncharted economic and socialpolitical category" (pp. 5–8, 23–24).

In this discourse, which is quite common in the US now, the ills and pathologies of American civil society curiously disappear, to be replaced surreptitiously by an idealized construction drawn from Locke and de Toqueville. Of course no one can claim that East Asian countries have the social pathology obvious on almost any street in any American city, and the recent elections in Taiwan had rates of voter turnout and exuberant participation far above those of American elections. But all that is forgotten in the conjuring of a Western civil society where well-informed citizens debate the important questions of politics and the good life without fear or favor, in contrast to the limited democracies, authoritarian systems, and general illiberalism of East Asia, illustrated mundanely in the caning of Michael Fay in Singapore, or more tellingly in the continuing crisis of governance in Japan.

Harvard political scientist Robert Putnam has been lauded across the American political spectrum, from the leftist *Nation* to the conservative *Economist*, for his recent book *Making Democracy Work*. A study of civil society in general and in the specific confines of Italy, it begins with a discussion of the widespread despair in the US about public institutions and democratic possibilities, continues with the exemplary civic virtue of northern Italy and the lack of it in southern Italy, and ends on a pessimistic note:

> Where norms and networks of civic engagement are lacking, the outlook for collective action appears bleak. The fate of the Mezzogiorno is an object lesson for the Third World today and the former Communist lands of Eurasia tomorrow, moving uncertainly toward self-government. (1993, p. 183)

Putnam thinks that Robert Dahl and Seymour Martin Lipset were right in stressing the contribution of modernization to democracy:

> Nothing is more obvious even to the casual observer than the fact that effective democracy is closely associated with socioeconomic modernity, both across time and space.

He also rehabilitates Almond and Verbal's *Civic Culture*, calling it "a modern classic" in the vein of de Toqueville's *Democracy in America* (p. 11).

Putnam's own theory draws heavily on the Weberian/Parsonian pattern variables that Almond and Verba used 30 years ago, renaming them as "norms of civic engagement," "social structures of cooperation," and the like. Machiavelli thought the character of a citizenry depended on its "civic virtue," and this "republican school," according to Putnam, gives us the best explanation for well-functioning civil societies and democracies. They rest on civic engagement, political equality, the attenuation of individual striving in the interests of community, "solidarity, trust, and tolerance," and a network of civic or secondary associations: indeed, a key indicator of "civic sociability" is the "vibrancy of associational life" (1993, pp. 86–91). Perhaps we can call this the conservative republican position.

The liberal republican position has its most sophisticated exposition in a new book by Harvard political theorist Michael Sandel (1996). He begins his account with a discussion of two great American worries:

> One is the fear that, individually and collectively, we are losing control of the forces that govern our lives. The other is the sense that, from family to neighborhood to nation, the moral fabric of community is unraveling around us.

Together, Sandel writes, these concerns "define the anxiety of the age (p. 3)."

Sandel's argument is that the ills of civil society have arisen from a one-sided emphasis on the rights of the individual (that is, libertarianism) and a corresponding decline in another form of American liberalism, called republicanism (that is, the civic virtue Putnam found in Northern Italy, but which Sandel also calls communitarianism). The master theorist of the first tendency is John Stuart Mill, and that of the second tendency (for Sandel) is the very same person the Cato Institute loves: Thomas Jefferson. The key distinction between Sandel and the Cato libertarians is not their worry about American civil society: they both agree that it is badly in need of repair. The distinction is that Sandel does not privilege the market, and seeks to retrieve a liberalism from the past that would control the worst effects of market capitalism through communitarian constraints.

This republican vision stresses the harnessing of individual liberty through the mediating effects of citizen activism, self-government, and the "moral bond" of the community. In place of individualism, it offers civic virtue; in place of a procedural political regime that guarantees individual rights, it offers a government that would seek the substantive goal of creating virtuous citizens. The republican tradition, Sandel argues, can thus "offer a corrective to our impoverished civic life," or even "repair the civic life on which democracy depends" (Sandel, 1996, pp. 37, 124–133, 351).

The key similarity in these texts by Putnam and Sandel is their disregard of radical, alternative constructions of civil society. From Raymond Williams we can learn that Sandel's reconstruction of republicanism is essentially an anachronistic discourse on the country and the city. The back side of Jefferson's rural community was disdain for newly risen industrial cities, a resistance to the simultaneous newly structured order and unruly chaos that any number of other critics declaimed in the early industrial era as they witnessed "a social dissolution in the very process of aggregation" (Williams 1973, pp. 142–64, 216). The recourse to ideas of civil society born of a bygone agrarian order ignores not only the impossibility of recreating them in our time, but the inequalities of that order when it existed, the isolation and frequent ignorance of the farms and villages, the slaves held by Jeffersonian Virginians, the oppressions of women, itinerant laborers, and the heterodox of all types, and the huge class of victims claimed by westward expansion. The pastoral ideal, as Williams says, is authentic and moving precisely to the degree of its unreality (p. 44).

Sandel privileges Jefferson because the political economy of the late nineteenth and early eighteenth centuries enabled Jefferson to have his cake and eat it too, that is, to be both individualistic and libertarian in regard to the (mostly nonexistent) central government, and to be communitarian through the lateral expansion to the Western frontier of replicative small towns and farming communities based on individual private property and government by "town meeting," yielding freedom and independence vis-à–vis superordinate power and the civic virtues of self-government (so long as the cavalry was not too far away) (Sandel 1996, pp. 137–42). In short, Sandel's vision is a sophisticated species of atavism. He offers not a single practical policy suggestion as to how republicanism can be reconstituted in 1990s America.

Sandel's anachronism is matched in Putnam's neo-Toquevillian account of civil society and democracy. However much Italians in certain wealthy regions (harboring cities like Venice and Florence that are showered every year with billions of tourist dollars) may be joiners and civic doers, de Toqueville's account of the 1840s American propensity to join voluntary associations and participate in politics has little relevance to "downsized" suburban couples working two or more jobs to make ends meet, collapsing exhausted into their chairs to let television entertain them before trying to get enough sleep to start the long workday again.

The most disturbing aspect of this recent literature, at least to me, is the cavalier identification of civil society and communitarian democracy with the West: these things originated in Western Europe and migrated to North America and the British Commonwealth, and hardly anywhere else. Non-Western societies are simply not suitable settings for civil society and republican democracy, Putnam suggests. *The Civic Culture* reported these Western conceits straightforwardly in 1963, a time of higher American self-confidence and less self-awareness; it was only in the United States and England that the authors found "a pattern of political attitudes and an underlying set of social attitudes that is supportive of a stable democratic process." In the other nations they studied (West Germany, Italy, and Mexico), "these patterns are less evident" (Almond and Verba 1963, p. x).

These writers share the prejudices of Max Weber, but not Weber's passionate and intelligent comparativist project—and in a time when Weber would certainly recognize his own provincialism, were he still talking about "only in the West. . . ." But perhaps we had better sample the original Weber, what he said then, since we don't know what he would say now:

> Only the occident knows the state in the modern sense, with a professional administration, specialized officialdom, and law based on the concept of citizenship. . . . Only the occident knows rational law. . . . Furthermore, only the occident possesses science. . . . Finally, western civilization is further distinguished from every other by the presence of men with a rational ethic for the conduct of life. (1981, pp. 312–14)

Democracy and Its Discontents in East Asia and Korea

The East Asian state-society configuration that van Wolferen, Putnam, Almond and Verba, Weber, and others find so wanting from a Western standpoint today bears close comparison to a particular Western experience, although it is not the Western experience that they talk about. It is instead the continental European pattern of development and democracy (or the lack thereof)—and therefore the East Asian version is by no means sui generis. Marx and Hegel could hardly have been more explicit about Germany's predicament: for Marx, it was that Germany "did not pass through the intermediate stages of political emancipation at the same time as modern nations" (Marx in Colletti 1975, p. 252); for Hegel, the optimist of course, it was the task of the state to overcome Germany's debilities:

> It is a prime concern of the state that a middle class should be developed, but this can be done only if the state is an organic unity . . . i.e., it can be done only by giving authority to spheres of particular interests, which are relatively independent, and by appointing an *army of officials* whose personal arbitrariness is broken against such authorized bodies. (Hegel, quoted in Colletti 1975, p. 116)

This is a theory of "late" state formation and of "late" democratization; Marx places the German domestic configuration in the time and space of the world system and declares the task hopeless, whereas Hegel conjures it in the thin air of an ideal type, and then foists the problem off on the bureaucrats. What is the problem? To create the middle class that is the presumed basis of democracy.

In German "state science" *(Staatswissenschaft)*, the conception of the *fused state* is thus born in the aftermath of the French Revolution, as a point of definitional anxiety and political reality (Wallerstein 1995, pp. 220–26).

It is then a short step to observe the disorders of that same revolution, to relate them to novel ideas about "popular will," and to conclude, well, who needs that? To put the point baldly, of what value is civil society in a race for industrialization? The Germans invented the fused state not to solve the problems of liberty, equality, and fraternity at the dawn of the industrial epoch, but to solve the mid-nineteenth-century problems of the second industrial revolution and, more importantly, catching up with England. A fused state is one that both subsumes civil society and tries to build it up—but not if these efforts get in the way of industrialization.

Here, in short, is a political theory of late development that put off to a distant future the magnificent obsession of the Anglo-Saxon early industrializers with questions of popular will, democratic representation, public versus private, or state versus civil society. It is also a theory that explains much about East Asia's democratic trajectory: Japan, a democracy after 1945 but only after the cataclysm of war and occupation; South Korea, a democracy in 1993 but only after the cataclysm of revolution, war, division, and decades of military dictatorship (1961 to 1987) and sharp political struggle; Taiwan, a democracy in 1996 but only after revolution, war, national division, and 40 years of martial law (1947 to 1987).

The struggle for Korean civil society and democracy was precisely situated in what Alasdair MacIntyre calls "sites of conflict" (1981, p. 153). Democratic struggles began in Korea on the day that Japan surrendered in August 1945 and have continued down to the present (Cumings 1997, chap. 7). The popular forces of the late 1940s wanted both democracy and social justice, that is, a cleansing revolution that would wipe away the influences of Japanese imperialism. They got a cleansing in North Korea but no democracy, little if any cleansing in South Korea and little if any democracy, and after a massively destructive civil war, a thoroughly divided and disjointed nation.

Within the constricted politics of the Rhee regime (1948 to 1960), where any sign of a leftist orientation meant a jail term if not death (the inconsequential progressive Cho Pong-am was executed in 1958, one of the better-known of many similar examples), a space for the intelligentsia cracked open enough that students, faculty, and intellectuals could be the vanguard for an overthrow of the First Republic, albeit when Syngman Rhee was on his last legs and the United States wanted him out. The tepid opposition organized the Second Republic through a weak cabinet system of government, where for a year (April 1960 to May 1961) civil society on the liberal model mushroomed rapidly. At this time South Korea had more college students per capita than England, more newspaper readers per capita than almost any country in the world, and a concentration of administrative, commercial, industrial, and educational energies in one great capital city—much like Paris (Henderson 1968). A very lively salon society animated the capital, publishers brought out thorough rewritings of modern Korean history, and students began to imagine themselves the vanguard of unification with the North.

General Park Chung Hee was the Korean agent of the Hegelian conception of the fused state, shutting down civil society with his coup d'état in 1961 and the three-year emergency junta that followed, and deploying the state as the initiator, guide, and financier of a classic type of "late" industrialization. Strong American pressure from the Kennedy administration forced Park to drop his plans for instant heavy industrialization and to don mufti and run for election in 1963, yielding "export-led development" and a contentious public sphere. The Nixon administration enlarged the sphere of Korean autonomy through the Guam doctrine and Nixon's neomercantilist "New Economic Policy" of August 1971, enabling Park to shut down civil society completely in 1971 and 1972 with barely a murmur from Washington (see Woo 1991).

The "Garrison Decree" of October 1971 and the Yusin system and martial law of autumn 1972 ensured an extensive and brutal deactivation of politics. To make a long and bloody story very short, we can say that Park misjudged the hidden strengths and growing maturity of civil society, which was overdeveloped in relation to the economy but still underdeveloped compared to the ubiquitous agencies of the expanding Yusin state: a vast administrative bureaucracy, huge, distended armed forces, extensive national police, a ubiquitous Central Intelligence Agency with operatives at every conceivable site of potential resistance, and thorough ideological blanketing of every alternative idea in the name of forced-pace industrialization.

Park's fused state thus set up an unending crisis of civil society that culminated in the disorders of Masan and Pusan in August and September 1979, leading to Park's assassination by his own intelligence chief in October, which led to the "coup-like event" mounted by Chôn Tu-hwan and No Tlae-u in December 1979, and the denouement at Kwangju in May 1980. The period of 1980 to 1987 will appear in history as a classic event out of Marx's famous *Eighteenth Brumaire*, with the luckless "nephew" (Chôn) acting on behalf of the dispatched "uncle" (Park), using the jail and the knout all the way, but compounding into farce the tragedy of Park Chung Hee (who truly was Korea's industrial sovereign, if not its Napoleon). The real tragedy, of course, had taken place at Kwangju, where an aroused, self-organized, and intersubjective citizenry (that is, not a bunch of rioters and miscreants) sought desperately to save itself from the new martial-law regime that Chôn had just announced, only to be slaughtered (a minimum of 600 killed, a maximum of 2,000—as with Tiananmen in 1989).

Civil society began to waken again with the February 1985 National Assembly elections, and by the spring of 1987 an aroused, self-organized, and intersubjective citizenry took over the streets of the major cities, with late-coming but substantial middle-class participation, thus forcing Chôn from office in June (see Greenberg 1992). A few months later the always-tepid opposition again split, allowing the emergence of an interim regime under the other, somewhat shrewder "nephew" (No Tlae-u), a regime that first accommodated and then sought to suppress a newly energized civil society that now included the liberated and very strong forces of labor (more strikes and labor actions occurred in 1987 and 1988 than at any point in Korean history, or most national histories).

In 1990 this regime sought to fashion the Japanese solution to democratic pressures, a "Democratic Liberal Party" (DLP) (reversing the characters of Japan's Liberal Democratic Party) that would encompass the moderate opposition in the form of Kim Young Sam and his Pusan-based political machine, bringing them under the tent of the southeastern Taegu-Kyôngsang elites (or "T-K Group") that had dominated the Republic of Korea (ROK) since 1961, thus to form a single-party democracy that would rule for the ages—or at least for the next generation. A host of analysts (not the least being the US Embassy in Seoul) came forward to laud this "pact" between soft-liners and hard-liners among the elite, which seemed to mimic the democratic transitions of the 1980s in Latin America.[1]

This was the Schumpeterian solution to the problems of an enlivened and growing civil society. The Austrian aristocrat Schumpeter never cared much about mass democracy; he was a classic elitist. He valued a democratic system that provided a circulation of elites through periodic elections, enough funds mediated by the banks or the state to keep business growing, enough cash from big business to keep the politicians happy, an occasional circus by the politicians to keep the people entertained, and little more than that. The Liberal Democratic Party followed this model closely in the period 1955 to 1992, perhaps too closely given its loss of power in the summer of 1993; the Democratic Liberal Party was the same (although no one quite imagined that it would provide such a circus!). Today it is gone, replaced by the *minjông* faction representing the T-K Group, and President Kim Young Sam's New Democratic Party.

The DLP solution could not last because, unlike Japan's system, it excluded labor (still today no political party has roots in Korea's massive working class), it failed to reckon with unresolved crises in postwar Korean history (especially Kwangju), and it merely masked over sharp splits within the political elite—above all, the continuing exclusion of representation for

the southwestern Chôlla people in the politics of Seoul, but also the continuing repression of anything smacking of a serious left (through the National
Security Law), and the restiveness of the *chaebôl* (conglomerate) groups under
continuing strong state regulation.

In 1995 a series of dramatic events and actions unfolded, with consequences no doubt unforeseen at the time but having the result of an auda-
cious assault on the military dictators who ruled Korea from 1961 onward
and their legacies, a reckoning that goes beyond anything in the global transition from authoritarianism that the world has witnessed in the past decade.
It goes beyond the Latin American cases, where (often at the urging of
American political scientists) the new regimes decided to let bygones be
bygones and let the military go back to the barracks; it goes beyond Rumania,
where a rough summary justice dispatched dictator Ceauçescu but let his system remain; and it goes beyond East Germany, where Honnecker was overthrown and expelled but where West Germany merely absorbed the old East
German system, rather than achieving a consensual merger between two
rather different civil societies.

Most commentary focuses on the actions of Kim Young Sam in the past
two years, with his backers arguing that he was a sincere reformer all along
who now wants to right the wrongs of modern South Korean history, and his
detractors saying he allowed the prosecution of Chôn and No on charges of
bribery because that would help him overcome the influence of the Taegu-
Kyôngsang group within the ruling party, and then was forced in November
1995 to allow both of them to be indicted for the December 1979 coup and
the suppression of the Kwangju citizenry because the "slush fund" scandal
was lapping too close to his own door. More important, in my view, has been
the emergence of a new generation of prosecutors, formed by the struggles of
civil society as they got educated and came of age, who now ingeniously use
"the rule of law" to go after their dictatorial antagonists. With Chôn and No
having been convicted and sentenced for both corruption and sedition, perhaps we have seen the end of that era. We can also draw some conclusions.

First, no "LDP" solution could work for the reasons given above, and thus
we are back to political parties grouped around prominent leaders (namely
the "three Kims"), based in regional political machines and patron-client ties
as always in postwar Korean history. Second, with the continuing exclusion of
labor from the governing coalition and the continuing suppression of the
nonviolent left under the National Security Law, the ROK still falls short of
either the Japanese or the American models of democracy and civil society.
Third, the falling-out among the ruling groups and the trials of Chôn and
No, as well as the full glare of publicity on the slush fund scandals, bathing
the state and the *chaebôl* groups in a highly critical light, opens the way to
another assertion of civil society and perhaps an authentic democracy that

would finally give Korea the noncoercive, intersubjective public sphere it has long deserved, a politics that would go beyond the halting and temporary jerry-built transitions to weak democracy in Latin America, the former Soviet Union and East Europe, and the Philippines. In any case, South Korea is now facing a crisis akin to that of the Alien and Sedition Acts in the early United States, and how it is resolved will determine the future of Korean democracy for a long time to come (see Lipset 1963).

We can conclude this brief consideration of recent Korean history with the observation that the contribution of protest to Korean democracy cannot be overstated; it is a classic case of "the civilizing force of a new vision of society . . . created in struggle" (Williams 1973, p. 231). A significant student movement emerged in Western Europe and the United States in the mid-1960s and had a heyday of perhaps five years. Korean students were central activists in the politics of liberation in the late 1940s, the overthrow of the Rhee regime and the politics of the Chang regime in 1960 and 1961, the repudiation of Korea-Japan normalization in 1965, and the resistance to the Park and Chôn dictatorships in the period 1971 to 1988. Particularly in the 1980s, through the mediation of *minjung* ideology and praxis (a kind of liberation theory borrowed from Latin America), Korean students, workers, and young people brought into the public space uniquely original and autonomous configurations of political and social protest—ones that threatened many times to overturn the structure of American hegemony and military dictatorship. This was a classic example of Jürgen Habermas's characterization of student protest in terms of a blurring of borderlines "between demonstration and civil disobedience, between discussion, festival, and expressive self-presentation" (Dews 1992, p. 234). Many students also adopted Antonio Gramsci's strategy, leaving the campuses to merge organically with the working class, often to find themselves jailed and tortured as "disguised workers," and always at the risk of their careers. Even if that part of the Korean public sphere is relatively quiescent now, it made an indelible contribution to Korean democracy in the 1980s.

One other conclusion is irresistible: so much for the Samuel Huntington—Lee Kwan Yew—van Wolferen idea that East Asians have a different view of human and civil rights from "us," that they prize order and even authoritarian direction, that they industrialized without Enlightenment and civil society, that "Confucianism" makes them this way, so on and so forth.

What Is Democracy?

This comparative inquiry into American and East Asian democracy has argued that the limited pluralism of American politics is the outcome of an abortive development of civil society under the pressures of the modern project itself over the past 200 years, and that when it comes to participation "without fear or favor" in the life of politics, not just the average American but the "vaunted students of the 1960s" cannot hold a candle to those who have struggled for democratic rights over the past half century in Korea and many other "developing" countries. But we have not really addressed a question prior to all this: What is democracy?

For Adam Przeworski, democracy exists if another party can win an election (Bagchi 1995, pp. 3–24, 24–27). Schumpeter also preferred this form, yielding a circulation of party elites. The premier democratic theorist in the United States, Robert Dahl, would not disagree; although he places more emphasis on political equality as a key prerequisite for democracy than does Schumpeter, their basic schemes of pluralist democracy are quite similar: "the Schumpeter-Dahl axis . . . treats democracy as a mechanism, the essential function of which is to maintain an equilibrium" between "two or more elite groups for the power to govern society" (Macpherson 1973, p. 78). In our terms, this is mere procedural democracy, less interested in developing civic virtue than in restraining civil society. Dahl's account is also marked by the implicit idea that democracy is what you get in the West, but not elsewhere for the most part (Dahl 1989, pp. 264, 322–23), and it is passively satisfied with the outcomes of procedural justice. Yet Dahl is the main theorist used by the political scientists who have produced most of the "transitions to democracy" literature.

A quite different view is presented by Michio Morishima, who argued recently that postwar Japan is both typically undemocratic in its cleavage between a favored upper stratum and all the rest (like other advanced industrial societies), and more democratic than the Western democracies by virtue of its "bureaucratic democracy," whereby each individual is treated equally, and there is little "us versus them" (that is, little class conflict). The situation of general equality and general education (to a high standard), with smaller maldistribution of wealth as compared particularly to the United States, means that Japan has satisfied a critical demand of Habermas's conception of the public sphere: that people enter it equal at the start. Thus the Japan model, he argues, is a challenge both to free-market-style development and to Western versions of democracy (Bagchi 1995, pp. 157–60). South Korea, also, has a more egalitarian distribution of wealth than does the US, high levels of general education, and, in my view, a much more developed civil society than one finds in Japan. So once labor and the left are also included in the system, perhaps it will be more democratic than the American system. But that is still not the democracy we need.

Another unusual perspective is provided in an excellent book entitled *Capitalist Development and Democracy* (Rueschemeyer, Stephens, and Stephens 1992). The authors begin by agreeing with Seymour Martin Lipset's famous judgment that economic development and pluralist democracy are positively related. But they offer very different explanations for this correlation. The political outcomes of development have to do with four elements, in their view: (1) the pattern of agrarian transition; (2) the empowerment of subordinate classes through industrialization (the middle class, but especially the working class); (3) the type of state structure; and (4) transnational power relations (something all the other accounts of democratization leave out). The authors also have a sense of *timing*, especially the persistence over time in certain "late"–developing countries of particular agrarian social relations, industrialization patterns, roles for the state, and variant positions within the world system. In other words they have systematized the conception of democracy that Marx was groping toward in his critiques of Hegel.

Capitalist development, according to the authors of this book, is associated with democracy because, as a by-product of growth, it transforms class structures, undermining old ones and creating new ones. The new middle classes, however, will fight to the point of their own democratic representation, but not beyond: after that, they will seek to restrict working-class representation (just like Mill and de Toqueville—in other words, a "yes," but then again a "no"). And here we have a nice explanation for the continuing absence of labor representation in South Korea and the fecklessness of the two "labor" parties in Japan—the socialists and the communists. In the United States, the Democratic Party functioned as a business/labor coalition from 1932 through the 1980s, but the "neodemocrats" now in power in Washington think they must attend to the interests of the middle class to the detriment of the old Democratic coalition. Perhaps this means that the middle class will also seek to disestablish working-class representation.

As for the international element, Rueschemeyer, Stephens, and Stephens rightly emphasize that geopolitical and other interests of great powers generated direct interventions and support for repressive states. For example, prewar Japan's authoritarianism was in part an outcome of the breakdown of the world economy and outside economic pressure from the United States and England (although neither supported its repressive state). Japan's postwar democracy was "nested" in an American-dominated security regime: American policing of East Asian security left Japan alone to be "developmental," and its status as an "economic animal" shorn of military and political clout in the world was a clear and conscious result of American strategy. We can also see in the authoritarian regimes that prevailed in South Korea and Taiwan until the end of the 1980s (and almost always supported by US policy) the *completion* of a Japan-centered economic and security sphere in Northeast Asia. At any rate, perhaps it is only in America that democratic theorists would think so little about the external sources of and obstacles to democracy.

C. B. Macpherson's work was imbued with the idea of substantive justice: democracy, for Macpherson, is that system which empowers a conception of man as a maker, as a fully realized human being. A truly democratic system must encourage the manifold development of human capacities in all people. Secondly, democracy in the world of inegalitarian distribution that we all live in is inseparable from "the cry of the oppressed." Democracy *is* and must be the means for a redress of human inequality, especially economic inequality. Without these two things, political equality is mostly meaningless (1973, pp. 3–8, 78–90).

The East Asia of today is far more democratic than it has been before. But the best example of such a politics—Japan—cannot be our model of democracy. The same is true of the new democratic systems in Taiwan, South Korea, and the Philippines. But then the American polyarchy cannot be the model to which democrats aspire, either. What is civil society? What is democracy? It has to be more than this, more than the Japan of the LDP, Korea of the DLP, or the American system. It is Macpherson's admonition to bring full human development to the many, not just to the few.

8

From Confrontation to Conciliation: The Philippine Path toward Democratic Consolidation

Gretchen Casper

The Philippine Path toward Democratic Consolidation

On February 25, 1986, Ferdinand E. Marcos was sworn in as president for the fourth time and then boarded a helicopter to flee Malacañang Palace. His authoritarian regime was overthrown by a diverse set of actors: businessmen, church members, students, workers, the middle class, economic elites, the New People's Army, Muslim guerrillas, political elites, and military rebels. Their success resulted in the installation of a fragile democracy and started the Philippines on a path toward democratic consolidation characterized by high levels of political conflict but also the potential to introduce significant reforms.

People Power in the Philippines—when hundreds of thousands of Filipinos stopped loyalist troops and forced Marcos to flee to Hawaii—was a dramatic transition from authoritarianism to democracy. However, People Power is less common, when compared both to democratic transitions in general and to Asian cases in particular. It is more likely that an authoritarian regime will volunteer or eventually agree to exit from power (Huntington

1991, p. 124). The regime may begin the transition process voluntarily because it has successfully installed certain guarantees or special privileges for itself. For example, the Turkish military regime agreed to hold elections in 1983 after gaining approval of an amnesty law and conversion of the National Security Council into an advisory Presidential Council. In Pakistan, General Zia ul-Haq announced in 1985 that the country would return to democracy after he had amended the constitution to increase presidential powers vis-à–vis those of the prime minister. Or the regime may realize that the opposition is gaining in strength and thus agrees to negotiate with the opposition while it has leverage to gain concessions and before it is overthrown. For example, General Chun Doo Hwan agreed to step down as president of South Korea in 1987 to escape Marcos's fate; and his handpicked successor, Roh Tae Woo, agreed to reopen debate with the opposition on constitutional reforms to increase his chances in the 1987 presidential elections.

It is less likely that an authoritarian regime will be adamant about remaining in power in the face of mounting opposition. However, if the leaders refuse to exit from power, then they will have to be removed by force. Nevertheless, few cases of regime overthrow result in the installation of a democratic government (Casper and Taylor 1996; Huntington 1991). Although the authoritarian regimes in Afghanistan (1973) and Iran (1979) were overthrown, they were replaced with other authoritarian regimes rather than democratic governments; in Myanmar, the opposition's attempt to oust the State Law and Order Restoration Council (SLORC) has stalled as of the late 1990s.

The Philippines, then, is a case of democratic transition that has successfully installed a democratic government by overthrowing an authoritarian regime. The overthrow of the Marcos regime started the country down a path toward democratic consolidation that has been characterized by conflict due to the high level of mobilization and the diversity of the actors required to overthrow Marcos. As a result, the democratic government that was installed was fragile, and the Aquino and Ramos administrations have been forced to focus primarily on the issue of stability. However, the Philippines' transition also created an opportunity for authoritarian rules to be dismantled and long-awaited reforms to be enacted. From 1986 to the present, then, the Philippines has been moving slowly from confrontation toward conciliation, and from restoration toward reform.

Martial Law: The Installation of an Authoritarian Regime

The Philippines was a colony of Spain from the late 1500s until 1898 and of the United States from 1898 to 1945 (Wurfel 1988, p. 7). At the end of World War II, the country became an independent democracy with a presidential form of government modeled after the American constitution. In 1969, Ferdinand Marcos was the first president to be reelected, having first won election in 1965. In 1972, near the end of his constitutional limit of two presidential terms, he declared martial law (Abueva 1979, p. 37). Although he ended martial law nominally in 1981, his regime remained in place until 1986, when it was overthrown.

President Ferdinand Marcos declared martial law on September 23, 1972, claiming that the government was "in urgent danger of violent overthrow, insurrection, and rebellion" (Rosenberg 1979, p. 17). The military immediately began arresting potential opponents, detaining over 30,000 people—including opposition politicians, journalists, students, and union leaders—in the first few weeks (Amnesty International 1976, p. 6).[1] Marcos released a new constitution in November 1972 that specified a parliamentary form of government (thus abolishing executive term limits) and included transitory provisions that allowed Marcos to implement the 1973 constitution at his discretion. The constitution also gave Marcos presidential powers under the 1935 constitution and prime ministerial powers under the 1973 constitution while martial law was in effect (Del Carmen 1979, p. 91). Marcos used referenda to ratify the 1973 constitution and to approve such actions as closing Congress, remaining in office, and delaying the opening of the interim National Assembly (Abueva, 1979; Del Carmen 1979). As the interim National Assembly was not created until 1978, there were no elections held from 1972 to 1978; instead, Marcos exercised legislative power during this period through the release of over 1,000 presidential decrees (Abueva 1979, p. 36).

Thus Marcos replaced the old democratic government with an authoritarian regime that he headed and that shared power with:

> the military; cabinet members, technocrats, and the bureaucracy under them; persons close to the president or Mrs. Marcos, whether relatives or loyal friends and former politicians; local officials, who also hold office by presidential appointment; and several big businessmen who enjoy the political stability and economic incentives [provided by the regime]. (Abueva, 1979, p. 54)

Martial law remained in force from 1973 to 1981. Marcos amended the constitution several times to increase and extend his powers; thus he was able to rule by decree even after martial law was lifted in 1981 and the regular National Assembly was constituted in 1984.

Early on, the moderate opposition criticized Marcos's 1973 constitution and his regime's human rights record. Marcos had manipulated the ratification of his 1973 constitution by using citizens' assemblies, which used voice vote and show of hands, rather than plebiscites with secret ballots (Del Carmen 1979, pp. 93–94; Abueva 1979, p. 38). When their petitions before the Supreme Court failed to declare the constitution invalid, the moderate opposition began organizing boycotts for subsequent referenda and were supported by the Association of Major Religious Superiors in the Philippines (AMRSP) (Wurfel 1988, pp. 119-20; Thompson 1995, p. 71). Moderate opposition and religious groups strongly protested the regime's human rights record: by 1977, over 70,000 people had been detained and many of them were tortured during interrogation (Amnesty International 1976, pp. 6-7; Wurfel 1988, pp. 124-25). Between 1975 and 1981, the church's Task-Force Detainees had documented 200 incidents of disappearances and 887 killings (Kessler 1989, p. 137; Youngblood 1990, p. 153). Support for the New People's Army (NPA), the military wing of the Communist Party of the Philippines (CPP), also increased after 1972. When Marcos declared martial law, it was estimated that there were only 800 NPA soldiers (Overholt 1986, p. 1140). By 1981, this number had risen to between 3,500 and 8,000 soldiers (Kessler 1989, p. 56). Thus, Marcos's installation of authoritarianism was criticized by the moderate opposition, religious groups, and the New People's Army.

To allay rising opposition, Marcos introduced several political changes in the late 1970s and early 1980s. In 1978, he opened the interim National Assembly, which served as the legislature until martial law was lifted and the regular National Assembly convened. The 1978 elections for the National Assembly were characterized by massive electoral fraud: out of 183 elected seats, Marcos's New Society Movement (NBL) won 169 seats compared with 14 seats for the opposition. Moderate opposition leaders and church members strongly protested the results and lodged a formal complaint with Vice President Walter Mondale when he visited the country several months later (Wurfel 1988, pp. 132-33). Any legitimacy the interim legislature had was further eroded by its restricted powers: it could only debate cabinet bills and legislation concerning local issues, and Marcos could implement his prime ministerial powers to close the legislature if it were "not doing its job properly" (Noble 1986, p. 97; Catilo and Tapales 1988, pp. 157-59).

In January 1981, Marcos announced that he would lift martial law. However, this event did not reduce his powers as he retained the power to release presidential decrees and to detain potential opponents through the use of national security laws (Wurfel 1988, p. 248.) Furthermore, he ensured that he would be able to control the regular National Assembly by having the interim legislature approve constitutional amendments that changed the governmental structure from a parliamentary form of government to a presidential-parliamentary one. Under the new government, the president would have a six-year term (with no term limits) and would appoint the prime minister and the cabinet members (Wurfel 1988, p. 250). When Marcos announced presidential elections in 1981, he was unable to find a credible candidate to run against him because the moderate opposition announced that it would boycott the elections. Marcos claimed that 80 percent of the voters turned out for the elections and that he had won 88 percent of the vote; however, the opposition claimed that fewer than 50 percent actually voted (Wurfel 1988, p. 253; Landé 1986, p. 139; Noble 1986, p. 107).

These political changes neither appeased the opposition nor legitimized Marcos's rule. By 1979, Cardinal Sin was calling for Marcos to step down (Casper 1995, p. 76). By 1983, the size of the NPA had grown to 8,000 to 10,000 soldiers, controlling 60 percent of the provinces (Kessler 1989, p. 56). The business community began to withdraw its support as Marcos continued to support crony corporations, while the economic growth rate declined from 5 percent in 1980 to 1.1 percent in 1983 (Thompson, 1995, p. 119). In 1982, the Reform the Armed Forces of the Philippines Movement (RAM) was formed by five junior officers close to Defense Minister Juan Ponce Enrile; by 1986, it had 4,000 members. While its official aim was to reprofessionalize the military, it was secretly preparing to overthrow Marcos's regime (Casper 1995, pp. 106–14).

When Marcos declared martial law in 1972, he dismantled the Philippines' democratic government and replaced it with an authoritarian regime that gave him legislative and executive power. Marcos refused to acknowledge the opposition's demands to step down. Instead, he kept changing the rules of the game in an effort to remain in power. By 1983, members of his support coalition began to defect, and the moderate opposition, religious groups, the NPA, business leaders, and military officers were preparing for a post-Marcos scenario.

People Power: From the Aquino Assassination to the EDSA Revolution

Up to the very end, Marcos assumed that he would be able to keep changing the rules of the game and control the electoral process, as he had in 1978 and 1981 (Overholt 1986). While Marcos wanted to remain in power, the moderate opposition, which fielded the slate of Corazon Aquino and Salvador Laurel for the 1986 elections, wanted Marcos's regime ousted and democracy restored. The military rebels—RAM and Defense Minister Enrile—wanted to install a military junta (Casper 1995, pp. 135–36).

It had been rumored since the late 1970s that Marcos was suffering from systemic lupus erythematosus (Wurfel 1988, pp. 234-35; Overholt 1986, p. 1152). He was hospitalized briefly in August 1982; when Marcos withdrew from the public for three weeks in August 1983, there was speculation that he was undergoing a kidney operation (Wurfel 1988, p. 255; Bonner 1987, p. 340). Benigno Aquino decided to return to the Philippines and ignored Imelda Marcos's warning that his safety could not be guaranteed in Manila (Wurfel

1988, p. 275; Bonner 1987, p. 341; Landé 1986, p. 115). Aquino landed in Manila on August 21, 1983, and was shot in the head seconds after being escorted off the plane by Aviation Security Command (AVSECOM) officers.

Aquino's assassination was the starting point of the Philippines' transition to democracy. Millions of people visited his coffin and watched the funeral procession (Bonner 1987, p. 342). Demonstrations erupted around the country implicating Marcos in the assassination and demanding that he resign; over the next three years, the demonstrations continued and escalated as more groups mobilized and joined the opposition. The church immediately condemned the assassination. Members of the business community joined the demonstrations and called on Marcos to institute political reforms, including "an honest and independent judiciary, restoration of public constitutional rights, relief from pervasive militarism, and clear legal provisions for a successor to the President" (Silliman 1984, p. 155). President Ronald Reagan, who had invited the Marcoses to Washington, D.C., for a state visit in 1982 and was planning a reciprocal visit to Manila in 1983, canceled his trip on the advice of the State Department. By 1985, senior officers in the State Department publicly acknowledged their fear that Marcos was losing control of his regime and would be overthrown by the NPA. To reassure the United States, Marcos declared in November 1985 on the ABC program *This Week* that he would hold presidential elections one year early, in 1986 (Bonner 1987, pp. 386–388).

Marcos thought that he would win the "snap elections" for two reasons: he would be able to control the ballot boxes, and the traditionally fragmented moderate opposition parties would not be able to field a unified slate. His efforts to stuff the ballot boxes were hampered by the National Movement for Free Elections (NAMFREL), an independent vote-counting organization that set up "Operation Quick Count" to verify returns announced by the government's Commission on Elections (COMELEC). Yet his assessment of the moderate opposition was correct: both Corazon Aquino (Benigno Aquino's widow) and Salvador Laurel registered as presidential candidates—Aquino for LABAN (Benigno Aquino's party) and Laurel for the United Democratic Organization (UNIDO). After heavy lobbying from Cardinal Sin, Aquino and Laurel agreed to unite: Aquino would run as the presidential candidate and Laurel as the vice presidential candidate, but they would run on the UNIDO ticket (Villegas 1987, p. 195; Youngblood 1990, pp. 198–199).

The elections on February 7, 1986, were characterized by the regime's "monopolization of the media, intimidation of the opposition, payoffs on an extraordinary scale, efforts to deprive the opposition of funds and transport, inadequate provision of time for the opposition to organize, stolen ballot boxes, [and] mistabulation of the results" (Overholt 1986, p. 1161). Voter lists disappeared: it was estimated that from 3.3 million to 5 million voters were barred from entering the polling places or were otherwise unable to vote. Election violence statistics ranged from 90 to 200 dead. Both Marcos and Aquino claimed they had won the election. Marcos sent the ballot boxes to the National Assembly for the final canvass, as delineated in the 1973 constitution. The National Assembly, in which the KBL controlled two thirds of the seats, declared Marcos the winner with 54 percent of the vote, the same figure that NAMFREL had announced as Aquino's share (Aquino 1986, p. 155).

Early in the vote-counting process, Senator Lugar, who was part of the US delegation observing the elections, stated that Marcos was trying to influence the outcome through the use of voter fraud. President Reagan initially supported Marcos, suggesting that there may have been "fraud on both sides" (Aquino 1986, p. 1955). However, after the moderate opposition strongly protested, he retracted his statement and sent special envoy Philip Habib to the Philippines to see whether or not a negotiated outcome could be reached between Aquino and Marcos. Aquino refused to concede. On February 15, she held a victory rally attended by over 500,000 people, and called for citizens to engage in civil disobedience until Marcos stepped down (Wurfel 1988, p. 300).

In late 1985, RAM had drafted a plan to overthrow Marcos's regime and install a junta (Nemenzo 1987, pp. 7–9; Wurfel 1988, p. 302; McCoy 1990, p. 10). RAM was debating whether or not to implement the coup when Marcos announced the snap elections. RAM members decided to wait until after the elections to see if Marcos would be defeated at the polls; however, after Marcos proclaimed his reelection, they returned to their original plan. On February 20, they contacted Aquino and proposed that she join forces with them to overthrow Marcos's regime and install a five-member junta that would include Enrile, Cardinal Sin, and Aquino. Aquino refused to go along with their plans, and the next day RAM decided to implement the coup without her (Bonner 1987, p. 434).

The tense period between February 22 and 25, 1986, is referred to by many names: the EDSA Revolution, the Miracle at EDSA, the Yellow Revolution.[2] On February 22, Marcos discovered RAM's plans and ordered the arrests of Defense Minister Enrile and acting chief of staff Lt. General Ramos. Enrile and RAM members fled to the Armed Forces of the Philippines (AFP) headquarters at Camp Aguinaldo, and Enrile asked Ramos to join him in defecting from Marcos; Ramos did and fled to Camp Crame, across the street (Arillo 1986, pp. 11–12). The two men held a joint press conference that evening, where they announced that Marcos had stolen the election and Aquino was the rightful winner, that they were withdrawing their support from Marcos, and that the AFP should not follow any orders given by Marcos (Arillo 1986, pp. 20–26). After the press conference, Cardinal Sin broadcast an appeal on Radio Veritas asking people to:

> leave your homes now. I am calling on our people to support our two good friends at the camp. Go to [Camp] Aguinaldo and show your solidarity with them in this crucial period. Our two good friends have shown their idealism. Take them food if you wish. Keep them safe. (Johnson 1987, p. 78)

Almost 50,000 people arrived at the camps that night in response to the cardinal's message (Arillo 1986, p. 39). Eventually, 800,000 Filipinos— People Power—stopped nine tanks and 2,000 marines from attacking the rebels, and demanded that Aquino be sworn in as president (Arillo 1986, p. 117; Johnson 1987, p. 103).

The size and intensity of People Power made the rebels realize that they could not successfully install a junta, and they began to negotiate with Aquino. They agreed to support Aquino's accession to the presidency in exchange for two government positions—for Enrile to be named secretary of defense and Ramos to be chief of staff (Johnson 1987, p. 83; Arillo 1986, pp. 99–100). They also asked, and claimed that Aquino agreed, that she consult with them before making decisions on a wide range of policy issues, from cabinet appointments to economic policy and political reforms (Casper 1995, p. 136).

On February 25, 1986, Marcos called Senator Lugar in Washington D.C. and asked whether the US would accept a power-sharing deal between Marcos and Aquino whereby "Aquino would be allowed to run the government, but [Marcos] would remain as president until his term expired in 1987" (Bonner 1987, pp. 439–440; Johnson 1987, pp. 233–234). Reagan vetoed a power-sharing deal and stated that Marcos should step down (Johnson 1987, p. 234). Thus, two inaugurations were held on February 25, 1986. Marcos was sworn in as president at Malacañang Palace; then he and his entourage boarded American helicopters and fled the country (Bonner 1987, p. 440). Corazon Aquino and Salvador Laurel were sworn in at a private country club near the rebel camps and began to install a democratic government.

Peaceful Succession: From Aquino to Ramos

The EDSA Revolution started the Philippines on a path toward democratic consolidation characterized by high levels of political conflict. Although Marcos had fled the country, the new government was faced with demands from mobilized actors with diverging interests. As a result, democratic stability became the main priority for both Aquino and Ramos. Because of conflicting demands, Aquino's coalition began to erode soon after she entered office. From 1986 to 1989, there were six coup attempts against her government, and it was almost overthrown in 1989 by RAM rebels and Marcos loyalists. Aquino's successor, President Ramos, was more successful in reducing the level of conflict by strengthening his legislative coalition and negotiating peace agreements with RAM and Muslim guerrillas.

President Aquino announced her provisional government in March 1986. The temporary Freedom Constitution allowed her to reestablish civil liberties and political rights, close the National Assembly, and exercise legislative powers until May 1987 (Hernandez 1986, pp. 181–82; Wurfel 1988, p. 309). The Constitutional Commission drafted a permanent constitution in October 1986, and it was ratified by a vote of 76 percent in February 1987 (Lapitan 1989, 239). The results of the May 1987 congressional elections, in which turnout was a record-setting 90 percent, gave 22 of the 24 Senate seats and 149 of 200 elected House seats to Aquino's coalition (Wurfel, 1988, pp. 318–319; Thompson 1995, p. 171). Marcos's old party, the KBL, received only 10 seats in the House (Thompson 1995, p. 171).

The coalition that helped Aquino gain the presidency was a highly mobilized group of actors with diverging interests:

> The regime created by People Power and military rebellion was a coalition broad enough to accommodate the political forces that contributed to its establishment—the military, the conservative politicians in UNIDO, a segment of the business elite, the mixture of progressive but increasingly traditional styles which characterized the PDP-Laban, and the progressives, who range from Christian liberals to nonparty Marxists. These forces were all assembled in the cabinet, the major political institution for more than a year, which temporarily performed the consultative function of a legislature as well as executive roles. (Wurfel 1988, pp. 305–6)

From the beginning of her administration, in February 1986, Aquino was pulled in conflicting directions. Progressive politicians wanted to take advantage of the return to democracy by implementing far-reaching reforms on a wide range of social issues, including peace negotiations with insurgency groups and land reform. The military and conservative politicians, however, were wary of dramatic change, particularly if it meant extending amnesty to the NPA or giving up their land.

While RAM had been unable to install a junta in 1986, it felt that "Corazon Aquino may have won the elections, but if the military had not intervened as it did in shifting loyalty from the dictator to Enrile and Ramos, there [was] serious doubt if she could have effectively claimed the presidency for herself" (Arillo 1986, p. 126). Aquino had kept her promise with RAM—she named Juan Ponce Enrile as secretary of defense and Fidel Ramos as chief of staff. However, RAM and Enrile quickly withdrew their support: they claimed that she had reneged on her promise to consult with them on major policy decisions, and that instead she was following advice from left-of-center politicians. Aquino moved to the right and shifted her priority from reform to stability to protect her government from coup attempts supported by RAM and Marcos loyalists.

From 1986 to 1989, there were six coup attempts against Aquino's government, led by Marcos loyalists or RAM members. The most serious threat to Aquino's government was the sixth coup attempt on December 1, 1989. The coup attempt was led by RAM but was financially supported by businessmen, opposition politicians, and Marcos loyalists. Over 3,000 RAM rebels attacked several military bases (including Camp Aguinaldo and Camp Crame) as well as government and business offices, luxury hotels, and residential subdivisions around Makati (Manila's business district). Over 100 people were killed and 300 wounded. The rebels finally surrendered only after the United States sent two air force F-4 Phantom jets to fly over their position as a show of American support for Aquino's government (Casper 1995, pp. 167–68; Timberman 1990, p. 176; Thompson, 1995, p. 165).

By the end of her term in 1992, Aquino had succeeded in restoring democracy and holding new elections from local governments to Congress. More importantly, perhaps, she had been able to withstand a series of coup attempts against her, and finished out her term. However, there was a rising sense of dissatisfaction within the country as "land reform under Aquino [had] been inconsequential; the state still [was] not able to effectively tax the rich; and half of the population [continued] to live below the poverty line in conditions of gross inequality" (Hutchison 1993, p. 193). Although the Philippines had expanded from a two-party to a multiparty system, almost "85 percent of the 200-member House of Representatives [came] from traditional political clans" (Coronel 1991, p. 167). People felt that the democratic transition in the Philippines was "more restoration than revolution" (Wurfel 1988, p. 311; Hutchison 1993, p. 199).

Given this dissatisfaction and demands for reform, it was not surprising that the theme of the 1992 presidential elections was *no trapos*—no traditional politicians. Indeed, of the seven presidential candidates, the top two vote-getters were nontraditional politicians—retired general Fidel Ramos, who received 24 percent of the vote, and former judge and immigration commissioner Miriam Defensor-Santiago, who gained 20 percent. Vice President Salvador Laurel, a traditional politician, polled seventh, with only 3 percent of the vote (Timberman 1992, p. 118). The 1992 presidential election also stood out because it was the first one held under the 1987 constitution and resulted in peaceful succession from Aquino to Ramos.

One hundred and twenty-four parties registered for the 1992 elections (Brilliantes 1992, p. 144). While Ramos was elected president, and had been supported by Aquino, he won by fewer than one million votes. In the congressional races, his party—LAKAS/NUCD (National Union of Christian Democrats)—received only 33 seats in the House of Representatives and two in the Senate. Thus, to strengthen his presidency and gain passage of his legislative agenda, Ramos's first task was to attract other parties to enter into a coalition with him. His coalition—LAKAS/NUCD and the Liberal Democratic Party (LDP, the largest party in Congress)—ended up with 122 out of 200 seats in the House and 18 out of 24 seats in the Senate (Timberman 1992, pp. 117–18). Furthermore, Ramos was able to strengthen his position after the 1995 congressional elections. Ramos's party significantly increased its control of the House, from 33 to 126 seats, thus gaining an outright majority. Thus Ramos has been successful not only in building a coalition but also in strengthening it.

Ramos was able to reduce the level of political conflict in the country by negotiating with RAM, Muslim guerrillas, and the CPP. His first legislative bill legalized the Communist Party of the Philippines. He released over 400 political prisoners, including communist and Muslim guerrillas as well as military rebels, and set up the National Unification Commission to conduct peace negotiations with all three groups (Brillantes 1993, pp. 226–27; Riedinger 1995, pp. 209–10). He was successful in reaching agreements with RAM and the MNLF.

In October 1995, Ramos's government signed a peace agreement with the RAM rebels. The government promised amnesty for their participation in coup attempts, allowed them to return to the armed forces, and promised to pay them back wages. In exchange for the government's generous terms, RAM members promised to surrender their weapons (Hernandez 1996, p. 145). Ten military rebels ran in the 1995 congressional elections and three of them won seats; Colonel Gregorio Honasan (one of the founders of RAM and the leader of the 1989 coup attempt) was elected as senator that year (Hernandez 1996, p. 143).

Ramos signed a peace treaty with the MNLF, the largest Muslim guerrilla group, in September 1996. The agreement appointed MNLF chairman Nur Misuari as the head of the Southern Philippines Council for Peace and Development. In exchange, Misuari and the MNLF renounced their goal of secession, and the guerrillas will join the Philippine army's ranks as regular soldiers. Furthermore, Misuari agreed to run as a LAKAS/NUCD candidate for governor of the temporary four-province autonomous government. A plebiscite will be held in fourteen provinces by 1999 to determine the exact composition of the permanent autonomous government (Hernandez 1996, p. 145; Hutchcroft 1996, pp. 10–11; Gargan 1996).

While Aquino successfully restored democracy to the Philippines in 1986,

Ramos worked toward ensuring its stability. He strengthened his presidency by building a legislative coalition and reducing the level of political conflict in the country by signing peace agreements with RAM and the MNLF.

The Future of Democracy in the Philippines

In 1986, the Philippines started down a path toward democratic consolidation that was characterized by high levels of conflict but also the potential to introduce significant reforms. Since then, both Aquino and Ramos have focused on stabilizing the fragile democracy. Ten years after the EDSA Revolution, the government has successfully strengthened its support coalition and negotiated peace agreements with military rebels and Muslim guerrillas. As the Philippines works toward achieving democratic consolidation, the government will be addressing the issues of stability and reform.

Both RAM and the MNLF have signed peace agreements and have shifted their struggle from the battlefield to the ballot box. The Philippine government is now considering peace accords with the CPP and with Muslim splinter groups. Ramos began talks with the CPP in 1992 to bring the 29-year war to an end, but these discussions have frequently collapsed. Regarding Muslim guerrillas, while the MNLF has signed a peace agreement with Ramos, Muslim splinter groups—such as the Moro Islamic Liberation Front (MILF) and the Abu Sayyaf group—have refused to negotiate with the Philippine government and are still committed to creating an independent Islamic state (Hernandez 1996, p. 146).

When Aquino became president in 1986, she restored the country's pre-1972 style of democracy, and Ramos focused on strengthening it. Now that the level of political conflict has declined, the government has an opportunity to implement significant political change. Three issues that the Philippines faces are agrarian reform, political reform, and foreign policy. Under Aquino's Comprehensive Agrarian Reform Program, more land was redistributed between 1988 and 1993 than during Marcos' fourteen-year rule. However, the government now faces implementing the more controversial stage: the "compulsory acquisition of private agricultural landholdings down to five hectares" (Riedinger 1995, pp. 212–13). Regarding political reform, the 1998 congressional elections will be the first time the country has implemented the constitutional provisions that party lists be used to select 20 percent of the House of Representatives' seats and that term limits become effective for members of both houses (Hutchcroft 1996, p. 13). Finally, the Philippines is redesigning its foreign policy. The country traditionally turned to the United States for military aid and trade agreements, and Aquino depended on American support to defend her government during the 1989 coup attempt. However, with the withdrawal of American bases, the Philippines is reducing its dependence on the United States by expanding ties with its Asian neighbors, through ASEAN, AFTA, and APEC (Hernandez 1996, pp. 149–50; Hutchcroft 1996, pp. 6, 16–17).

Since the EDSA Revolution in 1986, the Philippines has survived the first ten years on its path toward democratic consolidation. So far, the new democracy has achieved the first step toward democratic consolidation—by reducing levels of political conflict—and is slowly moving from confrontation to conciliation. In the next several years, the country will face the second step—introducing significant political change—to move the country from restoration to reform.

9

Modernization, Democracy, and the Developmental State in Asia: A Virtuous Cycle or Unraveling Strands?

Cal Clark

BY THE LATE 1980s and early 1990s, the "Third Wave of Democratization" (Huntington 1991) was rapidly spreading across Asia. Moreover, Asia had arguably become the most dynamic region of the world economically, as the longtime "economic miracles" of extremely rapid industrialization in Japan and East Asia's "Four Little Dragons" began to be replicated first by the ASEAN nations in Southeast Asia and China and then by the "laggards" in South Asia (Chan 1993; Fallows 1994). Since most of these countries pursued strategies of expor-toriented growth based on market liberalization, a good case could be made that Asia was heading toward a nirvana of "democratic capitalism" that Francis Fukuyama (1992), for example, optimistically proclaimed "the end of history."

Superficially at least, political and economic change in Asia over the last two decades appears to validate this "modernization model." As sketched in Figure 1, economic growth and industrialization have created sizeable middle classes in many Asian countries; and these middle classes often provided a central element in movements forcing political liberalization upon authoritarian Asian regimes. Internationally, the United States claims credit for at least some of Asia's political and economic success, since its pressure on its Asian clients to follow the U.S. model of capitalist economics and democratic politics helped bring these reforms to fruition. Thus the combination of democratic transitions and rapid economic modernization suggests that many Asian nations may be approaching a stable democratic capitalism in which economic prosperity and political freedom will coexist, thereby suggesting the existence of a "virtuous cycle" among economic freedom, political freedom, and the social change generated by industrialization and modernization.

Figure 1.

Modernization Interpretation of the Postwar Evolution of East Asian Political Economies

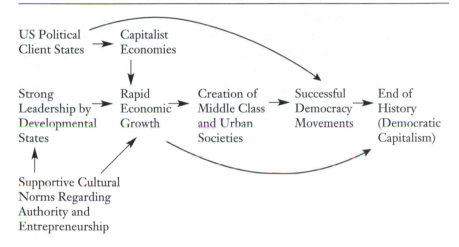

Yet Figure 1 is labeled a modernization model of "East Asian dynamism" (Chan 1993) because it incorporates two other factors that are commonly attributed to Asian political economies. First, rather than having laissez-faire economies, most Asian nations are seen as being guided by "strong and autonomous developmental states" that use government power to chart broad strategies of industrial transformation by concentrating resources and inhibiting rent-seeking behavior by economic elites (Amsden 1989; Johnson, 1982; Wade 1990). Second (in a departure from modernization's usual disparagement of traditional cultures and norms), it is often argued that the values associated with "Confucian capitalism" reinforced the organization and autonomy of developmental states in East Asia, while also providing incentives for individual entrepreneurship (Hofheinz and Calder 1982; Pye 1985). These aspects of the East Asian development model, therefore, present potential challenges to the virtuous modernization cycle just sketched. Over time, for example, modernization might erode the cultural values that under-girded "Confucian capitalism"; or democratization might impair the strength and autonomy of Asian developmental states (which could explain, for exam-ple, the severe "Asian flu" financial crisis of 1997 and 1998).

Such potential conflicts among the various strands of Asia's virtuous cycle should not be particularly surprising. The broad survey in William Glade's chapter of this volume, for example, found little consistency in the relation-ship between economic and political liberalization; and several of the other chapters on Africa, Latin America, and Eastern Europe (see the chapters by Peter Lewis, Ruth Berins Collier, and J. C. Sharman and Roger Kanet) sug-gest that market reforms may prove as challenging to democratic institutions as they are complementary. This chapter, hence, compares the virtuous cycle assumed by the modernization model to exist among market liberalization, industrialization, social change, democratization, and US policy with evi-dence that recent development in Asia may be creating pressures for "unrav-eling some strands" in what have been judged to be extremely successful political economies over the last decade or more. The first section considers whether modernization explains Asian democracy; and the second examines the relationships among democracy, developmental states, and economic per-formance in Asia.

Democratization and Modernization in Asia: A Questionable Connection

Figure 2 provides an overview of the nature of 24 political regimes in five Asian groupings (developed Oceania, the East Asian capitalist dragons, South Asia, Southeast Asia, and the once or present communist regimes) as a first step for testing the modernization model outlined above. The first two columns provide a tentative ranking of each country's current regime and dominant type of regime for the postwar period, using categories in fairly wide usage (Diamond et al. 1989a; Huntington 1991): (1) "consolidated democracies" in which democratic practices and organization have become strongly institutionalized; (2) "new democracies" where democratic institu-tions do not appear to have yet become fully consolidated and, thus, may be subject to challenge and reversal; (3) "semidemocracies" where elections coexist with political restrictions severe enough to render the label of full democracy unwarranted; and (4) authoritarian regimes of varying ideological hues (the following survey is based on *Asian Survey* 1996; Diamond et al. 1989b; Friedman 1994).

The first column in Figure 2 certainly supports the image of a democratiz-ing Asia that goes far beyond the traditional democracies in developed Oceania (Australia and New Zealand). If one includes the expanded representative bodies in Hong Kong in the decade before retrocession to China, some type of democracy can be found in all the East Asia dragons. Similarly, all of South Asia practices some level of democracy except Burma (Myanmar to its military rulers); and, in a sidelight on democratic outcomes, all the South Asian nations have elected women to head governments (primarily because of their family linkages to national heroes) despite having cultures that are normally considered rather derogatory toward women. Four of the six Southeast Asian nations (Malaysia, Papua New Guinea, the Philippines, and Thailand) have elected governments as well. Only among the six communist countries are democracies a minority (in part because most have pursued economic instead of political liberalization; see Figure 3 below); and even here, during the 1990s Mongolia opted for democratic reforms, while international pressure forced elections in Cambodia.

Comparing columns 1 and 2, furthermore, supports the image of democratic progress during the "third wave" of the 1980s and 1990s. Nine of the nations (South Korea, Taiwan, Pakistan, Bangladesh, the Philippines, Thailand, Papua New Guinea, Mongolia, and Cambodia in the order that they appear in Figure 2) improved their rankings; and, while not showing up in the table, significant liberalization occurred in many of the authoritarian/colonial regimes as well (China, Hong Kong, Indonesia, and Vietnam). Conversely, signs of deterioration are much harder to find (perhaps in civil-war-ravaged Sri Lanka and, depending upon how transitions are counted, the military coup against an elected government that never was in Burma).

If one considers that Australia and New Zealand were the only Asian democracies as the postwar era commenced, this is indeed dramatic and startling progress. Yet Asia certainly falls far short of reaching full democratization. Probably only five of the sixteen governments that fall into one of the democratic categories should be rated as "consolidated" (Australia, India, Japan, New Zealand, and Papua New Guinea); and, as argued in the next section, in all of these, the form of democratic government seems to be exacerbating current economic problems. Another four (Mongolia, the Philippines, South Korea, and Taiwan) are rated as "new democracies" and may well be just an election or two away from being "consolidated."

The seven "semidemocracies" fall into two very distinct groups. In the first, some less-than-democratic characteristics of the regime contribute to political stability and are thus seemingly acceptable to much of their citizenry. In Singapore and Malaysia, strong leaders of ruling parties (Lee Kuan Yew and Mahathir Mohamad respectively) specifically argue that they have created polities based on an "Asian democracy" that is superior to Western institutions. Similarly, Thailand's much more fragmented and volatile party system and even episodic military coups may not undermine effective government

Figure 2.

Synopsis of Asian Political Regimes

	Current Regime	Major Postwar Regime	Key for Regime Creation	Ethnic Frag	Major Parties
DEVELOPED OCEANIA					
Australia	Consolidated Democracy	Consold Democracy	Traditional Democracy	No	2
New Zealand	Consolidated Democracy	Consold Democracy	Traditional Democracy	No	2
EAST ASIAN DRAGONS					
Japan	Consolidated Democracy	Consold Democracy	New constitution during US occupation based on older political institutions & postwar antimilitarism	No	1+
South Korea	New Democracy	Military Rightist Authoritarian	Opposition & middle class protests during Chun-Roh transition	No	2+
Singapore	Semidemocracy	Semidemocracy	Lee & PAP's consolidation of power by "economic miracle"	Yes	1
Taiwan	New Democracy	Rightist Authoritarian	Gradual reforms by ruling KMT under pressure from middle class & opposition	Yes	2+
Hong Kong	PRC "Colonial"	British Colonial	Some representative organs at end of colonial era	No	–
SOUTH ASIA					
India	Consolidated Democracy	Consold Democracy	Postcolonial institutions	Yes	2+
Pakistan	Semidemocracy	Rightist Military Authoritarian	Military coups against shaky democratic govts	Yes	2

Sri Lanka	Semidemocracy	New Dem to Semidem	"Constitutional games" by ruling parties; ethnic civil war	Yes	2
Bangladesh	Semidemocracy	Rightist Military Authoritarian	Elections after mil regime forced out, but parliament boycott by opposition	No	2
Burma	Rightist Military Authoritarian	Leftist Military Authoritarian	Military coups vs. weak democratic governments	Yes	—
SOUTHEAST ASIA					
Philippines	New Democracy	Semidemocracy to Rightist Auth	Military opposition to Marcos in post-election showdown; some US pressure	Yes	Multi
Malaysia	Semidemocracy	Semidemocracy	BN's cross-ethnic coalition	Yes	1+
Thailand	Semidemocracy	Rightist Military Authoritarian	Royal intervention after popular opposition to harsh coup	Yes	Multi
Papua New Guinea	Consolidated Democracy	New Democracy	Postcolonial institutions	Yes	Multi
Indonesia	Rightist Military Authoritarian	Rightist Military Authoritarian	Military coup vs. Sukarno & semidemocracy	Yes	—
Brunei	Rightist Traditional Authoritarian	Rightist Trad Authoritarian	Postcolonial sultanate	No	—
COMMUNIST					
China	Communist Authoritarian	Communist Authorit	Suppression of Tiananmen Square	Yes	1
North Korea	Communist Authoritarian	Communist Authorit	Little change after regime established	No	1
Mongolia	New Democracy	Communist Authorit	Opposition wins 2nd elections (1996)	No	2
Vietnam	Communist Authoritarian	Communist Authorit	Won anticolonial wars	No	1
Cambodia	Semidemocracy	Rightist to Commnst	Internationally imposed elections	No	2+
Laos	Communist Authoritarian	Rightist to Commnst	Little change after regime established	No	1

because of strong executive and bureaucratic leadership coupled with a "soft-ball" political culture—for example, General Suthorn, who led the military coup that ousted Prime Minister Chatichai in February 1991, invited Chatichai to a party in his home the following October (Fry 1992). Elsewhere, in great contrast, semidemocracy connotes instability: the continuing threat and occurrence of irregular transfers of government in Pakistan and Bangladesh or the combination of civil war conditions with less-than-democratic political infighting in Sri Lanka and Cambodia.

A far more serious challenge to the modernization perspective than simply noting the partial characteristics of democracy in many Asian settings is presented by the data in column 3 of Figure 2, which summarizes the key phase or reason for the success or failure of recent democratic transitions. Starkly, democratization is little correlated with modernization or its leading indicator, the level of economic development. Democracy commenced in most of Asia with postcolonial institutions in poor (that is, unmodernized) nations. In many cases the formal institutions and informal political practices evolved as indigenous political leaders shaped them to local conditions, often in ways that did not totally conform to Western concepts of democracy (India, Japan, Malaysia, Papua New Guinea, Singapore, and Sri Lanka, fit this pattern). In addition, the democratic transition from a military regime in Bangladesh occurred in what must be considered a premodern period; and democratic and authoritarian regimes have alternated episodically in Thailand (going back to the 1930s), Pakistan, and the Philippines dating well back before "modernization" was much advanced.

Moreover, the most important political factors associated with modernization are not strongly correlated with the success of democratic transitions either. Globally, both ethnic/religious polarization and fragmentation in the party system have been shown to produce much less conducive contexts for stable democratic polities (Diamond et al. 1989a; Haggard and Kaufman 1995). Yet the last two columns in Figure 2 suggest that this has not been the case in Asia. The polities with multiple parties (Papua New Guinea, the Philippines, and Thailand) may not have the most fully developed democracies, but they do not stand out in terms of instability and democratic slippage either. Conversely, Sri Lanka's "textbook" party system, in which two major parties alternate in office with a fair degree of regularity, may actually undermine democratic performance, since competition between the two Sinhalese parties makes it hard to end the ethnic civil war with the Tamil Tigers. This does not mean, however, that ethnic cleavage provides a master explanatory variable explaining democratic success in Asia. For example, India and Sri Lanka arguably faced worse ethnic/religious polarization than Bangladesh and Pakistan; yet their democratic performance has clearly been superior.

Similarly, conflict between prosperous Chinese communities and indigenous populations can be found in Indonesia, Malaysia, and Thailand, despite their very different democratic experiences.

Thus the Asian evidence that is consistent with modernization theory is somewhat scanty. Only the recent democratizations of South Korea and Taiwan really conform to the pattern depicted in Figure 1; and even here, one might legitimately raise the question of why democracy was delayed until these two countries reached a much higher level of economic development than most other Asian democracies and semidemocracies. On the nondemocratic side, in addition, the Sultanate in Brunei might be considered a "premodern" government. There is also some, but far from overwhelming, support for Samuel Huntington's (1968) theory of political decay—that democracy can overwhelm fragile governments in developing countries with demands from the newly enfranchised citizenry, thereby leading to democratic collapse. Thus governmental breakdown from political fragmentation and polarization can arguably be seen as an important factor in coups ending democratic periods in Burma, Pakistan, Indonesia, and (in a few of many cases) Thailand. Still, these negative effects of polarization and fragmentation, as argued above, appear more historical than current.

Also contradicting the model presented in Figure 1, the data in column 3 are quite at variance with the belief that the United States can take much credit for the third (or any earlier) wave of democracy in Asia, buttressing the argument made in Steve Chan's chapter. For the oft-cited cases of Taiwan and South Korea, indeed, the very opposite might be argued: U.S. support for authoritarian Cold War client regimes may well have, if anything, delayed democracy. There are three clearly more positive cases of American influence, but even here the actions of the United States are only part of the story. The U.S. occupation in Japan imposed a democratic constitution, but this built upon the institutions of a previous semidemocracy (the Taisho Democracy) in the early twentieth century and reflected broad-based popular rejection of the 1930s and 1940s military regime. Similarly, US pressure was clearly significant in forcing Ferdinand Marcos to hold elections and very reluctantly abide by the results, but Cory Aquino's People Power and the pragmatic calculations of the Filipino military (General Ramos is now president) almost certainly take pride of place in explaining the return of democracy to the Philippines. Finally, the United States was part of the international pressure that forced the recent elections in Cambodia, but the key to this positive influence is being part of a broader international consensus. Surely the memory of the "human rights" Carter administration's and the "anticommunist" Reagan administration's opposition to replacing the Khmer Rouge as Cambodia's (then Kampuchea's) representative at the

United Nations for reasons of "Great Power gamesmanship" does not imply a stellar American record of promoting democracy in that ravaged nation.

Developmental States, Democracy, and Asian "Economic Miracles"

The economic success of the East Asian capitalist states is often explained by the "developmental state" model. This school of development studies argues that a strong developmental state—or BAIR ("bureaucratic authoritarian industrializing regime") in Cumings's (1984) less favorable terminology— could promote successful industrialization projects. State power, according to this perspective, is necessary to mobilize the requisite resources for overcoming the high "entry barriers" that late industrializers face, and can be used as a counterweight to the great disparities in structural power facing many developing nations. In particular, the power and leadership of a skilled technocracy could both chart a course for industrial upgrading and prevent the power of traditional elites from holding back change. The East Asian state elites, moreover, did not intervene in the economy to distort markets and protect monopoly rents. Rather, after short periods of "infant industry" protection, they pursued "market-conforming" strategies and promoted exports and integration into the world economy, in contrast to the "import-substitution" strategy of industrialization followed in most other parts of the Third World (Amsden 1989; Johnson 1982; Wade 1990).

Given the spread of East Asian export dynamism to Southeast Asia, China, and South Asia during the 1980s, it might seem reasonable to suppose that other nations in the region had finally learned from East Asia's model of "Confucian capitalism," including the positive economic leadership that developmental states supposedly provided. The brief summaries of the Asian political economies in the first two columns of Figure 3, however, cast considerable doubt upon such an interpretation. As the crude ratings of national economic and social performance in the last four columns demonstrate, the developmental states in capitalist East Asia have certainly been quite successful in promoting "growth with equity"—that is, they have good records in both the economic and social realms. Yet other types of regimes have displayed considerable success as well. Moreover, whatever else may be included among the causes and consequences of the recent economic transformations in other parts of Asia, leadership by a strong developmental state was certainly not one of their characteristics. In fact, even the successful developmental states in East Asia appear to be deteriorating.

The five East Asian capitalist nations have produced both rapid growth (except for the recent recession in Japan) and good social outcomes, as attested to by the standard indicators of education, health, and (to a somewhat more variable extent) income inequality, thereby escaping what is often assumed to be a trade-off between promoting economic growth and social equity. In fact, they have been used to support the argument that investment in "human capital" not only does not detract from economic performance, but is in itself an important positive influence on economic development (Clark and Roy 1997). The contrast with Australia and New Zealand in developed Oceania is striking. These longtime democracies had a huge advantage over East Asia (with the partial exception of Japan) in both wealth and human capital at the beginning of the postwar era. Instead of pushing industrial upgrading through exports, however, they relied on the export of primary products, while protecting inefficient local industries that had parliamentary clout. The resulting economic stagnation led one unfortunate Australian minister to refer to his country as a "fledgling banana republic" in the mid-1980s (Higgott 1987), supporting the statist contention that government "autonomy" from social forces can be very helpful in pursuing a successful developmental project.

Even East Asia, though, is not totally consistent with the argument that a strong developmental state comes close to being a necessary and sufficient condition for strong economic performance, since the role of developmental states varies considerably among these five political economies. Two of the East Asian dragons, Japan and South Korea, have archetypical developmental states that implemented strong industrial policies supporting the push of large domestic corporations to become "national champions" in most of the world's leading industries (Amsden 1989; Gerlach 1992; Hart 1992; Johnson 1982; Okimoto 1989). Yet, even in Japan, many industrial sectors do not conform to the developmental state model, either because business provided the primary leadership (sometimes directly ignoring government "guidance") or because business-government relations were primarily clientelistic (Calder 1993). Furthermore, as indicated in the second column of Figure 3, both these developmental states appear to be heading toward an eclipse. In Korea, democratization and the developmental state's very success in creating strong conglomerates or *chaebôl* have clearly undercut the autonomy and leadership power of the technocracy. Japan appears to be suffering from a variety of ills deleterious to its vaunted developmental state: political gridlock in the domestic arena, a state bureaucracy now primarily concerned with protecting its power over the economy, and gross corruption in business-government relations (Clark and Roy 1997).

The other East Asian dragons, furthermore, have significantly different types of political economies. Singapore also clearly has a strong developmental state, but it has pursued a very different strategy of growth-through-invitation-to-TNCs (transnational corporations). In stark contrast, Hong Kong has had what may be the closest approximation to a laissez-faire economy in the world. Taiwan occupies something of a middle position. It has

Figure 3.

State and Development in Asia

	Primary State Economic Role	Recent Change in Economic System	Economic Growth Pre-1997 Short Term	Long Term	Asian Flu	Social Outcomes
DEVELOPED OCEANIA						
Australia	Protectionism due to vested interests	No	Low	Medium	No	High
New Zealand	Protectionism due to vested interests	No	Low	Medium	No	High
EAST ASIAN DRAGONS						
Japan	Effective developmental state based on business-government cooperation	Growing bureaucracy & corruption undercut developmental state	Low	High	No*	High
South Korea	Effective developmental state with strong government leadership	*Chaebŏl* power & democracy undercut developmental state	High	High	Yes	High
Singapore	Strong developmental state: recruited TNCs & state corporations	No	High	High	No	High
Taiwan	Developmental state in heavy ind & regulating TNCs, but just created conducive atmosphere for small business	Low-tech manufactures move to PRC	High	High	No	High
Hong Kong	Essentially laissez-faire economy	Low-tech manufactures move to PRC	High	High	High	Some Impact

South Asia

India	Strong state control over economy for industrialization created huge inefficiencies	Significant liberalization in 1980s & 1990s	High	Low	No	Medium
Pakistan	Statist economy like India's	Significantly less reform than in India	Medium	Low	No	Low
Bangladesh	Statist economy like India's	Significantly less reform than in India	Medium	Low	No	Low
Sri Lanka	Statist economy & large social programs	Market liberalization in 1980s	Medium	Medium	No	High
Burma	Socialist autarchy	New military regime woos foreign capital	Low	Low	No	Low

Southeast Asia

Philippines	From crony capitalism to macroeconomic stabilization	No	Medium	Medium then low	Some impact	High
Malaysia	Some development policies but no strong state like E. Asian dragons	Market liberalization in switch from import-sub to export-based industry	High	Medium	Yes	Medium
Thailand	Similar development strategy to Malaysia	Liberalization for export-based industry	High	Medium	Yes	Medium
Indonesia	Similar to Malaysia & Thailand	Some liberalization but less than Malaysia & Thailand	High	Medium	Yes	Low
Brunei	Traditional economy	No	Medium	Medium	No	Low
Papua NG	Traditional economy	No	Low	Medium	No	Low

COMMUNIST	Primary State Economic Role	Recent Change in Economic System	Economic Growth PRE 1997 Short Term	Long Term	Asian Flu	Social Outcomes
China	Command economy, heavy industry push	Market lib & *guanxi* capitalism in 1980s	High	Medium	No	High
North Korea	Command economy, heavy industry push	No	Low	Medium	No	Medium then low
Mongolia	Command economy, heavy industry push	Market reforms in 1990s	Medium	Low	No	Medium
Vietnam	Command economy, heavy industry push	Market reforms in 1990s	Medium	Low	No	Medium
Cambodia	Command economy, heavy industry push	Market reforms in 1990s	Medium	Low	No	Medium
Laos	Command economy, heavy industry push	Market reforms in 1990s	Medium	Low	No	Medium

*Japan's financial problems are not included in the "Asian Flu" because they stem from a much earlier era (the collapse of the bubble economy at the beginning of the 1990s) and because they are not related to inflows of foreign capital.

been touted as a very successful developmental state (Haggard 1990; Wade 1990) because state policy instituted the major structural shifts in the economy; yet much of Taiwan's dynamism, especially in the key export sector, comes from small-scale firms with few ties to the government (Fields, 1995; Lam and Clark 1994; Skoggard 1996).

A survey of the other three regions also raises questions about the developmental state model. The communist countries had an ideology advocating what might be considered a superdevelopmental state. Yet only two of the six (China and North Korea) followed the pattern of European communism of an initially successful industrialization drive that raised the popular standard of living but which, over time, became increasingly inefficient and unproductive. The other four had far less impressive records in both the economic and social realms. A similar pattern can be seen in South Asia. Most particularly in India, these governments exercised strong state control over the economy to promote industrialization and attack widespread poverty and inequality. Yet the results were inefficient patronage-based state corporations, domestic businesses that were content to reap monopoly rents behind protectionist walls, and (unlike China and North Korea) rather poor progress toward alleviating poverty and creating "human capital"—with the very notable exception of Sri Lanka's outstanding record in the area of social outcomes (Clark and Roy 1997; Rudolph and Rudolph 1987). Thus simply having a strong state committed to industrialization and social change is clearly no guarantee that these goals will be achieved.

In Southeast Asia, the state structures tended to be somewhat weaker and more open to social, especially business, pressures. The results in both economic and social terms were generally better than in South Asia, but few if any analysts give much credit to state leadership. Rather, there were more clientelistic links between business and top leaders which were more marked by payoffs for doing business rather than positive state support, with the "crony capitalism" of the Marcos regime marking an extreme example. Perhaps more tellingly for testing the developmental state model, the transformation of these economies from import-substitution to export-orientation, which thus far appears to be quite successful, did not involve state-directed development policies à la Japan, South Korea, and Singapore. In direct contrast, economic reform in these countries, as in China (Vogel, 1989) and South Asia, was primarily based upon market and trade liberalization, that is, the *withdrawal*, not the intensification, of state controls (Haggard and Kaufman 1995; MacIntyre 1994).

This rather spotty record of the developmental state in Asia, with its decidedly non-laissez-faire economies (the Hong Kong exception ended in July 1997), turns attention to what causes "nondevelopmental" policies when states try to influence their economies. The most blatant problems arise in what Peter Evans (1995) has termed "predatory states," which simply use their monopoly of force to extract resources from society (the former Zaire represents an extreme example). The clientelistic states in Southeast Asia and China's "*guanxi* capitalism" (*guanxi* refers to "personal relations") represent "limited predation" in which state officials extract payoffs for allowing businesses to operate but seem to be smart enough not to kill the goose laying their golden eggs. A second type of problem arises from policy mistakes from developmentally committed officials. For example, Taiwan's attempts to promote the automobile industry ended in dismal failure (Arnold, 1989); and South Korea's heavy-industry drive in the 1970s seemed disastrous in the 1980s, although Korea ultimately succeeded in many of these industries (Haggard and Moon 1990).

When such "mistakes" are not rectified in fairly short order (for example, India's deteriorating economic performance over several decades), however, the question arises of alternative motives for state intervention. It is here that Mancur Olson's (1982) theory of "distributional coalitions" appears most applicable. According to Olson, stable democracies over time generate strong interest groups that use their political power to distort the economy for their own advantage, in reality reaping monopoly rents. This provides a good explanation for the economic stagnation of Australia and New Zealand noted above; and the closed Indian economy allowed both state corporations and private businesses to live comfortably from the resulting monopoly rents (Bhagwati 1993). There is little reason to think that such a process might not occur in other settings as well. Japan's ministries now seem less concerned with promoting development and structural transformation than with holding back market liberalization that would threaten their power over the economy.

This also raises the question of the impact of democratization upon economic policy and performance. A priori, democracy could have very different effects on these perversions of economic policy. On the one hand, popular power could be expected to check the abuses of "predatory" authoritarian states. On the other, democratic pressures could undermine a state's ability to implement strategic economic policy or could create pressures for more extensive "distributional coalitions." Unfortunately, the data in Figure 3 show democracy to be far more associated with policy perversions than with policy reforms in Asia. All five "consolidated democracies" display policy gridlock and strong distributional coalitions. Democratization does not seem to have resulted in much change in the clientelistic nature of business-government relations in Southeast Asia (for example, Hutchcroft 1994 argues that the Aquino government brought little change to the "booty capitalism" of the Philippines). Moreover, democratization actually seems to be associated with growing corruption and business abuses in South Korea (for example, the recent scandal involving the family of then-president Kim Young Sam) and Taiwan (Moon and Prasad, 1994).

The possible contribution of democratization to the recent Asian financial crisis is much more ambiguous, however. The crisis resulted from a perverse combination of external financial liberalization and internal distorted and/or corrupt financial systems in several Asian nations. Financial liberalization under US and IMF pressure in many (but not all) of the East and Southeast Asian nations during the 1990s brought a tremendous inflow of "hot" investment funds to profit from rapid Asian growth. In countries with poor financial controls, however, speculation and outright criminality ultimately produced huge losses that forced devaluations, thereby stimulating capital flight (Fischer 1998; Norton 1998). In several countries, democratization (for example, South Korea and perhaps Thailand) might bear some blame for weakening state controls over the financial sector. However, authoritarian protection of corrupt practices was clearly the major problem in several others (for example, Malaysia and particularly Indonesia).

Thus the Asian economic dynamism of the 1990s most emphatically cannot be explained by the developmental state model. Instead, a complex regional economy and division of labor appears to be evolving. What now appears to be the driving force in this regional economy are the linkages between transnational firms and indigenous businesses that often rest in informal connections, such as those that exist among Chinese business communities in many countries (Bernard and Ravenhill 1995). This growth of international "network production" obviously undercuts state power over the economy, leading to what Susan Strange (1996) has called "the retreat of the state," implying that international conditions are now becoming less favorable for developmental state activities.

Implications

This review of Asia's political economies, therefore, strongly challenges the modernization model presented in Figure 1. Most fundamentally, as summarized in Figure 4, modernization seems only vaguely related to democratic transitions and consolidations in Asia and does not appear to have had a positive impact upon the region's impressive economic performance. More derivatively for the theory sketched in Figure 1, the U.S. influence on Asia's "third wave" of democratization appears quite limited; and the "developmental state model" has only limited (and now clearly declining) applicability for explaining Asia's stellar economic performance. Rather, as highlighted by the boldfaced conclusions in Figure 4, each country's specific political economy appears to be shaped to a considerable extent by its own elite bargaining and political institutions, as well as by the culturally conditioned nature of society—consistent with recent theorizing about the nature of democratic transitions (Diamond et al. 1989a; Friedman, 1994; O'Donnell et al. 1986).

Figure 4.

Challenges to Assumptions of Modernization Interpretation

A. Causes of Democratic Transitions

1. Little correlation between democratic transitions and level of modernization in Asia, although partial support that a lack of modernization created "political decay" in earlier periods.

2. Democratic government fairly episodic in some countries.

3. Relationship between Asian culture and democratic goals contested (e.g., "Asian democracy" of Singapore and Malaysia).

4. While U.S. influence important in a few cases (Japan and the Philippines), it was immaterial to most.

5. Thus, nature of Asian regimes primarily determined by domestic elite bargaining (i.e., prerequisites for democracy only loosely important).

B. Results of Democratization

1. Longtime democracies (i.e., Australia, India, New Zealand, Sri Lanka, and, in 1990s, Japan) have subpar economic records.

2. Democratization seemingly undercutting effectiveness of Asian developmental states (and other types of regimes) following logic of "distributional coalitions."

C. Developmental State Model

1. Tremendous variation among East Asian political economies.

2. Southeast Asia, South Asia, and Dengist China have rapid growth without developmental state.

3. Similarly, Evan's "cultural embeddedness" explanation for success of East Asian developmental state does not apply elsewhere in Asia.

4. Spread of economic dynamism from East Asia based on regional linkages, reflecting "more than either market or state."

5. Thus, "state-in-society" more accurate than "developmental state" for conceptualizing Asia's recent economic success.

The weaknesses of applying the optimistic modernization faith in a new era of Western-style democratic capitalism to Asia should not be taken, however, to imply either a pessimistic outlook upon the future of the region or a "nattering nabobs of negativism" approach to the theory of development. Instead, the conclusion that Asia's political institutions and economic performance are primarily determined by indigenous factors should be optimistic.

Simplistically, since Asia is now marked by a goodly degree of democracy and (at least before the "Asian flu") by a generally strong economic performance, the essentially domestic derivation of these phenomena suggests that these "good things" may well continue in the future.

At a broader theoretical level, the developmental state model is now being challenged by what Joel Migdal and his associates (1994) term the "state-in-society" perspective—that is, national performance is not determined just by autonomous governments but by states in combination with broader social forces. For example, Peter Evans (1995) argues that many Asian governments have avoided becoming "predatory states" precisely because state elites are "embedded" within broader cultural and social structures. This brings us to a paradoxical perspective on Asian cultures and societies. On the one hand, scholars such as Lucian Pye (1985) have argued that the "cultural dimensions of authority" are substantially different in Asia than in the West. In particular, the greater emphasis on status and hierarchy in Asian conceptions of power creates a type of "paternalistic authority" that may be hard to reconcile with fully democratic institutions and practices. In short, Asian cultures may well inhibit the emergence of a "civil society," which the essays in this book by Stephen Macedo and Lucian Pye found to be central for democratization. Such an argument might be used to explain the "partial" nature of democracy in many Asian polities. Indeed, Larry Diamond (1989) argued that many Asian countries suffer from an "underdevelopment" of the normal institutions in a democratic polity (that is, parties, legislatures, specialized and expert bureaucracies).

Yet before we accept such an interpretation, it is certainly worth remembering the long-standing Weberian orthodoxy that Asian cultures stifled entrepreneurship and capitalism. Thus, just as aspects of Confucian culture are now seen as stimulating developmental activities (Hofheinz and Calder 1982; Fallows 1994; Pye 1985), the emphasis on family and group ties may well be quite functional for creating an independent sphere or "civil society" outside state control, which, while somewhat different from Western individualism and associational life, may serve as a viable foundation for democratic politics. For example, the essays in this volume by both Bruce Cumings and Lucian Pye start with the premise that Asia may be deficient in the normally conceived components of civil society, but then find substantial political activities outside state control in several Asian contexts, while Steve Chan directly argues that strong caution is needed in using Western premises to evaluate Asian polities because "Asian sandals do not fit Western feet" (that is, theories from modernization to Marxism). Certainly, even the very broad-brush overview presented here indicates that many Asian countries have found a way to reconcile active democratic politics with their own social and political institutions.

10

Democratic Inauguration
and Transition in East Asia

Steve Chan

Introduction

The recent "third wave" of democratization (Huntington 1991) has produced for the first time in history a majority of democratic states in the international system. This development has encouraged hopes for a more peaceful world, given the by-now well-known phenomenon that democracies seldom, if ever, fight one another (Russett 1993). Some observers even argue that the recent resurgence of democracy—and the decline of authoritarianism—signal an "end of history" (Fukuyama 1992), as the ideas of popular rule and human dignity have won a decisive final victory on the battlefield of ideologies. All that remains now is a matter of implementing these ideals.

Developments in East Asia seem to confirm such optimism. Long-term authoritarian regimes in Taiwan, South Korea, and Thailand have opened their political processes to mass participation and political opposition. Personal liberties—at least in terms of social and economic, if not political, freedoms—have made tremendous gains in China and Vietnam. With few exceptions (most notably, Burma and North Korea), civil society and the private economic sector have gained greater autonomy from and influence relative to the once-powerful "developmental states" in this region.

It even appears that the experience of the East Asian countries holds wider implications for theory and policy, because it offers an impressive example of "how democracy can be won." Although their political culture has been considered rather inhospitable to Western liberal ideals (see, for example, Huntington 1993; Pye and Pye 1985), their recent political transformation presumably demonstrates that these principles of governance have universal applicability beyond the latter's original European or European-heritage core. The experience of East Asia, or at least the capitalist, export-oriented part of that region, apparently validates the classic liberal thought and the once seemingly discredited "modernization" view that economic and political freedom (see, for example Friedman 1962; Hayek 1960), and democracy and capitalism (Olson 1993; Schumpeter 1942), and political and economic development (Cutright 1963; Burkhart and Lewis-Beck 1994) go hand in hand. The newly industrializing economies of East Asia show that such a "virtuous cycle" can be replicated outside Western Europe and North America, thus pointing the way for other developing countries to follow.

East Asia's experience seems to present another conclusion, namely, external influence can be pivotal. Above all, the U.S. is seen to have played the paramount role in opening up the markets and governments in this region. Had it not been for Washington's efforts, land reform, economic liberalization, and political competition would have been stifled or at least greatly delayed. The US is therefore given much credit for the breakup of Japan's prewar *zaibatsu*, the redistribution of land in Taiwan, the promotion of civilian technocrats as well as the moderation of military rule in South Korea and Thailand, and the legitimation of political opposition and respect for human rights in all countries in the region. Even when and where political dissidence is suppressed (such as China's Tiananmen Square crackdown), things would have been worse had it not been for the international protest led by Washington.

Such is at least the conventional wisdom on East Asia's "developmentalism." Yet while obviously containing some truth, these generalizations are not without some problematic aspects. The following discussion addresses several relevant concerns, including (1) the meaning of democracy, (2) historical conditions germane to its development in East Asia, and (3) speculations about the foreign policy implications of this region's democratization.

Conceptual Confusion

The meaning of democracy is not obvious. The Greek *polis* institutionalized direct participation by citizens, even though both citizenship and participation were severely limited to a minority of the adult population. The Lockean tradition emphasized the idea of social contract, suggesting that rulers must derive their right to rule from the consent of the ruled. The classic liberal conception is concerned with protecting civil liberties from infringement by the government. Marxian criticisms and the advent of the welfare state after the Great Depression helped to promote the notion of substantive democracy, justifying distributive justice and the fulfillment of basic needs as a government responsibility. Finally, in U.S. scholarship, democracy is frequently associated with and defined in terms of political participation and competition (see Dahl 1971). In this chapter, I will settle for the minimum definition of contested elections with full adult suffrage.

Nevertheless, the different perspectives, principles, and practices suggested by the various traditions lead to several observations. First, the concept of democracy is a matter of considerable intellectual—and indeed, political—contestation. Should it include or emphasize popular sovereignty, individual freedom, political participation, electoral competition, distributive equity, or mass welfare? In theory as well as practice, these desiderata stand in tension with each other. As attested by recent election returns in Algeria (for Islamic fundamentalists) and referendum results in the United States (for example, gay rights in Colorado, affirmative action in California), populism, official accountability, and political correctness do not necessarily coincide. Moreover, by ruling certain elements "in" (for example, regularly scheduled elections) as part of the definition of democracy, and other elements "out" (for example, the actual extent of political participation), one can arrive at very different "democracy" scores for countries.

Second, the concept of democracy has evolved over time. Before the twentieth century, liberalism—emphasizing personal freedom and the minimalist state—was the dominant theme. At the same time, republicanism—defined as the rule of law and equal rights for *qualified* citizens—was championed in some circles. At the turn of century, the bureaucratic state in the sense of the Weberian ideal type was much admired. More recently, governmental intervention to correct social injustices or market inefficiencies has become more identified with democratic practices. Often these different, even incompatible, ideas are conflated in contemporary discussion. For instance, although Immanuel Kant is routinely invoked as the first influential voice advocating democratic peace, his emphasis was distinctly on republicanism as a basis for interstate peace (Huntley 1996). Kant was rather skeptical about majoritarian rule, and indeed would not consider himself a democrat if democracy is defined as the rule of popular will. As another example, although Woodrow Wilson is widely seen as a proponent of national self-determination and as an advocate of universalizing democracy, he was less convinced by the virtues of mass sovereignty than by those of an efficient administrative state—with the Kaiser's Germany offering the most advanced example (Oren 1995).

Third, and as a result of the above tendencies, remarks about the extent and level of democracy for a particular country or era are subject to definitional confusion and historical revisionism. For instance, Owen (1994, p. 102) argues that compared to its contemporaries, Britain before the 1832 Great Reform Act was liberal but undemocratic, whereas the Confederacy during the US Civil War was democratic but illiberal—if by democracy one means that a relatively large percentage of the male adults had the right to vote. Imperial Germany was, until the outbreak of World War I, held up by leading Americans as the exemplar of efficient administration and progressive social programs (Oren 1995). More recently, authoritarian China outperformed democratic India when judged by the standards of local participation and mass welfare (Sorensen 1993). And, of course, during the era of the Cold War, all those joined the United States in opposing communism were granted automatic membership in the free world—regardless of the fact that many of these allies routinely engaged in severe domestic repression.

It is therefore not surprising that discourse on democracy has often been criticized as subjective, ethnocentric, inconsistent, incomplete, and biased (see, for example, Bollen 1993; Oren 1995; Scoble and Wiseberg 1981). This discourse also often "stretches" the concept of democracy (Collier and Levitsky 1997). More seriously, whether a country is considered democratic or not sometimes reflects changes in official policy. Thus Oren (1995, p. 147) argues that the values embodied in the definition of democracy "are the products, more than determinants, of America's past foreign political relations."

Assertions about the recent worldwide surge of democracy have typically focused more on the spatial spread of formally democratic structures than on their temporal resilience. Moreover, interests in the *broadening* or diffusion of democratic institutions across countries have generally not been matched by concerns about the *deepening* of democratic ethos within specific countries. Although more countries have recently adopted democratic *forms* in terms of the formal structures of governance (for example, universal suffrage, multiparty competition, contested elections, legislative oversight), it is not evident that their leaders and people have internalized democratic *norms* such as those regarding tolerance, compromise, and sharing power. Judged by the latter standards, it is unclear how effective the democratization process has been in East Asia. Indeed, the civic culture of even established democracies is a source of concern (see Sandel 1996).

When one looks at the mass and elite attitudes lying beneath the apparent structural transformation toward greater democracy, one finds rather important differences in the political cultures of East and West. The former countries tend to emphasize the values of group conformity and collective well-being, whereas personal freedom and civil liberties are stressed in the latter countries. There is in the former countries also a greater acceptance and even expectation that the government should serve as a custodian of public interests, thus justifying state intervention in the marketplace, promotion of public morality, and regulation of personal conduct, which tend to be seen in the West as illegitimate government interference in matters properly reserved for personal privacy and individual choice. As a general tendency, "the Lockean American is so fundamentally anti-government that he identifies government with restrictions on government" (Huntington 1968, p. 7). This preference for the virtues of a minimalist state is not shared in the East. Likewise, personal liberty has a distinctly less exalted place than social integration ("harmony") as a collective good. Moreover, good government is defined in terms of not so much the rule of law as the personal authority of especially virtuous leaders and just administration by an elite meritocracy (Chan and Clark 1992–93). Order and stability tend to be emphasized at the expense of competition and freedom (Pye 1967). The appearance of multiparty politics and electoral contest does not necessarily suggest a concomitant change in mass ethos. A civic culture of democratic norms generally follows imperfectly and belatedly the introduction of democratic institutions (Muller and Seligson 1994). Moreover, the success of democratic transition is more likely to be a result of negotiated pacts by elite factions than the politics of mass mobilization (Shin 1994).

Domestic Context

One recurrent theme of the companion chapters in this volume is that external influences are much less significant than internal ones in shaping a country's democratization. This view receives support from Ray's (1995) assessment of the relative role played historically by systemic-level and state-specific forces in motivating regime transformation. For each subperiod studied by him, the former turned out to be much weaker than the latter. For instance, systemic-level forces were responsible for only 2.7 percent (1865 to 1905), 1.4 percent (1905 to 1945), and 0.6 percent (1945 to 1985) of the changes in democratic scores for those countries included in his worldwide sample, compared to, respectively, 17.8 percent, 29.3 percent, and 28.5 percent accounted for by country-specific forces. These results do not encourage optimism in the efficacy of external intervention to promote democratization; they direct our attention instead to domestic conditions and processes.

Regime Legitimacy and Effectiveness

It is possible for a regime to recover its legitimacy through effective policy performance. Regime legitimacy was seriously deficient in the late 1940s and early 1950s because all the subsequent "miracle economies" of East Asia were suffering from the effects of debilitating domestic turmoil, disastrous military defeat, and/or unpopular alien occupation. Their ruling elites were seriously discredited because of terrible misrule producing rampant inflation, mass starvation, widespread graft, and war devastation.

At the end of World War II or their respective civil wars, the East Asian countries were hardly paragons of democratic virtue—indeed, Japan was under U.S. occupation, and Taiwan and South Korean were "garrison states" (Amsden, 1979) under authoritarian leaders who had been saved from their communist challengers only because the United States had come to their aid. The United States was at that time widely perceived as a defender of conservative political and economic interests, and a supporter of right-wing autocracies in the name of containing communism. Moreover, despite Washington's wartime proclamations in favor of national self-determination and democratic rule, its subsequent policies belied these ideals. In the ensuing contest between European colonialism (for example, the French in Vietnam) and Asian nationalism, it chose to support the former.

The legacies of Japanese colonialism, Chinese or Korean civil war, and American influence produced conservative ruling coalitions in the noncommunist countries of the region. With Washington's support, leftist political groups were banned or suppressed, and organized labor was domesticated and excluded from governance. The practically uninterrupted rule by a single conservative party, the concentration of economic power in large business conglomerates, the dominance of executive authority over legislative oversight, and the powerful influence and political autonomy of ministerial bureaucracies represent the hallmarks of these countries' political economies and can be traced to these legacies. The systematic and continuing exclusion of organized labor from the political process is an especially salient feature of the bodies politic of Taiwan, South Korea, and Japan, and distinguishes them from the social and plural democracies of Western Europe and North America, where workers' representatives command a large presence at the table of governance.

Whereas Western liberal discourse tends to stress procedural legitimacy defined in terms of partisan contest, political participation, mass suffrage, and regular elections, East Asia's experience demonstrates the importance of substantive legitimacy defined in terms of the regime's ability to provide tangible economic reward and persuasive evidence of merit-based social mobility. Regime legitimacy is more than a matter of implementing regular elections; it cannot be secured or sustained when there are widespread socioeconomic inequity and failure to meet basic needs. Effectiveness in addressing these problems distinguishes Taiwan and South Korea from the Philippines, which has had a longer history of electoral contests among oligarchs but less progress in advancing mass well-being. Taiwanese and Korean officials were more attuned to Huntington (1968) and Gerschenkron (1962) than to Locke and Smith. They perceived that their most pressing policy challenge, to paraphrase the former writers, was not to run elections but to organize society and launch industrialization. It would be wrong to dismiss these views, as political cultures in other transitional states such as those in East and Central Europe tend to also stress the state's substantive responsibilities relative to its procedural ones (see Cirtautas and Mokrzycki 1993).

In terms of the standard prerequisites for democracy such as industrialization, urbanization, education, and mass communication (Lipset 1994, 1963), the East Asian countries are overdue for democratization. Having already made substantial socioeconomic gains, Taiwan and South Korea do not have to deal simultaneously with the challenges of undertaking fundamental economic *and* political reforms, as the East European countries, for example, do. By implication, recently democratizing countries elsewhere face a severe challenge to the extent that they lack the favorable socioeconomic conditions characterizing the East Asians. Indeed, for many East Europeans, democratization and market reform have brought about both relative and absolute socioeconomic deprivation, therefore seriously undermining the legitimacy of the post communist leadership.

Reform from Above

The East Asian countries have been more effective than the rest of the developing world in dampening or skirting what conventional social science has taken to be the overriding development paradoxes. Simply put, these developmental paradoxes reflect the "stylized facts" that while modernity promotes democracy, modernization has the opposite effect. More specifically, at least since the classic works of Huntington (1968), Lipset (1963), Olson (1963), and Kuznets (1955), we understand that while a high *level* of economic development and its concomitants (for example, mass communication, literacy, urbanization) are conducive to democracy, a high *rate* of socioeconomic change tends to produce political instability and socioeconomic inequity. Significantly, democratic institutions and ethos are unlikely to be secured in an environment of widespread political turmoil and social frustration (Strouse and Claude 1976).

Arguably the East Asian countries have had much more success than other developing countries in achieving "growth with equity" and "growth with stability." Their democratic progress was more a by-product of this achievement than its initial inspiration. In economics as well as politics, the relevant endeavors were orchestrated by the ruling elites, who were initially more motivated by concerns with national security and competition with communist rivals than any commitment to mass sovereignty. These were, by and large, reforms undertaken by initiatives from above rather than due to pressure from below.

After being rescued by the United States from the brink of political extinction, the leaders of Taiwan and South Korea took steps to centralize and consolidate power in their respective territorial remnant. They created a relatively efficient "developmental state" and placed it at the commanding heights of their political economy. Overruling the objections of rural gentry, land was redistributed to the small farmers—thus laying the basis for raising agricultural productivity and for creating a relatively egalitarian society. Rural surplus, official credits, and U.S. largesse in turn facilitated export-driven industrialization. At least in the first years of this export drive, these countries as well as the other Asian little dragons pushed the only comparative advantage in their favor—namely, a cheap and abundant labor supply. As already noted, one of the most notable aspects of their political economy as well as that of Japan is the exclusion of labor from the "pact of domination" consisting of conservative politicians, powerful bureaucrats, and big businesses. This state of affairs has continued with only minor modifications to this date.

With the exception of Hong Kong, the post--World War II economic ascendance of Japan, the little dragons (Taiwan, South Korea, and Singapore), and the ASEAN (Association of Southeast Asian Nations) members following their path was orchestrated by their government (Amsden, 1989; Gold 1986; Hewison 1989; Johnson 1982; MacIntyre 1994; Wade 1990). In South Korea there was a strong and consistent bias for large conglomerates and heavy industries, ostensibly for the sake of national security. In Singapore, state entrepreneurship joined hands with large multinational corporations (Clark and Chan 1995; Deyo 1981). In these countries as well as Japan and Taiwan (Calder 1988; Chan and Clark 1992; Tien 1996), sustained economic growth provided the wherewithal for addressing the social and political conflict over competing distributive claims and, after a period of time, produced a sizeable middle class.

Political participation followed, and was until recently quite limited. Most have been ruled by a cohesive elite and their electoral processes dominated by a continuous ruling party (for example, Japan's Liberal Democratic Party, Taiwan's Kuomintang, Singapore's People's Action Party). In Hong Kong, where the authority of the appointed British governor was absolute, electoral contest and mass suffrage were not even given lip service until the last few years, after Britain agreed to return it to Chinese sovereignty (Cheek-Milby 1995).

In most East Asian countries, an effective accommodation seems to have been reached whereby politics has been kept out of those key sectors underpinning their successful export drives. In particular, monetary and fiscal policies have been depoliticized. To use Johnson's (1981) well-known remark, "politicians reign, bureaucrats rule." The latter have been deliberately insulated from social interests and electoral politics in order to give them greater autonomy. This phenomenon, of course, is very different from a view of democracy based on the organization, representation, and competition of rival interest groups for access and influence in the policy-making process.

Policy Sequence

As already implied, East Asia's experience shows that timing and sequence, as Huntington and Lipset reminded us long ago, are critical. The lesson offered by this experience is that order and growth should precede participation and distribution. The recent experiences of China and Russia present an especially dramatic contrast. Beijing promoted economic liberalization but resisted political liberalization. In Russia, economic reform came about a decade later than in China, and it followed glasnost and perestroika to change the political system. Mikhail Gorbachev's efforts, however, left the Communist Party and the state apparatus discredited and demoralized. This state of affairs led Samuel Huntington (1992–93, p. 12) to observe that:

> Liberalization, first, then democratization makes a great deal of sense for those who wish to achieve both goals. Opening up the political system first, in contrast, is likely to complicate economic reform. In 1989, I was told by top advisors to Gorbachev that they had made a horrible mistake in moving ahead with *glasnost* and a political opening, which had unleashed all sorts of political forces which were then making it very difficult to move toward economic reform. "We should have first concentrated power and pushed economic reform," they argued, "and let the political opening wait. Instead, we did the reverse, and now we no longer have the authority to do what is necessary."

Graham Allison (1992–93, p. 17) echoed the same view, noting that "the problem [for Russia] is not too much authority in the center, but rather too little." Moscow, therefore, has faced great difficulty in implementing the painful economic adjustment. In contrast, "the Chinese model is very interesting in this respect. While maintaining authority sufficient to take the actions required, China has been able to do—not in [a] big-bang mode, but in a gradual and deliberate mode—many of the hard things that needed to be done, such as feeding its population." That central authority should be consolidated to make the necessary economic adjustments and that economic development should come before political change lie at the core of the orthodox East Asian political thinking, and represent the received wisdom derived from the experiences of the Little Dragons. These views argue for setting priorities instead of mounting simultaneous reform on multiple fronts, and for settling for gradual but sustained gains as opposed to undertaking immediate and drastic changes (political or economic "shock therapy") in the hope of achieving systemic transformation overnight.

Security Environment

East Asia's "developmental state" has increasingly come under social pressure—very much as a result of its own success. Greater affluence and social awareness, as Lipset would have predicted, have followed socioeconomic development. There is, moreover, as observed elsewhere (Inglehart 1990, 1977), the ongoing process of *embourgeoisement* that accompanies rising mass affluence and education. These changes in turn have challenged bureaucratic discretion and the authority of ruling parties. Yet what do these changes—in favor of greater political influence for citizens, and more public accountability for officials—augur? One interpretation, that of the Kantian perspective already alluded to, would argue for political convergence among different states, leading to the possible formation of a "pacific union." As countries become more democratic, they share more values and institutions—thus reducing the areas of contention among them in the first place and, should disputes occur among them, improving the prospects that their differences will be resolved through peaceful means. Indeed, there is considerable empirical evidence to support this view (see Chan 1997 for a review of the literature).

But democratization can be a double-edged sword. In the context of two-level games (Evans et al. 1993; Putnam 1988), it can reduce the bargaining space for international negotiators faced with the problem of domestic ratification. More extensive interest mobilization and greater public influence may hinder rather than promote international agreements. One recent study argued that a more assertive public impeded Ukraine's compliance with the nuclear nonproliferation accord whereas, unconstrained by popular sentiments, authoritarian Kazakhstan was able to be more responsive to this convention (Kozhemiakin 1994). Another case study (Lehman and McCoy 1992), focusing on Brazil's debt problems, concluded that under conditions of severe internal constraints, fragile democracies may be more prone to engage in diplomatic brinkmanship and risk the collapse of international negotiations than their authoritarian counterparts (who may be both more willing and more able to impose internationally dictated concessions on their domestic constituents). Indeed, it is quite plausible that the United States will encounter a rising incidence of economic friction with the East Asians, whose politicians will come under increasing domestic pressure to resist Washington's demands for "fair trade."

Democracies may therefore face greater domestic *constraints* to making foreign concessions. They may also have greater *incentives* to initiate and escalate foreign conflict under certain circumstances. Authoritarian regimes are likely to use force to suppress domestic unrest. When faced with similar internal opposition and turmoil, democracies try instead to divert domestic attention by using force internationally. Gelpi's (1997, p. 278) statistical analysis shows a strong pattern suggesting that the "diversionary initiation of force is generally a product of democratic systems." A reluctance by the elite to engage in domestic repression, combined with the public's tendency to rally behind the flag, creates incentives to undertake violence abroad.

Although established democracies have almost never waged war against one another, the pacifism of newly democratizing countries is more questionable. Mansfield and Snyder (1995, p. 8) contend that "*democratizing* states—those that have recently undergone regime change in a democratic direction—are much more war-prone than states that have undergone no regime change, and are somewhat more war-prone than those that have undergone a change in an autocratic direction." The transition processes can in themselves be a source of elite vulnerability and political fragmentations, leading to ethnic mobilization, racial demagoguery, and assertive nationalism. Although Mansfield's and Snyder's evidence is challenged by some (Thompson and Tucker 1997), the view that democratization as a process—as distinct from a country's level of consolidated democracy—does not in itself promote international peace seems to be supported.

Quantitative studies of the democratic-peace proposition suggest two other possible concerns. The cross-national relationship between levels of democracy and propensity for conflict involvement appears to be curvilinear. The "partially free" states—alternatively known as "anocracies," which have both democratic and autocratic features—tend to be more prone to international conflict than full-fledged democracies and autocracies (see Rummel 1987; Vincent, 1987). Moreover, among the nondemocracies, those that are structurally more constrained by the need for power-sharing and political competition have actually had a higher percentage of their international disputes escalating to war than others that are not similarly constrained (Morgan and Schwebach 1992, p. 315). These patterns imply that as states embark on democratic transformation, their foreign conduct may not initially create a more peaceful external environment. The transitional nature of their regimes may actually produce the opposite effect.

Internal instability and turmoil in the democratic or democratizing states sometimes lead to foreign intervention. These states may be the initiator or the target of such intervention (sometimes undertaken by their fellow democracies). Kegley and Hermann (1995) have shown that the danger of military intervention is not removed between pairs of democracies. Significant normative and structural barriers discourage democratic regimes from waging outright war against each other (see Russett 1993). The relevant literature (Chan 1997), however, suggests that these constraints do not appear to bar them from undertaking conflict at lower levels of intensity. The United States, for example, has engaged in both covert subversion and overt intervention against popularly elected leftist governments (for example, in Guatemala, Chile, Iran).

Given the recency of democratic initiation in much of East Asia, its effects on the region's security environment are still uncertain. There is, however, some tentative and anecdotal evidence suggesting that the process of democratization may not produce a substantial immediate "peace dividend." For instance, military spending accelerated, at least in the short term, after the initiation of democratic opening in Taiwan, South Korea, and the Philippines (Chan 1998). As hypothesized by Huntington (1991), fragile civilian administrations facing serious domestic opposition and lacking institutional ties with the military—such as Corazon Aquino's government in the Philippines—appear to be especially inclined to increase the defense budget as a way of appeasing the armed forces and securing their support.

It also seems that the introduction of electoral competition can incline both the political incumbent and its opposition to engage in domestically popular but internationally destabilizing policies. Taiwan's "pragmatic diplomacy," including its recent efforts to gain entry into the United Nations, offers such an example. It is perceived by China as an attempt to change the status quo from de facto autonomy for the island to de jure independence, thus precipitating the cross-strait crisis in 1995.

Thus the domestic conditions of newly democratizing countries—in the form of both constraints and incentives—could have certain destabilizing effects internationally. Reversing the causal arrow, one may also ask how foreigners are likely to treat these countries in democratic transition. Naturally, democratic norms are not fully developed in the more recent and fragile democracies (Russett 1993, p. 34). Therefore they are not likely to be seen by their more established counterparts to be stable or dependable in their international conduct. Their constitutional pledges and formally democratic structures lack credibility since they have not met the test of time through customary and persistent practice. By implication, a more secure international environment depends not only on an expanding number of new democracies, but also on their ability to sustain and consolidate the relevant norms and institutions. The longevity of democratic regimes is important, as it signals reliability and resilience to foreigners.

But the perceived policy orientation of a regime also matters. Specifically, several recent studies have argued that democracies have historically been status quo powers, and as such, they are unlikely to *initiate* crises with the aim of challenging the existing international order (Gelpi 1997; Rousseau et al. 1996). Thus a "self-selection" process operates to reduce the incidence of crisis involvement by democracies compared to nondemocracies. Once they are in a crisis (often initiated by authoritarian challengers), however, democracies can be quite belligerent in their behavior toward the nondemocracies. It becomes therefore important to determine whether democracies are inherently more peaceful than nondemocracies because of the nature of their political systems, or whether these states are more peaceful because they have been satisfied with the international status quo. Would democracies still be less inclined to initiate or escalate crises if and when they became dissatisfied with a new international order?

This question is especially germane in a context of considerable status mobility in the international hierarchy. Schweller (1992) argues that, depending on the regime type of both the declining and ascending powers, the process of power transition may lead to a peaceful or a violent outcome. When faced with an unfavorable power shift, a declining authoritarian hegemon may wage a preventive war against the rising power. This option, however, is unavailable to a declining democratic hegemon, which is likely to accommodate an upstart if the latter is perceived as a fellow democracy inclined to preserve the status quo. It will seek to form a counterbalancing alliance if the challenger is perceived as an authoritarian and revisionist power. These hypothesized reactions to impending power transition are necessarily inferred from a relatively small number of historical cases. Most of these cases came from the North Atlantic area, where intraregional differences in political norms and institutions appear comparatively small when they are contrasted with those prevailing in other "civilizations" (Huntington 1993). The logic of Schweller's argument suggests that the rising status of China is likely to arouse much more concern in Washington than that of Japan, but neither of these countries enjoys the same degree of cultural proximity and political affinity that facilitated Britain's accommodation of US ascendancy. Moreover, Washington's reaction to Beijing's mounting capabilities is likely to involve the development of a blocking coalition joined perhaps by its members' common democratic experience.

Most standard accounts assume that democracies are also status quo powers, whereas authoritarian challengers seek to alter the prevailing order. If so, the increasing number of democratizing states in East Asia should, in the long run, produce a more stable environment, even though their short-term pacifying effects are more problematic, as already suggested. Democracies, however, can also be revisionist. The proposed expansion of NATO, increased economic embargo against Castro's Cuba (for example, the Helms-Burton Act), and mounting pressure on Beijing's performance on human rights could be perceived as deliberate attempts to change the status quo. An expansive vision of democratic crusade has been used in the past to justify covert subversion and overt intervention, and can itself become a source of international instability (Forsythe 1992; Kegley and Hermann 1995).

Conclusion

Starting from a serious legitimacy deficit at the end of World War II, the East Asian countries have been able to rebound on the basis of a sustained record of "growth with equity." The recent democratic reforms in Taiwan, South Korea, and indeed even Japan are suggestive of political reality playing catch-up to their considerable socioeconomic achievements. Significantly, efforts that led to the latter achievements were spurred by devastating setbacks in civil or foreign wars. In that sense, a challenging external security environment contributed to the urgency to undertake domestic socioeconomic reforms, which in turn helped later to facilitate the democratization process. These reforms were undertaken by a bureaucratic authoritarian state and a conservative elite buttressed by the legacies of Japanese colonialism and the US containment policy.

There is much empirical support for the proposition that established democracies rarely, if ever, go to war against each other. It is much more problematic, however, to infer from this proposition that the newly democratizing countries are also more peaceful in their international conduct. These states may instead face more severe constraints in making foreign concessions and have greater incentives to initiate diversionary crises. There is also some fragmentary evidence to suggest that when faced with serious domestic challenges, weak democracies may resort to appeasing the armed forces and appealing to ethnonationalist causes. Thus, the ongoing democratization process in East Asia may not produce a "peace dividend" in the short run. As the countries in this region gain greater democratic maturity in the longer run and as they deepen their economic interdependence, the prospects for regional security become brighter.

Part V

The Challenge of

Consolidation in Russia

and Eastern Europe

11

Regime Transition and Democratic
Consolidation: Federalism and
Party Development in Russia

Thomas F. Remington

Obstacles to Democratic Transition

The central problem of democratic transitions is that the very factors that break down an ineffective authoritarian regime also impede the consolidation of democracy in the successor regime (Huntington 1991). The compound economic and political crisis, the profound alienation of the populace from the state, severe social divisions, the weakness of mediating institutions between state and society—all are inherited by the new rulers. Under favorable circumstances they may enjoy a honeymoon period in which they can enact an austerity program to restore macroeconomic balance and channel political conflict into arenas that strengthen constitutional government. Under unfavorable conditions, the successor regime reverts to authoritarianism.

In the last decade, communist regimes throughout Eastern Europe and the former USSR have undergone revolutionary transformations. In some of the former communist states, democratic regimes have emerged from the process. In others, new forms of authoritarianism have arisen. In Russia, the outcome hangs in the balance. A new constitution, adopted in 1993, establishes a mixed presidential-parliamentary system. In it the president is given broad constitutional powers, including the right to issue decrees with the force of law. The greatest threat to the prospect for democratic consolidation in Russia, however, is not the character of its constitution, but the disorder in state institutions. The severity of this problem—marked by such pathologies as the state's inability to collect taxes or enforce the law in many parts of the country—tempts the leadership to turn to authoritarian solutions. Like many Russian rulers before them, they frequently claim sweeping powers over large domains of policy without establishing the means for implementing it. In 1998, the state's mounting insolvency reached the point where the central government could no longer meet its obligations to either domestic or foreign creditors, and, in effect, declared bankruptcy. The financial system broke down and many banks failed. Yet the basic framework of constitutional structures continued to operate. The political institutions established in Russia's transition from communism are proving to be more resilient than the new market-oriented economic institutions.

If democratic institutions succeed in becoming consolidated in Russia, it will be because they serve the interests of the country's national and regional leaders in being represented in policy-making. Two sets of new, representative political institutions are especially noteworthy: a system of competitive national political parties, and a mechanism for balancing the powers of central and regional governments. Both have proven to be adaptable in the face of the profound social and economic turmoil of the 1990s. Each is likely to be a necessary feature of any stable, working, democratic order in Russia.

Russia faces particularly steep obstacles to the establishment of democracy in the aftermath of communist rule. Russia was the world's first state to undergo communist revolution, and its rulers actively spread the communist system throughout Eastern Europe and much of Asia by means of revolutionary propaganda, active political intervention, and direct military occupation. In turn, it was Russian political leadership that initiated the deep structural reforms in the Soviet system that led—very much against the desires of the Soviet leaders themselves—to the collapse both of the communist regime and of the very Soviet Union. The effects of this transformation rippling outward resulted in the collapse of communist regimes throughout Eastern Europe and their replacement by a variety of postcommunist successor states, some democratic, some authoritarian. This transformation also resulted in the breakup of the federated states that had attempted to maintain political unity among different ethnic nationalities. Besides the USSR itself, the other two ethnic federations in the communist world that split apart were Yugoslavia and Czechoslovakia.

Thus the transformation of regimes in the communist world has had enormous consequences for the peoples of those countries and for the balance of power in the world. A successful outcome of the transition in Russia, by the same token, will affect the processes of regime change that are still continuing in many of the former communist states.

While it is useful to apply models of regime transition developed in the context of Southern Europe and Latin America to these communist cases, it is important as well to bear in mind the peculiar features of communist regimes that have made these transitions so much more difficult and have lowered the odds of a democratic outcome (Linz and Stepan 1996). Among these are the far greater degree of economic centralization that characterized communist regimes. As a result of their attempt to eliminate private property and the power of the capitalist class, the state owned and administered the means of production through central planning. This placed enormous power over the economy in the hands of the state bureaucracy and the political leadership. And, unwilling to tolerate challenges to their monopoly on political power, the communist authorities suppressed alternative ideologies to their own Marxist-Leninist doctrine, and prevented any rival political force from organizing. As a result of these economic and political controls, communist states typically had very weak civil societies. That is, there were few voluntary, autonomous public associations that could organize people, mediate between their demands and the state, and channel their demands into constitutional avenues of political activity. Organized social groups that could provide bases of support and serve as pools of leadership for new political parties were weak or absent in most communist states. These conditions help us understand why in many cases the breakdown of the communist regime has resulted in wars and nationalist dictatorships. They help explain the rise of separatist movements, often fueled by ethnic-national grievances and resentment against a distant and exploitative central government. The absence of market-supporting institutions and the pervasive atmosphere of uncertainty have undermined the chances for functioning market systems to emerge. Widespread bureaucratic rent-seeking and corruption undercut Russia's halting progress toward the rule of law.

These challenges, characteristic of the new postcommunist systems throughout the region, are more acute in the republics of the former Soviet Union than in the countries of Central Europe (Rose, Mishler, and Haerpfer 1998). Except for the three Baltic states of Estonia, Latvia, and Lithuania, none of the former Soviet republics has achieved a stable democratic system; Russia is one of the few where democratic institutions exist even in partial, incomplete form. In view of the government's dismal performance in social and economic policy, the survival of its representative institutions—parties and federalism—invites us to take a closer look and ask how they came into being and what makes them reasonably sturdy in the face of formidable obstacles.

A number of political scientists have argued that simply strengthening executive power in fragile new democracies will not overcome the problems associated with the weakness of civil society and the fragmentation of states along regional and ethnoterritorial lines (Lijphart 1984; Hellman 1998; Weingast 1993, 1997). Centralization under such circumstances may succeed in imposing a kind of praetorian order, but will not stimulate markets and democracy.

Notwithstanding the utopian Marxist vision of abolishing conflict from society, it has proven impossible to eliminate contests of power and interest in new states. Rather, to succeed, new democracies must find means of structuring and channeling the expressions of conflict that strengthen rather than weaken democratic institutions. Historically, rulers intent on increasing their state's wealth and power have often found it more rewarding to tie their own hands through the rule of law and the marketplace, so as to stimulate productive efforts by others, than to try to exercise impossibly broad control over society's behavior. Representative institutions such as parties and federalism have therefore contributed not only to the democratization of states, but also to *effective* government. Parties connect the public with state policy-makers, establishing legitimacy, choice, and accountability in relations between governors and governed. Federalism in large and regionally diverse states balances the rights and responsibilities of the center with those of the regions, easing tendencies toward regional separatism and checking the power-aggrandizing temptations of the central government.

In the belief, therefore, that parties and federalism will be essential features of any future democratic order in Russia, let us ask how these institutions were created through the strategic choices of Russia's own political actors. Then let us examine how they are working in practice, to seek evidence about how they may evolve in the future. We will place particular emphasis on *parliamentary* politics, because the interaction of the two chambers of the new Federal Assembly can tell us a good deal about the way conflicts are structured by Russia's new institutional landscape.

Political Dilemmas, Institutional Solutions

The health of a competitive party system in Russia is critical to the character of its politics. As many scholars have argued, a system of opposing political parties supplies crucial public goods for a democracy, including electoral choice, governmental accountability, and policy-making capacity (Powell 1982; Aldrich 1995; Mainwaring and Scully 1995; Linz and Stepan 1996). In a postcommunist setting, where politicians discount the future heavily and opponents mistrust one another, commitment to democratic procedures is costly to enforce: mutual scrutiny by opposing parties lightens the burden on a weak central authority. Their tacit agreement to compete for power under common constititional and electoral rules reinforces democratic stability.

Although there is general agreement on the importance of a party system for democratic consolidation, scholars debate what most influences a party system's formation and development. Must a young democracy wait until a civil society has achieved a certain level of maturity before parties will form that can provide the benefits of democratic legitimation, representation, and governance? Or can constitutional designers engineer a party system into being without being overly concerned about economic and social precondi-tions? Some observers emphasize the social determinants of party systems. Others argue that political actors have wide latitude to devise rules and strate-gies governing the development of party systems. Doubtless a full account of the subsequent development of a party system will require explanation of the strategies of key actors and the constraints on their actions, particularly at moments when basic institutions are being established. The collapse of the communist regime in Russia gives us a rare opportunity to observe the influ-ence of such choices on the evolution of the party system.

The choices made over parliament's structure have been decisive in shap-ing both the party system and federalism. These choices are embodied in the constitution of 1993, which was written and adopted largely at the initiative of President Boris Yeltsin. Not surprisingly, therefore, the constitution pro-vides for an extremely strong presidency: the president is directly elected and has far-reaching powers of veto and decree-making. Yet the bicameral Federal Assembly has significant powers as well, including the right to pass legislation, to override a presidential veto, to deny its confidence to the gov-ernment, and to remove the president through impeachment.

Of greater importance for our purposes is the fact that the two chambers of the Federal Assembly employ different rules of representation and operate under different rules of procedure. The lower, popular chamber, the State Duma, divides its 450 seats into two categories: 225 are filled by the results of plurality elections in single-member districts, and 225 are filled through elec-tion of candidates from party lists according to the share of the vote each party received in a single, Russia-wide electoral district, subject to a 5 percent threshold. The upper house, the Federation Council, comprises 178 mem-bers, 2 from each of the country's 89 federal "subjects," or constituent terri-tories. These two members are the heads of the legislative and executive branches of government in each subject. As full-time leaders in their home regions, therefore, they are "senators" on a part-time basis only and come to Moscow for Federation Council business only a few days a month.

Of crucial importance is the fact that in the State Duma, partisan factions have acquired collective power over the legislative process and management of the chamber (Remington and Smith 1995, 1996). The Duma is steered by its council, which is composed of one member from each party faction or registered deputy group; committee chairs do not have a vote in the decisions of the Council of the Duma. The factions divide up chamber and committee leadership positions among themselves roughly in proportion to their number of members. Factions also possess other rights and privileges under the Standing Orders, a fact that encourages members to affiliate with one or another faction or registered group. Even deputies who ran as independents usually join a faction.

In the Federation Council, however, factions are not recognized. This is not simply because the rules of the chamber assign no place to political factions. The members, after all, could readily amend the rules to give party factions rights. The members of the Federation Council themselves prefer not to organize the chamber by party.

These differences in the rules between the two chambers survived the 1995 and 1996 elections. Neither the new deputy corps of the Duma elected in 1995 nor the new membership of the Federation Council that entered following the wave of regional elections in 1996 has altered them in any major way. The different relationships between electoral system and rules of procedure that are evident in the two chambers appear to have stabilized. In the Duma, members adopted a strongly party-dominated organizational structure, while in the Federation Council, politics is played out without regard to partisan affiliations. In neither chamber, moreover, does any one party or political tendency possess a clear majority. Following the 1995 elections, the largest party in the Duma—the Communist Party of the Russian Federation (CPRF)—gained one third of the seats and has a near-majority when the two factions closest to it vote with it. But the communists did not attempt to overturn the rules and transform the Duma into an instrument of a partisan majority. Thus not only is the party-oriented structure of governance preferred by a majority of the members, but so is the nonmajoritarian way in which the chamber is managed.

The constitution provides that laws originate in the Duma and, once passed there, are considered by the Federation Council. Deadlock in the Duma thus means that the parliament cannot act. The Duma can override the Federation Council if the latter rejects a bill that the Duma has passed. Usually, though, the two chambers form a conciliation commission to iron out their differences. The president can veto any bill that comes to him for signature. While parliament can override a presidential veto, a two-thirds majority in each chamber is required. Moreover, the president has the power to issue decrees with the status of law so long as his decrees do not violate federal law or the constitution. Therefore when parliament fails to act, the president can sometimes set policy by decree. By choosing when and where to push parliament, then, the president can often get what he wants or at least prevent parliament from getting what it wants.

Is a party system beginning to arise in Russia? Certainly Russia's parties are weak and fragmented: there are many parties but few are able to mobilize voters or influence national policy. Forty-three electoral associations—only a few of them formally identified as partiesæran lists of candidates for the 1995 parliamentary elections, diverting so many votes away from the major political parties that fully half the popular vote went to parties that failed to cross the 5 percent threshold to parliamentary representation. Candidates running in single-member districts are apt to run *against* parties, to the extent of concealing their party affiliation from voters on the grounds that most voters express a strong antipathy to the very notion of party (White, Rose, and McAllister 1996). This practice declined somewhat in 1995 compared with 1993, however.

Political camps are also highly polarized, with conflict between Yeltsin loyalists and opposition forces not only harsh in rhetoric but even, in 1993, reaching the point of armed confrontation between Yeltsin's opponents and the armed forces that ultimately backed him against the uprising by the radical opposition.

Political scientists often distinguish among three aspects of political parties: their activity in government, including parliament; their internal organization; and their support in the electorate. Let us consider each of these three aspects of Russia's parties in turn.

Russian voter identification with political parties remains very low, although it may be growing. Voters have higher levels of mistrust of political parties than of any other political institution (White, Rose, and McAllister 1996, pp. 52–53). Only around one fifth identify with any political party, and of those, the largest share is made up of Communist Party supporters (White, Rose, and McAllister 1996, pp. 135–37). Still, voters form preferences for parties based on their evaluation of the party's stance on policy and on their view of the party leaders (Oates 1996, p. 29). And parties have made an impression on the voters. A survey in late 1998 by a Russian polling firm found that 44 percent of the voters could remember which party they voted for in 1995, while 21 percent could not; and 30 percent claimed to have some knowledge of what that party was doing in the Duma. But when it came to knowing something about their district representatives in the Duma, only 19 percent claimed to have some knowledge of their activity in parliament, while 77 percent knew nothing about it (*Segodnia*, December 26, 1998). Against the background of generally weak ties between Russia's populace and electoral representatives, parties seem to figure more prominently in the voters' consciousness than do individual deputies.

Russia's parties can be distinguished by the social bases of their support. For instance, studies show that the communists draw most heavily from among the elderly and least-educated segments of the population as well as soldiers and industrial workers. The communists also do well in the rural areas. Extreme nationalist Vladimir Zhirinovsky's Liberal-Democratic Party of Russia (LDPR) also attracts substantial support from workers and soldiers. His support among women, however, is half the level of his support among men. Administrators and managers are about equally likely to support the communists, the government party Our Home Is Russia, and reformer Grigorii Yavlinsky's party, Yabloko. Support for other democratic reform parties also tends to be concentrated among upper-income groups, the highly educated, and the young (Wyman 1996, p. 282). Thus there is a somewhat coherent social basis for party support in Russia.

As to the second face of parties, that of their internal organization, Russia's parties vary considerably. The major parties have adopted differing strategies for making use of the resources that they have to wage their election campaigns. The Communist Party of the Russian Federation, which is the direct successor of the old ruling party, the Communist Party of the Soviet Union, possesses a cohesive organization. Its officeholders are loyal and disciplined in their behavior. Personality is downplayed, and the party's campaigns are characterized by intense get-out-the-vote efforts among their followers. Similarly, the Agrarian Party has concentrated its effort on reaching a particular segment of society, using its strong base among collective and state farm managers, and a relatively strong central organization. Our Home Is Russia, LDPR, and Yabloko have relatively weak electoral organizations and are dominated by their officeholders at the central level, in parliament and in government. Generally speaking, parties' staff and financial resources are extremely modest, and ties between central and local party activists are usually tenuous (Fish 1995). It is an ironic effect of the Russian transition that the communists' very cohesiveness and discipline, in an environment where the allergy to party allegiances is widespread among voters and politicians, prompt other parties to close ranks to fight them more effectively. In this way, the communists are serving as a catalyst for the development of a new, democratic system of political parties. Still, by far the most important organizational resource for parties is the prominence of their leaders; most parties are little more than organized followings around high-visibility personalities.

It is at the third level of parties' functioning—their interaction with the structures of government—that they are exerting real influence on Russian policy-making and political development. The challenge they face is to link large national segments of the electorate with the policy choices and government of the country. In the parliament, however, Russia's nascent parties have been able to maintain a relatively high level of *intraparty* cohesion and to negotiate and uphold a number of *interparty* agreements to facilitate legislative decision-making. To a much greater extent than outside observers appreciate, the party-oriented legislative process in the State Duma has resulted in some significant legislative achievements. Among these are:

1. Enactment of budget laws every year that, even if they invariably fail to meet their revenue and spending targets, reflect crucial political compromises over fiscal allocations across branches of government;

2. A series of reforms of the judicial and legal systems that include a constitutional law reorganizing the judicial system, a new federal criminal code, Parts I and II of a new federal Civil Code; and a new federal criminal corrections code;

3. Constitutional laws on the Human Rights Commissioner and Constitutional Court;

4. Five major electoral laws (a law establishing uniform rights for voters throughout the federation; a law governing elections to the State Duma; a law on presidential elections; a law on referenda; and a law governing the composition of the Council of the Federation);

5. And agreement on a set of stable rules about parliamentary organization, including the distribution of leadership posts and other rights.

On the other hand, on other issues, parliamentary parties in the Duma remain deadlocked. A number of major bills remain stuck in parliament. Some major property-rights-related laws either cannot get through the Duma at all or cannot clear all three successive hurdles to enactment: Duma passage, Federation Council passage, and the president's signature. A case in point is the "Land Code," which is a comprehensive law regulating the rights of citizens to purchase and sell land. As of the end of 1998, it had spent five years in the toils of the legislative mill, unable to win concurrent assent of the Duma, the Federation Council, and the president in a form acceptable to all sides. Similar stories may be told of other property-rights-related legislation, such as the package of laws on production-sharing; tax reform; and replacement of comprehensive social welfare entitlements with targeted, need-based social policy. Similarly, parliament and president have deadlocked over the parliament's efforts to weaken the president's constitutional powers through constitutional amendment.

Generally speaking, the Duma has been able to reach agreement more readily on issues that do not directly concern the great struggle over the transformation of property rights. Measures that move Russia toward a capitalist, market economy regularly reach an impasse within the Duma; when they finally pass the Duma, they run up against the president's opposition.

And when they finally are signed into law—examples are the laws legalizing mortgage loans, regulating production-sharing agreements, and regulating the privatization of state enterprises—they have been so eviscerated in the course of the legislative process that they emerge toothless and ineffective. In many cases, policy in these vital matters has been set by presidential decree instead. As a result, much of the conflict over the constitutional balance between legislative and executive branches stems from parliament's acute dissatisfaction with the president's policies, coupled with its inability to set policy on property rights through legislation. This leads parliament in turn to seek a mechanism for revising the constitution so as to weaken the president's powers, but the president has of course repulsed all such efforts.

Yet on federalism issues—matters affecting the balance of power between central government, regional and local governments, and individuals—the Duma has been more effective in reaching internal agreement and in allying with the president. In these areas, the Duma has been able to pass a number of laws, sometimes overriding the Federation Council's veto to do so. What is significant about this fact is that a majority in the Duma is necessarily a cross-party coalition, since no one party or coalition commands a majority. Passage always requires negotiating an interparty agreement as well as an effort by party leaders to keep their troops in line. The wider the distance separating the political camps in the Duma, the harder they find it to find a compromise position that can win a majority. Party positions reflect the divisions in society over the transition, but party leaders make it possible to achieve workable legislative agreements.

The Federation Council acts if and when the Duma has spoken, and it often blocks laws passed by the lower house. Usually the Duma is unable to override the upper house, so that the two chambers form an agreement commission and try to hammer out a compromise. Here the president's position is very important. If he favors the Duma's position, he can sometimes pressure the Federation Council into passing a bill close to what he and the Duma want. But when he defers to the regional power elites who make up the membership of the upper house, he can block the Duma's bill. And if he cannot get a bill he likes out of parliament, he can veto the parliament's product and issue a decree or leave the status quo in place. It is a system with multiple veto players, making alterations to the status quo difficult (Tsebelis 1995). On federalism issues, therefore, although the Duma is regularly able to take a position favoring the prerogatives of the federal government, its bills have been blocked or gravely weakened by the regional leaders sitting in the Federation Council.

Thus there are, in effect, two great axes of political conflict on which the politicians line up: one over market reform, and the other over the powers of the central government vis-à–vis regions. Political parties in the Duma tend to align themselves along the first axis, while the two chambers of parliament line up on opposing sides of the second.

The reason that politics in the two chambers is so different is because of the different ways in which they are formed. The Duma is dominated by political parties because of the fact that the electoral law and Duma's procedural rules favor political parties as the principal actors both in the elections and in the chamber. The Federation Council is made up of the regional chief executives and assembly speakers, who lock horns with the Duma over the powers of the federal government vis-à–vis the regions. The two chambers differ because of the way each is elected; they *represent* Russian citizens differently. It is for this reason that alignments form very differently in the two chambers. Understanding why these two different systems of representation were adopted will help us to judge how they are likely to affect the development of the party system and federal relations in the future.

Electoral Law, Political Conflict, and Party Competition

Russia's nascent party system is a classic product of institutional engineering, in both its weaknesses and its strengths. Like other political institutions in Russia, the parties were organized "from above" rather than "from below" and therefore are more developed as players in central politics than as organizations or vessels of popular representation. In this respect Russia's protoparties are not so very different from the eighteenth- and nineteenth-century predecessors of today's parties in Western Europe. Early on, parties in the West also served as institutional solutions to politicians' interest in retaining the benefits of office, inducing loose coalitions of politicians pressured by an expanding franchise to devise electoral committees and seek public support. Parties, after all, are politicians' vehicles for solving a variety of tasks, some related to their interest in influencing policy, others connected to their political ambitions (Cox 1987; Strom 1990; Cox and McCubbins 1993; Aldrich 1995).

It makes sense, therefore, to ask what Russian politicians wanted from the electoral system and constitutional framework they devised, given the particular political landscape in which they operated: strong popular antipathy to parties; organizational resources and experience inherited from the single-party state and particularly the continuing organizational network possessed by the communists; the deep division between democrats who believed that liberty and democracy required a market economy with secure property rights, and the large sector of society dependent on state socialism for their livelihoods. The dismantling of state socialism, therefore, created a line of intense conflict along which a party system could arise.

In Russia, as conflict between Yeltsin and his communist-nationalist opposition deepened over Yeltsin's radical reform policies in the period between

1990 and 1993, both Yeltsin and the opposition forces had reasons to favor an electoral system and parliamentary structure giving parties a stronger role. Yeltsin's use of his decree power simply to put a new electoral law into force in 1993 cut the Gordian knot of confrontation over the country's direction in an abrupt, unconstitutional way. But it is important to understand that the electoral system he put into place for the new parliamentary elections that he demanded for December 1993 was one which had been extensively discussed by all political camps. And most accepted the idea that the new electoral system should combine single-mandate district elections for a certain share of the seats in the new parliament with a proportional representation system where voters chose among party lists to fill the rest of the seats. None of the organized political groups could be sure whether they would be more advantaged in local district races or in the national party-list race. They therefore tended to accept the notion of mixing the two electoral procedures so that they could try their luck both ways. Most agreed, moreover, that a system of competitive national parties was beneficial to Russia. This position was motivated perhaps less by their interest in democracy in the abstract than by their concern with giving leaders ways of attracting followers. A system of national party lists gave leaders incentives to build electoral organizations and coalitions of support.

This fact helps to explain the willingness of politicians who otherwise vehemently opposed Yeltsin to enter into the electoral contest opened up by Yeltsin's decrees of September and October 1993. Privileged representation for parties in the future parliament was a valuable and low-cost organizational resource for ambitious politicians, and the automatic translation of a certain share of the vote for a particular leader or party into parliamentary seats would help allow the heads even of embryonic partisan movements to offer their followers sufficient incentives to accept their leadership. The prospects of career advancement to higher office; the opportunity to enjoy various forms of privilege; and the considerable benefits that a proportional representation (PR) system offered for future reelection were all attractions as well, and encouraged the proliferation of leader-dominated smaller parties willing to take the chance of winning 5 percent of the vote.

The parties campaigned as national organizations; the national party-list system encouraged the "nationalization" of political issues. As a result, parties tended to line up along the dominant axis of Russian political conflict, which divided market-oriented, westward-looking reformers from state-socialist, nationalist conservatives. Some parties strove to position themselves as "centrists" between these camps. Party competition for the 1993 parliamentary elections, therefore, was influenced both by the way the rules of the game were set up, and by the predominance of the fight over market reform among the great policy issues facing the country. In turn, the parties preserved essentially the same electoral system for the 1995 elections that had been used in 1993, and following the 1995 elections, they retained the same party-oriented legislative process in the Duma. Parties make use of their status in parliament to showcase favored issues and achieve policy benefits; they hold press conferences and parliamentary hearings, make televised speeches on the floor, sponsor, push, or block legislation, and so on, with larger policy and electoral considerations in mind. The major parties have fought to create distinct political identities based on their programs and on the personalities of their leaders. The parties have shaped both the electoral law and the governance of parliament in such a way as to further their own influence over policy-making and elections in Russia. The rules regulating elections give both politicians and voters reasons to associate their own interests with those of parties. As a result, a pluralistic, multiparty system is beginning to develop.

So, moreover, is the suggestion of constitutional evolution toward parliamentary government. Until the crisis of August 1998, the president considered himself free to appoint a prime minister without taking into account the balance of party forces in the Duma, so long as he could pressure the deputies to confirm his choice by threatening them with parliamentary dissolution and early elections. In September 1998, amidst the gravest financial crisis of the decade, the Duma forced the president to withdraw his candidate and instead to name as prime minister an individual much more to parliament's liking. Evgenii Primakov, as soon as he was confirmed as the new prime minister, in turn named a prominent member of the communist faction in the Duma to be his first deputy prime minister in charge of economic policy-making. The faint outlines of an incipient parliamentary system of government began to emerge as economic policy shifted considerably leftward.

Federalism and Bicameralism

A different set of political problems shaped the formation of Russia's federalism but, like those structuring the party system, they include both power and policy motivations. Once again, the arrangements inherited from the old regime were important as well.

Federalism in the Soviet Union was largely a device for accommodating ethnic-national minority groups within the Soviet state, and existed largely as an organizational formality. It served to grant nationalities a recognized administrative jurisdiction, political identity, and certain formal rights, so long as these did not jeopardize CPSU policy powers in any essential way. The Communist Party, of course, was highly centralized. Within the Russian Republic (RSFSR), federalism had a comparable purpose. Unlike the Soviet federation, however, Russia, which was the only nominally federal republic of the union, comprised both ethnic-national and ordinary constituent territories. These differed in legal status, however. Ordinary regions (*oblasti* and *kraia*) were units to which the federal state delegated some administrative powers: they did not have sovereign power. Republics, however, had the legal attribute of sovereignty, much as union republics were legally considered sovereign. A republic therefore enjoyed certain capacities that ordinary regional organs of power lacked, among them the rights to adopt a constitution and to enact laws. The regions thus were and remain today asymmetric in their legal relationships with the federal center, an anomaly comparable in some respects to the asymmetric unions in Canada, Scotland, and Spain.

Not surprisingly, as political transition commenced, leaders of the ethnic territories refused to give up any of their former rights in exchange for a greater degree of political democracy. Rather, they demanded to retain the legal rights they had enjoyed and to infuse them with actual political power over their territories. At the same time, leaders of regular subdivisions demanded parity of status with republics. The conflict between these groups remains one reason there has been no "regional rights" party in Russia.

As is the case with his handling of the electoral system issue to stimulate political parties and diffuse opposition to his policies, Yeltsin made federalism an instrument for short-term political gains. Devolution of power to the regions was a strategy for winning over the support of the regional elites in his battles against Gorbachev in 1990 and 1991 and then again against the communist-nationalist opposition in parliament in 1992 and 1993.

Again, the setting for the development of the new institutions was the intense conflict over economic policy. Once Yeltsin's team of young reformers, led by Egor Gaidar as First Deputy Prime Minister, had enacted their plan for macroeconomic stabilization by presidential decree beginning on January 2, 1992, the political reaction was immediate. As prices soared and state spending fell, Yeltsin's reserve of political support in the Congress began sliding sharply. To defend his flanks, Yeltsin accelerated the pace of the program of privatization of state assets—for which support from many industrial managers could be generated so long as they were given privileged rights to claim shares of privatized state assets for themselves—and made concessions to regional elites. Throughout 1992 and 1993, Yeltsin sought to win the support, or at least neutrality, of governors using various institutional devices designed to give them a collective voice in national policy (Slider 1994). Federalism in Russia was effectively a concession to the regional power elite in return for their acceptance of Yeltsin's radical economic reforms.

As their antagonism deepened, Yeltsin and Supreme Soviet Chairman Ruslan Khasbulatov began to appeal to competing bases of support in the regions. Yeltsin built up the power of the governors; Khasbulatov, that of the Soviets. Each sought to create corporate bodies amplifying the collective power of these respective constituencies. Khasbulatov convened grand assemblies of heads of regional and local Soviets, emphasizing his claim that constitutionally, the Soviets were the supreme instance of state power. Yeltsin in turn created a "Council of Heads of Republics" in October 1992 and a "Council of Heads of Administration" in March 1993 (Slider 1994, pp. 261–62). The central government began to include the regional chief executives in its meetings.

In March 1993 the leaders of both Soviet and executive branches in 73 regions proposed the creation of a Council of the Federation to serve as the upper chamber of a future parliament. Although rejected by the Congress, the proposal then regularly resurfaced in the texts of new draft constitutions that were then actively circulating (Slider 1994, p. 262). This was the first airing of a *Bundesrat*-style model of an upper house in Russian constitutional debate. Yeltsin then employed a similar sort of representation—an equal fixed number of delegates from each subject—when he convened a Constitutional Assembly in June 1993: along with two experts, each subject of the federation was invited to send the heads of its legislative and executive branches. Yeltsin again proposed such a model for his new constitutional scheme in the draft presented for national referendum in December 1993. The new parliament's upper house would be called the Federation Council and would consist of two representatives from each subject, one from the executive, the other from the legislative branch. The council was given considerably more than purely advisory powers. Its consent was to be required for any legislation pertaining to federal budget policy, regional policy, treaties, customs, peace and war, and for any override of a presidential veto of legislation.

For the first time in Russian history, a federal constitution granted the constituent territories enforceable powers. The product of Yeltsin's strategy of satisfying the demands of regional leaders for influence over policy, it was an arrangement that prevented a coalition of communists and regional leaders from forming that might have reversed macroeconomic stabilization.

Formation of the Federation Council was characteristic of Yeltsin's use of institutional reform to solve political problems. Yeltsin created a different alignment with which to win over a key pivotal constituency. The regional interest was internally divided over a variety of issues—regions versus republics, donors versus recipients, and urban-rural divisions—but governors as a body desired greater collective influence over the policy of the federal government in areas of immediate concern to them, and Yeltsin devised a means to grant it to them. The partitioning of conflict in this way has had a stabilizing influence, but the cost has been high. The central government's ability to enforce federal law is gravely threatened by the weakness of its sanctions for violations and by President Yeltsin's tendency to give special exemptions and privileges to individual regions in return for delivering him votes or other benefits.

Yeltsin's policy of using carrots and sticks in his relations with the regional governments averted some immediate problems—particularly the constitutional impasse of 1992 and 1993—but made it extremely difficult for the central government to establish a uniform constitutional framework for the enforcement of federal law throughout the country. The central government will not soon repeat a bloody and disastrous campaign of the sort it pursued in Chechnia, where federal troops fought from December 1994 until October 1996 to suppress an independence-seeking republican government. On the other hand, none of Russia's other regions has attempted to declare its complete independence. Future federal relations will most likely be the product of a long-term process of negotiated mutual accommodation that will give substantive meaning to Russia's newly real federalism.

Early Returns

Russia's experience with the 1993 constitution is still very limited, and it would be unwise to draw any firm conclusions about the future of the political arrangements it has created. Moreover, President Yeltsin's infirmity and the depth of the financial crisis make it impossible to speak of the consolidation of the current constitutional system. Many of the most important legislative issues remain in suspended animation in the Duma while the deputies devote a good deal of time to political posturing. A case in point is the drive spearheaded by the hard-liners among the communist faction to remove Yeltsin through impeachment.

Yet the basic institutions that are coping with these stresses continue to be a party system aligned along the left-right cleavage and a model of federalism that gives regional governors substantial authority to influence national policy. Stabilization of these features of the new postcommunist political system would provide routinized means for the articulation of the major political conflicts in its environment. Bargaining and compromise will characterize their resolution, although at the expense of strong and effective central government. The system offers certain advantages to a society torn by profound economic and political dislocation. It provides avenues for ambitious politicians to seek office and in small ways to shape policy, and it keeps Russia's nascent postcommunist institutions from being overloaded with the full burden of political choice. On the other hand, unless the two chambers of parliament can address the country's real financial and economic problems, it is unlikely that the present constitution can survive.

We have examined parties and federalism separately, observing that each is reflected in the politics of one of the two chambers of parliament. In fact, of course, they are closely related. As Peter Ordeshook has recently argued, a stable system of federalism requires that the relationship between central government and the territorial subdivisions of the federation be balanced between mutual dependence and autonomy. The constituent units of the federation must be able to maintain spheres of independent jurisdiction in order to prevent encroachments on their power by the federal center, but they also need the federal government to enforce the federal framework and prevent particular regions from "free riding" on the other regions. Political parties, he points out, can play a crucial role in maintaining this equilibrium. Parties give politicians at local, regional, and national levels of government reasons to maintain relations of reciprocal dependence and respect, since the political fortunes of party politicians at any given level are tied to some degree to those of their copartisans at other levels. Party systems in which electoral competition at the regional level is detached from competition at the central level give local and regional politicians no reason not to run "against" the federal center, and give politicians at the center no reason not to encroach on the power and perquisites of the regions. In such systems, regional separatism flourishes (Ordeshook 1996).

So far, Russian parties have done relatively little to integrate the country territorially. Regional and local races are only loosely tied to the competition among national parties, in contrast to political life at the central level. Yet there are reasons to expect that time will bring a closer coordination of party contests at different levels of government. The communist legacy means that control over many resources remains highly concentrated at the center. It is simply not possible for regional governments to solve the deep problems of economic transition in their own regions—problems such as converting a heavily defense-oriented economy to civilian needs, for instance, and problems of attracting new investment—without joining forces with like-minded leaders in other regions and hammering out a common policy for the country. Therefore, however much the regional and local politicians may consider parties a nuisance and a distraction from the real work of governing, they will increasingly find that they need to link their own fortunes to those of their counterparts in other regions sharing similar interests. There are incentives, therefore, in the institutional landscape that are conducive to the development of a party system integrated across levels of government. This will be all the more true to the extent that meaningful local self-government can arise, serving as a counterweight to the control possessed by regional executives over their territories' land and resources.

Yeltsin's intense struggle against the USSR's central government led him to adopt a political and economic framework in the Russian Republic designed to make the transition from communist rule irreversible. In this, he had a wide range of international experience from which to borrow. Most of the institutional features discussed here—the mixed electoral law, bicameral parliament, federalism, dual executive, and Constitutional Court—were adapted from foreign models. If there is a lesson here for policy-makers in our own and other Western countries, it is that we can help establish the facilitating conditions in which Russia's political actors can create a self-sustaining path of constitutional democracy by adapting universal models of political instutions for their own political struggles. But the institutions they employ must suit their own—not our—purposes.

12

The Longest Transition

Joseph S. Berliner

I TAKE MY TITLE from a witticism that made the rounds in Eastern Europe some years ago: "Communism is the longest road from feudalism to capitalism." In all the regions considered in this volume, the notion of transition connotes a change from one type of political-economic system to a different one. In the former European communist world, however, transition also conveys a sense of finally coming home again. That is particularly the case in the westernmost of them. Czechoslovakia was a pearl of democratic capitalism before 1948, and Hungary and Poland were essentially capitalist, although politically authoritarian. The Russian Empire had been a "developing" country, to use the language of a later generation, but by 1914 virtually all of its industry, trade, commerce, finance, and much of its agriculture, were vigorously capitalist (Nove 1969, ch. 1).

A second difference between the former communist countries and the other regions is that in the latter the transition to democracy is taking place in societies in which the basic economic structure is not under challenge; the center of controversy is how best to manage it. In the former communist world, however, the political transition is occurring at the same time as the economy is undergoing a wrenching transformation of fundamental structure. There are in fact at least three kinds of transformation, each of which is the source of enormous disruption. One is the transfer of ownership of the entire productive property from the state to individual citizens. The second is the creation of entirely new economic institutions of finance, accounting, corporate governance, and commercial law. The third is the massive change of the structure of capital stock from the military and heavy industry that dominated the past to the consumer goods and services demanded under the nascent market institutions.

Any one of these economic transformations would place a great strain on the process of political democratization going on at the same time. Coming all together, they leave one awestruck at the task, particularly in the former Soviet Union, where the communist period lasted, as the disheartened say, for "70 lost years."

It is all the more remarkable that this great transition was not at all what the Soviet political leadership had in mind when they voted Mikhail Gorbachev into the office of general secretary of the Communist Party in 1985. They had a much more limited goal in view.

The Origin

Politburo members were united in their anxiety over the "stagnation" that had set in during the long tenure of Leonid Brezhnev. There were widely differing views, however, on how to reform the economic system (Aslund 1989, ch. 2). The fundamental difference, in the language of the time, was whether to rely on "administrative" or "economic" measures. Administrative measures meant the restoration of economic discipline by tightening central control over the economy; to coerce workers into putting in a full day's work, to compel managers to increase their efforts to overfulfill plan targets, and to improve central planning and expand the scope of its control. Economic measures meant the wider use of incentives rather than ministerial sanctions to motivate workers to exert greater effort and to motivate managers to express greater initiative in reducing costs and expanding output.

In electing Mikhail Gorbachev as general secretary, the Politburo threw its weight on the side of economic measures. At the time, however, there did not exist a clearly articulated and long-debated program for incorporating such measures into the planning framework. A small group of economists had been cautiously promoting the wider use of economic incentives, but their proposals did not amount to full reform programs.[1] The set of initiatives that Gorbachev introduced should not, therefore, be viewed as a clear reform strategy, but rather as the product of improvisation and political compromise.

The two directions of Gorbachev's reforms that turned out to have the greatest influence on the course of events were the legalization of certain limited forms of private enterprise and of marketlike transactions. Initially private enterprise was limited to the formation of small cooperatives, in handicrafts such as dressmaking and in consumer services such as taxi transport and food catering. The new cooperatives, together with the older form of private enterprise known as the "collective farm market," constituted a small but vibrant sphere of market transactions in which prices reflected the play of supply and demand.

In 1988, these reforms were extended to a portion of the state sector in a move that mirrored the Chinese reform, the stunning success of which was then astounding the world (Berliner 1994). A new Law on the State Enterprise authorized managers to lease portions of their enterprises' property to groups of workers who formed cooperatives to run the shops themselves and to share in the profit, after paying a portion of the profit as rent to the enterprise. The managers were also authorized to use a certain portion of their plant and equipment to produce and sell goods outside of the planning system, in contrast to the past, when their entire capacity was dedicated to plan fulfillment. The overplan output could be sold to whomever they wished at whatever prices they could get, with the profit to be used to supplement the personal incomes of management and workers. The new law therefore added to the flow of goods produced and exchanged under market conditions, while the scope of output produced and exchanged under the central planning mechanism contracted.

These measures were designed to engage the energy and initiative of the population by permitting a portion of the increased productivity to be directly rewarded by larger income, which was what "economic measures" were supposed to do. Like all major reforms, however, they had certain unintended consequences, the most destructive of which was inflation.

The retreat of the state from control over a growing portion of economic activity was followed by an accelerating loss of control over the financial system. Among the major causes was a sharp increase in the state budget deficit, which was financed by the issue of currency. Many things contributed to the deficit, some the consequence of government policy (a drop in tax revenue because of an antialcohol campaign) and some due to bad luck (Chernobyl). The reform program was also partly responsible, however, for enterprise officials developing ways of using their expanded autonomy to convert growing portions of their formerly frozen bank deposits into cash.[2] The volume of money in circulation began to rise much more rapidly than the volume of goods that could be bought with cash.

Accustomed to a planned economy in which finance was regarded as of no great importance, the government paid little attention to the rising state budget deficit until its effects began to hit consumer goods markets. By 1990 the volume of money in circulation was so large that demand for consumer goods far outstripped the supplies in the state stores, where goods still had to be sold at the old fixed prices. The result was that the shops were increasingly denuded of their goods, which found their way smoothly into the new markets, both newly legal and illegal, where they sold at multiples of the fixed state-store prices. It was the long rows of completely empty shelves in the state stores that contributed, more than anything else, to the growing sense of panic. By 1991 the economy had also begun to reel under the economic effects of political developments that disrupted interrepublic and interbloc trade. It was widely felt that the economy was in a tailspin and the government was incapable of doing anything about it. When the Soviet flag was hauled down from the Kremlin in 1991 and the Russian flag raised in its place, the economy was on the verge of collapse.

The perilous condition into which the economy had fallen in 1991, however, was not the consequence of the state of the pre-Gorbachev economy. It was rather the consequence of the unsuccessful effort to improve it. The patient was ill, but it was the botched operation that did him in.

The Motivation for Change

The foregoing implies that international factors were of little significance in the decision in 1991 to abandon Soviet-type socialism in favor of a market economy. The critical state to which the economy had fallen was the consequence of domestic political and economic developments and not of pressures from abroad.

That was not the case in 1985, however. The decision of the Politburo to elect a general secretary whose program consisted of a radical but unspecified economic reform cannot be understood without reference to the rest of the world. For at that time the Soviet economy was not at all in a state of crisis.

There was, to be sure, a sense of deep dissatisfaction with the performance of the economy. In the two decades after World War II, the leadership of the USSR and other communist countries felt fully a part of the world's technological and economic progress. Growth rates were well in the range of the advanced capitalist countries, and with the dramatic Soviet achievements in military and space technology there was no reason to suspect that anything was amiss, or that their system was not capable of keeping abreast of, and even overtaking, the West. Had things not changed, there would have been no transition.

From the mid-1960s on, however, things did begin to change. Postwar growth decelerated everywhere, but it slowed down more in the communist countries than in the West (U.S. Directorate of Intelligence 1988, p. 33).[3] Even more alarming was the growing technological gap, which was indeed a major source of the widening growth rates. The technological gap was most evident in such leading-edge technologies as electronics and biotechnology, but it was apparent in the quality of goods generally. The growing disparity was no doubt communicated to the leadership by the Soviet scientists, engineers, and managers who were visiting the West with increasing frequency under the various scientific and economic exchange programs.

Perhaps even more alarming was the rise of the new economic powers in the East. The economic superiority of the West has been a Russian concern for centuries, and the challenge facing the communist leadership could be seen as but another chapter in a long story going back to Peter the Great. To be left behind by its old enemy, Japan, in its remarkably rapid rise to world leadership in economic and technological attainment was another matter. The spread of that development process to other countries of the Pacific Rim drove the point further home. And finally, with the explosive growth of the Chinese economy under the liberalization following the death of Mao, it was inescapable that something very big was happening throughout the world that was not happening in the USSR and Eastern Europe. Reform-minded forces began to write that unless something were done, the USRR would soon be find itself in the status of a Third World country.

It was only in that comparative perspective, however, that the country could be regarded as in deep distress. In absolute terms the picture was not nearly so bleak. Output and consumption continued to increase slowly, although at a declining rate.[4] There was no significant unemployment, workers continued to enjoy job security for life, and the relaxed pace of labor was reflected in the popular slogan, "They pretend to pay us and we pretend to work." The necessities of life were fully if scantily provided for, and some luxuries were available as well. There was no mass hunger or starvation, although significant numbers of people lived in poverty—10 percent by one estimate (Gregory and Stuart 1986, p. 334). Education and medical care remained free, housing was practically free, and all retired workers, including farmers, received meager but liveable pensions. The managerial and professional elite lived sufficiently better than the masses to give them a sense of personal attainment and social privilege. There were only two groups that were deeply disaffected by the system at that time; dissidents, on political or ethnic grounds, and a small group of intellectuals and Party officials who worried about where the USSR would be in the future unless things turned around.

That state of affairs contrasts sharply with that of China in 1976. A few years after the catastrophe of the Great Leap Forward, in which millions died of starvation and many more suffered extreme deprivation, the country was thrust into the maelstrom of the Cultural Revolution. Many of the political and intellectual elite were thrown out of power, humiliated, and packed off to work at manual labor in remote villages. It was the desperate peasants in the poorer provinces who broke up the communes and returned to traditional household farming, initially in defiance of the Party. When, after the death of Mao, the Party sanctioned their actions and gradually legalized private initiative, there were large numbers of people throughout the country who, having been put through a political and economic wringer, were eager for a radical change. In the USSR and Eastern Europe, in contrast, there were no peasants storming the gates for the right to break up the collective farms. In the USSR today they remain staunch enemies of private farming and land ownership reform, while millions of workers think back nostalgically to the security they had enjoyed in the old days.

Hence if the Soviet Union had been the only country in the world, there was nothing in its economic condition in 1985 that would have motivated its leadership to unleash a major economic reform. The vitality and dynamism of the postwar capitalist countries, however, set a standard that the communist world proved unable to meet, and it was that which generated the pressures for change. It is in that sense that international factors were decisive in motivating the changes that culminated in the transition to capitalism. One might say that the Soviet transition reflects not so much the failure of communism as the success of capitalism.

The launching of the Soviet transition unleashed the long-suppressed forces in its own national minorities and in Eastern Europe for independence from Russian domination. Once Gorbachev declared that Soviet armed forces would not come to the support of communist governments elsewhere, it was just a matter of time before those Soviet-imposed governments would be overthrown and the Soviet-imposed economic system discarded. The international factor, in the form of the Soviet transition, was therefore decisive in the launching of the transition in Eastern Europe.

The Cold War

That is the main part of the story of international influence on the economic transition. Another part is the influence exerted by the Cold War. There were many channels through which that influence flowed. One was the limitation on the rate of transfer of technological knowledge and hardware to the communist countries. The magnitude of that influence may be gauged by imagining how Japan's economy would have been affected if the country had as little access to the universities, research centers, business firms, and markets of the West as the USSR had. There is no doubt that its technological performance would have been smaller, possibly by a very large amount. A second channel was the huge military budget of the Soviet government. The size of Soviet defense expenditures remains a subject of controversy, but even under the CIA's relatively conservative estimate of about 15 to 17 percent of GDP, it was exceedingly large by international standards.

In the absence of these consequences of the Cold War, the lag of Soviet economic performance behind that of the West would surely have been smaller than it was in 1985. How much smaller is impossible to say, but one can say with assurance that the lag would still have been substantial because of the profound deficiencies of the Soviet economic system itself. In the case of technology transfer, for example, if the Soviets had had the same access to Western technology as the Japanese, they are unlikely to have reaped the same benefit, for the resistance to technological innovation was deeply embedded in the structure of the economy (Berliner 1976). Soviet managers did not have the powerful incentives or the supportive conditions that drove Japanese managers to seek out new products and processes and to introduce them into production.

The influence of the defense burden is more complex. One line of argument credits the defeat of communism to the toughness of US policy, because it forced upon the Soviets a defense burden so large that it bankrupted the economy. A popular variant of that view is that the Strategic Defense Initiative (SDI) was the straw that broke the camel's back.

The controversy has now generated a large literature that is too complex to be dealt with adequately here, but I offer some evidence that sheds light on an economic aspect of the matter.[5] The basis of the claim that the large defense burden was responsible for the low growth rate is that it tied up resources that would otherwise have been used for investment. The strength of that claim depends on the productivity of Soviet investment; the lower its productivity, the smaller the growth-retarding effect of the diversion of resources from investment to defense. The fundamental defect of the Soviet economy, however, was precisely the low level of productivity. The reason it lagged behind the West was not that it lacked resources, but that it got too little output from the resources that it did have. The most careful study of the subject found, for example, that a bundle of resources used in the communist economies in 1975 produced 25 to 34 percent less output than the same bundle produced when used in capitalist countries (Bergson 1989, p. 22). As for investment resources in particular, the rate of return on investment was barely above zero in 1980, having declined drastically from a respectable rate of 25 percent in the 1950s (Easterly and Fischer 1994).

Hence, counterintuitive though it may seem, the large defense burden bore little responsibility for the decline in Soviet growth, for the decline would not have been appreciably smaller had the defense burden been smaller. The order of magnitude is suggested by the finding of an econometric exercise that if the Soviets had frozen defense expenditures at their 1980 level, the growth of GNP would have risen by little more than one tenth of one percentage point (Bond and Levine 1983, pp. 18–19).[6] The economy was still able to convert its resources into an adequate level of consumption, but it had lost the ability to convert them into growth.

My own assessment, which I believe most analysts of the Soviet economy hold, is that the weaknesses in the economy were increasing in severity but there was no evidence that it was near the edge of a precipice (Hewett 1988, ch. 2). The SDI did indeed dump another straw on the camel's back, but there is no reason to believe that the camel could not have stumbled on. The decision to embark on a path of radical change was taken because some influential members of the leadership had long been aware that the old-style economy was utterly incapable of meeting the economic and technological challenges of the day. Radical change was impossible during the long political coma of Leonid Brezhnev, but his death provided the first opportunity in a generation to acknowledge openly the relative decline of the Soviet economy and to try to do something serious about it. The decision to entrust the country's future to a young Party secretary eager to lead the risky transformation would have been taken at that time even if the SDI had never been invented.

Consolidating the Market Economy

A centrally planned economy is like a mechanical system. It can be built and put into operation fairly quickly by an effective government, and it can be demolished in an instant. A market economy, in contrast, is like an ecological system. A regiment of chain saws can cut it down in an instant, but the strongest of governments cannot bring it into being quickly. The best it can do is plant the seeds, fertilize the ground, and wait for the trees to emerge and grow.

Gorbachev's policies reduced the range of commodities that were controlled by the central planners, and expanded the scope of marketlike transactions. It remained for Yeltsin's government, however, to finish off the planned economy with the stroke of a pen. With the virtually complete elimination of price controls on January 1, 1992, the foundations of planning were demolished. No one expected that a fullblown market economy would spring to life at once. What they sought to accomplish was to create the initial conditions under which markets could sprout and perhaps eventually thrive.

The second major component of the transition strategy was the privatization program. By the end of 1995, 122,000 formerly state-owned enterprises had been privatized (Blasi, Kroumova, and Kruse 1997, p. 189). In addition, almost 900,000 small private companies have been started up, now accounting for about 12 percent of the GDP (Kennan Institute Meeting Report 1997).

With the twin measures of price liberalization and privatization, the Yeltsin government set the country firmly on the road to capitalism. If an authoritarian paramilitary government should come to power on a wave of popular discontent, it might try to restore extensive government controls over production, prices, and wages, but it is unlikely to reintroduce full-scale central planning or to renationalize the productive property, which would have to be done if central planning were to be restored.

The Yeltsin program administered a shock to the economy from which it has not yet recovered. GDP declined every year until 1997, when it grew very slightly, but 1998 is expected to be another year of decline (OECD 1998, p. 149.) Open unemployment has doubled, and real household income has declined by 40 percent (Blasi, Kroumova, and Kruse 1997, p. 190). The program of "shock therapy" is mired in controversy. Its critics contend that a more gradual approach would have made for a smoother and less painful transition (Millar 1995). Its supporters offer a variety of economic arguments, among them that the cost of transition has been smaller in countries that reformed rapidly (such as Poland) than in countries that did not (such as Ukraine). One of the main arguments is political, however. The sudden collapse of the state in 1991 produced a weak new Russian government facing a deeply divided Duma, and saddled with an entrenched rent-seeking administrative apparatus prepared to undermine any reform that would weaken its power. A gradual reform would have had to be implemented by that bureaucracy, which would have administered it to death. Under those circumstances it "would have been lethal to hesitate or move slowly" (Aslund 1995, p. 11).

I now believe that judgment was correct. If the architects of the Yeltsin program had designed a sophisticated program of close regulation and gradual change, and turned it over to the bureaucracy to implement, the economy would have been so tightly controlled that the transition would be barely further along today than it was in 1991. It is true that one cost of that policy is that many former Party and industrial leaders were able to amass large fortunes in the form of private ownership of the former state property, and by other means as well. It is difficult, however, to imagine any way of privatizing the entire property of that huge nation without much of it falling into the hands of people of power and influence.

Thus the Yeltsin program took the economy beyond the point of no return. The question now is what the regime can do to consolidate the nascent market economy and set it on a vigorous growth path. The conditions required for the resumption of growth fall into two groups: the maintenance of macroeconomic stability, and the strengthening of the institutions that support a market economy.

On the first count, the Yeltsin government's performance has been mixed. On the positive side, the ruble held stable until 1998 and inflation was tamed, declining by 1997 to the acceptable annual rate of 11 percent. There was a growing looming threat, however, in the form of a persistent government budget deficit that stood at 7 percent of GDP in 1997 (OECD 1998, p. 149). The succession of annual deficits had been financed by large-scale borrowing, both at home and abroad, much of it short-term and at high interest rates. By mid-1988, the short-term debt held by Russian commercial banks and foreign investors (about $25 billion) substantially exceeded Russian international reserves ($15 billion) (Aslund 1998, p. 313). The Asian financial crisis and the drop in the world price of oil further reduced investors' willingness to continue buying Russian treasure bills. Confronted with the prospect of a massive flight from the ruble to the dollar, on August 17, 1998, the government recognized the inevitable; it declared a moratorium on its debt payments, the ruble fell sharply, and inflation accelerated to an annual rate of 60 percent (*Financial Times*, December 9, 1998, p. 3). The new Primakov government has not yet committed itself to a program that promises a solution to the budget-deficit problem; nor are there any proposals on the horizon that inspire confidence that macroeconomic stability is within reach.

Progress in strengthening the supporting institutions of capitalism has also been slow, and the prospect is bleak. To note a few of the items on the long litany:

> The institutions of law and order are unable to control the criminal organizations that extort large sums from business enterprises, virtually with impunity. The business risk is compounded by the threat of personal violence.

> The courts of law are too feeble to enforce contracts. Firms do not expect to get satisfaction from the courts for goods contracted for but not received or for the failure of a customer to pay for goods shipped. Legitimate firms therefore sometimes turn to criminal organizations to collect bills due.

> Government regulation of banks, financial markets, and corporate governance is weak. There are no conflict-of-interest laws, and victims of fraud have little recourse.

> Clear title to land and productive assets is difficult to establish and defend. A firm that buys a building or a tract of land may find its ownership contested by a city or regional government that claims ownership.

> Private ownership of farm land is particularly difficult to establish, and people who have defied the collective farms by trying to operate their private farms have confronted enormous obstacles.

> Taxes are levied and rates changed arbitrarily.

> The extraction of bribes by government officials, including police officers, judges, customs officials, and others whose authorization is required for the conduct of business, is endemic..

To list those items is to identify the fundamental obstacle to consolidation of the market economy. All of them require a strong federal government supported by a reasonably competent and honest administrative staff, but political and social conditions make it unlikely that such a government will emerge in the near future. The electoral system is bound to give the anticapitalist forces a strong hold on the Duma for some time, and government power has slipped from the hands of the reformers into those of the prereform *nomenklatura* led by Prime Minister Primakov. Regional (Siberia), ethnic (Bashkir), and sectoral (collective farm) interests compound the difficulty of collecting taxes and executing national policy. Under these conditions there is little prospect that the government can make rapid headway in establishing law and order and strengthening the institutions upon which a market economy thrives.

That does not at all mean that the transformation will not eventually succeed. Markets, like weeds, are able to seize hold and grow in the most inhospitable of environments. What it does mean is that the process of economic consolidation and growth in Russia will be slow until the new society matures sufficiently to generate an effective democratic political system.

Consolidation proceeded more rapidly in the Baltic countries and Eastern Europe, where the rejection of communism was more enthusiastic because of its association with Soviet domination. The establishment of institutions supportive of markets also proceeded more rapidly because the older population had grown up and lived under such institutions before their countries came under communist control. Hence, while they also suffered an initial decline in output, growth resumed quite rapidly in many of them, starting with Poland as early as 1992. With the exception of the Baltic states, in the other former Soviet republics consolidation proceeded slowly and output continued to decline (World Bank 1996, p. 173).

The International Role

The outside world has made its major contribution to the consolidation of the new economies by what it has *not* done. By not taking full advantage of Russia's present military weakness, it has enabled that much-troubled country to concentrate on the rebuilding of its society without having to deal with a hostile foreign environment. The NATO expansion is a small cloud on that otherwise benign horizon, but it is unlikely to place a significantly larger military burden on the strained state budget.

There are times when a timely and large infusion of foreign resources can make a crucial contribution to a country's recovery. The Marshall Plan made such a contribution after World War II, and the West has been criticized for not having risen to the occasion in the case of the transition countries (Soros 1997, p. 47). In fact, however, the international community was quick to organize a set of new programs to support the transition process, and in the case of Central and Eastern Europe, official aid flows came to about the same proportion of GDP as under the Marshall Plan (World Bank 1996, p. 48). Aid flows came later to the countries that were slower to undertake reforms, which include Russia and many of the former Soviet republics. Yet Russia has now become the third largest client of the World Bank, which had lent it $6.5 billion as of mid-1996 (*Transition*, May 1996, p. 25). It is also the largest client of the IMF, accounting for a fifth of all of the IMF's outstanding loans. By qualifying for IMF loans, Russia improved its credit rating sufficiently that it was able to raise $34.2 billion in private capital markets (*Financial Times*, December 9, 1998, p. 3). International organizations have also provided a large volume of valuable technical assistance in the areas of their expertise, such as finance, tax collection, and statistics. The United States, the European Union, and other governments and agencies have also provided technical assistance to Russia and other transition countries in a great many areas, including accounting and auditing methods, economics education and analysis, and corporate law and governance.

It is often said that what developing countries need more than grants and loans from official organizations is access to the markets of the richer countries. That is particularly true of the former communist countries, which had traded excessively with each other and too little with the rest of the world. The European Union is the natural market for many of the transition countries' exports, and has indeed become a major importer from those countries, but it has been unwilling to subject its own farmers and manufacturers fully to that new competition. The reduction in those trade barriers could make a significant contribution to the transition process, particularly in Eastern Europe, but the prospect looks dim.[7]

The big disappointment in the case of Russia is the scanty inflow of private capital. Foreign direct investment could make a major contribution to the transition because it brings with it not only physical capital but human capital —particularly knowledge of world quality standards, marketing, cost accounting, finance, and other such matters that played no role in the working lives of people who grew up in the planned economies. Moreover, the volume of worldwide foreign direct investment dwarfs the flow of international official funds; the flow to developing and transition countries alone amounted to $1.6 trillion during 1990 to 1995 (World Bank 1996, p. 136). The enviable growth performance of many Asian countries derives from their ability to tap into that capital flow. Some of the East European transition countries have also attracted a substantial quantity of foreign capital; by mid-1997 the stock of foreign direct investment per capita in Russia amounted to $70, compared to $140 in Poland and $1,300 in Hungary (OECD 1997, p. 69).

The potential is there, and Western business recognizes it.

Russian securities are known to be greatly underpriced; a dollar invested in Russian oil shares buys ownership of about 15 times as many barrels of reserves as a dollar invested in Exxon shares. Yet, writes a businessman, "you think not of the *return on* the money you invest, but the *return of* the money" (Biggs 1996, p. 3). Many companies have nevertheless invested directly in small enterprises and joint ventures in order to establish a presence in the Russian market. They are making a valuable contribution toward the diffusion of Western business and managerial experience in Russia, but their commitment of funds has been small and their present inclination is to wait and see. The cautious attitude applies to Russian citizens as well. The transition process has enabled many Russians to accumulate substantial wealth, with $40 to 50 billion of it parked abroad (*Transition*, April 1997, p. 10).

The international community could provide more official aid than it has. Russia has not reached the limit of what it can profitably absorb, in such forms as technical assistance and funds to support the social safety net. However, there is little prospect that those programs will be greatly expanded. At a time when governments are under pressure to cut their own social expenditures, it would be hard to make the case for additional help to the Russians in that respect.

Nor is there reason to believe that a large further expansion of technical assistance would make a critical difference. The key to accelerating the transition lies not in official aid but in private investment. Russia could use more people with training in business management and tax law, but it is not the shortage of such skills that discourages foreign businessmen from risking their funds in Russia. It is the absence of an economic environment that would provide investors with the confidence that their funds would be secure and the returns competitive with other parts of the world. It is doubtful that an increase in official aid can do very much to promote the establishment of that environment. Economic change waits upon political change, reports the World Bank (*Transition*, May 1996, p. 2), and the source of political change lies deep within the society itself, well beyond the reach of the best-intentioned international community.

13

International Influences on Democratization in Postcommunist Europe

J. C. Sharman and Roger E. Kanet

THE STUDY OF democratic regimes has been marked in the last two decades by a switch from the search for socioeconomic prerequisites for democracy, in line with the tenets of modernization theory, to the analysis of interdependent choices and decisions made by actors in the open and fluid context of democratic transitions. The wave of such transitions beginning in Portugal and Spain in the mid-1970s refocused the attention of students of comparative politics on the contingent outcomes produced by various strategies employed by elite political groups within authoritarian governments and prodemocracy oppositions.[1] The contrasting circumstances and different paths to democracy across Southern Europe and Latin America cast increasing doubt on those approaches that stressed particular class configurations, education levels, and other structural variables. Spanning the divide between the two schools, however, is the assertion that domestic factors, whether elite bargaining and negotiation or economic development, are paramount in determining whether a nation makes the transition to democracy and is successful in entrenching the new postauthoritarian constitutional arrangements. In their seminal work on democratic transitions, one of the most confident conclusions reached by Guillermo O'Donnell and Philippe Schmitter is that for each of their contemporary cases, "domestic factors play a predominant role in the transition. . . . there is no transition whose beginning is not the consequence—direct or indirect—of important divisions within the authoritarian regimes itself" (1986, p. 19). Even those later commentators detailing the role of international factors have continued to uphold the centrality of domestic conflicts and coalitions.[2]

The collapse of communism, first in Eastern Europe[3] and then in the Soviet Union, has returned questions concerning the role of international influences on the process of democratization to center stage, for both scholars and policy-makers. This is not only because of the role played by the Soviet policies of glasnost and perestroika in undermining the communist regimes in Eastern Europe and in the abandonment of the Brezhnev Doctrine in late 1989, but also because, above all else, the temporal proximity of the various transitions from authoritarian communism constituted one of the most noticeable commonalties across the former Soviet bloc. Even in Yugoslavia and Albania, long independent of Soviet control, the *ancien régimes* failed to outlive the "people power" revolutions in East Germany and Czechoslovakia by more than a few years. In the absence of formal political learning, a diffusion effect culminated in the institution of democratic governance across Eastern Europe and most of the Soviet successor states. In this regard, the importance of international factors—first, the Soviet decision no longer to impose its views on Eastern Europe, and second, a diffusion or contagion effect—were qualitatively greater in the former communist countries than in earlier Southern European and Latin American transitions.

With the emergence of around 20 new democracies by the beginning of 1992, the role of international political and economic variables in fostering the continued development and consolidation of representative governments and capitalist economies ("market democracies" in current parlance) has become a matter of importance to the West, which has identified crucial humanitarian, economic, and security interests riding on the long-term success of the transition. "Democratic enlargement" has become a key slogan of the Clinton administration's foreign policy (see Brinkley 1997; Carothers 1995), while the European Union has coordinated the largest part of the economic aid program directed toward the postcommunist states.

Given the epochal nature of the democratic revolutions of 1989 to 1991 and the vital Western interests at stake in the success of the European third-wave transitions, much effort has been devoted to ascertaining the role of international influences in the consolidation of the new political arrangements in Eastern Europe, Russia, and the other Soviet successor states and determining how the West can most effectively aid this process of democratic consolidation. However, despite the attention that these issues have attracted, the role of international factors remains poorly understood. Partially as a result, some Western assistance programs have proved to be of limited value or even to be counterproductive. Apart from an unwillingness by many Western countries, particularly in the European Union, to sacrifice immediate narrow economic goals in favor of bolstering the consolidation process (discussed later), there has been a fallacious tendency to assume that "all good things go together": democracy, political stability, economic restructuring, and peace. It is the authors' contention that, although international factors strongly affect the context and direction of democratic consolidation in postcommunist Europe, attempts to help this process along have often run afoul of the conflicting imperatives of governmental stability, representativeness, and economic reform.

Contrary to Western official beliefs concerning the complementary and mutually reinforcing nature of democratic consolidation and the replacement of the command economy by the market, as often as not international efforts directed at promoting one goal may be irrelevant or even deleterious to the achievement of others. Confronted with trade-offs, countries have made choices on an ad hoc basis, commonly without adequate information. At the narrowly political level, these trade-offs have arisen from the tension between assistance programs directed to achieve a consolidated regime, as opposed to the prerequisites of a more democratic one. Economically, the desire to implement macrostabilization policies in line with IMF prescriptions in a technocratic fashion has often come at the expense of consultation and negotiation. National security concerns have also had differing effects on the process of democratization. In order best to demonstrate the trade-offs and limitations of Western assistance programs, it is necessary first to identify the role of international influences in general on the democratization process, and then to survey the dominant, and sometimes erroneous, conventional wisdom that has so far informed Western efforts to entrench democracy across the former Communist bloc.

Democratic Consolidation

In speaking about the process of democratization, an initial distinction must be made between transition and consolidation. The first refers to the changeover from an authoritarian to an elected representative government no longer beholden to the previous authoritarian rulers. Consolidation is a separate issue in that, even though a transition to democracy has been made, it may be reversed. Scholars have often bemoaned the inconsistent manner in which the term is employed, charging that consolidation is an unclear, unbounded concept without a commonly agreed-upon definitional core (Schedler 1998). Nevertheless, consolidation most often refers to the process by which democratic arrangements become stabilized, institutions take root, and actors' expectations and goals are modified to work within the strictures of the prevailing system. For present purposes, when discussing the causal effect of international factors on the process of democratization in the former Soviet Union and Eastern Europe, we are interested in democratic consolidation. Transitions have already occurred in the postcommunist states (with the exception of Belarus, Serbia, and much of the Southern tier of the former USSR), while the tasks of consolidation are very much unfinished, and it is here that the West has sought to make its mark.

As Adam Przeworski puts it, democracy is consolidated when "it is the only game in town" (1991); others speak of when "the rules according to which political and distributional conflicts are carried out are relatively immune from becoming themselves the object of such conflict" (Elster, Offe, and Preuss 1998, p. 28). Although it is very difficult to determine just when a democracy has become consolidated, there are three broad sets of characteristics associated with such a condition. These criteria can be divided into those relating to the degree to which the exercise of power is institutionalized and consistent with formal rules laid out in the constitution, the development of a stable party system and appropriate links between civil society and the political system, and finally the extent to which democratic ideals and institutions have gained subjective acceptance and legitimacy among both political elites and the population at large. Perhaps the most representative work on the subject, Juan Linz's and Alfred Stepan's *Problems of Democratic Transition and Consolidation*, also adopts a tripartite definition based on behavioral, attitudinal, and constitutional factors:

> Behaviorally, democracy becomes the only game in town when no significant political group seriously attempts to overthrow the democratic regime or secede from the state. . . . Attitudinally, democracy becomes the only game in town when, even in the face of severe political and economic crises, the overwhelming majority of the people believe that further political changes must emerge from within the parameters of democratic formulas. Constitutionally, democracy becomes the only game in town when all of the actors become habituated to the fact that political conflict will be resolved according to established norms and that violations of these norms are likely to be both ineffective and costly. (Linz and Stepan 1996, p. 5)

As can be seen, both of the last two criteria are in fact attitudinal, one referring to the attitudes of the masses and the other to elite attitudes. Because consolidation is not just a matter of formal constitutional arrangements or observable behavior, but also of subjective beliefs and values, the study of democratic consolidation is indeed an inexact science; nevertheless the characteristics listed above provide an adequate starting point for analysis.

International Influences on Democratization

At the broadest level, international influences on the process of democratization can be divided into two groups. The first is connected with the issue of Western Europe, and the West in general, serving as a role model. The presumption is that liberal democracy and capitalism represent both the normal path of development, in contrast to the communist "experiment" or deviation, and the goal to be achieved. The particular mixture of peace, prosperity, and democracy enjoyed by the nations of the European Union is the example before all the nations of postcommunist Europe, and is in large part the driving force behind the whole process. The lack of ideological competitors brought about by the bankruptcy of Soviet-style socialism and the global retreat of the left has meant that even nominally socialist parties, upon accession to power in Hungary, Poland, Lithuania, the Czech Republic, and elsewhere, have continued to privatize state firms, reform the price system, and pursue conservative fiscal policies broadly in line with Western desires and the policies of their anticommunist predecessors. Although diffuse, the democratic zeitgeist, the unchallengeable success of the West in providing civil rights and material welfare to its citizenry, and the lack of alternative visions have contributed more to the continued efforts of the former communist countries to democratize and reform their economies than any other factor, domestic or international. In this sense the West can provide the greatest impetus for the ongoing transformations merely by continuing to satisfy the demands of its own population and maintaining pervasive diffusion of Western culture (see Pridham 1994).

The second group of international influences includes those deliberate policy measures taken by the West to assist democratic consolidation. For, beyond providing exemplars of the objectives to which the current social dislocation and trauma of political and economic transformation will hopefully give way, the United States and the European Union countries have sought actively to foster the consolidation of postcommunist democracies. This support has been extended directly, through democratic assistance and traditional foreign policy means, and indirectly, through economic support. By some measures the amount of aid given to former communist countries during the years 1990 to 1994 was greater in inflation-adjusted figures than that provided to Western Europe by the United States through the Marshall Plan.[4] Rhetorical commitment has been of a similar magnitude: "Clinton officials stock almost every general foreign policy speech with the argument that promoting democracy abroad advances US interests" (Carothers, 13). European Union and US statesmen repeatedly point out the interest that the West has in the long-term success of the democratic transitions, because of a whole series of interrelated virtues exhibited by consolidated democracies. As the official in charge of American aid to the Soviet successor states put it, American policy "rests on a simple principle: the security of the United States and the rest of the world is immeasurably enhanced if Russia, Ukraine and the rest of the NIS [Newly Independent States] are stable market democracies" (Morningstar 1997). Stable market democracies are held to be peaceful by nature, better trading partners, as well as less likely to engage in or support terrorism (Talbott 1996).

To reach the goal of a stable market democracy, not only must the command economy be dismantled, but an acceptable rate of economic growth must also be attained whereby people's standard of living is brought to (at least) the level they enjoyed under communism. A consensus exists on a package of measures that must be taken in order to traverse the path of economic reform and halt and reverse the catastrophic drop in production levels that has afflicted most of the region's economies since the early 1990s. Once again goals are viewed as mutually reinforcing; economic restructuring and the increasing prominence of market mechanisms reinforce democratization by reducing the power of the government in the everyday lives of its citizens, and the economic growth that results blunts the acrimony of political conflict, as people become more satisfied and distributional questions can be resolved with growing resources rather than within a static or shrinking pie.

The relationship between wealth and democracy is no longer as clear as it was once held to be, but severe economic depression is still counted as a mortal threat to democracy, and especially unconsolidated democracy (see Przeworski and Limongi 1997; Londregan and Poole 1996). That version of modernization theory that centers around the natural development of representative government with increasing affluence has been eclipsed, but with the collapse of the Weimar Republic still the paradigmatic case of the breakdown of democracy, scholars continue to stress the zero-sum nature imparted to political competition in an environment of economic uncertainty and widespread poverty (Linz and Stepan 1978). With the majority worse off than before the collapse of communism, no longer able to rely on pervasive consumer subsidies and security of employment but exposed to the conspicuous consumption of the wealthy few, economic growth is touted as the most certain way to bring tangible benefits to the broad masses of the population and thereby give them a stake in the transformation being wrought. That evenly distributed growth would improve the chances of democratic consolidation is commonsensical; that Western policies currently being pursued are optimal for achieving this end is another matter. Additionally, there has been a failure to appreciate that the methods by which Western assistance have been directed and Western economic advice imposed, far from strengthening the consolidation of democratic institutions and practices, has often actually undermined them.

Finally, even direct political assistance devoted to democratic consolidation has often been misdirected or fallen victim to the hybrid nature of the task at hand: Which is valued more, the stability of existing arrangements, or the advancement and deepening of democratic procedures? As with the issues raised above, the point is not that different goals are mutually exclusive or that favoring one goal ahead of others is wrong, but that Western political and economic attempts to further the processes of democratization in former communist Europe have often misfired because goals that were assumed to be all of a piece have actually involved trade-offs between conflicting objects. A greater awareness of these trade-offs would allow more informed choices to be made about where to direct resources and how to set priorities, while also avoiding policies that undo the results of earlier efforts or retard democratic consolidation more than advancing it.

The "Democratic Peace," European Security, and NATO

The national security benefits derived from stable democracies across Eastern Europe and the former Soviet Union rest on the assumptions of the "democratic peace" thesis. In fact, the thesis has a substantial proviso that, while democracies do not fight other democracies, or do so only very rarely, they are just as likely to go to war as are authoritarian states against non-democratic states (see Russett 1993).[5] History has so far lent strong support to the general argument that democracies do not fight one another, and thus it is assumed that each stable democracy is a country that can be crossed off the list of threats to the Atlantic Alliance. The reasons why democracies have not fought each other are not fully understood, with theories ranging from the historical rarity of democracies, to shared cultures, to the slow-moving nature of decision-making in democratic systems of limited governments (Lynn-Jones et al. 1995). Whatever the case, the most commonly advanced justification for the diversion of scarce Western resources to its former enemies is enlightened self-interest in terms of the security benefits obtained at a price far lower than Cold War–level military spending. The assumption is that money spent promoting democracy also preserves or promotes peace because stable market democracies are inherently pacific and conversely that, as war tends to subvert democracy, effort devoted to ending wars in Yugoslavia and elsewhere will ease the path to democratization.

Although Western security concerns have been the commonly advanced reason for American and European taxpayers to help underwrite the transition from communism to democracy and the market, the security concerns of the East European and Soviet successor states themselves have also had powerful ramifications for democratic consolidation. Most drastically, the transition to democracy was largely stillborn in those former Yugoslav and Soviet republics recently involved in large-scale hostilities: Croatia, Bosnia-Herzegovina, Serbia-Montenegro, Armenia, Azerbaijan, and Tadjikistan. Although it is not possible to ascribe the failure of transition exclusively to the various conflicts, the difficulty of contesting existing government policy without being branded as traitors and the rigors of a wartime environment have been formidable obstacles.

Western governments have attempted to assuage the security concerns of East Europeans to reduce the risk of further outbreaks of nationalist wars, but also as part of a deliberate effort to foster democratic consolidation. In fact, one of the most common arguments in support of NATO expansion into Central Europe has emphasized the support that it will provide to the democratization process under way in the region (see Goldgeier 1998). The objective of expanding and establishing a range of security-related international organizations has been both to build confidence between states no longer locked into opposing alliances, and to establish a system of rewards and punishments to encourage democratization. The idea of "conditionality," whereby Western assistance and favors are dependent upon free and fair elections, the observance of civil rights, and the like, has been central to Western policy since 1989, particularly for the European Union. Conditionality in security matters is most noticeable in the Organization for Security and Cooperation in Europe (OSCE) and in relation to discussions over expanding NATO membership. The OSCE has had a modest, though significant, impact in promoting consolidation, but NATO expansion has had a more ambivalent effect, positive with respect to Poland, the Czech Republic, and Hungary (the first countries admitted), but negative in Russia.[6]

During its Cold War history, NATO did not specify that its members must be democracies; at times authoritarian states like Portugal, Greece, and Turkey retained full membership rights and privileges. NATO was first linked to democratic consolidation efforts with the admission of Spain in 1981, a move in part motivated by the desire to engage the military further in professional activities and thereby lessen the temptation to meddle in domestic politics. Recent moves toward expansion have been explicitly conditional, being dependent on democratic governance and civilian control of the military (necessitating a change in Polish defense ministers). As such, the lure of NATO membership has provided a strong incentive for continued democratization among realistic contenders for membership (the above mentioned three, plus Slovenia and Romania), and to some extent even unrealistic contenders such as the Baltic states. NATO expansion has had a far less benign effect on political developments in Russia. Reformers in Russia have often remarked that, in failing to allow for wounded Russian national pride and in riding roughshod over Russian national interests, the West has only advanced the position of antidemocratic and anti Western forces. That the Russian government, in May 1997, bowed to the inevitable and accepted the idea of NATO expansion into Central Europe, despite having most of its substantive demands rejected, only increases the chance that a future Russian regime will live up to the way it is typecast in the West, and particularly in Eastern Europe, as a threat to the stability and independence of its neighbors. Measures that can entrench democracy in one country can, thus, substantially complicate consolidation in another.

Western Development Assistance

By monetary value alone, the lion's share of Western assistance has been devoted to the task of economic restructuring and stabilization.[7] In keeping with the "stable market democracy" formula, the switch away from bureaucratic to market coordination mechanisms is seen to provide the best prospects for growth which, in turn, enhances the opportunities for democratization and helps to consolidate those advances already made. In this sense very little economic aid is exclusively economic in intent; because economic stability is seen as a prerequisite for political stability, grants and credits have a definite political purpose, and most of the aid is explicitly or implicitly conditional on governments acting within a democratic-constitutional framework. The main economic assistance programs have been run through the Commission of the European Union, the Washington-based financial institutions (the International Monetary Fund and the World Bank), the European Bank for Reconstruction and Development, and various U.S. bilateral funding arrangements.

The then European Community began stepping up its relations with Eastern Europe in 1988, but these efforts were quickly superseded with the overthrow of communism. The European Community's (EC) economic assistance has been divided between technical assistance programs and trade agreements. In July 1989 at the Paris G7 summit the PHARE program (Pologne Hongrie: aide à la restructuration Économique) was initiated, at first directed at Poland and Hungary, but subsequently extended to Bulgaria, Czechoslovakia, Romania, Yugoslavia, Albania, and the Baltic states. Although a combined effort by the G7, the Organization for Economic Cooperation and Development, and the European Community, the last-mentioned was entrusted with administering the program. PHARE was later matched by TACIS (Technical Assistance for the Commonwealth of Independent States), and in combination they account for the bulk of Western technical support to Eastern Europe and the former Soviet republics. Both PHARE and TACIS include strong conditionality components. Romania, for example, was excluded from PHARE aid from mid-1990 to January 1991 after miners were brought into Bucharest to suppress antigovernment student demonstrations.

A second tier of West European development activities has comprised the European Union's signing a series of Association Agreements (or "European Agreements") involving a limited trade liberalization with former communist countries. Once again a strongly conditional aspect is included. The agreements are based on five principles of "the establishment of the rule of law; respect for human rights; the introduction of multi-party democracy; the holding of free and fair competitive elections; and the development of market-oriented economies" (Hyde-Price 1994, pp. 233–34). Aside from trade matters, there are also subsidiary sections dealing with consultation among the countries and the regulation of the movement of people and capital. The heart of the agreements, however, is a ten-year schedule for freeing up trade in manufactures between the EU and the Eastern European countries. Reductions take place asymmetrically, with the EU lowering its barriers earlier in line with its stronger economic status.

The Association Agreements include considerable limitations, which are symptomatic of broader shortcomings in the European Union's strategy for encouraging the growth of stable market democracies in Eastern Europe and, to a lesser extent, in the Soviet successor states. First, the Association Agreements clearly do not include membership or even a promise of future membership in the EU. The prospect of membership in the European Community was a major factor in the transition to and consolidation of democracy in Portugal and Spain (Whitehead 1986), but because of self-absorption on the part of the EU, stemming first from the implementation of the terms of the Maastricht Treaty and then monetary union, even the "fast-track" postcommunist states can expect admission only after 2005 (*Economist* 1998).

The consolation prize of Association Agreements was also marked by serious flaws, which led to the initial negotiations of 1990 and 1991 being much longer and acrimonious than had been expected. This hinged on the problem that West European markets continued to be closed to precisely those products that Eastern Europe had the best chance of exporting: steel, agricultural products, textiles, and apparel. In these areas, nontariff barriers such as antidumping regulations, voluntary export restraints, restrictive technical standards, quota restrictions, and restrictive health and sanitary regulations effectively shut out goods from the East (Organisation for Economic Cooperation and Development 1992). Thus, "there was considerable ironic bitterness in Central Europe that, while EC members lectured them on the virtues of the free market, it looked at one stage as if the negotiations might collapse over protection of French and Irish beef, Spanish steel and textiles, and Scottish raspberries" (Gower 1993, p. 292). The plausible suspicion existed that the agreements were designed to minimize adjustment pressures on the EU rather than to effect an East European recovery (Csaba, 1995, pp. 256–60). The single most important measure that the European Union could take to boost economic recovery and thereby contribute to consolidating the new democracies would be to open its markets, in line with both East European requests and Western economic advice.

A final European Union commitment to East European economic recovery has been the European Bank for Reconstruction and Development, set up in London on the initiative of the French government. The EBRD had an extremely slow start, for several years spending more on its own setup costs than was actually disbursed to the former communist countries, and has come in for considerable criticism (Hutchings 1997, pp. 207–8; Csaba 1995, p. 263).

U.S.' aid, both bilateral and that coming under the auspices of the Washington-based international financial institutions, has included a greater grant component than is included in the European aid, which has tended to consist of loans and trade credits, in response the Europeans' claim they have provided six times more to Eastern Europe than has the United States (*Economist* 1997). A greater proportion of the American aid has been directed toward the former Soviet republics and particularly Russia; indeed, some East European countries have suffered from the shift of attention after 1991 that resulted in a sharing of aid with all the Soviet successor states. Aside from assistance provided to ensure compliance with arms treaties, economic aid has had the purpose of helping to build "stable market democracies." The confidence expressed that economic transition assists democratic consolidation is, however, often misplaced. This is not only because of the hardships and inequalities that result, but more because of the manner in which decisions have been taken and implemented; in effect, to avoid those institutions of democratic government that might slow, review, or reject measures in line with societal interests, and thereby stymie technocratic prescriptions.

From the collapse of the Soviet Union in 1991 to October 1995, the United States obligated about $15 billion to the Soviet successor states, not including IMF and World Bank support (Menges 1996). Roughly half of this aid has gone to Russia, with the rest going to the other republics, particularly, in the last few years, to Ukraine and Armenia. The International Monetary Fund, ostensibly concerned with technical economic matters, has in fact coordinated with other Western institutions in the pursuit of foreign-policy objectives. IMF approval for a sizable loan came just in time to lend the appearance of plausibility to Boris Yeltsin's reelection promises in 1996, and further IMF money was proffered as a reward for Russian cooperation on NATO expansion. Such economic aid is thus strongly imbued with political conditionality, in terms of narrow foreign-policy objectives, but more importantly because of the purported mutual reinforcement of the market economy and democratic polity. In economic terms such credits have usually gone toward macroeconomic stabilization, microeconomic restructuring (including privatization), and currency stabilization.

Despite the benefits accruing from IMF support (in Eastern Europe if not Russia), the tendency to date of Western donors to evade democratic institutions and social consultation and to rely instead on cliques with narrow bases of institutional and popular support has been profoundly harmful to democratic consolidation. Przeworski holds that one of the major differences between democracy and authoritarianism is the fact that in the former the rules are certain but the outcomes are uncertain, in contrast to dictatorships, where the rule of law is forsaken to achieve the outcome favored by the rulers (1991). Democracies are different not so much in the particular policies they adopt, as in the rules that govern the process by which policy is formulated. Political agency must be institutionalized (Elster, Offe, and Preuss 1998). The technocratic approach to economic reform undermines democracy in its insistence that certain policy measures must be implemented and, thus, that those rules or institutions that delay or amend the necessary measures must be evaded or preempted. In Russia, virtually none of the regulations governing economic reform have gone through the legislature, rather, they have been promulgated by presidential decree. In addition, the United States Agency for International Development (USAID) has set up a variety of semi-private organizations to carry though economic reform measures, avoiding both parliamentary scrutiny and the control of the relevant ministries (Wedel 1996). The persistent desire of both those in charge of American economic aid programs and those few of the recipients charged with administration to evade the slowing effects of divided government and democratic processes does nothing to foster the institutional culture and participatory decision-making that are so necessary for the consolidation of democracy. It sets a poor precedent to rule that a certain class of decisions is "too important" to be subjected to public scrutiny or to the compromises inherent in divided government, particularly when the measures in question will have such a lasting impact on society and impose severe privations on large sections of the population.

The corollary of this impatience with due process has been the habit of relying on a very narrow base of support, usually clustered around one key personality. Not only does this behavior tend to mortgage democracy to the welfare of one personality (as the United States was criticized for being over-reliant on Gorbachev for too long), but the schematic representation of "reformers versus the rest" tends to be highly misleading, except to the degree that it is self-fulfilling. In contemporary Russia the chosen few (apart from Yeltsin himself), formerly the St. Petersburg group around Anatoly Chubais, were somewhat hyperbolically referred to by a top official of

USAID as "the Adam Smiths of Russian reform economics" (Dine 1995, p. 29). The strategy of "picking winners" retards or reverses democratic consolidation in the same way as does shielding economic reform from ministerial, legislative, and public comment and amendment. Furthermore, it tends to be even more prevalent at the level of direct democratization aid, where the United States has tried not only to pick but also to create winners.

Political Assistance

Direct political aid has come from both the United States and the European Community, in the form of both government programs and those sponsored by a wide variety of private and semiprivate institutes (see Quigley 1997). Western advice has been sought and proffered on constitutional design and electoral systems. Observers have supervised and certified the free and fair nature of most postcommunist elections, while the OSCE and Council of Europe have been particularly active in the cause of promoting human rights. A huge number of conferences and seminars have been held dealing with the mechanics of democratic governance, from passing legislation to judicial review. Finally, there have been consistent attempts to contribute to the rebuilding of civil society after the suppression of independent associational life under communism, including building links with political parties, trade unions, media networks, environmental groups, churches, civil rights organizations, and so on.

The United States set up direct democratization assistance with the program entitled Support for East European Democracy shortly after the 1989 revolutions, initially to help run the first set of free elections, and thereafter to promote many of the type of civil associations listed above. Funding has been provided for this and other programs from the USAID, the National Endowment for Democracy, and other governmental agencies. For example, the Department of Defense has provided democratization assistance to formerly communist militaries through a series of programs that have not been especially clear in either their purpose or their execution (Ulrich 1996, pp. 350–403).

The OSCE set up the Office for Free Elections in Warsaw, and the Council of Europe has provided the Demosthenes Program from 1990 to promote pluralist democracy and the rule of law in a series of seminars requested by a number of postcommunist countries. The council has further established the European Commission of Democracy through Law, or Venice Commission, to provide advice on constitutional design (Hyde-Price, 1994). Private West European bodies such as the Westminster Foundation for Democracy and the Konrad Adenauer Foundation have sponsored exchanges and conferences (Shin 1994; Lazar 1996). The greatest private contribution to the consolidation of democracy in Eastern Europe has been from the Soros Foundation, which, apart from setting up the Central European University, has also instituted a variety of decentralized "Open Society" projects across the region. Although the amounts invested in such programs has tended to be an order of magnitude smaller than those devoted to economic reform and adjustment, they have established a wide coverage across the new democracies of Eastern Europe and, to a lesser extent, the Soviet successor states (Quigley 1997, pp. 87–102).

In Lieu of Conclusions

Because of the vast array of factors contributing to the success or failure of democracy, and the modest and usually unquantifiable contribution that direct democratization assistance makes to consolidation in any particular country, it is difficult to assess their overall effectiveness. However, it seems apparent that some generalizations may be ventured, as similar assumptions underlie different assistance efforts throughout the region, and persistent misapprehensions have clouded their potential contribution in the same way as with the administration of economic aid. Perhaps the most incisive assessment of Western democracy assistance aid has been made by Thomas Carothers (1996). He notes, first of all, that at best such aid will have a marginal effect on consolidation. Even if the amounts devoted were increased tenfold, the intangible cultural basis and legitimacy of democratic institutions and democracy in general are attained through the passage of time and the successful workings of the system; this sort of major attitude change cannot be bought.[8] This is all the more so when it is remembered that most of the money devoted to democratization assistance is spent on Western consultants and intermediary organizations.

The degree to which external actors can promote democracy is examined by Laurence Whitehead in a study of United States attempts in Latin America (1991). He concludes that the imposition of democracy can be reliably achieved only by incorporating the country into an existing democratic state (his example is Puerto Rico), and somewhat less dependably by invasion and occupation, as in the cases of post–World War II West Germany and Japan. In other words, short of major efforts akin to those undertaken by the Western occupying power in Germany and Japan in the wake of World War II,[9] democracy will become consolidated, remain unstable, or fail in Eastern Europe and the Soviet successor states to the extent that it attracts domestic support and legitimacy, and is dependent on the skill and foresight of native politicians. A partial exception to this might occur were there to be a thoroughgoing European Union trade liberalization in steel, textiles, and agriculture, or early admission of East Central European countries to the union itself, neither of which seems likely within the crucial next five years.

Despite the essentially limited nature of democratization assistance, it has had a significant effect on the dynamics of postcommunist politics, not always in a positive fashion. Western donors have often succumbed to the "picking winners" approach discussed above in relation to economic aid. Two contrasting instances of this tendency have occurred in Russia, where the incumbents have been the favored party, and in Romania, where the opposition received the bulk of support (and has subsequently formed a government). In both cases a highly simplified assessment of the political landscape has resulted in a dichotomous division of pro- and antireform camps. The standard credentials of reformers exacerbate this rather arbitrary categorization: "Western orientation; ability to speak English and converse in donor vernacular of 'markets,' 'reform,' and 'civil society'; already established Western contacts . . . having traveled to and/or studied in the West; and, perhaps the most important, self identification . . . as a reformer and association with other reformers" (Wedel 1996, p. 575). Carothers writes of the early decision by the U.S. government that the Romanian government that had taken power after the 1989 overthrow of Ceauçescu was antireform and therefore antidemocratic, particularly during the period 1990 to 1992, and consequently sought to build up the opposition Democratic Convention as a suitable replacement. The notion of American impartiality between government and opposition became an increasingly transparent fiction:

> Most US officials—and most of the Americans working in the various US organizations involved in democracy assistance programs—had no qualms about the United States taking sides in the Romanian electoral process. . . . In this view . . . it was necessary for the United States to play a partisan role in the elections in order to further the goal of promoting democracy. (Carothers 1996, p. 30)

The opposite bias in Russia may have inculcated the view among Yeltsin officials that the West had anointed them to rule, even in the event of a communist victory in the 1996 presidential elections. A debate about whether to honor the election result took place among presidential aides in the run-up to the election as the president himself, newly fortified by a $10 billion IMF loan, vetoed a bill on establishing the rules for an orderly transfer of power for the stated reason that he would win and thus there was no need for the legislation (White, Rose, and McAllister 1997, p. 242).

All of this is not to say that democratization assistance is bound to backfire or to constitute a waste of time. Such aid can have a moderate positive impact, provided that its application is properly targeted and researched (Quigley, 1997, pp. 103–14). Above all, this means being aware that, although the desired end point is the hybrid entity of (pacific) stable market democracies, not all of these elements are in harmony with each other all the time; on the contrary, striving too hard for one portion of the final objective may mean undoing progress made toward accomplishing the others. Relatively generous financial aid to Ukraine to ensure its stability and independence may detract from incentives to reform the economy and put it back on a productive footing. Pushing through market reform in Russia by using backdoor techniques and informal personal networks has not built confidence in the workings of the fragile democratic processes. Setting priorities and making trade-offs between desirable alternatives may well be inevitable, but donor nations and international organizations should be cognizant of these trade-offs. The phenomenon of democratic consolidation is still poorly understood, but it seems clear that it is a medium- to long-term prospect, reversible under the wrong conditions. Perhaps the most reassuring feature of the West's efforts to promote democracy in postcommunist Europe is the fact that it most powerfully aids this goal simply by doing what it has in the past done better than any competing system: securing and extending the civil rights of its own populations, providing a historically unprecedented standard of living, and exporting its cultural habits and artifacts around the world.

Acknowledgments

The authors wish to express their appreciation for financial support from the Hackett Studentship program of the University of Western Australia (for Dr. Sharman) and from the Office of the Provost of the University of Illinois at Urbana-Champaign which has made the research for this article possible. A German-language version of the article has appeared in *Osteuropa* 48, no. 11–12, (1998): pp. 1069–86, with the title "Internationale Einsflüsse auf den Demokratisierungsprozeb in Osteuropa." A related article entitled "The Challenge of Democratic Consolidation in Postcommunist Europe" has been published in *International Politics*, 35 (September 1998), pp. 1–19.

Part VI

The Colonial Legacy

and Sponsored Transitions

in Africa

14

Understanding Ambiguity during Democratization in Africa

Jeffrey Herbst

ROUGHLY THREE DOZEN countries in Africa are now involved in some type of process of political liberalization. However, democratization across the continent has been problematic. African political institutions are weak, previous efforts at democratization have often failed, and there is frequently a long history of military involvement in politics. Finally, almost all African countries are extremely poor: per capita income on the continent is only $460 (1995 U.S. dollars) (World Bank 1996, p. 189), when it is now estimated that a per capita income of $6,000 is needed to ensure democratization. Indeed, recent data suggest that democracies with a per capita income of less than $1,000 will not last more than eight years (Przeworski and Limongi 1997, p. 165). African democratization represents an unprecedented attempt by a large number of poor countries to liberalize well before they have achieved the level of institutional development and material prosperity typically associated with democracy.

Not surprisingly, there is considerable analytic confusion over what success and failure, especially over the short term, means for poor countries in Africa, and elsewhere, that are trying to democratize. Previous studies of democratic failure largely focused on relatively established democracies where restoration was the major issue. For instance, the well-known Linz and

Stepan project on the breakdown of competitive democracies specifically excluded postcolonial countries from the study (Linz 1978, p. 7). As a result, African countries, despite the fact that they account for a very large percentage of the world's polities (roughly one quarter), have not been included in many studies of democratization (Bratton and van de Walle 1994, p. 453).

Indeed, in a sure sign that the analytic moorings of current scholarship on African democratization are weak to nonexistent, there has been an enormous fluctuation in opinion over the prospects for democracy in Africa. After the first autocrats were overthrown in the early 1990s, there was a tremendous exuberance about the prospects for democracy. For instance, Professor Georges Nzongola-Ntalaja wrote: "The democratic process in Africa today is irreversible. There may be setbacks here and there. . . . But two factors seem to promise hope for the future: The people can no longer be intimidated by the ruling oligarchies. . . . [and] The neocolonial umbrella relied upon by corrupt and discredited regimes to stay in power has collapsed" (Nzongola-Ntalaja 1992, p. 7). Only a few years later, not even a blink in the histories of most countries, opinion is migrating to the other extreme. Thus the *Economist* wrote, "Democracy, at least of the conventional kind, is not working in Africa. . . . African elections are now seldom genuine tests of popular opinion. Except in one or two places, notably South Africa, democratic travesty is the pattern" (*Economist* 1996, p. 20; see also, Caruthers 1997, p. 87). Others are almost as pessimistic about the future. For instance, Dr. Larry Diamond argues that, globally, "We may or may not see the emergence of a few new electoral democracies. But a further sizeable increase seems unlikely" (quoted in Wright 1997, p. 1).

The reasons for these sharp swings of opinion are relatively clear. First, some feel betrayed because the overthrow of a number of African autocrats in the early 1990s has not produced more and better results. Second, since the democratic experience in Africa is so short, analyses are vulnerable to sharp swings due to small changes in the documentary base. Of course, previous analytic disasters in Africa—including the rush to judgment on the viability of the initial postindependence political arrangements, the attribution of characteristics to political parties and militaries that turned out to be incorrect, and the failure to understand the determinants of ethnicity—came about in part because scholars let what they wanted to see influence them in an environment where information was scarce. Finally, and most important, the major conclusions regarding democratization rest on the frail shoulders of elections, arguably the least understood part of the admittedly spotty democratic record in Africa. There has been little attempt to go beyond elections in understanding what has happened in Africa's liberalizing polities. Indeed, the *Economist*, following most others, argues that good news regarding democracy in Africa can be found solely in electoral transitions—as happened in Malawi and Zambia—and that otherwise, "the old dictators and party bosses, with varying degrees of fiddling and bullying, kept their hold on power. In the Gambia, a military dictator arranged for his own election, following the example of Jerry Rawlings in Ghana" (*Economist* 1997, p. 46). Naturally, the reality is both more confused and more interesting. It cannot be said that democratic backsliding in Africa is simply a return to the old authoritarianism that existed across the continent from the 1960s to the 1980s. Indeed, whatever else has happened, it is clear that the old order— characterized by one-party states that had complete control over the media and public life and that faced little domestic or international opposition to their continued rule—is dead. Neither large segments of many African polities nor, critically given the income levels of African countries, donors will stand for the kind of political stagnation that was previously taken for granted. Even the military leaders who had taken power from civilians in Niger and Gambia or, as in Nigeria, from fellow soldiers, have felt compelled to announce that they will hold elections as part of an attempt to legitimate themselves. Usually these elections are farcical but they demonstrate how far some of even the most troubled African polities have traveled from the 1960s and 1970s, when military rule was announced with no hint of an end point and when there were at least some attempts to construct an ideology for the one-party state or rule by the man on horseback.

At the same time, it is hardly the case that democracy is inevitable in Africa, even if the problems posed by low per capita incomes can somehow be breached. Rather than profoundly democratic movements, many of the oppositional movements that confronted African autocrats in the late 1980s and early 1990s were concerned mainly with displacing the incumbent. As Crawford Young has argued, "The widespread perception of the state as predator will not dissolve with a single election. Indeed, a disquieting amount of the energies of democratization draw upon this vast supply of disaffection with the personalized summit of power and the state apparatus as a whole" (Young 1994, p. 244). Indeed, most of the revolts since 1989 against African authoritarianism were largely urban affairs and did not involve the majority of the population that still, in most countries, live in the rural areas (Bratton and van de Walle 1992, p. 31). As a result, few, if any, of the political parties that have come into existence since 1989 have strong rural roots, indicating that one fundamental aspect of African politics—the primacy of the urban population due to its ability to threaten the stability of the government—has not changed.

There is, in fact, little evidence that most of the oppositional movements that forced differing degrees of political liberalization in African countries had any explicit program beyond overthrowing the single leader. These "civilian coups," to borrow Pauline Baker's deft phrase, are weak reeds upon which to build democracies. Indicative of their hasty beginnings and the frequent lack of an accompanying societal consensus, transitions in African countries have been notable in that most lack pacts, agreements that observers have credited for much of the durability demonstrated by South American democracies. Indeed, many have been skeptical about transitions that are not guided by elite agreements (see Karl 1990, p. 9; and Stepan, 1986, p. 78). For instance, little attention has been devoted to social pacts with soldiers that would help develop some kind of consensus that the military should withdraw from politics. Nor, in general, have there been agreements on individual soldiers' culpability for past human rights abuses or theft. Even the national conferences being held in francophone Africa cannot be considered pacts because leaders do not speak for well-defined groups (van de Walle 1994, p. 149).

Similarly, many African countries that have experienced democratic transitions have not evidenced much work in building the foundations of a democratic society. In many countries, the rules that govern the current elections are not significantly different from those inherited from the respective metropoles (district-based systems for anglophone countries, proportional representation for francophone ones) before independence. In few African countries can there be said to be a clear consensus around a democratic theory or even many attempts to construct such an ideology. For instance, most countries do not have a clearly defined role for the military that would keep soldiers permanently out of politics.

Finally, the history of democratization elsewhere suggests that democratization is not a unilinear process and that repeated failure may be an integral part of learning how to succeed. Democratization in Europe took hundreds of years and, while learning how to create democracies can certainly have spread widely, there is little reason to believe that political liberalization can be accomplished in a very short period of time. Indeed, as Lijphart has consistently pointed out, even European democracies vary widely. For instance, the United Kingdom has a highly centralized political system that encourages a small number of parties to compete for power, and does not have a written constitution. In contrast, Switzerland has a decentralized system of power with a proportional representation system that encourages many parties to operate according to a highly detailed constitution (Lijphart 1984, chapters 1 and 2). These nuanced political systems developed in response to the particular political and social conditions existing in their respective countries. They evolved over decades, at least in part in response to political failures.

African countries, if they are to be successful in democratization, will need equally nuanced political systems, each designed to cope with a unique constellation of political, economic, and social forces. Such complex political arrangements cannot be created overnight and will probably evolve only in response to failure. Indeed, even Indian democracy, one of the notable successes in the Third World over the last 40 years, may not yet have developed a set of institutions capable of withstanding the stresses of cultural pluralism (Kohli 1990). While it is not usually considered politic to say, in this democratic age, the truth is that some of the multiparty democracies overthrown in the past in Africa—including the regimes of Hilla Limann in Ghana (overthrown in 1981), Shehu Shagari in Nigeria (1983), and Sadiq el-Mahdi in Sudan (1989)—were highly dysfunctional, although the militaries that succeeded them were not necessarily better governors. There will undoubtedly be other dysfunctional regimes that need to end before their countries can go forward.

If successful, African democratization will be a process that, in most countries, will take decades. As a result, it is likely that there will be considerable confusion regarding the course of African democratization, among both the principals involved and observers, for the foreseeable future. As I noted in 1994, in the near term, it may be clear that many of the upheavals currently occurring across Africa were the precursors of more open, viable political systems. It is far more likely that in a few years the current attempts at political openness will be seen as simply the beginning of an extraordinarily complex process from which emerged a few clear successes, some disasters, and many countries only beginning the struggle to design political systems that are appropriate for their own local circumstances (Herbst 1994, p. 184). The fall from grace of Zambia, to take only the most obvious example, from a country that was widely perceived as leading the democratic transition in Africa in 1991 to one that has come to be seen as heading the democratic retreat because of President Frederick Chiluba's electoral machinations, is a cautionary tale on how fast quick judgments can turn bad.

Obviously, the question becomes: What more can we say about ambiguity during democratization, given the indeterminate state of politics in many African countries? In particular, it would be extremely useful to develop a more nuanced understanding of democratic politics outside of elections. That may appear to be paradoxical, because routine elections are the most significant feature of institutionalized democracies. However, elections are unlikely to be the full story of African democratization for some time. At the same time, it would be useful to be able to learn more from democratic setbacks rather than simply to classify a country as having missed the third wave. Some countries learn from failure, and the setbacks are viewed as useful learning experiences. Other democratic reversals are seen, in retrospect, as unmitigated disasters that derailed a country's progress for a nontrivial period.

Evolution of African Democratization

Table 1 classifies African countries according to their recent democratic history as of the beginning of 1997. At that point there were very few countries that fulfilled Huntington's basic definition of a democracy having at least two transitions of power through free and fair elections (Huntington 1991, p. 267). Ironically, Benin and Madagascar, which joined this category in 1996, both saw the autocrats who lost elections during the first wave of democratization regain power as their successors could not gain the confidence of their constituents.

Table 1: African Countries by Electoral Experience (as of March 1997)

Two Transitions

Benin
Madagascar
Mauritius

Elections, One Transition

Cape Verde
Central African Republic
Comoros
Congo
Lesotho
Malawi
Mali
São Tomé and Principe
Zambia

Civilian Government Overthrown by Military and Ruled by Soldiers

Burundi
Nigeria
Sierra Leone

No Elections

Eritrea
Liberia
Rwanda
Somalia
Sudan
Swaziland
Zaire

Elections, No Transition

Angola	Guinea-Bissau
Botswana	Kenya
Burkina Faso	Mauritania
Cameroon	Mozambique
Chad	Namibia
Côte d'Ivoire	Niger
Equatorial Guinea	Senegal
Ethiopia	Seychelles
Gabon	Tanzania
Gambia	Togo
Ghana	Uganda
Guinea	Zimbabwe

A significant number of countries have also had elections and one transition of power. Inevitably, the democratic credentials of this group are more confused. Indeed, there have already been several defections from this category. Niger had a highly disappointing coup in January 1996 after a long period of government deadlock. The coup not only signaled the end to an important democratic experiment but was the first military intervention in politics in francophone Africa since 1990, suggesting that France would tolerate the overturn of some democratic regimes. Niger's military rulers subsequently had a sham election (thus placing Niger in the elections but no transition category) that demonstrates just how little predictive power one transition can have. The fate of Burundi after its transition election is even more dramatic evidence of the long road that African countries must still travel. In June 1993, Metchior Ndadaye, a representative of the majority Hutu, defeated the then incumbent president Major Paul Buyoya and became the country's first democratically elected president. Ndadaye was assassinated in October 1993 by elements of the army (still controlled by the Tutsi), and his successor, Cyprien Ntaryamira, was killed in the plane crash that also killed the Rwandan president Juvenal Habyarimana in April 1994. Finally, in July 1996, Buyoya overthrew then-president Sylvestre Ntigantunganya to return the military, and the Tutsi minority, to power. In May 1997, Sierra Leone had a relatively unsurprising coup that displaced an extremely fragile democratic government that had come to power after a civil war. Other countries, such as Zambia, are still in the one-transition category but have experienced significant backsliding. Indeed, Zambian President Frederick Chiluba has attracted international opprobrium for changing citizenship and electoral laws to prevent former president Kenneth Kaunda and other prominent opposition leaders from running for office.

Even more difficult to understand is the next category, countries that have had elections that vary in quality from free and fair to farce, but that have not had transitions. In some cases, for instance Kenya and Zimbabwe, the elections are held by civilians and are quite unfair, as the rules and procedures do not allow for serious contestations of political power. Similarly, some elections (including, in 1996, Gambia and Niger) have been held by soldiers to provide the barest fig leaf of legitimacy for their seizure of power. In others, for instance Ghana, while it is still uncertain that the incumbent would have allowed power to be transferred through elections, the November 1996 election was free and fair, and the results were accepted by the opposition. Finally, there is Botswana, where there is a long tradition of free and fair elections and a free press but where the population continues to vote for the same party, no doubt in part because of the government's excellent overall management of the economy.

The "elections but no transition" category is by far the largest (21 countries) and when it is combined with the "elections and one transition" category (11 countries), a total of 32 of the 46 countries in sub-Saharan Africa can be considered ambiguous democratizers. Indeed, it is likely that this combination of categories will hold the majority of African countries, and be a good classification of many developing countries around the world, for some time to come. Certainly, many of the countries in the "overthrown" or "no elections" categories will hold elections of varying quality in the years to come. At the same time, it is unlikely that a very large number of countries will migrate to the less ambiguous category of two transitions, for the reasons enumerated above.

Analyzing Partial Democratization

As a first cut toward understanding ambiguous democratization, I have classified African countries across the civil liberties rankings published by Freedom House in its 1995–96 publication *Freedom at Issue*. The civil rights index (ranging from 1, the best ranking, to 7, the lowest) is formed by a checklist of eleven questions including, most relevant for this discussion: "Are there free and independent media, literature, and other cultural expressions"; "Is there open public discussion and free private discussion"; "Is there freedom of assembly and demonstration"; and "Is there freedom of political and quasi-political organization (Freedom House, 1996, p. 531). Freedom House notes that it does not assume that simply because there are constitutional guarantees, freedom exists in practice. While several African countries achieved the worst ranking, none was judged to have the highest level of civil rights. Freedom House classifies those countries getting a ranking of 1 to 2.5 as "free," 2.5 to 5.5 as "partly free," and greater than 5.5 as not free (p. 534).

The civil-liberties checklist provides a relatively good measure of whether a climate of open political discussion and debate exists. This is especially important for Africa's ambiguous democratizers. Countries in the midst of difficult political liberalizations (in Africa, there is probably no other kind) need a substantial amount of public debate and discussion to develop a public consensus on how to move forward. There will be no other way to develop the nuanced structures and ideologies that each country needs. Freedom of political parties is absolutely essential, as alternative groupings to the party in power must be able to operate freely to convince everyone that a transition via elections is at least possible. In largely peasant societies, freedom of assembly will be especially important, as peasants often find it necessary to demonstrate outside of the electoral cycle in order to bring their concerns to politicians in the cities. Finally, the civil-liberties checklist measures important changes in political liberalization—notably freedom of the press—that are not immediately captured by examining simply whether there has been a change in power due to elections but which may have a profound impact on everyday politics and peoples' perceptions of the future.

I did not use Freedom House's more famous political-rights checklist because that index, appropriately, starts with a series of questions concerning the actual mechanics of elections, including whether the head of state had been elected through free and fair elections, whether the legislature had been elected through free and fair elections, and whether there are fair electoral laws. Precisely because this paper examines ambiguous democratizers, I wanted a measure that classified countries according to the workings of politics outside of directly competitive elections.

Table 2 arrays the countries according to the classifications in Table 1 and the categories of civil liberties developed by Freedom House.[1] Not surprisingly, countries are grouped in a diagonal with the countries having completed two or more transitions showing the best civil rights record. Indeed, all of the countries with two transitions are considered "free" (at least for civil liberties) by Freedom House, suggesting that the two-transitions benchmark is consequential. Correspondingly, those that have not had elections or that have experienced a coup d'état tend toward the lowest ranking. There is more variation among the countries that have had one transition, although they still garner relatively high ratings.

More importantly, there is significant variation within the "elections but no transitions" category. Here countries range from Botswana, which misses the best ranking in part because of repressive laws regarding sedition and detention without trial that are seldom used but are still viewed as deterrents to freedom of expression, to countries such as Angola and Equatorial Guinea, which are viewed as not free and, in fact, managed to garner among the worst possible civil-liberties ranking (Freedom House 1996, p. 153). What is even more notable is that many relatively well established polities have low rankings, including Kenya (at 6 and therefore "not free") and Côte d'Ivoire and Senegal (at 5 and therefore just "partly free).

A similar variation within categories is demonstrated by Table 3, which arrays countries by their recent democratic history against a set of rankings derived from Freedom House's publication *Press Freedom World Wide: 1996*. A 100-point scale is derived by coding, for both print and broadcast journalism, four issues: "laws and regulations influence media control"; "political pressures and controls on media content"; "economic influences over media content" (all three scored on a 0-to-10 basis); and "repressive actions" that include physical violence against journalists (scored on a 0-to-20 basis). Freedom House considers countries that have a score of 30 or less to have a "free" press, those that score 31 to 60, a "partly free" press, and 61 to 100, a "not free" press (Freedom House 1996). In Table 3, I divide the "partly free"

Table 2: African Countries Categorized by Recent Democratic History and Civil-Rights Ranking

Civil Liberties	Two Transitions	Elections, One Transition	Elections, No Transition	Civilian Government Overthrown	No Elections
2	Benin Madagascar Mauritius	Cape Verde São Tomé	Botswana		
3		Malawi Mali	Namibia Seychelles		
4		CAR Comoros Congo Lesotho Zambia	Burkina Gabon Ghana Guinea-Bissau Mozambique Uganda		Eritrea
5			Cameroon Chad Côte d'Ivoire Ethiopia Guinea Niger Senegal Tanzania Togo Zimbabwe		Swaziland
6			Angola Gambia Kenya Mauritania	Sierra Leone	Liberia Rwanda Zaire
7			Equatorial Guinea	Burundi Nigeria	Somalia Sudan

category in half in order to provide more detail. The numbers in parentheses next to each country are the raw scores.

The press-freedom indicator is another especially useful window on democratic politics outside of elections. If countries without a history of transitions via elections have a relatively free press, it will be possible to begin a national debate over democratic institutions and start a process that may end up in a fully free electoral process. Correspondingly, transitions in countries that do not have a particularly free press should be viewed with suspicion because the transition may simply have been the collapse of an old authoritarian regime (important, of course, in itself) rather than the clear start of democratic politics.

Again, not surprisingly, the same pattern of within- and across-category variation repeats itself. The countries with at least one transition generally have high press scores, while those without a history of transition or elections tend to gravitate toward the bottom. The press-freedom and civil-liberties scores are, of course, highly correlated, because press freedom is a component of the civil liberties score. However, there is not a perfect correlation. Senegal, for instance, with a score of 31 (just outside the "free" press range), has a somewhat freer press than its civil-liberties score of 5 (just above "not free") would suggest. However, in general, it does not appear that the rank order of countries within a particular category changes that much between Table 2 and Table 3.

Understanding Variation in Africa's Democratic Experience

The common charge that elections mean nothing in most African countries clearly has to be modified. In some countries, elections have been part of a process that has resulted in a notably freer political environment, even if these polities have not yet achieved the benchmark of having a transition in power via an election. For instance, Ghana, which the *Economist* viewed as a paradigm of a country holding elections but not liberalizing, has actually undergone a considerable transformation since A. Adu Boahen, Rawlings's principal critic, decried "the culture of silence" in 1989. Indeed, Boahen wrote, "We have not protested or staged riots not because we trust the PNDC [Provisional National Defense Council] but because we fear the PNDC! We are afraid of being detained, liquidated or dragged before the CVC [Citizens Vetting Committee] or NIC [National Investigation Committee] or being subjected to all sorts of molestation" (Boahen 1989, pp. 51–52). Compared to when Flt. Lt. Jerry Rawlings and the PNDC were in power in the 1980s, the Ghana of the 1990s under now-president Jerry Rawlings and the National Democratic Congress (to some, admittedly, the old PNDC without the "Provisional") is a more liberal polity. The press is freer, there is open political debate, including in the parliament, and the government is occasionally forced to rescind measures (such as a widely unpopular value added tax) that do not have public support. These changes have come despite the president's own limited ambitions for democracy. For instance, soon after being sworn in, he warned that the military may intervene in the future even if civilian democracy is reestablished: "a soldier may be a professional fighter, but does that take away his or her social and political responsibility" (quoted in Morna 1991, p. 23).[2] However, liberalization may take on a momentum of its own that even those initially ambivalent about the process may find irresistible.

Table 3: African Countries by Recent Democratic History and Press-Freedom Ranking

Press Freedom Ranking	Two Transitions	Elections, One Transition	Elections, No Transition	Civilian Government Overthrown	No Elections
0 to 30	Mauritius (25)	Mali (24)			
31 to 45	Benin (31) Madagascar (32)	Cape Verde (32) Comoros (35) Malawi (36)	Botswana (30) Namibia (30) Senegal (31) Burkina (37) Mozambique (36) Uganda (38)		
46 to 60		Congo (52) Lesotho (55) Niger (54) São Tomé (48) Zambia (60)	Ethiopia (57) Gabon (49) Guinea-Bissau (49) Niger (54) Seychelles (50) Tanzania (49) Zimbabwe (56)		
61 to 100		CAR (65)	Angola (69) Cameroon (72) Chad (72) Côte d'Ivoire (74) Equatorial Guinea (78) Gambia (62) Ghana (62) Guinea (61) Kenya (62) Mauritania (71) Togo (70)	Burundi (85) Nigeria (92) Sierra Leone (75)	Eritrea (68) Liberia (70) Rwanda (74) Somalia (79) Sudan (80) Swaziland (69) Zaire (84)

Similarly, countries such as Burkina Faso and Uganda, which have now had elections but have not had a transition, and Eritrea, which is still to hold an electoral contest, have civil-liberties rankings that are relatively good. These countries have clearly managed to make some fundamental changes in politics even if their electoral politics are yet to be fully democratic.

Uganda is, in fact, a good example of how distorting reading only electoral tea leaves can be. President Moseveni has been seen as bucking the democratizing trend in Africa because of his insistence on "no-party" elections and his frequent protestations that multiparty competition is not appropriate for African countries. However, in June 1993, Museveni restored the traditional leaders of the Buganda, Toro, Bunyoro, and Busoga (Mutebi II 1996, p. 578). These traditional leaders, during both the colonial and postindependence periods, had been seen as potential competitors to the state for power and the allegiance of the population. Legalizing the traditional kings was an important step in decentralizing authority and thus in liberalization in Uganda. It was a particularly significant reform because reaching an accommodation with traditional leaders, who are often viewed as far more legitimate than the faraway state by many citizens, will be critical to the long-term stability of many African countries.

At the same time, there have been elections and, in a surprising number of cases, transitions in countries where there is, at the very least, a deficit in democratic politics as measured by freedom of the press, of assembly, and of debate. Clearly, the countries that have had one transition but still have a relatively low civil-liberties score have not been able to use the democratic transition to propel fundamental changes in politics that are concomitant with their implied level of electoral competition. Thus the Central African Republic (CAR), Comoros, Congo, Lesotho, and Zambia must still reform significant portions of their political systems before they can reasonably be viewed as being as democratic as their electoral politics imply. In fact, CAR and Lesotho have experienced highly destabilizing protests against the regimes by the security forces, and Congo has also had considerably instability. Zambia, as noted above, has been one of the more significant disappointments of the third wave in Africa.

Conclusion

A great deal more attention needs to be devoted to what might be called democratic sequencing. To date, debates about sequencing have largely focused on whether economic liberalization should precede, go with, or follow democratic transition (Bienen and Herbst 1996). However, understanding whether a country has developed the necessary societal consensus about the future of democratic institutions is critical to understanding the long-term fate of many of Africa's liberalizing polities. Indeed, an argument can be made that countries that are developing a relatively impressive record on civil rights and on freedom of the press, in particular, will be in a better position to have an institutionalized democracy than those countries that go directly to a transition without creating or allowing the necessary civil liberties and press freedoms to develop. The development of a free press, a climate where debate is possible, and the right to assembly reflect a set of decisions to devolve power that may have much greater impact on society and be much harder to revoke than one transition happening in the urban capital. Free debate may also lead to the design of the localized democratic structures that still have to be theorized and developed in Africa. Twenty years from now, it may become clear that the development of a more liberal polity was a better predictor of which countries experienced real transitions after the fall of autocrats in the late 1980s than who had the first transition from an authoritarian leader.

Notions of democratic failure must also accordingly be revised. For instance, the election of an autocrat may indicate, as was the case in Kenya and Zimbabwe, that the electoral rules have changed slightly but there is no process of liberalization occurring. Or the election of an autocrat may indicate, as is potentially the case in Ghana, Burkina Faso, Uganda, and elsewhere, that a country is liberalizing although electoral politics may change more slowly than some other aspects of the polity. In some cases, only time will tell. Certainly, the holding of one and possibly several elections is not a particularly good predictor of a country's long-term democratic trajectory.

The analytic perspective adopted here in the end departs from much of the democratization literature in the amount of time full-scale liberalization is assumed to take. Even if not writing on the European cases that were the foci of early studies of democratic decline, many writers have still assumed that liberalization is a process of years, or at most, a decade. The lightning-fast fall of the communist regimes in Central Europe and the demise of the Soviet Union have only reinforced the assumption that the end of democratization is in sight from the beginning of liberalization. That is, a logical process can be mapped out, with the electoral process providing the major road marks. Thus the focus has been on the immediate strategic moves of leaders in designing pacts to hasten the fall of old regimes so that new democratic structures can take their place. In Africa, and probably in many other parts of the world, the basic assumption regarding the relatively short time frame within which democratization will proceed must be rejected. African democratization, if it occurs, will happen in a much slower, more convoluted and confusing manner than our current assumptions allow for. Thus a much greater focus must be devoted to the construction of democratic fundamentals while, of course, continuing to study elections.

15

A Virtuous Circle?
Democratization and Economic
Reform in Africa

Peter M. Lewis

Introduction

Over the past decade, sub-Saharan Africa has reflected a sweeping set of political and economic changes. At the beginning of the 1980s, the region was beset by an economic crisis of broad dimensions. Most countries reflected declining growth rates, stagnant production, rising external debt, and widening domestic poverty. Many governments, in the face of acute fiscal problems and balance of payments shortfalls, turned to the International Monetary Fund and the World Bank for new resources or debt relief. With the sponsorship of these international financial institutions (IFIs) and other donors, a majority of African states embarked upon stabilization or structural adjustment programs. The effectiveness of these measures varied greatly, but at the end of the 1980s economic policies had changed markedly in numerous African countries, and some economies showed hesitant signs of recovery.

The uneven process of economic reform was joined in the early 1990s by a dramatic wave of political renovation. Concurrent with the East European revolutions and political opening in South Africa, pressures for democratization and political change gained considerable momentum. Within a few years, most countries in sub-Saharan Africa had shifted from relatively closed, restrictive, and noncompetitive politics to more open and competitive politics. In 1989, nearly half the countries in Africa were ruled by military regimes and most of the remaining states had long-standing single-party or dominant-party regimes. By 1994, only a handful of military regimes remained across the continent, while more than 30 countries had legalized multiparty politics and permitted competitive elections. At least fourteen new democracies could be counted across the region.

The interaction of economic and political reform has emerged as one of the paramount issues in contemporary African development. Largely by historical coincidence, many African countries are concurrently engaged in economic and political liberalization. As is the case in Eastern Europe, a number of African states face basic problems of economic reorganization while seeking to strengthen and stabilize competitive political institutions. Analysts have speculated on the optimal sequencing of these reforms, an issue complicated by the suddenness of democratization in Africa and the rudimentary state of economic restructuring in the region (Haggard and Kaufman, 1994; Encarnacion, 1996).

In recent decades African economies have performed more poorly than those of other developing regions, and economic reform has been comparatively slow. Political reform has prompted an unprecedented wave of political openness, participation, and contention in many states, creating possibilities for new directions in economic policy-making. Alterations in the governing institutions of African countries also raise prospects for improvements in the general setting for economic growth. Yet democratic politics and regime change might also give rise to political dynamics and social forces that would impede economic recovery. The implications of political change for economic performance remain indeterminate. Two essential questions surround these processes: First, can Africa's new democracies manage the demands of economic liberalization? Second, will economic performance influence the survivability of democracy in the region?

Debates about the relation of economic and political reform have yielded disparate positions (Armijo, Biersteker, and Lowenthal 1995). One view, rooted in the modernization perspective, views economic and political liberalization as mutually reinforcing. Some 40 years ago, Seymour Martin Lipset emphasized the correlation between market economies and stable democracies (1959). Lipset strongly implied that the direction of causation ran mainly from economics to politics, as the process of economic modernization generated a panoply of effects that were conducive to democratic politics. The spread of education and communications, the growth of an articulate middle class, and the moderating effects of higher incomes were prominent factors fostering competitive political systems.

The association observed by Lipset has been confirmed by many subsequent studies (Diamond, 1992; Rueschemeyer, Stephens, and Stephens 1992). The affinity between democracy and capitalism has been interpreted even more forcefully by some recent analysts who argue that a "virtuous circle" exists between market economies and pluralist politics. In this view, economic liberalization will tend to encourage political liberalization, and political opening, in turn, will advance market reform. By increasing general welfare, dispersing social power, and freeing resources from the grip of central authorities, market economies undermine the control of the centralized state while giving rise to social forces that contest the arbitrary power of rulers. Economic well-being also encourages moderation and political stability. Conversely, democratization gives voice to such groups as private business and the professional middle classes, who have a stake in a liberal economy and a strong motivation for responsible economic management. A number of observers, most notably the major international donors, have explicitly advanced this position.

A contrasting perspective holds that economic and political liberalization are basically antagonistic. Democratic politics will tend to frustrate economic reform, and stagnant economies will undermine fledgling democracies. Rather than a virtuous circle, a vicious cycle is more likely. In this view, economic reform gives rise to disruptive social tensions that erode political stability, and competitive regimes may be especially vulnerable to such pressures. Economic liberalization redistributes opportunities and resources, prompting a variety of interests to defend their entrenched positions. Urban workers, government employees, middle-class wage earners, and import-competing manufacturers are among the groups who mobilize against the loss of entitlements. Governments—particularly those that are accountable to voters—are often susceptible to lobbying from these important constituencies (Olson 1982). Consequently, political leaders are faced with the alternatives of retreating from reform or pushing ahead through authoritarian means. Emerging democracies that fail to cope with severe economic problems may be seriously disrupted or deposed. These considerations suggest that democratic settings are not generally conducive to economic liberalization. The obverse side of this perspective considers the potential advantages of authoritarian regimes in pursuing stabilization and economic growth. Cases as diverse as Korea, Chile, and Ghana suggest that under certain circumstances nondemocratic regimes can muster the autonomy necessary to pursue politically risky economic restructuring. While analysts have been careful to qualify their arguments, the conditional association of authoritarianism and development has been widely recognized (Deyo 1987; Haggard 1990; Callaghy 1993).

Between these poles of debate, another viewpoint can be discerned from some recent analyses of new democracies. The connection between economic and political reform may be more logical than real; in fact these processes can be separate and even self-contained, at least in the near term. This argument holds that democratization is a good in itself, and that democratic governments gain legitimacy from such attributes as elections, more open participation, improved human rights, and greater accountability. Citizens in new democracies tend to identify economic performance with particular leaders rather than with whole political systems (Duch 1995; Haggard and Kaufman 1994). In addition, there is considerable leeway for skilled leaders or political parties to manipulate policies and public perceptions so as to evade the adverse effects of economic restructuring. In sum, regimes are not necessarily doomed by economic failure, and clever politicians can utilize democratic institutions to manage reform.

When assessing these arguments in the African context, it is important to consider the origins of democratization in the region and the character of new democratic regimes. The next section discusses the background to reform in Africa and the sources of Africa's democratic wave, focusing particularly on the role of economic crisis in prompting political liberalization. This is followed by an overview of the context of economic change in the region, with consideration of the political factors essential to economic recovery. The fourth section considers the effects of democratic reform on economic policy and performance. I conclude with general observations about the course of economic and political reform in Africa.

Economy and Democracy in Africa

What were the sources of change in Africa leading to recent political transitions? Appraisals of the region's democratic movements have offered differing interpretations. Some observers have stressed the external stimulus for democratization, arguing that political change was impelled mainly by international diffusion effects and by leverage from donors (Uzodike 1996). A contrasting view attributes democratic pressures to domestic forces, with local social and political groups leading the drive for change (Bratton and van de Walle 1992).

There are similarly divided accounts of the impact of economic crisis on political reform. A set of writers has linked democratic pressures to popular protests against the effects of economic adjustment, underscoring a contradiction between economic and political liberalization (Baregu 1994). Another group has argued that the impulse for democracy was animated by a rejection of economic statism and corruption; from this vantage, pressures for economic and political liberalization are united (Westebbe 1994).

Ultimately, any single-cause explanation of Africa's diverse political changes is unsatisfactory. We can identify a convergence of domestic and international factors influencing democratic reform in Africa. The broad political changes after 1989 reflected changes in domestic social and political structures, as well as shifts in the global economy, the realignment of international strategic balances, and the influence of new ideas and social networks.

A central factor running through the political transformations of recent years has been the weakening of traditional ruling elites and state institutions across the region. Africa's personalized authoritarian regimes have frequently been described as "neopatrimonial" in character (Clapham 1982; Bratton and van de Walle 1994; Lewis 1994). Neopatrimonial systems reflect the outward features of institutionalized administrative states while operating essentially along patrimonial lines. Beneath a facade of formal administration and law inherited from the colonial state, neopatrimonial states have been organized by kinship, faction, and patron-client networks. Power in such regimes is concentrated and personalized, and the prerogatives of the ruler typically override the authority of laws and organizations. Since material inducement is essential to clientalist systems, neopatrimonial regimes require a regular flow of resources to loyalists and strategic supporters.

Two consequences of neopatrimonial rule have been especially important for the advent of political reform. First, these regimes fostered weak and unstable economies. Political concerns disposed most African governments toward statist policies and relatively closed economies (Sandbrook 1985). Patronage and corruption also gave rise to chronic fiscal crises. Interventionist economic policies and capricious management discouraged investment and productive activities. In addition, the personalization of authority created weak institutions in most countries. Neopatrimonial states commonly fomented economic stagnation and fragility.

Second, neopatrimonial regimes have been especially dependent on external patronage and support. Aid dependence is higher in Africa than in other regions of the world, as development assistance and concessional finance have provided a significant proportion of the official budgets for many countries. Despite pervasive concerns over economic self-reliance, most African economies continue to rest heavily on a narrow range of primary commodity exports, making African economies highly susceptible to trade fluctuations. In the political and military realm, the region's authoritarian regimes have also counted on external patronage and intervention, which were encouraged for many years by Cold War rivalries among the major powers. These multiple sources of dependence have rendered governments vulnerable to shifts in strategic balances and the world economy. The adverse economic management of African states and the ensuing economic malaise throughout the continent have accentuated these problems.

With these factors in mind, we can identify both international and domestic sources of political change. The regional economic crisis following the oil price shocks of the 1970s and the debt pressures of the early 1980s created repercussions that weakened neopatrimonial regimes. Fiscal problems and dwindling foreign exchange dried up sources of patronage and rents through which leaders secured political allegiance. The need for debt relief also accentuated the role of the international financial institutions in promoting policy reform. Measures such as trade liberalization and privatization, commonly introduced through donor conditionality, had the effect of loosening state control over resources. Cutbacks in government spending further reduced outlets for political patronage. By the early 1990s, some bilateral lenders had explicitly linked economic reform with political liberalization, pressing for political change as a requisite for new resources.

Strategic changes also undercut the international support for authoritarian rule in Africa. The end of the Cold War meant that northern governments were less willing to prop up unpopular regimes for strategic gain (Huntington 1991). The loss of external aid and support, including security assistance, weakened many established leaders. Moreover, liberalization in other regions raised the specter that investment and aid would flee to more hospitable areas of the globe. These factors encouraged some elites to initiate political reforms in an effort to preempt more difficult challenges.

While external factors often influenced political transitions, they were rarely the driving element in the reform process. On balance, there is not a strong case for the contention that democratization in Africa was mainly a product of donor conditionality or international diffusion effects. The timing of African transitions certainly suggests that the demise of Cold War rivalries and the withdrawal of external patrons were consequential for political change. Moreover, the impact of events in Eastern Europe and South Africa, combined with a potent "neighborhood effect" in the region, certainly propelled political changes after 1990. However, there are relatively few instances where democratic pressures were essentially motivated by foreign events or where the actions of donors were decisive for reform outcomes.[1]

In most African countries, political change was driven by intensifying pressure from domestic societal groups. Protracted economic malaise fostered popular restiveness and eroded much of the support coalition for incumbent regimes. A variety of popular sectors, including labor, students, business associations, women's organizations, and the professions, mobilized around economic issues and increasingly aimed their protests at official corruption and mismanagement. Austerity measures also penalized important constituencies such as civil servants, professionals, and the military, causing strategic interest groups to part ways with authoritarian regimes. Protests in many countries originated with economic grievances, but they became increasingly political as important segments of society turned against incumbent regimes and embraced demands for fundamental change (Bratton and van de Walle 1992).

As authoritarian regimes contended with growing domestic dissent in the late 1980s, the crucial determinants of change were the relative strategies and organizational capacities of government and opposition. The results of political contestation have varied from democratization in Benin and Zambia to managed transition in Ghana, stymied reform in Kenya and Cameroon, democratic failure in Niger, and civil catastrophe in Burundi. These disparate outcomes have been influenced mainly by domestic forces and structures, and cannot be explained by focusing on external actors.

In sum, there has been a strong linkage between economic crisis and democratic reform in Africa. The failure to promote economic development provided a major source of public antipathy to authoritarian rule. The social impact of austerity also incited considerable popular protest, leading ultimately to direct political opposition. These influences suggest overlapping or additive effects moving from economic failure to political change. Yet we should recognize that a rejection of the old regime does not imply an embrace of economic reform. The prevailing political context of economic change must be considered when assessing the possible directions of the region's new democracies.

The Context of Reform in Africa

Africa embodies a distinctive setting for political and economic reform. While the region's political changes have been associated with the broader international trend toward democratization in the late 1980s, liberalizing countries in Africa differ significantly from transitional countries in other regions. Aside from their limited experiences with democracy, most African countries do not reflect the attributes historically associated with democracies elsewhere. Low levels of economic development, meager educational endowments, large unmobilized rural populations, social fragmentation, weak institutional legacies, and an inheritance of instability all create basic challenges for democratic development (Young 1994; Diamond, Linz, and Lipset 1995). These conditions reinforce a general skepticism about the viability of democracy in poor countries.

The existing state of economic reform is also noteworthy. Unlike most of Eastern Europe, African countries embarked on liberalization measures prior to democratization, and an array of policy reforms were already under way when political change occurred. Compared with many parts of Latin America and East Asia, however, these efforts have displayed modest success. African reforms have been comparatively halting, uneven, and inconsistent (World Bank, 1994). While nominal price reforms in such areas as exchange rates and agricultural producer prices have been enacted, broader policy and institutional changes have been slower to materialize. Moreover, many governments have delayed, suspended, or reversed adjustment packages, leading investors and donors to question the reliability of reform.

African economies reflect a number of problems that raise doubts about their possibilities for rapid recovery. Structurally, most economies in the region embody weak foundations of human capital, infrastructure, and productive facilities. Essential institutions such as financial markets, legal codes, and regulatory mechanisms are often inadequate or lacking. Africa's position in the international economy is also problematic, as the region has experienced growing isolation from global trade and capital markets in recent decades. This marginality has meant that economic reform often fails to elicit new investments, trade, or financial resources. Many governments, facing the sacrifices of austerity with few apparent returns, have loosened or abandoned reforms.

The organization of interest groups in Africa has not been conducive to assertive mobilization on behalf of economic reform. Politics in much of the region has been structured along the lines of ethnic alliances and patron-client networks, and political parties do not generally reflect strong class or ideological appeals (Bienen and Herbst 1996). Moreover, key social groups with a likely interest in economic liberalization, such as export-oriented farmers or urban business elites, are often divided or diffident in their political behavior. There are few constituencies to impel democratic regimes in the direction of greater liberalization. In consequence, economic reform has typically been guided by state elites without substantial public support.

These regional patterns suggest some requisites for altering the political context of economic development. Significant changes in executive leadership and the character of state elites are integral to a shift in policy and management. The social coalitions underlying regimes are also crucial, since constituencies for change are strategically important in democratic settings. Finally, it is essential to renovate or revive the institutional setting for economic growth. If new governments cannot amend the traditional shortcomings of state administration and the provision of public goods, then regime change is unlikely to produce significant improvements in economic performance.

Democracy and Economic Change in Sub-Saharan Africa

The sustainability of political reform, and the implications of political opening for economic liberalization, are leading issues for many African countries. Democratic consolidation in Africa is contingent upon a host of factors, including civil-military relations, ethnic accommodation, the establishment of effective democratic institutions, the behavior of emergent political elites, and the growth of active civil societies. Alongside these other challenges, economic performance and popular welfare are likely to be important determinants of democratic stability.

Assuming that democratic regimes endure, it is not evident that they will provide a more favorable climate for economic management. A key question is whether new democracies can overhaul the structures and coalitions associated with neopatrimonial regimes, or if traditional politics will be resurrected in a different guise. As noted above, there are three aspects to this problem: the nature of political leadership; the composition of support coalitions; and the capacities of public institutions.

Democracy provides ostensible grounds for a transfer of elites, yet there is considerable evidence of elite continuity in many of Africa's new democracies. Despite popular calls for a renovation of politics, reform has often been implemented by incumbent leaders and veteran politicians (Bates 1994). The top-down character of liberalization in many countries raises the possibility that clientalist politics will reemerge under democratic auspices. In many countries, parties and notables from the early postindependence period have been instrumental in political opposition. In Benin and Madagascar, former authoritarian rulers were returned to power in the second posttransition elections, while in Ghana, the incumbent president has maintained power in a process of "creeping democratization." Even where there has been a decisive change of elites, democratic leaders are often drawn into the logic of distributive politics as readily as the deposed patrons, and transition can yield a superficial circulation of elites with little change in the substance of economic management.

The changing composition of support coalitions is another important dimension of transition. Political opening provides new opportunities for organized interests to enter politics, raising the possibility that such groups will exercise greater influence in favor of economic change. It is reasonable to suggest that political liberalization will alter the context for economic policymaking, as increased participation and freer associational activity give rise to new outlets for the expression of popular groups. This naturally depends upon the sectors that are mobilized into politics, as well as the organizational resources at their disposal. The composition of new party systems also influences the ways in which interests are politically represented (Remmer 1991).

While political inclusion may encourage interests with a concern for liberalization, it also brings forward groups who are opposed to economic reform, such as civil servants, students, or import-competing manufacturers. Consequently, democratization can easily give rise to populist lobbying rather than support for adjustment. Groups with a traditional stake in the entitlements of the old regime may press for expansionary fiscal policy as well as continued subsidies, services, and protection. It is equally possible that interest groups with a stake in reform will remain politically marginal. Rural constituencies commonly face collective-action problems that limit their organizational strength. There is no prominent example of assertive rural interest associations in any of the region's new democracies. Business groups, although better organized, may be co-opted through patronage or estranged because of their association with opposition parties. In Ghana, for example, business groups complain of governmental discrimination because of their association with the political opposition (Hart and Gyimah-Boadi 1997). Consequently, private-sector elites may be politically neutralized under democratic rule and will not play an assertive role in reform.

Finally, the enhancement of institutions presents a formidable challenge to transitional governments. Fledgling democracies confront the legacies of administrative weakness and societal alienation inherited from their autocratic predecessors (Young 1994). The new regimes face a double burden of moribund economies and feeble state institutions. Many of these debilities have arisen from the predatory actions of authoritarian rulers, though additional problems have emerged from orthodox adjustment programs. Many reform packages have induced wide-ranging cutbacks in state personnel and funding, along with a contraction of services and regulatory roles. State restructuring is a necessary component of economic reform, but democratic regimes will face serious limitations on their abilities to rehabilitate public institutions. Caught between the budget constraints of donor assistance and the pressures of popular constituencies for expedient spending, elected governments have little latitude for marshalling expenditures toward administration, infrastructure, or regulatory reform. In the final analysis, democratization cannot be viewed as a panacea for the establishment of an institutional framework for growth.

What is the evidence from the brief tenure of Africa's posttransitional regimes? Thus far, there are few indications of major revisions of policy or practice in new democracies. Most countries have maintained existing relations with the IFIs, implying continued policy dialogue, conditional lending, and adherence to basic features of stabilization and adjustment. There are, however, signs of departure from the status quo. Fiscal policy in several countries has shown the effects of electoral competition, with public sector deficits and monetary expansion ballooning during election years. Ghana and Zambia in particular have reflected the swings of politically induced spending cycles. Moreover, some governments have responded to public pressure by temporizing on important policies such as revenue levies, subsidy cuts, or privatization measures. Not only has macroeconomic policy been erratic, but several democratizing countries have shown signs of corruption and illicit activities. The charges of corruption surrounding Frederick Chiluba's administration in Zambia and the spread of drug trafficking in that country illustrate such problems.

The general impression of policy inertia is mirrored by the pattern of economic performance. Although political transitions in Africa are recent, so far there is scant indication of economic recovery in liberalizing states. Taking only the crude indicator of growth, new democracies have generally displayed flat performance, although a few, such as Benin, have made marginal improvements, while others, including the Congo and Madagascar, have registered slight declines. A similarly lackluster picture is evident when looking at such indicators as fiscal deficits, money supply, inflation, and investment.[2] Bearing in mind the short period since the change of regime, we do not yet see clear evidence that democracy has a systematic effect on economic performance in Africa.

These circumstances present an adverse setting for democratic consolidation. Economic stagnation has the potential to erode public confidence in new democracies. Scarcity also accentuates the stakes of political power. These conditions can give rise to ethnic contention and electoral misconduct, while also coaxing politicians to employ patronage politics. It is not inevitable for economic stasis to threaten the survival of democracies, and there are tentative signs that voters in countries with severe economic difficulties are willing to reject incumbents rather than challenge entire regimes. However, events in Niger and Nigeria show that economic malaise and failed reform can be a liability for democratic change.

In view of these inconclusive patterns, three future trajectories can be suggested. One path is the virtuous circle, in which democratic politics yield changes over time in the quality of economic management and performance, with salutary effects on democratic stability. A second route is a turn toward populism, and a breakdown of reform, yielding an insecure regime and a moribund economy. A third possibility is democratic failure, fostering an authoritarian regime that might pursue reform, populism, or predation. In all likelihood, we will see each of these scenarios fulfilled in some African countries in the years to come.

Conclusions

The speed and scope of political reform in Africa have led some observers to speak of the region's "second liberation," comparing the current period to the heady days of the independence era. Certainly there has been no incidence of regime change as dramatic or widespread in the past three decades (Joseph 1991). The old regime has been decidedly eclipsed in numerous countries, yet most of these transformations remain halting and uncertain.

Economic liberalization can create important structural changes that serve to bolster political pluralism, as the legacies of economic statism and personal rule in Africa point to the necessity of dispersing social and economic power. Economic performance constitutes an important factor in the endurance of new democracies, and the ability of these governments to sustain macroeconomic stability and restructure their economies is an important test of political change.

Economic policy-making in Africa's liberalizing regimes has reflected conflicting tendencies. There is evidence that political-fiscal cycles are emerging in several new democracies, reflecting both the cost of elections and the side payments disbursed by incumbents. In several states, populist tactics are evident in expansive fiscal and monetary policy, the preservation of consumer subsidies, and a reluctance to pursue risky policies of taxation or state sector reform. Yet there has not been an instance of wholesale abandonment of economic liberalization, nor a decisive shift toward populist strategies, in any of Africa's new democracies. Indeed, the most dramatic policy reversal of recent years occurred under authoritarian rule in Nigeria, when military rulers unveiled a statist economic program in 1994, curtailing several years of adjustment efforts. This reminds us that democratization is not the central liability for economic reform.

A variety of influences shape economic policies in Africa's democratizing states. Democratic politics undoubtedly give rise to new pressures on regimes for spending, subsidies, and rents. Though some constituencies press for a populist direction in economic policy, there are also contrasting forces that may favor elements of liberalization. Business groups as well as organized labor gain a new voice under democratic rule, and the pressures on policymakers are often disparate. Executive commitment to economic liberalization in such countries as Ghana, Mali, and Benin has been sufficient to maintain reform under democratic auspices.

Political leaders are mindful of the demands of electoral competition and popular expression, yet they are also constrained by pressures from donors and the international economy. A significant loss of foreign exchange, debt relief, or investment can be as consequential for political stability as challenges from domestic constituencies. Ultimately, African states have few alternatives to continued economic adjustment, however hesitant and erratic it might be. The international political and economic environment creates a tacit inducement to sustain a course of reform.

While policy continuity is important for growth and stability in the near term, most African countries face the fundamental challenges of enhancing basic state capabilities and establishing credibility within international markets. The extended processes of institution-building and the reorganization of support coalitions will be decisive for economic recovery. Democratization has opened a window of opportunity to meet these challenges, though the opening is narrow and perhaps transient. When assessing the course of reform in the region, it is important to avoid the undue optimism that accompanied independence three decades ago, as well as the pervasive pessimism surrounding analyses of the region in recent years. The viability of democratic capitalism will be an important question for African development over the next decade.

Page 272 blank

Part VII

Conclusion

16

Democratization, International Relations,

and U.S. Foreign Policy

Ben Hunt

Introduction

When asked the difference between economics and political science, Hans
Morgenthau described the former as defining interests in terms of money and
the latter as defining interests in terms of power. Economists seem to have
staked out the easier turf, at least from this definitional vantage point. Power
is simply a far more slippery concept than money, at whatever level of specificity, and as a consequence, political scientists have been far less successful
than economists in efforts to apply scientific rigor to their respective fields. In
fact, political scientists lack agreed-upon definitions for many of their most
central concepts, especially those concepts in practice. That problem plagues
the topic at hand in this volume—democracy—and its attendant concepts,
such as democratic transitions.

Fortunately for political science as an academic discipline, theorizing can
withstand quite a bit of uncertainty at its definitional core without losing all
semblance of usefulness. Certainly many political scientists talk past each
other rather than with each other, in large measure because they define core
concepts differently, but as long as a critical mass of researchers share the
same language—whatever that language might be—intellectual progress can

take place within that group of researchers. Policy-makers are not so lucky. The devices of policy are tangible goods, such as money or bullets, rather than ideas or theories. Everyone agrees what money and bullets are—no one talks past each other here—and similar agreement on how to identify the object of these devices, in this case democratic transitions, is necessary for an effective policy commitment. That is, without some reasonably clear standards (or definitions) of the behaviors we wish to reward or punish with the tangible devices of our decisions, policy-making is necessarily capricious. Before we can ask what policies should be implemented to encourage and support democratic transitions, we must answer another question first. How do we know a democratic transition when we see one?

I will not presume to answer the ultimate question regarding specific policies for specific cases. One common thread to the contributions in this volume is that the pathway to any democracy is idiosyncratic, beset by a host of domestic political and cultural concerns particular to the nation in question. One would presume that the associated foreign policies implemented by the United States or any other nation to support that individual transition would of necessity be largely idiosyncratic as well. And, too, the confounding effects of domestic politics within the United States or other foreign supporters make it virtually impossible to predict or argue for any specific policy in the abstract. I will, however, attempt to provide a framework for analyzing the prior question of how to recognize and evaluate the progress of democratic transitions. If we can agree on a set of evaluative standards, then we will have gone a long way toward providing a theoretical foundation for future policy debates.

Make no mistake about it—such policy debates regarding democratic transitions will only increase in number and scope over the next decade. The kudzulike spread of liberal democracy around the world is of immense practical importance to the very national security of fellow democracies, if we are to believe the similarly rampant "democratic peace" literature (Russett 1993). Policy-makers in the United States are concerned with democratic transitions in other countries not only because they believe liberal democracy to be a blessing to these lucky foreign citizens, but also because they increasingly believe that the spread of liberal democracy is advantageous to the safety and security of their *own* citizens.

Cold War issues dominated these concerns of safety and security for 45 years, and with good reason. With the end of the Cold War, however, two questions arise: How can the United States avoid a second hegemonic military struggle with another great power? And how can the United States best achieve other national goals (such as economic growth) now that the overriding goal of national preservation has been largely secured? Global liberal democracy offers a coherent answer to both questions—a separate sphere of democratic peace on the one hand, and an expanding economic pie through greater international trade on the other. Debate regarding the accuracy of these answers, as well as the proper means to achieve those ends, promises to be fierce, as we are discussing nothing less than the appropriate grand strategy for the United States and its allies for the twenty-first century. Perhaps we should agree on the pertinent and recognizable features of liberal democratic transitions, then, before embarking on such a daunting task.

Blind Men and the Democratic Elephant

The definitional debate here boils down to a question of where to look for the true nature of democracy. To be sure, just as the proverbial blind men touched an elephant's separate parts and came away with completely different notions of the true nature of elephants, so do we risk missing an understanding of democracy's whole by emphasizing one aspect or another. I argue this is a risk worth taking, given the need for identifiable standards to serve as a foundation for any coherent policy. And fortunately, democracy is not quite as disparate from trunk to tail as is an elephant.

Two aspects of democratic practice have been widely suggested as the proper place to look for the essence of democracy: the institutional rules and procedures that provide the structure for meaningful elections, and the substantive political norms that provide for an underlying ethos of popular participation—the "citizenship and community" of which Stephen Macedo writes. Many a tome has been written in support of the former or latter claim, and it would be futile to try to recapture that debate in a paragraph or two. In practice, however, and from a policy-evaluation perspective, the debate becomes this: Which polity is more democratic — one that holds regular elections where the usual suspects are reelected time and again, or one that allows significant political participation and mobility within a nonelectoral framework?

The chapters in this volume suggest different answers to that question, but most seem to suggest that we should *not* focus the lion's share of our attention on elections, but rather on the existence or lack thereof of some inchoate social commitment to participative government. For example, Bruce Cumings writes that American citizens "cannot hold a candle" to Korean citizens in terms of essential participation in political life, and that Korean civil society is thus more genuinely democratic than U.S. civil society, despite the more tenuous existence of elections in Korea. Lucian Pye, after noting Robert Dahl's largely institutional requirements for polyarchy/democracy, goes on to write that "liberal democracies, however, need more than just these institutional requirements" as he makes the case for the importance of a liberal "civic culture." Likewise, Jeffrey Herbst argues that "understanding whether a country has developed the necessary societal consensus about the future of democratic institutions" is more important than noting an election result in efforts to estimate the long-term health of a democratic transition.

Contributing to the definitional confusion is the role of economic theory and practice. We are accustomed to muttering "free market system" and "democratic government" in the same breath, as if the two were simply sides of a single coin. And in fact, they *are* hardly separable, despite what our friends in Beijing might claim. The precepts of liberalism, when applied to the economic and political realms, yield open markets in the former and open elections in the latter. But just as many of the authors here point out a sharp distinction between the trappings of liberal democracy and its substance, so must we also make a distinction between the trappings of a liberal market system and its substance. For example, Indonesia has all the institutional prerequisites for a free market system, yet its economy in practice is light-years away from what the West would call liberal.

This definitional interweaving between free markets and democracy means that analysts must evaluate both in order to evaluate either. That is, in most cases it makes little sense to talk about a democratic transition separate from a concurrent market transition, and vice versa. Quadrants I through IV in Figure 1 describe the universe of possible cases along these two dimensions.

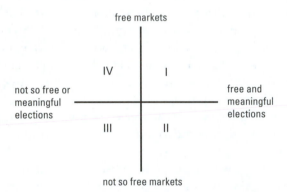

Note that with the addition of this second dimension of economic concerns, our efforts to establish criteria and standards for democratic transitions are made even more difficult. Which polity is more liberal and more democratic—that with a stronger commitment to free elections or that with a stronger commitment to free markets?

The easy answer to this question of how to identify a genuine democratic transition is that we would want to see both an institutional and a social commitment to democracy, plus a far-reaching implementation of liberal market principles. We would want to see a polity firmly entrenched in Quadrant I before putting another notch on democracy's belt. The real world, of course, is not so cooperative. In fact, it is precisely those countries on the margins of democracy or nondemocracy, close to the borders of one quadrant or another, that we are most interested in evaluating for policy purposes.

Most of the contributions to this book are from country or regional specialists who were asked to evaluate a nation or group of nations in terms of the dimensions outlined above. One of the most striking points about these evaluations is how closely the regional experts agree with each other, despite the lack of common standards to categorize democratic transitions. Apparently the elephant of democracy is recognizable enough, and distinguishable enough from other regime creatures, to allow a general consensus among experts as to its existence. To paraphrase Justice Potter Stewart and his famous comment regarding how the Supreme Court defined obscene material, we know democracy when we see it. And although we are no closer to a standard definition of democracy at the conclusion of this volume than we were at the outset, we can at least place the examined nations in relative position to each other on these quadrants. At the risk of oversimplifying matters greatly, I would summarize the regional assessments as saying that we see genuine democratic transitions fairly widely in East Asia and Latin America, that we see them hardly or not at all in Africa, and that we see glimmers of democratic transitions in Russia and Eastern Europe but that it is too early to tell whether they will stick or not.

We can also distill some specific pieces of policy advice from these expert area assessments.

South and Central America

No need here for heroic measures, as the clear trend in the region is toward successful consolidation of democratic regimes. Felipe Agüero notes that the military, the traditional enemy of democracy in the region, is surprisingly docile in almost all of these countries. Arturo Valenzuela suggests that US policy should focus on early warning efforts to anticipate potential coup activity; if so warned, the United States should work through multilateral institutions, such as the OAS, to make clear that a coup would result in multilateral economic isolation. Bilateral efforts alone are unlikely to provide a sufficient stick, as regional economic integration (either via NAFTA or MERCOSUR) is the primary carrot fostering regional liberalization.

East Asia

While over a period of time we might expect economic liberalization to foment political liberalization (through the creation of a politically active middle class, and so on), such a causal relationship is particularly tortuous,

long, and uncertain in East Asia. In practical terms, this means that while liberal trade policies between the United States and China may be good for
business, we are kidding ourselves if we think that such policies are creating
significant political pressures to liberalize in Beijing. Steve Chan notes that
most East Asian regimes already see themselves as both economically liberal
and politically democratic, albeit in a largely non-Western, more communitarian political form (if it even makes sense to speak of "communitarian liberal democracy"), and that the United States should expect to meet stiff
resistance if it should have the temerity to suggest that true liberal democracy
requires meaningful multiparty elections and issue-based party systems.

Africa

The prolonged downturn in various international commodity markets and
the reliance of many African economies on a single commodity export (for
example, copper and Zambia) has created a disastrous economic crisis in
many countries that severely undercuts the sustainability of *any* government,
democratic or otherwise. Combining commodity price shocks with the threat
and reality of predatory rule, institutionalized corruption, and war makes any
African civil society remarkably fragile, much less any realized government.
The surprise is not that we see so little democracy, but that — given the
endemic economic and security problems of the region — we see so much. As
Jeffrey Herbst argues, the future path of African political development is by
no means certain to reach a democratic destination, but there has been a
quantum change from the political processes of the past. Democratic liberalization, as measured by civil liberties rather than elections, proceeds fitfully
and could be supported by tailored foreign policies that seek to promote
these basic liberties, such as press freedom.

Russia and Eastern Europe

Overall, the commitment to liberal democracy in this region appears to be a
mile wide and an inch deep. Within the region, Jason Sharman and Roger
Kanet see democratic civil society as weakest in Russia and Slovakia,
stronger in East Central Europe. Absent some external shock, however, the
area experts here see no inherent reason why any of these ostensibly democratic systems should necessarily fail. Thomas Remington argues that while
the Russian constitution is clearly propresidential, allowing more than a hint
of authoritarian rule-by-decree, the system is actually rather flexible, "allowing all major constituencies to win at least some battles." Wise U.S. policy
under such conditions would be to avoid providing such an external shock
and to stay the course on conditional economic aid administered through
multilateral institutions. Sharman and Kanet suggest that efforts to encourage a liberal civil society through educational exchanges and support, per-

haps along the lines of George Soros's philanthropy in the region, would be similarly helpful.

A Modest Proposal: KISS (Keep It Simple, Stupid)

Analyzing individual nations closely and placing them roughly and relatively in their appropriate quadrant is of immense value for academic theory and research. The specific policy recommendations that stem from this analysis are well considered and well meaning. I want to argue that, unfortunately, such analysis is *too good* to provide either a practical bearing or practical advice to actual policy-makers.

Keep in mind that the people who ultimately decide critical foreign policies are rarely expert country analysts who can see entire elephants at once. Every experienced State Department bureaucrat has his or her own collection of horror stories regarding how the decision-making process at the level of "high politics" mangled or subverted an expert country analysis. Nuanced country analysis and detailed position papers are, as often as not, ignored in the final determination of policy, either because of some pathology of the bureaucratic decision-making process (Jervis 1976; Janis 1982; Levy 1986) or because a more salient issue is considered to be at stake and takes precedence. Support for democratic transitions is only one facet of foreign policy (and perhaps not a particularly important facet depending on the larger foreign policy picture), and foreign policy itself is only a slice of the larger pie of national security and national interests.

And, too, policy is a blunter tool than theory, with far more inertia behind it. Ideas are like a speedboat on a lake, easy to steer in one direction or another depending on the immediate decisions of the driver. Policy is like a gigantic barge, where even the smallest course correction requires tremendous time, effort, and coordination. Changing the course of a barge is a very expensive undertaking, as is changing the course of foreign policy. By expensive I do not mean costly in terms of money (although this, too, may be true), but costly in terms of information collection and information-processing resources (Schelling 1960; Jervis 1970). The great advantage to simple decision-rules is that they require very little in the way of collection or processing resources. Provided that a simple identification principle or decision-making rule gives us most of the information we need most of the time, ignoring a thorough yet expensive expert country analysis in favor of this simple yet inexpensive rule is perfectly rational. If we make a decision on the basis of simple and less accurate information, we are more likely to make a poor decision than if we use expert and more accurate information. But if the costs of acquiring that more accurate information are much higher than the costs of acquiring the simple information, then the overall expected utility of the fast and simple decision will be greater than the overall expected utility of the slow and expert decision.

For both sets of reasons mentioned above—bureaucratic efficiency and the ponderous nature of policy itself—I argue that it makes sense to have an extremely simple and clearly visible standard for the establishment of democracy or lack thereof. This sine qua non for democratic transition policy determination should be the existence of multiparty elections. To be sure, a focus (in the words of one conference participant, a "fetish") with elections per se runs a substantial risk of confusing the trappings of democracy with its substance. But the alternative—developing an expert country analysis and correspondingly nuanced policy, explaining said analysis and policy to nonexpert policy-makers and their constituents, convincing them that the policy recommendation makes sense even given the inertia of prior policy and the perhaps-conflicting demands of other national and political interests—is so difficult and costly to achieve that the most likely outcome is paralysis.

We can easily imagine exceptions that we might want to make to a general policy rule of supporting regimes that hold multiparty elections and withholding support from regimes that cancel multiparty elections. For example, should we really protest too loudly if a government calls off elections that are likely to be won by an illiberal party, one that might well dismantle the entire democratic institutional structure if elected into office? Both Thomas Remington and Jason Sharman and Roger Kanet point out, in their respective chapters on Russia and East Central Europe, that the specter of a "red-brown" coalition, a potential pairing of vanguard parties from the communist left and the fascist right, is never too far removed from electoral prognostications for their region. Expert analysts of Algeria and Turkey (indeed, most of North Africa, the Middle East, Central Asia, and South Asia) would add green or religious fundamentalist parties to the color swatch of potentially illiberal election candidates.

Similarly, should we implement sanctions against a military junta that overthrows a democratically elected civilian government if that civilian government was profoundly corrupt? Peter Lewis points out that such predatory governments in Africa have not been limited to authoritarian forms but have occasionally taken on a democratic face. Similarly, Southeast Asian nations such as Thailand and the Philippines have had actual or threatened military coups to curb the rampant corruption of elected officials. While the generals who attempt coups are generally more willing to seize power than they are to implement a schedule for the resumption of regular elections, it is difficult to imagine how any civilian leader, no matter how well intentioned, could transform the profoundly illiberal polity of, say, Zaire/Congo without using guns and extralegal means.

But even with these two possible exceptions to a general rule of fetishizing elections, we can easily make an argument that the advantages of swift and consistent policy in support of elections outweigh the dangers of either an elected illiberal party (which can suffer sanctions if it indeed moves to cancel future elections) or an elected predatory leadership (which can suffer sanctions for its actions or be voted out of office for its misdeeds). Moreover, once it becomes common knowledge that such a simple rule is firmly in place, it can have a preemptive dampening effect on antidemocratic plots. For example, several of Yeltsin's closest advisers suggested strongly (and by most accounts, successfully) that Yeltsin should cancel the most recent national election for the Russian presidency if any of his opponents were even close to winning, with the international excuse that any other candidate would back Russia off its path toward liberal market institutions. If it were common knowledge that such a pretense would simply not wash with the United States, that a canceled election would be prima facie evidence of authoritarian subversion of democratic rule and would result in immediate suspension of aid and loans, then it is hard to imagine that such a plan to cancel elections would have been as easy to contemplate as it apparently was. For all these reasons, then, even if we ultimately decided to turn a blind eye toward a particular subversion of democratic institutions, I argue that it still makes sense to set an extremely high threshold of tolerance for elections, however imperfect, and a strong presumption of disapproval if multiparty elections are canceled.

Market Reforms and Policy Standards

While the argument here is that the trappings of democracy—elections per se—are as important as the substance of democracy for setting clear standards for policy decisions, the same reasoning does not hold for the trappings of liberal market systems, such as stock exchanges or convertible currencies. We can have no confidence that the trappings of a market-oriented economy provide the necessary foundation for a liberal polity, as we can with elections.

The econometric evidence regarding correlations between democracy and market-oriented economic policy is fairly clear (data from Przeworski and Limongi 1997). There is a significant correlation between per capita GNP and the stability of a democratic regime. That is, no democracy has ever fallen with a per capita GNP of $6,055 or more. Dictatorships, on the other hand, have fallen to more democratic regimes even with a high per capita GNP. But we cannot say that dictatorships fall to democracy *because* of economic development. That is, there is little or no statistical evidence that liberal market reforms create pressures to push dictators out of office. Rather, the evidence is that liberal market reforms create pressures to keep democrats in office. Whatever pressures exist to turn dictatorships into democracies are largely independent of the regime's success or failure in growing the economy or implementing liberal market reforms. There is still a relationship between open markets and free elections, both theoretically from liberalism and practically from regime survival data, but the relationship is not a causal one from the standpoint of a democratic transition. Our linkage between markets and elections, as in Figure 1, is not wrong, but we cannot simply expect a policy shift in one magically to engender a complementary policy shift in the other. There is no evidence to suggest that if an authoritarian regime establishes a stock exchange today, it will call for multiparty elections tomorrow or at any time in the future. This is precisely William Glade's point when he writes that free market policies, in the absence of additional social and political reforms to create a vibrant liberal polity, are at least insufficient and potentially detrimental for democratization.

But since democratic and market transitions are linked, albeit not causally, we should still want our foreign policy to promote the substance of liberal market reform even as we refuse to be fooled by its trappings into believing that elections and other democratic institutions are just around the corner. To distinguish the trappings of liberal markets from the substance, we need to focus on the regulatory policies of the nation in question, as well as popular attitudes regarding market behavior. Taken in tandem, these practices can provide some benchmarks for our foreign-policy formation regarding liberal democratic transitions, although neither is as clear-cut an indicator as elections are.

The former indicator—regulatory policy—really has two components. First, to the degree that the government in question owns majority shares in a broad swath of large corporations, to the degree that regime policies determine prices and create inefficiencies in production and consumption, then regulatory policy subverts the creation of a liberal market. I am not claiming that only laissez-faire systems are truly liberal (even Adam Smith adamantly rejected that notion), and in fact every advanced industrial nation since World War II has intentionally and cooperatively maintained a significant degree of government intervention, what John Ruggie (1982) calls embedded liberalism. But at some point, too much state direction pushes a polity from Quadrant I into Quadrant II (or IV to III). Such a nation might well provide a wide array of social services for its citizens (services that, confusingly for our purposes, are described as liberal policies), but such a nation is, in toto, less liberal than its Quadrant I neighbors. The point at which a regime's economic policies cross the line, so to speak, is impossible to say with precision, despite various empirical efforts to do just that.[1] There is no election corollary here to provide a clear standard for our foreign policy.

A second aspect of regulatory policy, however, is both more easily identified from afar as well as perhaps more indicative of a genuine commitment to the underlying liberal principles that go hand in hand with democracy. All liberal transactions, from ideas and conversation, to money and trade, to votes and elections, are based on a free (in the sense of voluntary) exchange of information. That exchange is predicated on the availability of such information as well as a significant degree of transactional transparency. For example, if I knowingly sell cubic zirconium rings to the public as genuine diamond rings, then I am operating within an open market but not a liberal market. For a government to inspect my rings and insist on full disclosure of their content is a perfectly legitimate, in fact necessary, form of intervention to ensure a truly liberal market. Such regulation designed to promote transactional transparency is of a different nature from regulation designed to influence prices and the unfettered clearing of markets. Price-setting policy is almost inherently illiberal; disclosure requirements, on the other hand, are a sine qua non of liberal markets.

Significantly for our foreign-policy-making efforts, disclosure regulations are more clearly identifiable as placing a regime on one side or another of some theoretical quadrant line than the more general set of regulations designed to provide some measure of state control over macroeconomic behavior. Disclosure regulations are by their nature public and transparent, there is little disagreement in policy circles as to the content of effective disclosure legislation (Sudweeks 1989), and we can further operationalize regime commitment to disclosure efforts by measuring budget allocations to financial regulatory agencies.

The latter indicator of liberal market substance—popular attitudes regarding market behavior—is a murkier concept and harder to operationalize than regime disclosure regulations, but similarly indicative of a broad-based commitment to the substance rather than just the form of liberal markets. The basic idea here is that a nation's citizens must enjoy a proper liberal education before that nation's markets will be liberal in fact as well as name.[2] That is, market participants must understand the essential nature of efficient price setting to be through supply and demand rather than through government directive, else behavior within those markets is necessarily flawed. This problem is especially pronounced in those countries where the state formerly directed virtually every aspect of economic life, notably Russia, the former Soviet Republics, and the former Warsaw Pact nations of Eastern and Central Europe.

A related "perversion" of liberal market practice, at least in term of popular attitude or education, is the degree to which market behaviors are seen as gambles, as exercises in luck rather than exercises in supply and demand. For example, a brokerage house in Taipei or Jakarta resembles nothing more than an off-track betting parlor, where patrons spend the day watching the tote board and placing bets on hourly changes in stock prices. Many "investors" in these markets (especially the mainland Chinese markets of Shanghai and Szenzhen) take their holdings out in cash at the end of each day, as holding equity shares in a company, even just overnight, is just too abstract a practice for comfort. The recent collapse of pyramid investment schemes in Albania and Russia is another variation on this theme. In both cases, and especially in Albania, the purveyors of the pyramid investments were rather up-front regarding the gambling aspect of the enterprise: that future profits relied on a continuing stream of greater fools. Popular demands in the wake of the collapse of these schemes was not so much that the originators be punished or their assets seized (although certainly that, too), but that the government step in and reimburse shareholders for their losses, as if the failure of an immensely speculative pseudo-confidence game were really no different from the failure of a bank. To be sure, this casino approach to market institutions is practiced by many in the United States and other well-established market systems, where we call it speculation rather than gambling, but there is a quantum difference in the breadth and depth of such practices in the nascent markets of Asia, Africa, and Eastern Europe.

Democratic Transitions and National Security

Finally, we need to ask ourselves how salient democratic transitions in other countries really are to our national interests. It pretty much goes without saying that U.S. policy-makers think that liberal democracy is a good thing in and of itself and that, all other things being equal, U.S. foreign policy should support democratic transitions and help consolidate them when they occur. But all other things are never equal. During the Cold War, U.S. policy-makers determined that it was more important for a foreign country to be aligned with the United States against the Soviet Union than for that foreign country to be a liberal democracy. Of course it would be nice if a country could be both an ally and a liberal democracy, but when forced to choose between the two, U.S. policy-makers uniformly favored an anti-Soviet stance over democracy. With the end of the Cold War, the United States has a great deal more flexibility in its foreign policy to pursue goals—such as the spread of liberal democracy around the globe—that have always been important to U.S. policy but not as important as a long-term strident conflict with a military superpower like the USSR.

Today's absence of hegemonic competition is hardly a certain predictor of perpetual peace. In fact, a central tenet of realist international relations theory is that conflict between great powers is a constant, that balancing behavior will occur to set the United States at odds with a new constellation of competitor nations—perhaps a resurgent Russia, perhaps an expansionist China—at some point in the not-too-distant future. Given this potential for direct national security threats to reemerge in the world, should foreign policies designed to promote or consolidate democratic transitions be at the top of the policy to-do list or somewhere in the middle? After all, if ten years from now the United States ends up fighting a cold or hot war with China, it will be more important for U.S. interests that India and Russia be our allies than that they be democracies. To answer this question, to determine the proper salience of policy in support of democratic transitions, depends on whether you believe in a separate sphere of democratic peace.

A robust set of observations suggests that liberal democracies are just as likely to fight wars as nondemocracies, but that, statistically speaking, they are pacifist toward each other (Russett 1993, and works cited therein). If true, then supporting democratic transitions serves a national security interest for the United States as well as a philanthropic one. By helping to establish liberal democracies in foreign nations, the United States simultaneously reduces the universe of potential military adversaries and increases the universe of likely allies. If true, the establishment of a stable democracy in Russia means that the United States should fear a future war with Russia as much as it fears a war with Belgium.

Recent scholarship has directly investigated the possibility that these observations of a democratic peace are simply artifacts of geographic propinquity or economic wealth. Maoz and Russett (1993) find that they are not, that regime type is both the most influential and the most significant source of variation in war-proneness, as well as a robust indicator across different operationalizations. On the other hand, Layne (1994) is openly critical of the strength of the empirical data, Mansfield and Snyder (1995) argue that nascent or transforming democracies are prone to fight anyone, and Farber and Gowa (1995) claim that while the statistical evidence for a democratic peace is plausibly strong in the post–World War II era, there were simply not enough potentially warring democracies prior to World War II to substantiate the broad historical claims of democratic peace's more ardent supporters.

A statistical correlation between peace and interdemocratic relations, regardless of whether it extends only since World War II or has been in effect across all of modern history, is a weak reed on which to base foreign policy. We need a plausible theory, an understanding of *why* liberal democracies are unlikely go to war with each other, before we can have any real confidence in the truth of the data.

Maoz and Russett characterize different attempts to explain democratic peace as falling into one of two categories—normative or structural.[3] In simplest terms, normative approaches claim that one democracy behaves peacefully toward another because of trust. As Doyle (1986) argues, not only do the citizens and leaders of liberal states prefer negotiation to violence in their domestic affairs, but they would like to see those same political norms extended internationally. Unfortunately, nations have often paid a heavy price for cooperating with aggressive states that do not negotiate in good faith. In order not to be duped, then, a democracy will extend its domestic norms of cooperation and compromise to its international relations with another country only if it believes that this other country shares these norms of cooperation and compromise; that is, only if this other country is a fellow democracy.

Structural approaches contend that the domestic constraints of certain political institutions tend to keep a government from waging war, and that these constraints are far more pronounced in liberal democratic regimes than in their more authoritarian counterparts. For example, Bueno de Mesquita and Lalman (1992) point to the existence of an organized opposition political party as the single greatest impediment to the exercise of war powers. At first glance, such a claim would not seem to support the democratic peace observations, as such a structural impediment would logically make democracies more pacific vis-à-vis all nations, not just fellow democracies. As Morgan and Campbell (1991) point out, however, some nondemocratic regimes may also be highly constrained along structural lines (the spread of decision-making powers among individuals and institutions, for example), accounting for an overall equivalence in the pacific behavior when comparing the two groups, as well as strong evidence of peace when two democracies confront each other.

The academic jury is still out regarding an underlying theory for a separate sphere of democratic peace, and attempts to develop a critical test between the two families of explanations proposed by Maoz and Russett have not been particularly successful. There is a greater level of academic consensus on the statistical evidence regarding democratic peace, albeit with the important caveats described by Farber and Gowa (1995). Current policy-makers appear to have a similar level of grudging confidence in the precepts of democratic peace. In his contribution to this volume, Arturo Valenzuela cites speech by Bill Clinton stating that the U.S. commitment to securing democratic transitions around the world was clearly in the security interests of the United States as democracies were more likely to be stalwart allies than nondemocracies. Likewise, George Bush defined his concept of a New World Order as a global collective security alliance made up of nations with a shared commitment to furthering liberal democratic principles domestically and internationally.

From a policy perspective, then, it seems clear that the concerns of this volume are both vital and salient. Policy-makers in the United States and abroad are acting on the assumption that encouraging and consolidating democratic transitions serve a vital national interest. The chapters here provide a wealth of information—theory, analysis, and facts—for both students and practitioners of international politics as they seek a better understanding of the political economy of democratic transitions in various regions and countries. My argument has been that the trappings of democracy—multiparty elections in and of themselves—are important, too, as long as foreign-policy makers must act swiftly and consistently within an environment that sharply penalizes long and costly information searches. Then again, perhaps if the ideas within this book were taken to heart and its information absorbed by the movers and shakers of foreign policy, such a simple identifying signal for democratic transitions would be unnecessary and policy decisions could be made on the basis of shared expert assessments of genuine democratic substance. Perhaps then the specific policy recommendations made by the authors herein would find a happy home in the corridors of power, rather than find themselves in an uphill battle simply to be understood. Would that any collection of academic chapters were so influential!

About the Contributors

Felipe Agüero (Ph.D., Political Science, Duke) is associate professor in the School of International Studies of the University of Miami. He previously taught in the Department of Political Science at Ohio State University and has been a fellow at the Kellogg Institute in the University of Notre Dame and the Institute for Advanced Study in Princeton. He is the author of *Soldiers, Civilians, and Democracy: Post-Franco Spain in Comparative Perspective* (Johns Hopkins, 1995) and coeditor of *Fault Lines of Democracy in Post-Transition Latin American* (North-South Center, University of Miami, 1998).

Joseph S. Berliner taught economics at Syracuse and Brandeis Universities. His field of specialization was comparative economics, notably the USSR and other socialist countries. He served as president of the American Association of Slavic Studies and of the Association for the Study of Socialist Economies. He is the author of numerous articles and several books on the subject, including most recently *The Economics of the Good Society*.

Gretchen Casper is an associate professor of political science at Pennsylvania State University. She is the author of *Fragile Democracies: The Legacies of Authoritarian Rule* and *Negotiating Democracy: Transitions from Authoritarian Rule* (with Michelle M. Taylor). She is currently researching why democracy survives in "least likely cases" and fails in "most likely cases."

Steve Chan is professor of political science at the University of Colorado (Boulder). His teaching and research interests lie in the general areas of international relations and political economy. His recent publications address questions pertaining to democratic peace, defense allocation, foreign direct investment, and Asia Pacific regionalism.

Cal Clark is an alumni professor of political science at Auburn University whose research and teaching specialties include East Asian political economy and comparative public policy. He received his Ph.D. from the University of Illinois. His recent books include the coauthored *Comparing Development Patterns in Asia* (1997), *Flexibility, Foresight, and Fortune in Taiwan's Development* (1992), and the coedited *Beyond the Developmental State* (1998) and *Democracy and the Status of Women in East Asia* (2000).

Ruth Berins Collier is professor of political science at the University of California, Berkeley. Her work has focused on regime change across several world regions. She is the author of *Regimes in Tropical Africa: Changing Forms of Supremacy, 1945–1975*; *The Contradictory Alliance: State-Labor Relations and Regime Change in Mexico*; and *Paths toward Democracy: The Working Class and Elites in Western Europe and South America*. She is also the coauthor of *Shaping the Political Arena: Critical Junctures, the Labor Movement, and Regime Dynamics in Latin America*.

Bruce Cumings is the Norman and Edna Freehling Professor of International History and East Asian Political Economy at the University of Chicago. He is the author or coauthor of eight books, including a two-volume study, *Origins of the Korean War* (Princeton University Press, 1981, 1990), and *Parallax Visions: Making Sense of American–East Asian Relations at Century's End* (Duke University Press, 1999), and more than 70 articles in various journals.

William Glade is professor of economics and director of the Mexican Center in the University of Texas at Austin and a senior scholar at the Woodrow Wilson International Center for Scholars in Washington, D.C. His fields of teaching are development (particularly Latin American development) and comparative economic systems. His research interests fall within those fields and also include the economics of culture. He has over the years lectured and consulted widely in this country and abroad, and served in the Bush administration as associate director for educational and cultural affairs in the United States Information Agency.

Jeffrey Herbst is an associate professor of politics and international affairs at Princeton University's Woodrow Wilson School. He has been on the faculty of the University of Zimbabwe, the University of Ghana, Legon, the University of Cape Town, and the University of the Western Cape.

James F. Hollifield received his doctorate in political science at Duke University in 1985. Currently he is professor of political science and director of international studies at Southern Methodist University. He is the author of many articles and books, including *Searching for the New France* (Routledge, 1990) with George Ross, *Immigrants, Markets and States* (Harvard, 1992), *Controlling Immigration* (Stanford, 1994) with Wayne Cornelius and Philip Martin, and *L'Immigration et l'état-Nation* (L'Harmattan, 1997). His most recent work, *The Myth of Globalization*, looks at the rapidly evolving relationship between trade, migration, and the nation-state. His teaching and research interests lie primarily in the areas of international and comparative political economy, with a specific focus on issues of immigration and citizenship.

Ben Hunt is an associate professor in the Department of Political Science and the associate director of the John Tower Center for Political Studies, both at Southern Methodist University. His research deals principally with security studies, with a specific focus on information transfer and international conflict. He is the author of *Getting to War: Predicting International Conflict with Mass Media Indicators* (University of Michigan Press, 1997), coauthor with Michael Laver of *Policy and Party Competition* (Routledge, 1992), and author of numerous journal articles and book chapters.

Roger E. Kanet is professor and dean of the Graduate School of International Studies of the University of Miami and professor emeritus of political science and former associate vice chancellor for academic affairs and director of international programs and studies at the University of Illinois at Urbana-Champaign, where he joined the faculty in 1973. His recent publications include *Coping with Conflict after the Cold War*, coedited with Edward A. Kolodziej (Baltimore: Johns Hopkins University Press, 1996); *The Foreign Policy of the Russian Federation*, coedited with Alexander Kozhemiakin (London: Macmillan, 1997); *The Post-Communist States and the World Community*, coedited with William E. Ferry (London: Macmillan, 1998); and *The Resolution of Regional Conflicts* (Champaign: University of Illinois Press, 1998).

Calvin Jillson received his B.S. in political science from Oregon State University in 1971 and his M.A. and Ph.D. degrees in government and politics from the University of Maryland, College Park, in 1976 and 1979. He taught at Louisiana State University (1980 to 1987) and at the University of Colorado (1987 to 1995). Professor Jillson chaired the Department of Political Science at the University of Colorado, Boulder, from 1989 to 1993, and served as founding director of the Keller Center for the Study of the First Amendment from 1993 to 1995. He joined the faculty of Southern Methodist University in July 1995 as professor and chair in the Department of Political Science. He also serves as director of the John G. Tower Center for Political Studies.

Peter M. Lewis is assistant professor at the School of International Service, American University, Washington, D.C. His work centers on economic reform and political liberalization in developing countries, with a focus on sub-Saharan Africa. He has written extensively on Nigerian political economy, as well as on broader regional issues of participation, democratic transition, and economic adjustment in Africa. He is currently finishing a book on the comparative political economies of Indonesia and Nigeria.

Stephen Macedo holds the Michael O. Sawyer Chair in Constitutional Law and Politics at the Maxwell School of Citizenship and Public Affairs at Syracuse University. He has also been an assistant and associate professor in the Government Department at Harvard University. His written works include *Liberal Virtues: Citizenship, Virtue, and Community in Liberal Constitutionalism* (Oxford: Oxford University Press, 1990), and *Diversity and Distrust: Civic Education in a Multicultural Democracy* (forthcoming from Harvard University Press, 1999). His articles have appeared in scholarly journals such as *Ethics, Political Theory*, the *Review of Politics*, and the *Georgetown Law Journal*. He has also written for the *New Republic*, the *New York Times*, and the *Wall Street Journal*.

Lucian W. Pye is Ford Professor of Political Science Emeritus at the Massachusetts Institute of Technology. He is a specialist on the political cultures of Asia, particularly with respect to the challenges of modernization and political development. He is the author of, among other books, the *Spirit of Chinese Politics* and *Asian Power and Politics*.

Thomas F. Remington is professor of political science at Emory University. He is author of a number of books and articles on Soviet and post-Soviet politics, including *Politics in Russia* (1998). His current research focuses on the development of political institutions in post-Soviet Russia, particularly the legislative branch and legislative-executive relations.

J. C. Sharman recently completed his Ph.D. in political science at the University of Illinois at Urbana-Champaign, where he is now an instructor. He is especially interested in state-society relations and the role of social movements in communist and postcommunist states; his dissertation dealt with "State Obstacles to Collective Action in Communist System." He has coauthored several long review essays that appear in the scholarly journal *Osteuropa*; in addition, several of his articles on social movements in communist states have appeared in scholarly journals.

Arturo Valenzuela is professor of government and director of the Center for Latin American Studies at Georgetown University. His academic work has focused on regime breakdown and democratic consolidation. He is the author of several books on Chilean politics and the recently published volume *The Failure of Presidential Democracy*, coedited with Juan Linz. He served as deputy assistant secretary of state for inter-american affairs in the first Clinton administration, charged with regional issues such as democracy, human rights, environment, immigration, and U.S. bilateral relations with Mexico.

Notes

Introduction

1   Even though it ignores many of the normative issues associated with democratic develop-
    ment, Schumpeter's definition of democracy as "competition for political leadership" is
    widely accepted among social scientists as a workable definition. See Joseph A. Schumpeter,
    Capitalism, Socialism and Democracy (New York: Harper & Row, 1952), pp. 269 ff.
2   A new and extensive literature has grown up around the issues of democratic transition and
    consolidation. One of the best recent works on this topic is Stephan Haggard and Robert R.
    Kaufman, *The Political Economy of Democratic Transitions* (Princeton, NJ: Princeton
    University Press, 1995). Cf. also the multivolume work by Larry Diamond, Juan J. Linz, and
    Seymour Martin Lipset, eds., *Democracy in Developing Countries* (Boulder, CO: Lynne
    Rienner, 1988, 1989), vols. 1–4.
3   In spite of the recent wave of democratic transitions, Robert Putnam sees a decline of civil
    society and social capital, especially in the more advanced democracies such as the United
    States. See Robert Putnam, *Making Democracy Work: Civic Traditions in Modern Italy*
    (Princeton, NJ: Princeton University Press, 1993), pp. 163 ff., and Putnam's various articles
    about "bowling alone."
4   The reference here is to the political revolution in France (1789) and the industrial or eco-
    nomic revolution in Britain. See E. J. Hobsbawm, *The Age of Revolution, 1789–1848* (New
    York: Mentor, 1962), pp. 44–100. Cf. also Karl Polanyi, *The Great Transformation* (Boston:
    Beacon Press, 1944).
5   See David S. Landes, *The Unbound Prometheus* (Cambridge: Cambridge University Press,
    1969).
6   Samuel P. Huntington, "Democracy's Third Wave," *Journal of Democracy* 2, no. 2 (spring
    1991): 12–34.
7   One could cite many examples of the modernization argument, but for a good summary see
    Seymour Martin Lipset, "Some Social Requisites of Democracy: Economic Development
    and Political Legitimacy," *American Political Science Review* 53, no. 1 (1959): 69–106. Also
    Gabriel Almond and G. Bingham Powell, *Comparative Politics: A Developmental Approach*
    (Boston: Little Brown, 1966). On the importance of political parties in the modernization
    process, see Joseph LaPalombara and Myron Weiner, eds., *Political Parties and Political
    Development* (Princeton, NJ: Princeton University Press, 1966).
8   Cf., G. W. F. Hegel, *The Philosophy of History* (New York: Dover, 1956) and Francis
    Fukuyama, *The End of History and the Last Man* (New York: Free Press, 1992).
9   Polanyi, *The Great Transformation*, passim.
10 Barrington Moore Jr., *Social Origins of Dictatorship and Democracy* (Boston: Beacon Press,
    1966), pp. 413 ff.
11 This is the well-known thesis of "late development," expounded by, inter alia, Alexander
    Gerschenkron, *Bread and Democracy in Germany* (New York: Howard Fertig, 1966).
12 See Theda Skocpol, *States and Social Revolutions* (Cambridge: Cambridge University Press,
    1979), pp. 19–33.
13 On the confrontation between traditional (non-European) and modern (European) cul-

tures, see David A. Apter, *The Politics of Modernization* (Chicago: University of Chicago Press, 1965), pp. 81 ff. Also, James Scott, *The Moral Economy of the Peasant* (New Haven, CT: Yale University Press, 1976).

14 Most contemporary theorists of international relations (in contradistinction to Woodrow Wilson) recognize the centrality of power and the role of "hegemonic states" in creating and maintaining international peace and order. On the theory of hegemonic stability, see, for example, Robert Gilpin, *The Political Economy of International Relations* (Princeton, NJ: Princeton University Press, 1987), pp. 72–80.

15 Another important feature of the changing international context, which was a by-product of "mass politics," was the increasingly close linkage between public opinion and foreign policy. "In democratic countries, this manifested itself in an excessive preoccupation with the mood of the electorate and a consequent tendency of governments to follow rather than lead opinion." Gordon A. Craig and Alexander L. George, *Force and Statecraft* (New York: Oxford University Press, 1995), p. 52.

16 The original classic work on dependency is Fernando Henrique Cardoso and Enzo Faletto, *Dependency and Development in Latin America* (Berkeley and Los Angeles: University of California Press, 1979). See also André Gunder Frank, *Capitalism and Underdevelopment in Latin America* (New York: Monthly Review, 1967).

17 Eric Nordlinger, *Soldiers in Politics* (Englewood Cliffs, NJ: Prentice Hall, 1977), and Samuel P. Huntington, *The Soldier and the State* (Cambridge, MA: Harvard University Press, 1957).

18 Juan Linz and Alfred Stepan, eds., *The Breakdown of Democratic Regimes* (Baltimore: Johns Hopkins Press, 1978), and David Collier, ed., *The New Authoritarianism in Latin America* (Princeton, NJ: Princeton University Press, 1979), especially the article by Guillermo O'Donnell, "Tensions in the Bureaucratic-Authoritarian State and the Question of Democracy," pp. 285–318.

19 See J. Samuel Valenzuela and Arturo Valenzuela, "Modernization and Dependency: Alternative Perspectives in the Study of Latin American Underdevelopment," *Comparative Politics* 10 (July 1978): 535–57, and Immanuel Wallerstein, *The Capitalist World-Economy* (Cambridge: Cambridge University Press, 1979).

20 For a nice overview, see Samuel P. Huntington, "Will More Countries Become Democratic?" *Political Science Quarterly*, 99 no. 2 (summer 1984): 193–218.

21 Huntington's *Political Order in Changing Societies* remains the classic, if not definitive, work on this subject. In *The Leviathan*, Hobbes argued that providing order is the most basic and important function of government, upon which rests the social contract. Authoritarian regimes are best at fulfilling this function; hence his defense of absolutism in the England of his day. But in *Two Treatises on Government*, John Locke argued that the legitimacy of government stems not just from its ability to provide order for society and protection for the individual, but from the trust conferred by the people upon government, which in turn must agree to respect the "natural rights" and liberties of the individual. Locke felt that the Stuart monarchy had violated this trust and that the English people were therefore justified in overthrowing it (during the Glorious Revolution). This did not mean that English civil society would collapse, as Hobbes feared, but rather it would be strengthened by the creation of a new political society and civic culture.

22 As Stephen Macedo (in this volume) points out, building and maintaining a civic culture is as big a problem in highly developed democracies like the United States as it is in newly created democracies. Cynicism, alienation, corruption, and ethnic and racial conflict are problems found in almost every democratic society.

23 Seymour Martin Lipset and Stein Rokkan, eds., *Party Systems and Voter Alignments* (New York: Free Press, 1967).

24 Cf. Dankwart Rustow, "Transitions to Democracy," *Comparative Politics* 2, no. 3 (1970), and Juan J. Linz, "Transitions to Democracy," *Washington Quarterly* 13, no. 3 (1990).

25 Cf. Jeffrey Sachs, *Developing Country Debt and Economic Performance* (Chicago: University of Chicago Press, 1989); Jeffrey Sachs, ed., *Poland's Jump to the Market Economy* (Cambridge, MA: MIT Press, 1993); and Alejandro Portes, "Neoliberalism and the Sociology of Development:

Emerging Trends and Unanticipated Facts," *Population and Development Review* 23, no. 2 (June 1997): 229–259.

26   For a review of the development literature, see Gabriel A. Almond, "The Development of Political Development," in Myron Weiner and Samuel P. Huntington, *Understanding Political Development* (Boston: Little Brown, 1987), pp. 437–490.

Chapter 1

1   Francis Fukuyama's eye-catching phrase, "the end of history," has been widely misunderstood. He did not intend to suggest that human affairs would not continue to be filled with its ups and downs, its conflicts and disagreements. He was picking up Kant's and Hegel's idea that "universal history" is the striving for the grand ideal for human society, which now turns out to be not communism or fascism, but liberal democracy.

2   Fukuyama charts a relatively smooth acceleration in the spread of democracy from only 3 states in 1790, then 13 in 1900, 25 in 1919, 36 in 1960, and 61 by 1990, with only slight drops in 1940 and 1975. Fukuyama, *The End of History and the Last Man* (New York: The Free Press, 1992), pp. 49–50.

3   Putnam suggests that the prime cause for the decline is television viewing. See Putnam 1996; Michael Schudson, Theda Skocpol, and Richard Valelly challenged Putnam's thesis and analysis in *American Prospects*, spring 1997.

Chapter 2

1   A recent OECD report (OECD 1992) calls economic and political pluralism necessary supports for development and notes : "For all OECD donors, human rights and democratic values have become a consideration in decisions about aid allocation. Aid programmes have been developed to help build and strengthen democratic institutions." Along with policy reforms to correct the profligate macroeconomic policies, unrealistic exchange rates, and distorting regulations that led to misshapen investment decisions in both public and private sectors, there is renewed attention to development of leadership capacity and popular participation, to fortify the democratic structures on which the whole enterprise of development must, it is assumed, be based if it is to be sustainable.

2   The size of the traded-goods sector in Germany was a critical variable, for in time the external sector accounted for an exceptionally high percentage of GDP—exerting a much greater influence on the organization of the whole economy than happened in Japan or other Asian exporters.

3   It could be argued that the GATT negotiations were initiated in a belief that liberalized trading regimes, by reversing prewar nationalisms, would foster prosperity and improve the environment for democratic governments—just as the IMF sought to undo the cumbersome and often complicated restrictions that had cluttered the exchange rate systems of the 1930s and 1940s.

4   Marklew's analysis, coming after regionalization and globalization had been shaping the environment even longer, shows how the boundaries between the private- and public-sector firms have become increasingly ambiguous.

5   It is probably significant that in both Taiwan and Korea, the postwar era was ushered in with an agrarian reform and a governmental commitment to strengthen the rural sector that was almost wholly absent in contemporary Latin America, save for Bolivia.

6   Sheahan's "Market-Oriented Economic Policies and Political Repression in Latin America" provided typically dark reading, but until recently Latin American intellectuals in general, because of the association between restructuring and heavy-handed rule in Chile, looked askance at structural adjustment.

7   The World Bank's devastatingly critical *Report on Cuba* (1951) contained an astonishing

exposé of public-sector failings, but its candor in this respect was unique among the country studies put out by that institution.

8   Otero 1996 tackles the relationship of political regime to economic reform from a variety of perspectives, but the analysts in this book find nothing unarguably assertable about it.

9   For Peru, see Sagasti et al. 1994 for a thoughtful exploration of the problematic relationship in a country that has enjoyed only brief intervals of reasonably democratic rule but whose bold restructuring has yielded significant returns in the short run. The authors forthrightly note that the problems the country confronts today have been centuries in the making.

10   The strategic business alliance of Televisa with the PRI and the Mexican government, which was much commented on in the last presidential elections, is a prime case in point.

11   Leigh Payne (1992), suggests that business interests may also come to see authoritarian regimes as too costly in terms of the systemic transaction costs they impose, thus hampering their own competitive standing in the international economy.

Chapter 4

1   Appraisals are much less critical of the Southern European democracies inaugurated in the 1970s (Greece, Portugal, and Spain), which, in spite of problems of democratic governance, occasionally quite severe, are generally regarded as consolidated democracies with problems of a much lesser magnitude than the ones confronting Eastern Europe, the republics of the former Soviet Union, or Latin America (Linz and Stepan 1996; Gunther, Diamandouros, and Puhle 1995).

2   This chapter follows Stepan's definition of military prerogatives (1988, p. 93).

3   For other ways of classifying transitions in the literature, see Mainwaring (1992) and McGuire (1995).

4   The distinction of transition paths of compromise and no compromise made in Bruszt and Stark (1992, pp. 16–19) is useful here.

5   Sarney had been elected as vice president on the opposition ticket, but Tancredo Neves, the president-elect, suffered a stroke on the eve of the transfer of power and died a few weeks later. Until six months before the election, Sarney had headed the official party that supported the military. He then led a splinter faction to join the opposition. The alliance of Sarney's group with the opposition allowed for their victory in the electoral college. Neves's death, however, lessened the successor's government break with the past. Sarney ruled with substantial military support, which helped him resist pressures to shorten his term. Also, the military intervened in a wide array of policy areas.

6   These decrees establish, for instance: a new National Defense System, which is led by the president but gives ample prerogatives within it to the military; a mobilization system that prescribes that individuals must make information available to the armed forces; a National Intelligence System and Service that may obtain any information required from public or private agencies; the power of the military to intervene in university locales, prisons, and areas not declared in state of emergency; the expansion of military prerogatives in areas declared in state of emergency; an amnesty (granted in June 1995) to military personnel for crimes committed in the fight against subversion since 1980. For a detailed description of these decrees see Degregori and Rivera (1994) and Basombrío (1997).

7   For an account of the constitution's mixed success for the military, see Hunter (1997, pp. 57–60).

Chapter 5

1   Harry C. Katz, "The Decentralization of Collective Bargaining: A Literature Review and Comparative Analysis," *Industrial and Labor Relations Review* 47, no. 1, (October 1993); and Kathleen Thelen, "Beyond Corporatism: Toward a New Framework for the Study of Labor

in Advanced Capitalism," *Comparative Politics* 27, no. 1, (October 1994).

2   Ruth Berins Collier and David Collier, *Shaping the Political Arena* (Princeton, NJ: Princeton University Press, 1991), chaps. 6 and 7.

3   James G. Samstad and Ruth Berins Collier, "Mexican Labor and Structural Reform Under Salinas: New Unionism or Old Stalemate?" in *The Challenge of Institutional Reform in Mexico*, ed. (Boulder Riordan Roett, CO: Lynne Rienner Publishers, 1995), p. 15.

4   Yemile Mizrahi, "La nueva relación entre los empresarios y el gobierno: el surgimiento de los empresarios panistas," *Estudios Sociológicos* 14, no. 41, (1996), pp. 493–515; Carlos Arriola, *Ensayos sobre el PAN* (Mexico City: Miguel Angel Purrua Grupo Editorial, 1994).

5   Ruth Berins Collier, *The Contradictory Alliance* (Berkeley: University of California, Berkeley International and Area Studies, 1992), p. 100.

6   The analysis of this law can be found in ibid., pp. 142–44.

7   Samstad and Collier, "Mexican Labor"pp. 18–21.

8   Ibid., pp. 21–24.

9   The candidate, Luis Donaldo. Colosio, wass assassinated before the election.

10 Latin American Data Base, *SourceMex* 7, no. 14 (April 3, 1996), p. 7.

11 Wayne Cornelius, *Mexican Politics in Transition* (San Diego: University of California, San Diego Center for U.S.-Mexican Studies, 1996), p. 36.

12 This orientation was evident in the defense of the governor of Tabasco (who was accused of wild violations of campaign spending limits) and in the setbacks in the new electoral law, which were demanded by groups within the party whose opposition erupted in the move to open the party to broader participation. *Latin American Weekly Review* 95, .no. 38, (October 5, 199): p. 445.

13 Mexico2000 e-mail newslist, Reuters, January 12, 1997; and *Washington Post* January 1, 1997, p. A35

14 James Samstad, "Mexican Labor after Fidel Democratization and the Erosion of Corporatism during the Zedillo Administration," paper presented at the Latin American Studies Association (LASA) annual conference, September 1998.

15 Ibid., p. 19.

Chapter 6

1   In addition to works cited, this section and chapter relies heavily on the works of leading experts on U.S.–Latin American relations (Atkins 1995; Carothers 1991; Lowenthal 1987; Pastor 1992; Schoultz 1981, 1987; Smith 1996.)

Chapter 7

1   The key texts in this literature are Guillermo O'Donnell, Philippe C. Schmitter, and Laurence Whitehead, eds., *Transitions from Authoritarian Rule: Comparative Perspectives* (Baltimore: Johns Hopkins University Press, 1986); same authors, *Transitions from Authoritarian Rule: Latin America* (Baltimore, 1986). same authors, *Transitions from Authoritarian Rule: Tentative Conclusions about Uncertain Democracies* (Baltimore, 1986); For my critique, which compared several Latin American cases with South Korea, see "The Abortive Abertura," *New Left Review*, Spring 1989.

Chapter 8

1   Senator Benigno Aquino was one of the first politicians arrested. He was held in solitary confinement for seven years on murder charges, and was eventually sentenced to death. He was allowed to go to the United States for heart bypass surgery with the understanding that

he would not return to the Philippines. Although he was allowed to leave the country, his death sentence was not commuted (Landé 1986, 113; Wurfel 1988).

2 EDSA refers to the main highway—Epifanio de los Santos Avenue—that runs by the two military camps where RAM, Enrile, and Ramos fled after Marcos discovered the plans for the coup. The events were considered by some to be "miraculous"—that divine intervention helped People Power stop the loyalist tanks. The color yellow was associated with Benigno Aquino after he was jailed, and was adopted by the moderate opposition during the snap election campaign.

Chapter 12

1 It was not until the death of Brezhnev in 1982 that his successor, Yuri Andropov, relaxed the censorship sufficiently to permit a serious, if still limited, public discussion of economic reform (Hewett 1988, p. 260).

2 Under central planning, enterprise bank accounts served primarily to pay for goods and services received from other enterprises. They could be converted into cash only for specific planned purposes such as the payment of wages.

3 From 1961 to 1965, the Soviet growth rate of GNP (4.9 percent) was 92 percent of the OECD growth rate (5.3 percent). From 1981 to 1985, Soviet growth (1.8 percent) had fallen to 69 percent of OECD growth (2.6 percent) (US Directorate of Intelligence 1988, p. 33).

4 The CIA estimated that Soviet GNP grew at 2 percent per year from 1980 to 1985. Some analysts contend that growth had ceased entirely some time before 1985, but most observers regard the CIA estimates as most authoritative (Aslund 1989, p. 15).

5 Contrasting points of view are developed in Schweizer 1994 and Garthoff 1994.

6 The growth rate would rise from from 3.15 percent to only 3.27 percent per year. The growth rate of per capita consumption would increase by somewhat more— from 2.03 percent to 2.68 percent per year. That would have been a tangible improvement for the consumer, but the effect on the overall growth gap was too small to have affected the course of events. Those results are consistent with a recent multiple regression study of 101 countries that found defense expenditures to have no effect on the growth rate (Kim 1996).

7 It has been estimated that if Poland, with one quarter of its population still engaged in farming, could export farm products to the EU under its Common Agricultural Policy, its farm incomes would increase by 48 percent. *Financial Times*, February 17, 1997, p. 12.

Chapter 13

1 This so-called "third wave" of democratization began in the 1970s in Europe and expanded to Latin America and portions of the developing world before taking root in Central and Eastern Europe (see Huntington 1991).

2 International factors have been seen as catalysts or triggers for domestic processes. The failure of the Greek military to deter or counter Turkey's invasion of Northern Cyprus, the fruitless struggle to retain Portuguese colonies in Africa, and the Argentinean defeat in the Falklands War all fall into this category, with the critical actors, decisions, and events in the transition process still located at the domestic level (see Pridham 1994).

3 The term "Eastern Europe" will be used throughout this essay to refer to the former communist countries of East Central Europe and the Balkans.

4 The Marshall Plan was worth US$ 13 billion at the time, or, adjusted for inflation in the intervening period, US$ 85 billion. In total, the amount spent by the United States and Europe from 1990 to 1994 was US$ 107 billion, the big difference being that Marshall aid was in the form of direct grants, while most of the aid to the former communist countries has been in the form of trade credits and loans (Weiss 1997).

5   Various authors have challenged the "democratic peace" argument. See, for example, Mansfield and Snyder 1995 and Kozhemiakin 1998.
6   Since the focus of this argument is not on NATO expansion or Russian reactions to it, we have limited our discussion to a general assessment of the relationship of the proposed expansion to democratic consolidation. For a discussion of NATO and European Union expansion, see Kanet and Lund, in press.
7   For an assessment of EU democratization assistance, see Pinder, 1994.
8   On the importance and difficulty of changing political culture, see Kürti and Langman 1997 and Plasser and Ulram 1996.
9   On the role of the occupying forces in democratizing Germany and Japan, see Ginsberg 1996 and Hoffmann 1996.

Chapter 14

1   It should be noted that the two sets of classifications are not completely compar-able because the Freedom House data appears to end in early 1996 while the classification of countries by democratic history goes to the beginning of 1997. However, none of the rankings appears egregiously wrong. For instance, Burundi, Niger, and Sierra Leone had the lowest civil-liberties ranking in the one-transition category before they experienced their coups.
2   Rawlings's warning is especially ominous because he initially intervened in politics in 1979, only to hand power over to a civilian government after a bloody "housecleaning" of the then-current military regime. In 1981, he undertook a second coup d'état that ended Ghana's third attempt at multiparty democracy.

Chapter 15

1   Kenya provides one such example, but even here the influence of the donors was important in a tactical sense—influencing the pace of political reform at a crucial juncture—rather than providing a fundamental source of democratic pressure.
2   These conclusions are drawn from a comparison of leading economic indicators from 1985 to 1995 for the following countries: Benin, Congo, Ethiopia, Ghana, Madagascar, Malawi, Mali, and Zambia. The dates of political transition ranged from 1991 to 1994. The transitional countries were compared with a set of countries that did not experience political transitions: Côte d'Ivoire, Kenya, Togo, Uganda, and Zimbabwe. The indicators included annual GDP growth, government fiscal balance, inflation, and growth of the money supply. Figures were taken from the World Bank (1996).

Chapter 16

1   Well-known efforts on this score, such as the indices constructed by Freedom House, are contentious precisely because there is no definitional agreement on what liberal markets should look like.
2   See Stephen Macedo, *Liberal Virtues: Citizenship, Virtue, and Community* (Oxford: Clarendon Press, 1992), for further exposition of this idea.
3   Other authors may disagree on the semantics of the distinction—for example, T. Clifton Morgan calls the categories cultural and structural ("Democracy and War: Reflections of the Literature," *International Interactions* 18, no. 3, pp. 197–203)—but the meaning of the categories is identical.

Bibliography

Chapter 1

Almond, G. A. and S. Verba. *The Civic Culture: Political Attitudes and Democracy in Five Nations*. Princeton, NJ: Princeton University Press, 1963.
de Schweinitz, K. "Industrialization, Labor Controls and Democracy." *Economic Development and Cultural Change* 7 (July 1959).
Diamond, Larry, Juan J. Linz, and Seymour Martin Lipset, eds. *Democracy in Developing Countries*. 4 vols. Boulder, CO: Lynne Rienner, 1988–89.
Diamond, Larry. "Economic Development and Democracy Reconsidered." In Gary Marks and L. Diamond, eds., *Reexamining Democracy: Essays in Honor of Seymour Martin Lipset*. Newbury Park, CA: Sage Publications, 1992.
Ehrenhalt, Alan. *The Lost City: The Discovering of the Forgotten Virtues of Community in the Chicago of the 1950s*. New York: Basic Books, 1995.
Etzioni, Amitai. *The New Golden Rule: Community and Morality in a Democratic Society*. New York: Basic Books, 1997.
Fukuyama, Francis. *The End of History and the Last Man*. New York: The Free Press, 1992.
Galenson, W. "Introduction." In Galenson, ed., *Labor and Economic Development*. New York: Wiley, 1959.
Gerschenkron, Alexander. *Economic Backwardness in Historical Perspective*. Cambridge, MA: Harvard University Press, 1962.
Huntington, Samuel P., and Joan Nelson. *No Easy Choice: Political Participation in Developing Countries*. Cambridge, MA: Harvard University Press, 1976.
Huntington, S. P. *The Third Wave: Democratization in the Late Twentieth Century*. Norman: University of Oklahoma Press, 1991.
King, Anthony. *Running Scared*. New York: The Free Press, 1996.
Lipset, S. M. *The Social Bases of Politics*. New York: Doubleday, 1960.
Mansfield, Edward D., and Jack Snyder. "Democratization and War." *Foreign Affairs*, May/June 1995, pp. 79–97.
O'Donnell, Guillermo, and Philippe Schmitter. *Transition from Authoritarian Rule*. Baltimore, MD: Johns Hopkins University Press, 1986.
Przeworski, A., and F. Limongi. "Modernization, Theories and Facts." *World Politics* 49, no. 2, (January 1992): pp.155–83.
Putnam, Robert. "Bowling Alone: America's Declining Social Capital." *Journal of Democracy*, January 1995.
———. "The Strange Disappearance of Civic America." *American Prospects*, winter 1996.
Root, Hilton L. *Small Countries, Big Lessons: Governance and the Rise of East Asia*. Hong Kong: Oxford University Press for the Asian Development Bank, 1996.
Rustow, D. A. "Transitions to Democracy: Toward a Dynamic Model." *Comparative Politics* 2, (April 1970): 337 ff.
Schudson, Michael, Theda Skocpol, and Richard Valelly. *American Prospects*, spring 1997.

Chapter 2

Aharoni, Yair. *The Evolution and Management of State-Owned Enterprises*. Cambridge, MA: Ballinger, 1986.
Aspe, Pedro. *Economic Transformation the Mexican Way*. Cambridge, MA: MIT Press, 1993.

Baklanoff, Eric N., ed. *Mediterranean Europe and the Common Market: Studies of Economic Growth and Integration.* Alabama: University of Alabama Press, 1976.

Balassa, Bela A., et al. *Toward Renewed Economic Growth in Latin America.* Mexico City: Institute for International Economics, 1986.

Bartell, Ernest, and Leigh A. Payne, eds. *Business and Democracy in Latin America.* Pittsburgh: University of Pittsburgh Press, 1995. A compilation of studies done at the Kellogg Institute, some of which are listed separately here for convenience in location.

Camp, Roderic A. *Politics in Mexico.* New York: Oxford University Press, 1996.

Commons, John R. *Industrial Goodwill.* New York: McGraw-Hill, 1919.

Conaghan, Catherine M. "The Private Sector and the Public Transcript: the Political Mobilization of Business in Bolivia." Working Paper #176, Helen Kellogg Institute for International Studies, University of Notre Dame, June 1992.

Dornbusch, Rudiger, and Sebastian Edwards, eds. *The Macroeconomics of Populism in Latin America.* Chicago: University of Chicago Press, 1991.

Foxley, Alejandro. *Latin American Experiments in Neo-Conservative Economics.* Berkeley: University of California Press, 1983.

Friedman,. Milton. *Capitalism and Freedom.* Chicago: University of Chicago Press, 1962.

Fuentes Irurozqui, Manuel. *Una experiencia interesante en el Perú; del intervencionismo a la libertad económica.* Madrid: Ediciones Cultura Hispanica, 1952.

Giersch, Herbert, et al. *The Fading Miracle: Four Decades of Market Economy in Germany.* Cambridge: Cambridge University Press, 1994.

Griffin, Keith. *Alternative Strategies for Economic Development.* New York: St. Martin's Press, 1989.

Hart, Jeffrey A. *Rival Capitalists: International Competitiveness in the United States, Japan, and Western Europe.* Ithaca, NY: Cornell University Press, 1992.

Hayek, Friedrich H. Von. *The Constitution of Liberty.* Chicago: University of Chicago Press, 1960.

Holland, Stuart, ed. *The State as Entrepreneur—New Dimensions for Public Enterprise: The IRI State Shareholding Formula.* London: Weidenfeld and Nicolson, 1972.

International Monetary Fund. *World Economic Outlook, May 1997: A Survey by the Staff of the International Monetary Fund.* Washington, D.C: IMF, 1997.

Jenny, Frédéric. "Competition and Competition Policy." In William J. Adams, ed., *Singular Europe: Economy and Polity of the European Community after 1992.* Ann Arbor: University of Michigan Press, 1995.

Johnson, Chalmers. *MITI and the Japanese Miracle: The Growth of Industrial Policy, 1925–1975.* Stanford: Stanford University Press, 1982.

Koo, Bon Ho, and Dwight H. Perkins, eds. *Social Capability and Long-Term Growth.* New York: St. Martin's Press, 1995.

Lustig, Nora. *Mexico: The Remaking of an Economy.* Washington, D.C.: Brookings, 1992.

Mallon, Richard D., and Juan V. Sourrouille. *Economic Policymaking in a Conflict Society: The Argentine Case.* Cambridge, MA: Harvard University Press, 1975.

Marklew, Victoria. *Cash, Crisis, and Corporate Governance: The Role of National Financial Systems in Industrial Restructuring.* Ann Arbor: University of Michigan Press, 1995.

Maxfield, Sylvia, and Ben Ross Schneider, eds. *Business and the State in Developing Countries.* Ithaca, NY: Cornell University Press, 1997.

Mazzolini, Renato. *Government Controlled Enterprises: International Strategic and Policy Decisions.* New York: Wiley, 1979.

OECD. *Development and Democracy: Aid Policies in Latin America.* Paris: OECD, 1992.

Otero, Gerardo, ed. *Neo-Liberalism Revisited: Economic Restructuring and Mexico's Political Future.* Boulder, CO: Westview Press, 1996.

Packenham, Robert. "The Politics of Economic Liberalization: Argentina and Brazil in Comparative Perspective." Working Paper #206, The Helen Kellogg Institute for International Studies, University of Notre Dame, April 1994.

Payne, Leigh A. "Brazilian Business and the Democratic Transition: New Attitudes and Influence." Working Paper #179, Helen Kellogg Institute for International Studies,

University of Notre Dame, August 1992.

Petras, James, ed. *Latin America: Bankers, Generals, and the Struggle for Social Justice*. Totowa, N.J.: Rowman and Littlefield, 1986.

Ramos, Joseph. *Neoconservative Economics in the Southern Cone of Latin America, 1973–1983*. Baltimore, MA: Johns Hopkins Press, 1986.

Richardson, Elliot. *Confessions of a Radical Moderate*. New York: Pantheon Books, 1996.

Sagasti, Francisco, Pepi Patron, Nicolas Lynch, and Max Hernandez. *Democracia y buen gobierno. Proyecto agenda: Perú*. Lima: Editorial Apoyo, 1994.

Schydlowsky, Daniel M., and Juan J. Wicht. *Anatomía de un fracaso económico: Perú 1968–1978*. Lima: Universidad del Pacífico, 1979.

Sheahan, John. "Market-Oriented Economic Policies and Political Repression in Latin America." *Economic Development and Cultural Change* (1980), pp. 267–91.

Smyser, W. R. *The German Economy: Colossus at the Crossroads*. New York: St. Martin's Press, 1993.

Solimano, Andrés, et al. *Rebuilding Capitalism: Alternative Roads after Socialism and Dirigisme*. Ann Arbor: University of Michigan Press, 1994.

Valdés, Juan Gabriel. *Pinochet's Economists: The Chicago School in Chile*. New: York: Cambridge University Press, 1995.

Vernon, Raymond, ed. *Big Business and the State: Changing Relations in Western Europe*. Cambridge, MA: Harvard University Press, 1974.

Williamson, John. *Latin American Adjustment: How Much Has Happened?* Washington, D.C.: Institute of International Economics, 1990.

Wade, Robert. *Governing the Market: Economic Theory and the Role of Government in East Asian Industrialization*. Princeton, NJ: Princeton University Press, 1990.

Webb, Richard C. *Government Policy and the Distribution of Income in Peru, 1963–1973*. Cambridge, MA: Harvard University Press, 1977.

Whitehead, Laurence. "The Alternatives to Liberal Democracy: A Latin American Perspective," *Political Studies* (1992), special issue, pp. 146–59.

World Bank. *The East Asian Miracle: Economic Growth and Public Policy*. Washington, D.C.: published for the World Bank by Oxford University Press, 1993.

World Bank, Economic and Technical Mission to Cuba. *Report on Cuba: Findings and Recommendations of an Economic and Technical Mission Organized by the International Bank for Reconstruction and Development in Collaboration with the Government of Cuba in 1950*. Baltimore, MA: Johns Hopkins Press, 1951.

Chapter 3

Alexander, Christopher, et al. *A Pattern Language: Towns, Buildings, Construction*. New York: Oxford University Press, 1977.

Almond, Gabriel A., and Sidney Verba. *The Civic Culture: Political Attitudes and Democracy in Five Nations*. Princeton, NJ: Princeton University Press, 1963.

Arendt, Hannah. *The Human Condition*. Chicago: University of Chicago Press, 1958.

Banfield, Edward. *The Unheavenly City Revisited*. Boston: Little, Brown, 1974.

Beito, David. "Mutual Aid for Social Welfare: The Case of American Fraternal Societies." *Critical Review* 4, no. 4, (1990): 709–36.

Bienen, Henry, and Jeffrey Herbst. "The Relationship between Economic and Political Reform in Africa." *Comparative Politics*, October 1996.

Chan, Alfred L., and Paul Nesbitt-larking. "Critical Citizenship and Civil Society in

Contemporary China." *Canadien Journal of Political Science* 28, no. 2 (June/July 1995): 293–309.

Constant, Benjamin. "The Liberty of the Ancients Compared with that of the Moderns." Speech given at the Athenee Royale, 1819, in Biancamaria Fontana, ed., *Benjamin Constant: Political Writings*, ed. Cambridge, UK: Cambridge University Press, 1988.

Di Palma, Giuseppe. "Legitimation from the Top to Civil Society: Politico-Cultural Change in Eastern Europe." *World Politics* 44 (October 1991):. 49–80.

Durkheim, Emile. *Professional Ethics and Civic Morals.* Glencoe, IL: Free Press, 1957.

Hamilton, Alexander, James Madison, and James Jay. *The Federalist Papers*. New York: Mentor, 1961.

Hobbes, Thomas. *Leviathan.* Harmondsworth, UK: Penguin, 1981.

Holmes, Stephen. "Cultural Legacies or State Collapse? Probing the Postcommunist Dilemma." Collegium Budapest/Institute for Advanced Study, Public Lecture #13, November, 15, 1995.

Ignatieff, Michael. "On Civil Society: Why Eastern Europe's Revolutions Could Succeed." *Foreign Affairs* 74, no 2 (March/April 1995): 128–36.

Isaac, Jeffrey C. "The Meanings of 1989." *Social Research* 63, no 2 (summer 1996): 291–344.

Jacobs, Jane. *The Death and Life of Great American Cities.* New York: Random House, 1961.

Kammen, Michael. *A Machine That Would Go of Itself.* New York: Knopf, 1986.

Kornhauser, William. *The Politics of Mass Society.* Glencoe, IL: Free Press, 1959.

Lane, Robert. "The Joyless Polity: Contributions of Democratic Process to Ill-Being." Paper prepared for conference on Citizen Competence sponsored by Committee for the Political Economy of the Good Society, University of Maryland, Washington, D.C., February 10--11, 1994.

Lee, Su-Hoon. "Transitional Politics in Korea, 1987–1992: Activation of Civil Society." *Pacific Affairs* 66 (fall 1993): 351–67.

Lewis, Peter M. "Economic Reform and Political Transition in Africa. *World Politics* 48, October 1996.

Ling, L. H. M., and Chih-yu Shih. "Confusionism with a Liberal Face: The Meaning of Democratic Politics in Contemporary Taiwan." *Review of Politics* 60, no. 1 (January 1998): 55–82.

Lipset, Seymour M. "Some Social Requisites of Democracy: Economic Development and Political Legitimacy." *American Political Science Review*,. 53 (1959).

Locke, John. *Two Treatises of Government.* Edited by Peter Laslett. New York: Mentor, 1963.

Macedo, Stephen. *Liberal Virtues: Citizenship, Virtue, and Community in Liberal Constitutionalism.* Oxford: Clarendon Press, 1992.

MacIntyre, Alasdair. *After Virtue.* Notre Dame, 1981.

———. *Whose Justice? Which Rationality?* Notre Dame, 1988.

Mill, John Stuart. *On Liberty.* Edited by. David Spitz. New York: W. W. Norton, 1975.

Nagle, John. "Ethnos, Demos, and Democratization: A Comparison of the Czech Republic, Hungary and Poland," *Democratization* 4, no. 2 (summer 1997): 28–56.

Nelson, Daniel N. "Civil Society Endangered." *Social Research* 63, no. 2 (summer 1996): 345–68.

Plato. *The Republic.* translated by Allan Bloom. New York: Basic, 1968.

Przeworski, Adam, and Fernando Limongi. "Modernization: Theories and Facts," *World Politics* 4,(January 1997): 155–83.

Putnam, Robert. *Making Democracy Work.* Princeton, NJ: Princeton University Press, 1994.

———."Tuning In, Tuning Out: The Strange Disappearance of Social Capital in America." *PS: Political Science and Politics* 27, no. 4, (1995) 664–83.

Rawls, John. *A Theory of Justice.* Oxford: Oxford University Press, 1971.

———. *Political Liberalism.* New York: Columbia University Press, 1993.

Rose, Richard. "Postcommunism and the Problem of Trust." *Journal of Democracy* 5. (July 1994): 18–50.

Rousseau, Jean-Jacques. *On the Social Contract.* Translated and edited by Donald Cress. Indianapolis: Hackett, 1983.

Sandel, Michael. *Liberalism and the Limits of Justice.* Cambridge: Cambridge University Press,

1992

———. *Democracy's Discontents: America in Search of a Public Philosophy*. Cambridge, MA: Harvard University Press, 1996.

Shifter, Michael. "Tensions and Trade-offs in Latin America." *Journal of Democracy* 8, no. 2, (1997): 114–28.

Siedentop, Larry. "Two Liberal Traditions In." ed., Alan Ryan, *The Idea of Freedom: Essays in Honor of Isaiah Berlin*. Oxford: Oxford University Press, 1979.

Smith, Adam. *An Inquiry into the Nature and Causes of the Wealth of Nations*. Edited by. R. H. Campbell, A. S. Skinner, and W. B. Todd. vol. 2.Oxford: Clarendon Press, 1979

Soros, George. "The Capitalist Threat," *Atlantic Monthly* February 1997.

Taylor, Charles. *Philosophy and the Human Sciences: Philosophical Papers, II*. Cambridge: Cambridge University Press, 1985.

de Tocqueville, Alexis. *Memoir, Letters, and Remains of Alexis de Tocqueville*. vol. 1. London, 1861

———. *Democracy in America*. Edited by J. P Mayer. Garden City, NJ: Doubleday, 1969.

Walzer, Michael. "Philosophy and Democracy." *Political Theory* 9 (1981): 379–99.

———. *Spheres of Justice: A Defense of Pluralism and Equality*. New York: Basic Books, 1983.

Chapter 4

Agüero, Felipe. "Democratic Consolidation and the Military in Southern Europe and South America." In Richard Gunther, P. Nikiforos Diamandouros, and Hans Jürgen Puhle, eds., *The Politics of Democratic Consolidation: Southern Europe in Comparative Perspective*. Baltimore: Johns Hopkins University Press, 1995a.

———. *Soldiers, Civilians, and Democracy: Post-Franco Spain in Comparative Perspective*. Baltimore and London: The Johns Hopkins University Press, 1995b.

Anderson, Charles. *Politics and Economic Change in Latin America*. Princeton, NJ: Princeton University Press, 1967.

Basombrío, Carlos. "La subordinación de los militares a la democracia en la América Latina de los noventa." Paper presented to the international seminar "La cuestión cívico-militar en las nuevas democracias de América Latina," Buenos Aires, Universidad Torcuato di Tella, May 22, 1997.

Bruszt, László, and David Stark. "Remaking the Political Field in Hungary: From the Politics of Confrontation to the Politics of Competition." In Ivo Banac, ed., *Eastern Europe in Revolution*. Ithaca and London: Cornell University Press, 1992.

Comisso, Ellen. "Legacies of the Past or New Institutions? The Struggle over Restitution in Hungary." *Comparative Political Studies* 28 (1995): pp. 200–238.

Crawford, Beverly, and Arend Lijphart. "Explaining Political and Economic Change in Post Communist Eastern Europe: Old Legacies, New Institutions, Hegemonic Norms, and International Pressures." *Comparative Political Studies* 28 (1995): 171–99.

Dahl, Robert A. *Democracy and Its Critics*. New Haven, CT: Yale University Press, 1989.

de Brito, Alexandra Barahona. *Human Rights and Democratization in Latin America: Uruguay and Chile*. Oxford: Oxford University Press, 1997.

Degregori, Carlos Iván, and Carlos Rivera. "Perú 1980–1993: Fuerzas armadas, subversión y democracia." *Instituto de Estudios Peruanos* Documento de Trabajo No. 53, 1994.

Ensalaco, Mark. "Accounting for the Past: Human Rights in Democratic Chile." Paper presented at the XXI International Congress of the Latin American Studies Association, Washington, D.C., 1995.

Franko, Patrice. "De Facto Demilitarization: Budget-Driven Downsizing in Latin America." *Journal of Interamerican Studies and World Affairs* 36 (1994): 37–74.

Friedheim, Daniel V. "Bringing Society Back into Democratic Transition Theory after 1989: Pact Making and Regime Collapse." *East European Politics and Societies* 7 (1993):. 482–512.

Garretón, Manuel Antonio. "Human Rights and Processes of Democratization." *Journal of Latin American Studies* 26 (1994): 221–24.

Geddes, Barbara. "A Comparative Perspective on the Leninist Legacy in Eastern Europe."

   Comparative Political Studies 28 (1995): 239–74.
Gross, Jan T. "Poland: From Civil Society to Political Nation." In Ivo Banac, ed., *Eastern Europe in Revolution*, pp. 56–71. Ithaca, NY: Cornell University Press, 1992.
Gunther, Richard, Nikiforos P. Diamandovros, and Hans Jourgen Puhle. *The Politics of Democratic Consolidation.* Baltimore: Johns Hopkins University Press, 1995.
Hagopian, Frances. "Democracy by Undemocratic Means? Elites, Political Pacts and Regime Transition in Brazil." *Comparative Political Studies* 23 (1990): 147–70.
———. "Democracy and Political Representation in Latin America in the 1990s: Pause, Reorganization or Decline?" Paper presented at the conference "Fault Lines of Democratic Governance," North South Center, University of Miami, May 5–6, 1995.
———. *Traditional Politics and Regime Change in Brazil.* Cambridge: Cambridge University Press, 1996.
Holston, James, and Teresa Caldeira, P. R. "Democracy, Law and Violence: Disjunctions of Brazilian Citizenship." Paper presented at the conference "Fault Lines of Democratic Governance," North-South Center, University of Miami, May 5–6, 1995.
Hunter, Wendy. *Eroding Military Influence in Brazil: Politicians against Soldiers.* Chapel Hill: University of North Carolina Press, 1997.
Jowitt, Ken. "The Leninist Legacy." In Ivo Banac, ed., *Eastern Europe in Revolution*, 207–24. Ithaca and London: Cornell University Press, 1992
Karl, Terry Lynn, "Dilemmas of Democratization in Latin America." *Comparative Politics* 23, (1990): 1–21.
Karl, Terry Lynn, and Philippe C. Schmitter. "Modes of Transition in Latin America, Southern and Eastern Europe." *International Social Science Journal* 128 (1991).
Lamounier, Bolivar. "Brazil: The Hyperactive Paralysis Syndrome." In Abraham F. Lowenthal and Jorge I. Domínguez, eds., *Constructing Democratic Governance: Latin America and the Caribbean in the 1990s.* Baltimore and London: The Johns Hopkins University Press, 1996.
Linz, Juan J. "The Future of an Authoritarian Situation or the Institutionalization of an Authoritarian Regime." In Alfred Stepan, ed., pp. 233–54. *Authoritarian Brazil: Origins, Policies, and Future.* New Haven: Yale University Press, 1973.
——— "Presidential or Parliamentary Democracy: Does It Make a Difference?" In Juan J. Linz and Arturo Valenzuela, eds., *The Failure of Presidential Democracy: Comparative Perspectives*, pp. 3–87. Baltimore and London: The Johns Hopkins University Press, 1994.
Linz, Juan J., and Alfred Stepan. *Problems of Democratic Transition and Consolidation: Southern Europe, South America, and Post-Communist Europe.* Baltimore and London: The Johns Hopkins University Press, 1996.
Loveman, Brian. *The Constitution of Tyranny: Regimes of Exception in Spanish America.* Pittsburgh and London: University of Pittsburgh Press, 1993.
Lowenthal, Abraham F., and Jorge I. Domínguez. "Introduction: Constructing Democratic Governance." In Abraham F. Lowenthal and Jorge I. Domínguez, eds., *Constructing Democratic Governance: Latin America and the Caribbean in the 1990s.* Baltimore and London: The Johns Hopkins University Press, 1996.
Mainwaring, Scott. "Transitions to Democracy and Democratic Consolidation: Theoretical and Comparative Issues." In Scott Mainwaring, Guillermo O'Donnell, and J. Samuel Valenzuela, eds., *Issues in Democratic Consolidation: The New South American Democracies in Comparative Perspective*, pp. 294–341 Notre Dame: University of Notre Dame Press, 1992.
———. "Democracy in Brazil and the Southern Cone: Achievements and Problems." *Journal of Interamerican Studies and World Affairs* 37 (1995): 113–179.
Malloy, James M. "The Politics of Transition in Latin America,"in James M. Malloy and Mitchell A. Seligson, eds. *Authoritarians and Democrats: Regime Transition in Latin America.* Pittsburgh: University of Pittsburgh Press, 1987.
Mauceri, Philip. "State Reform, Coalitions, and the Neoliberal *Autogolpe* in Peru." *Latin American Research Review* 30, 1995, pp.7–37.
McGuire, James W. "Interim Government and Democratic Consolidation: Argentina in Comparative Perspective." in Yossi Shain and Juan J. Linz, eds., *Between States: Interim*

Governments and Democratic Transitions, pp. 179–210. Cambridge: Cambridge University Press, 1995.

Mesquita Neto, Paulo de. "From Intervention to Participation: The Transformation of Military Politics in Brazil, 1974–1992." Ph.D. dissertation, Columbia University, 1995.

Norden, Deborah L. *Military Rebellion in Argentina: Between Coups and Consolidation.* Lincoln: University of Nebraska Press, 1996.

O'Donnell, Guillermo. "Transitions, Continuities, and Paradoxes." In Scott Mainwaring, Guillermo O'Donnell, and J. Samuel Valenzuela, eds., *Issues in Democratic Consolidation: The New South American Democracies in Comparative Perspective.* Notre Dame: University of Notre Dame Press, 1992.

———. "On the State, Democratization and some Conceptual Problems: A Latin American View with Glances at some Postcommunist Countries." *World Development* 21 (1993): 1355 –69.

———. "Delegative Democracy." *Journal of Democracy* 5 (1994): 55–69.

———. "Illusions about Consolidation." *Journal of Democracy* 7 (1996): 34–51.

O'Donnell, Guillermo, and Philippe C. Schmitter. *Transitions from Authoritarian Rule: Tentative Conclusions about Uncertain Democracies.* Baltimore and London: Johns Hopkins University Press, 1986.

Oliveira, Eliezzer Rizzo de. "Constituinte, forças armadas e autonomia militar." in Eliézer Rizzo de Oliveira et al., eds., *As forças armadas no Brasil.* Rio de Janeiro: Espaço e Tempo, 1987.

Pion-Berlin, David. "The Armed Forces and Politics: Gains and Snares in Recent Scholarship." *Latin American Research Review* 30 (1995): 147–62.

———. *Through Corridors of Power: Institutions and Civil Military Relations in Argentina.* College Station: Penn State University Press, 1997.

Przeworski, Adam. *Democracy and the Market: Political and Economic Reforms in Eastern Europe and Latin America.* Cambridge: Cambridge University Press, 1991.

———. "Economic Reforms, Public Opinion, and Political Institutions: Poland in the Eastern European Perspective." In Luiz Carlos Bresser Pereira, José María Maravall, and Adam Przeworski, eds., *Economic Reforms in New Democracies: A Social Democratic Approach*, pp. 132–98. Cambridge: Cambridge University Press, 1993.

Remmer, Karen L. "New Theoretical Perspectives on Democratization." *Comparative Politics*, October 1995, pp. 103–22.

Rial, Juan. "Uruguay: From Restoration to the Crisis of Governability." In Abraham F. Lowenthal and Jorge I. Domínguez, eds., *Constructing Democratic Governance: Latin America and the Caribbean in the 1990s.* Baltimore: Johns Hopkins University Press, 1996.

Shain, Yossi, and Juan Linz. "Part I: Theory." In Yossi Shain and Juan J. Linz, eds., *Between States: Interim Governments and Democratic Transitions*, pp. 3–123. Cambridge: Cambridge University Press, 1995.

Smith, William C., and Carlos Acuña. "Future Politico-Economic Scenarios for Latin America." In William C. Smith, Carlos H. Acuña, and Eduardo A. Gamarra, eds., *Democracy, Markets, and Structural Reform in Latin America.* North South Center, University of Miami. New Brunswick and London: Transaction Publishers, 1994.

Stepan, Alfred. *The Military in Politics: Changing Patterns in Brazil.* Princeton, NJ: Princeton University Press, 1971.

———. "Paths towards Redemocratization: Theoretical and Comparative Considerations." In Guillermo O'Donnell, Philippe C. Schmitter, and Laurence Whitehead, eds., *Transitions from Authoritarian Rule: Comparative Perspectives.* Baltimore and London: The Johns Hopkins University Press, 1986.

———. *Rethinking Military Politics: Brazil and the Southern Cone.* Princeton, NJ: Princeton University Press, 1988.

Stokes, Susan C. "Democratic Accountability and Policy Change: Economic Policy in Fujimori's Peru." *Comparative Politics* 29 (1997): 209–26.

Valenzuela, Arturo. "Party Politics and the Crisis of Presidentialism in Chile: A Proposal for a Parliamentary Form of Government." In Juan J. Linz and Arturo Valenzuela, eds., *The Failure of Presidential Democracy: The Case of Latin America*, pp. 91–150. Baltimore: Johns

Hopkins University Press, 1994.

Valenzuela, J. Samuel. "Democratic Consolidation in Post Transitional Settings: Notion, Process, and Facilitating Conditions." In Scott Mainwaring, Guillermo O'Donnell, and J. Samuel Valenzuela, eds., *Issues in Democratic Consolidation: The New South American Democracies in Comparative Perspective*, pp. 57–104. Notre Dame: University of Notre Dame Press, 1992.

Zaverucha, Jorge. "The Degree of Military Political Autonomy During the Spanish, Argentine and Brazilian Transitions." *Journal of Latin American Studies* 25 (1993): 283–99.

———. *Rumor de sabres: tutela militar ou controle civil?* São Paulo: Editora Ática, 1994.

———. "Sarney, Collor, Itamar, FHC e as Prerrogativas Militares (1985–1998)." Presented to the XXI International Congress of the Latin American Studies Association, Chicago, September 24–27, 1998.

Chapter 6

Acevedo, Domingo E., and Claudio Grossman. "The Organization of American States and the Protection of Democracy." In Tom Farer, ed., *Beyond Sovereignty: Collectively Defending Democracy in the Americas*. Baltimore: Johns Hopkins University Press, 1996.

Atkins, G. Pope. *Latin America in the International Political System*. Boulder, CO:-Westview, 1995.

Bailey, John, and Arturo Valenzuela. "The Mexican Transition to Democracy." *Journal of Democracy* 8, no. 4 (October 1997): 43–57..

Bethell, Leslie. "From the Second World War to the Cold War: 1944-1954," in Abraham Lowenthal, ed., *Exporting Democracy: The United States and Latin America*. Baltimore: Johns Hopkins University Press, 1991.

Booth, John. "The United States and Central America: Cycles of Containment and Response." In John D. Martz, ed., *United States Policy in Latin America*. Lincoln: University of Nebraska Press, 1995.

Carothers, Thomas. "The Reagan Years: The 1980s." In Abraham Lowenthal, ed., *Exporting Democracy: The United States and Latin America*. Baltimore: Johns Hopkins University Press, 1991.

Castañeda, Jorge G. *Utopia Unarmed: The Latin American Left after the Cold War*. New York: Alfred A. Knopf, 1993.

Epstein, Leon. *Political Parties in Western Democracies*. New York: Praeger, 1967.

Hartlyn, Jonathan, and Arturo Valenzuela. "Democracy in Latin America, since 1930." In Leslie Bethell, ed., *The Cambridge History of Latin America*, vol. 6. Cambridge and New York: Cambridge University Press, 1994.

Hartlyn, Jonathan. "Political Continuities, Missed Opportunities and Institutional Rigidities: Another Look at Democratic Transitions in Latin America." In Scott Mainwaring and Arturo Valenzuela, eds., *Politics, Society and Democracy: Latin America*. Boulder, CO: Westview Press, 1997.

Levinson, Jerome, and Juan de Onis. *The Alliance That Host Its Way: A critical Report on the Alliance for Progress*. Chicago: Quadrangle Books, 1970.

Lowenthal, Abraham.. *Partners in Conflict: The United States and Latin America*. Baltimore: Johns Hopkins University Press, 1987.

O'Donnell, Guillermo, *Modernization and Bureaucratic Authoritarianism: Studies in South American Politics*. Institute of International Studies, University of California, Berkeley: Politics of Modernization Series no. 9, 1973.

O'Donnell, Guillermo. Philippe C. Schmitter, and Laurence Whitehead. *Transitions from Authoritarian Rule*. Baltimore: Johns Hopkins University Press, 1986.

Pastor, Robert. *Condemned to Repetition: The United States and Nicaragua*. Princeton, NJ: Princeton University Press, 1987.

———. *Whirlpool: U.S. Foreign Policy toward Latin America and the Caribbean*. Princeton, NJ: Princeton University Press, 1992.

Rockefeller, Nelson. *The Rockefeller Report on the Americas*. Chicago: Quadrangle Books, 1969.

Schoultz, Lars. *Human Rights and United States Policy toward Latin America*. Princeton, NJ: Princeton University Press, 1981.

———. *National Security and United States Policy toward Latin America*. Princeton, NJ: Princeton University Press, 1987.

Smith, Peter. *Talons of the Eagle: Dynamics of U.S. Latin American Relations*. New York and London: Oxford University Press, 1996.

Stepan, Alfred. *The Military in Politics: Changing Patterns in Brazil*. Princeton, NJ: Princeton University Press, 1971.

Valenzuela, Arturo. "Estados Unidos: Doctrinas de Desarrollo y América Latina." in Heraldo Muñoz, ed. *Crísis y Desarrollo Alternativo en Latinoamérica*. Santiago: Editorial Aconcagua, 1985.

———. "Chile: Origins, Consolidation and Breakdown of a Democratic Regime," In Larry Diamond, Juan J. Linz, and Seymour Martin Lipset, eds., *Democracy in Developing Countries: Latin America*. Boulder, CO: Lynn Rienner, 1989.

———. "Paraguay: The Coup That Didn't Happen." *Journal of Democracy* 8, no. 1 (January 1997): 43–55.

———. "Latin America and the Caribbean." In Roger Kaplan, ed., "1997 Freedom Around the World." *Freedom Review* 28, no. 1 (January-February 1997): 173–85.

———. "The Challenge of Mexico to U.S. Foreign Policy." In *The Foreign Policy Project*. A Collaboration of the Henry L. Stimson Center and the Overseas Development Council, Occasional Paper 4, June 1997.

Walker, Ignacio. *Socialismo y Democracia: Chile y Europa en perspectiva comparada*. Santiago: CIEPLAN-Hachette, 1990.

Chapter 7

Almond, Gabriel, and Sidney Verba. *The Civic Culture: Political Attitudes and Democracy in Five Nations*. New York: Little, Brown, 1963.

Bagchi, Amiya, ed. *Democracy and Development*. New York: St. Martin's Press, 1995.

Colletti, Lucio. *Karl Marx: Early Writings*. Translated by. Rodney Livingstone and Gregor Benton. New York: Vintage Books, 1975.

Cumings, Bruce. *Korea's Place in the Sun: A Modern History*. New York: W. W. Norton, 1997.

Dahl, Robert. *Democracy and Its Critics*. New Haven: Yale University Press, 1989.

Dews, Peter, ed. *Autonomy and Solidarity: Interviews with Jürgen Habermas*. Rev. ed. New York: Verso, 1992.

Greenberg, Marcia, et al. *Broken Promises, Unfulfilled Dreams: Human Rights and Democracy in South Korea*. New York, 1992.

Henderson, Gregory. *Korea: The Politics of the Vortex*. Cambridge, MA: Harvard University Press, 1968.

Huntington, Samuel P. "The Clash of Civilizations." *Foreign Affairs* 72 (summer) 22–49.

Lipset, Seymour Martin. *The First New Nation*. New York: Basic Books, 1963.

MacIntyre, Alasdair. *Virtue After*. (South Bend: University of Notre Dame Press, 1981), p. 153.

Macpherson, C. B. *Democratic Theory: Essays in Retrieval*. New York: Oxford University Press, 1973.

Putnam, Robert D. *Making Democracy Work: Civic Traditions in Modern Italy*. Princeton, NJ: Princeton University Press, 1993.

Rueschemeyer, Dietrich, Evelyne Huber Stephens, and John D. Stephens. *Capitalist Development and Democracy*. Chicago: University of Chicago Press, 1992.

Sandel, Michael J. *Democracy's Discontents: Americas in Search of a Public Philosophy*. Cambridge, MA: Harvard University Press, 1996.

van Wolferen, Karel. *The Enigma of Japanese Power: People and Politics in a Stateless Nation*. New York: Alfred A. Knopf, 1989.

Wallerstein, Immanuel M. *After Liberalism*. New York: New Press, 1995.

Weber, Max. *General Economic History*. Translated by Frank H. Knight, introduction by Ira J.

Cohen. New Brunswick, NJ: Transaction Books, 1981.

Williams, Raymond. *The Country and the City*. New York: Oxford University Press, 1973.

Woo, Jung-en (Meredith Woo-Cumings). *Race to the Swift: State, Finance and the Industrialization of South Korea*. New York: Columbia University Press, 1991.

Chapter 8

Abueva, Jose Veloso. "Ideology and Practice in the 'New Society.'" In David A. Rosenberg, ed., *Marcos and Martial Law in the Philippines*, pp. 32–84. Ithaca.NY: Cornell University Press, 1979.

Amnesty International. *Report of an Amnesty International Mission to the Republic of the Philippines*. London: Amnesty International Publications, 1976.

Arillo, Cecilio T. *Breakaway*. Manila, Philippines: CTA and Associates, 1986.

Aquino, Belinda A. "The Philippines: End of an Era." *Current History* 85, no. 507 (April 1986): 155-58, 184-185.

Bonner, Raymond. *Waltzing with a Dictator*. New York: Times Books, 1987.

Brillantes, Alex. "The Philippines in 1991: Disasters and Decisions." *Asian Survey* 32, no. 2 (February 1992): 140–45.

———. "The Philippines in 1992: Ready for Take Off?" *Asian Survey* 32, no. 2 (February 1993): 224–30.

Casper, Gretchen. *Fragile Democracies: The Legacies of Authoritarian Rule*. Pittsburgh: University of Pittsburgh Press, 1995.

Casper, Gretchen, and Michelle M. Taylor. *Negotiating Democracy: Transitions from Authoritarian Rule*. Pittsburgh: University of Pittsburgh Press, 1996.

Catilo, Aurora C., and Prosperina D. Tapales. "The Legislature." In Raul P. De Guzman and Mila A. Reforma, eds., *Government and Politics of the Philippines*, pp. 132–163. Singapore: Oxford University Press, 1988.

Coronel, Sheila S. "Dateline Philippines: The Lost Revolution." *Foreign Policy*, no. 84, (fall 1991): 166–85.

Del Carmen, Rolando V. "Constitutionality and Judicial Politics." In David A. Rosenberg, ed., *Marcos and Martial Law in the Philippines*, pp. 85–112. Ithaca, NY: Cornell University Press, 1979.

Gargan, Edward A. "Filipino Foes Meet to End Muslim Revolt." *New York Times*, August 20, 1996, sec. A, p. 5.

Hernandez, Carolina G. "Reconstituting Political Order." In John Bresnan, ed., *Crisis in the Philippines: The Marcos Era and Beyond*, pp. 176–199. Princeton, NJ: Princeton University Press, 1986.

———. "The Philippines in 1995: Growth amid Challenges." *Asian Survey* 36, no. 2 (February 1996): 142–51.

Hutchcroft, Paul D. *The Philippines at the Crossroads: Sustaining Economic and Political Reform*. New York: Asia Society, 1996.

Huntington, Samuel P. *The Third Wave: Democratization in the Late Twentieth Century*. Norman, OK: University of Oklahoma Press, 1991.

Hutchison, Jane. "Class and State Power in the Philippines." In Kevin Hewison, Richard Robison, and Garry Rodan, eds. *Southeast Asia in the 1990s: Authoritarianism, Democracy, and Capitalism*, pp. 191–212. Boston: Allen and Unwin, 1993.

Johnson, Bryan. *The Four Days of Courage*. New York: Free Press, 1987.

Kessler, Richard J. *Rebellion and Repression in the Philippines*. New Haven: Yale University Press, 1989.

Landé, Carl H. "The Political Crisis." In John Bresnan, ed., *Crisis in the Philippines: The Marcos Era and Beyond*, pp. 114–44. Princeton,NJ: Princeton University Press, 1986.

Lapitan, A. E. "The Re-Democratization of the Philippines: Old Wine in a New Bottle." *Asian Profile* 17, no. 3 (June 1989): 235–42.

McCoy, Alfred W. "RAM Boy Series (Special Issue)." *Philippine Daily Inquirer*, February 1990.

Nemenzo, Francisco. "A Season of Coups." *Kasarinlan* 2, no. 2 (1987): 5–14.

Noble, Lela Garner. "Politics in the Marcos Era." In John Bresnan, ed., *Crisis in the Philippines: The Marcos Era and Beyond*, pp. 70–113. Princeton: Princeton University Press, 1986.

Overholt, William H. "The Rise and Fall of Ferdinand Marcos." *Asian Survey* 26, no. 11 (November 1986): 1137–63.

Riedinger, Jeffrey. *Agrarian Reform in the Philippines: Democratic Transitions and Redistributive Reform.* Stanford, CA: Stanford University Press, 1995.

Rosenberg, David A. "Introduction: Creating a 'New Society.'" In David A. Rosenberg, ed. *Marcos and Martial Law in the Philippines*, pp. 13–31. Ithaca, NY: Cornell University Press, 1979.

Silliman, G. Sidney. "The Philippines in 1983: Authoritarianism Beleaguered." *Asian Survey* 24, no.2 (February 1984): 149–58.

Timberman, David G. "The Philippines in 1989: A Good Year Goes Sour." *Asian Survey* 30, no. 2 (February 1990): 167–77.

———. "The Philippines at the Polls." *Journal of Democracy* 3, no. 4 (October 1992): 110–24.

Thompson, Mark R. *The Anti-Marcos Struggle: Personalistic Rule and Democratic Transition in the Philippines.* New Haven: Yale University Press, 1995.

Villegas, Bernardo M. "The Philippines in 1986: Democatic Reconstruction in the Post-Marcos Era." *Asian Survey* 27, no. 2 (February 1987):, 194–205.

Wurfel, David. *Filipino Politics: Development and Decay.* Ithaca: Cornell University Press, 1988.

Youngblood, Robert L. *Marcos against the Church.* Ithaca: Cornell University Press, 1990.

Chapter 9

Amsden, A. H. *Asia's Next Giant: South Korea and Late Industrialization.* New York: Oxford University Press, 1989.

Arnold, W. "Bureaucratic Politics, State Capacity, and Taiwan's Automobile Industrial Policy." *Modern China* 15 (1989): 178–214.

Asian Survey. vol. 36, nos. 1–2 (1996) Special issues surveying individual Asian nations.

Bernard, M., and J. Ravenhill. "Beyond Flying Geese and Product Cycles: Regionalization, Hierarchy, and the Industrialization of East Asia." *World Politics* 47 (1995): 171–209.

Bhagwati, J. N. *India in Transition: Freeing the Economy.* Oxford: Clarendon, 1993.

Calder, K. *Strategic Capitalism: Private Business and Public Purpose in Japanese Industrial Finance.* Princeton, NJ: Princeton University Press, 1993.

Chan, S. *East Asian Dynamism: Growth, Order, and Security in the Pacific Region*, 2nd ed. Boulder, CO: Westview, 1993.

Clark, C., and K. C. Roy. *Comparing Development Patterns in Asia.* Boulder, CO: Lynne Rienner, 1997.

Cumings, B. "The Origins and Development of the Northeast Asia Political Economy: Industrial Sectors, Product Cycles, and Political Consequences." *International Organization* 38 (1984): 1–40.

Diamond, L. "Introduction: Persistence, Erosion, Breakdown, and Renewal." In L. Diamond, J. J. Linz, and S. M. Lipset, eds. pp. 1–52. *Democracy in Developing Countries: Asia*, Vol. 3. Boulder, CO: Lynne Rienner, 1989.

Diamond, L., J. J. Linz, and S. M. Lipset, eds. *Democracy in Developing Countries.* 4 vols. Boulder, CO: Lynne Rienner 1989a.

Evans, P. *Embedded Autonomy: States and Industrial Transformation.* Princeton, NJ: Princeton University Press, 1995.

Fallows, J. M. *Looking at the Sun: The Rise of the New East Asian Economic and Political System.* New York: Pantheon, 1994.

Fields, K. J. *Enterprise and the State in Korea and Taiwan.* Ithaca, NY: Cornell University Press, 1995.

Fischer, S. "The Asian Crisis: A View from the IMF." Address to the Midwinter Conference of the Bankers' Association for Foreign Trade, Washington, D.C., 1998.

Friedman, E., ed. *The Politics of Democratization: Generalizing East Asian Experiences.* Boulder, CO: Westview, 1994.

Fry, G. "Thailand's Political Economy: Change and Persistence." In C. Clark and S. Chan, eds., *The Evolving Pacific Basin in the Global Political Economy: Domestic and International Linkages,* pp. 83–105. Boulder, CO: Lynne Rienner, 1992.

Fukuyama, F. *The End of History and the Last Man.* New York: Free Press, 1992.

Gerlach, M. L. *Alliance Capitalism: The Social Organization of Japanese Business.* Berkeley: University of California Press, 1992.

Haggard, S. *Pathways from the Periphery: The Politics of Growth in the Newly Industrializing Countries.* Ithaca, NY: Cornell University Press, 1990.

Haggard, S., and R. R. Kaufman. *The Political Economy of Democratic Transitions.* Princeton, NJ: Princeton University Press, 1995.

Haggard, S., and C. I. Moon. "Institutions and Economic Policy: Theory and a Korean Case Study." *World Politics* 42 (1990): 210–37.

Hart, J. A. *Rival Capitalists: International Competitiveness in the United States, Japan, and Western Europe.* Ithaca, NY: Cornell University Press, 1992.

Higgott, R. "Australia: Economic Crises and the Politics of Regional Economic Adjustment." In R. Robison, K. Hewison, and R. Higgott, eds., *Southeast Asia in the 1980s: The Politics of Economic Crisis,* pp. 177–217. Sydney: Allen & Unwin, 1987.

Hofheinz, R. Jr., and K. E. Calder. *The East Asia Edge.* New York: Basic Books, 1982.

Huntington, S. P. *Political Order in Changing Societies.* New Haven, CT: Yale University Press, 1968.

———*The Third Wave: Democratization in the Late Twentieth Century.* Norman: University of Oklahoma Press, 1991.

Hutchcroft, P. "Booty Capitalism: Business-Government Relations in the Philippines." In A. MacIntyre, ed., *Business and Government in Industrializing East and Southeast Asia,* pp. 216–43. Sydney: Allen & Unwin, 1994.

Johnson, C. A. *MITI and the Japanese Miracle: The Growth of Industrial Policy, 1925-1975.* Stanford: Stanford University Press, 1982.

Lam, D. K. K., and C. Clark. "Beyond the Developmental State: The Cultural Roots of 'Guerrilla Capitalism' in Taiwan." *Governance* 7 (1994): 412–30.

MacIntyre, A., ed. *Business and Government in Industrializing East and Southeast Asia.* Sydney: Allen & Unwin, 1994.

Migdal, J. S., A. Kohli, and V. Shue, eds. *State Power and Social Forces: Domination and Transformation in the Third World.* New York: Cambridge University Press, 1994.

Moon, C. I., and R. Prasad. "Beyond the Developmental State: Networks, Politics, and Institutions." *Governance* 7 (1994): 360–86.

Norton, J. J. "The Korean Financial Crisis, Reform and Positive Transformation: Is a Second 'Han River Miracle' Possible?" *Global Economic Review* 27 (1998): 3–36.

O'Donnell, G., P. C. Schmitter, and L. Whitehead, eds. *Transitions from Authoritarian Rule: Prospects for Democracy.* Baltimore: Johns Hopkins University Press, 1986.

Okimoto, D. I. *Between MITI and the Market: Japanese Industrial Policy for High Technology.* Stanford, CA: Stanford University Press, 1989.

Olson, M. Jr. *The Rise and Fall of Nations: Economic Growth, Stagflation, and Social Rigidities.* New Haven, CT: Yale University Press, 1982.

Pye, L. W. *Asian Power and Politics: The Cultural Dimensions of Authority.* Cambridge, MA: Harvard University Press, 1985.

Rudolph, L. I., and S. H. Rudolph. *In Pursuit of Lakshmi: The Political Economy of the Indian State.* Chicago: University of Chicago Press, 1987.

Skoggard, I. A. *The Indigenous Dynamic in Taiwan's Postwar Development: The Religious and Historical Roots of Entrepreneurship.* Armonk, NY: M. E. Sharpe, 1996.

Strange, S. *The Retreat of the State: The Diffusion of Power in the World Economy.* Cambridge: Cambridge University Press, 1996.

Vogel, E. F. *One Step Ahead in China: Guangdong Under Reform.* Cambridge, MA: Harvard University Press, 1989.

Wade, R. *Governing the Market: Economic Theory and the Role of Government in East Asian Industrialization.* Princeton, NJ: Princeton University, 1990.

Chapter 10

Allison, Graham, Stephen Cohen, and Timothy Colton. "Staggering Toward Democracy: Russia's Future Is Far From Certain." *Harvard International Review* 15 (1992–1993): 14–17, 60–62.

———. *Asia's Next Giant: South Korea and Late Industrialization.* New York: Columbia University Press, 1989.

Amsden, Alice H. "Taiwan's Economic History: A Case of Etatism and a Challenge to Dependency Theory." *Modern China* 5 (1979): 341–79.

Bollen, Kenneth. "Liberal Democracy: Validity and Method Factors in Cross-National Measures." *American Journal of Political Science* 37 (1993): 1179–1206.

Burkhart, Ross E., and Michael S. Lewis-Beck. "Comparative Democracy: The Economic Development Thesis." *American Political Science Review* 88 (1994): 903–10.

Calder, E. Kent. *Crisis and Compensation: Public Policy and Political Stability in Japan.* Princeton, NJ: Princeton University Press, 1988.

Chan, Steve. "In Search of Democratic Peace: Problems and Promise." *Mershon International Studies Review* 41 (1997): 59–92.

———."Democratic Change and Defense Allocation in East Asia." In Frank P. Harvey and Ben Mor, eds., *New Directions in the Study of International Conflict, Crisis and War*, pp. 272-87. London: Macmillan, 1998.

Chan, Steven and Cal Clark. *Flexibility, Foresight, and Fortune in Taiwan's Development: Navigating between Scylla and Charybdis.* London: Routledge, Chapman, and Hall, 1992.

———. "The Price of Economic Success: South Korea and Taiwan Sacrifice Political Development." *Harvard International Review* 14 (1992–93): 24–26, 64.

Cheek-Milby, Kathleen. *A Legislature Comes of Age: Hong Kong's Search for Influence and Stability.* Hong Kong: Oxford University Press, 1995.

Cirtautas, Arista Maria, and Edmund Mokrzycki. "The Articulation and Institutionalization of Democracy in Poland." *Social Research* 60 (1993): 787–819.

Clark, Cal, and Steve Chan. "MNCs and Developmentalism: Domestic Structures as an Explanation for East Asian Dynamism." In Steve Chan, ed., *Foreign Direct Investment in a Changing Global Political Economy*, pp. 84–103. London: Macmillan, 1995.

Collier, David, and Steven Levitsky. "Democracy with Adjectives: Conceptual Innovation in Comparative Research." *World Politics* 49 (1997): 430–51.

Cutright, Phillips. "National Political Development: Its Measurement and Social Correlates." In Nelson W. Polsby, Robert A. Dentler, and Paul A. Smith, eds., *Politics and Social Life: An Introduction to Political Behavior*, pp. 569–82. Boston: Houghton Mifflin, 1963.

Dahl, Robert A. *Polyarchy: Participation and Opposition.* New Haven, CT: Yale University Press, 1971.

Deyo, Frederic. *Dependent Development and Industrial Order: An Asian Case.* New York: Praeger, 1981.

Evans, Peter B., Harold K. Jacobson, and Robert D. Putnam, eds. *Double-Edged Diplomacy: International Bargaining and Domestic Politics.* Berkeley: University of California Press, 1993.

Forsythe, David P. "Democracy, War, and Covert Action." *Journal of Peace Research* 29 (1992): 385–95.

Friedman, Milton. *Capitalism and Freedom.* Chicago: University of Chicago Press, 1962.

Fukuyama, Francis. *The End of History and the Last Man.* New York: Free Press, 1992.

Gelpi, Christopher. "Democratic Diversions: Governmental Structure and the Externalization of Domestic Conflict." *Journal of Conflict Resolution* 41 (1997): 255–82.

Gerschenkron, Alexander. *Economic Backwardness in Historical Perspective: A Book of Essays.* Cambridge, MA: Harvard University Press, 1962.

Gold, Thomas B. *State and Society in the Taiwan Miracle.* Armonk: M. E. Sharpe, 1986.

Hayek, Friedrich A. *The Constitution of Liberty*. London: Routledge and Kegan Paul, 1960.

Hewison, Kevin. *Bankers and Bureaucrats: Capital and the Role of State in Thailand*. New Haven, CT: Yale University Southeast Asian Studies, 1989.

Huntington, Samuel P. *Political Order in Changing Societies*. New Haven, CT: Yale University Press, 1968.

———. "The Clash of Civilizations?" *Foreign Affairs* 72 (1993):.22–49.

———. "What Cost Freedom: Democracy and/or Economic Reform." *Harvard International Review* 15 (1992-93):.8–13.

———. *The Third Wave: Democratization in the Late Twentieth Century*. Norman: University of Oklahoma Press, 1991.

Huntley, Wade. "Kant's Third Image: Systemic Sources of the Liberal Peace." *International Studies Quarterly* 40 (1996): 45–76.

———. *The Culture Shift in Advanced Industrial Society*. Princeton, NJ: Princeton University, 1990.

Inglehart, Ronald. *The Silent Revolution: Changing Values and Political Styles among Western Publics*. Princeton, NJ: Princeton University Press, 1977.

———. *MITI and the Japanese Miracle*. Stanford, CA: Stanford University Press, 1982.

Johnson, Chalmers. "Introduction—The Taiwan Model." In James C. Hsiung, ed., *Contemporary Republic of China: The Taiwan Experience, 1950–1980*, pp. 9–18. New York: Praeger, 1981.

Kegley, Charles W. Jr., and Margaret G. Hermann. "Military Intervention and the Democratic Peace." *International Interactions* 21 (1995): 1–21.

Kozhemiakin, Alexander V. "Democratization and International Cooperation: Comparative Analysis of Ukraine's and Kazakhstan's Responses to the Nuclear Non-Proliferation Regime." Paper presented at the Midwest meeting of the International Studies Association, Columbus, 1994.

Kuznets, Simon. "Economic Growth and Income Inequality." *American Economic Review* 45 (1955):1–28.

Lehman, Howard P., and Jennifer L. McCoy. "The Dynamics of the Two-Level Bargaining Game: The 1988 Brazilian Debt Negotiations." *World Politics* 44 (1992): 600–644.

———. "The Social Requisites of Democracy Revisited." *American Sociological Review* 59 (1994): 1–22.

Lipset, Seymour M. *Political Man: The Social Bases of Politics*. Garden City, NY: Doubleday, 1963.

MacIntyre, Andrew, ed. *Business and Government in Industrialising Asia*. Ithaca, NY: Cornell University Press, 1994.

Mansfield, Edward D., and Jack Snyder. "Democratization and the Danger of War." *International Security* 20 (1995): 5–38.

Morgan, T. Clifton, and Valerie Schwebach. "Take Two Democracies and Call Me in the Morning." *International Interactions* 17 (1992): 305–20.

Muller, Edward N., and Mitchell A. Seligson. "Civic Culture and Democracy: The Question of Causal Relationships." *American Political Science Review* 88 (1994): 635–52.

———. "Dictatorship, Democracy, and Development." *American Political Science Review* 87 (1993): 567–76.

Olson, Mancur Jr. "Rapid Growth as a Destabilizing Force." *Journal of Economic History* 23 (1963): 529–52.

Oren, Ido. "The Subjectivity of the 'Democratic' Peace: Changing U.S. Perceptions of Imperial Germany." *International Security* 20 (1995): 147–84.

Owen, John M. "How Liberalism Produces Democratic Peace." *International Security* 19 (1994): 87–125.

Putnam, Robert. "Diplomacy and Domestic Politics: The Logic of Two-Level Games." *International Organization* 42 (1988): 427–60.

Pye, Lucian W., *The Authority Crisis in Chinese Politics*. Chicago: University of Chicago Press, 1967.

Pye, Lucian W., and Mary W. Pye. *Asian Power and Politics: The Cultural Dimensions of Authority*. Cambridge: Belknap Press, 1985.

Ray, James L. *Democracy and International Conflict: An Evaluation of the Democratic Peace Proposition.* Columbia: University of South Carolina Press, 1995.

Rousseau, David L., Christopher Gelpi, Dan Reiter, and Paul K. Huth. "Assessing the Dyadic Nature of the Democratic Peace, 1918–1988." *American Political Science Review* 90 (1996): 512–33.

Rummel, Rudolph J. "On Vincent's View of Freedom and International Conflict." *International Studies Quarterly* 31 (1987): 113–17.

Russett, Bruce M. *Grasping the Democratic Peace: Principles for a Post–Cold War World.* Princeton, NJ: Princeton University Press, 1993.

Sandel, Michael. *Democracy's Discontents: America in Search of a Public Philosophy.* Cambridge, MA: Harvard University Press, 1996.

Schumpeter, Joseph. *Capitalism, Socialism and Democracy.* New York: Harper and Brothers, 1942.

Schweller, Randall L. "Domestic Structure and Preventive War: Are Democracies More Pacific?" *World Politics* 44 (1992): 235–69.

Scoble, Harry M., and Laurie S. Wiseberg. "Problems of Comparative Research on Human Rights." In Ved P. Nanda, James R. Scarritt, and George W. Shepherd Jr., eds., *Global Human Rights: Public Policies, Comparative Measures, and NGO Strategies*, pp. 152–63. Boulder: Westview, 1981.

Shin, Doh Chull. "On the Third Wave of Democratization: A Synthesis and Evaluation of Recent Theory and Research." *World Politics* 47(1994) 160–79.

Sorensen, Georg. *Democracy and Democratization.* Boulder: Westview, 1993.

Strouse, James C., and Richard P. Claude. "Empirical Comparative Rights Research: Some Preliminary Tests of Development Hypotheses." In Richard P. Claude, ed., *Comparative Human Rights*, pp. 51–67. Baltimore: Johns Hopkins University Press, 1976.

Thompson, William R., and Richard Tucker. "A Tale of Two Democratic Peace Critiques." *Journal of Conflict Resolution* 41 (1997): 428–54.

Tien, Hung-mao, ed. *Taiwan's Electoral Politics and Democratic Transition: Riding the Third Wave.* Armonk, NY: M. E. Sharpe, 1996.

Vincent, Jack E. "Freedom and International Conflict: Another Look." *International Studies Quarterly* 31 (1987): 103–12.

Wade, Robert. *Governing the Market: Economic Theory and the Role of Government in East Asian Industrialization.* Princeton, NJ: Princeton University Press, 1990.

Chapter 11

Aldrich, John H. *Why Parties? The Origin and Transformation of Political Parties in America.* Chicago: University of Chicago Press, 1995.

Cox, Gary W. ,*The Efficient Secret: The Cabinet and the Development of Political Parties in Victorian England.* Cambridge: Cambridge University Press, 1987.

Cox, Gary W. and Matthew D. McCubbins. *Legislative Leviathan: Party Government in the House.* Berkeley: University of California Press, 1993.

Fish, M. Stephen. "The Advent of Multipartism in Russia, 1993–1995." *Post-Soviet Affairs* 11 (1995): 340–83.

Huntington, Samuel. *The Third Wave: Democratization in the Late Twentieth Century.* Norman: University of Oklahoma Press, 1991.

Hellman, Joel S. "Winners Take All: The Politics of Partial Reform in Postcommunist Transitions," *World Politics* 50(1), 1998, pp. 203–234.

Lijphart, Arend. *Democracies: Patterns of Majoritarian and Consensus Government in Twenty-One Countries* New Haven, CT: Yale University Press, 1984.

Linz, Juan J., and Alfred Stepan. *Problems of Democratic Transition and Consolidation: Southern Europe, South America, and Post-Communist Europe.* Baltimore: Johns Hopkins University Press, 1996.

Mainwaring, Scott and T. R. Scully. "Introduction: Party Systems in Latin America." In *Building Democratic Institutions: Party Systems in Latin America*, pp. 1–34 Stanford, CA: Stanford

University Press, 1995.

Oates, Sarah. "Vying for Votes on a Crowded Campaign Trail." *Transition* 2, no. 4 (1996): 26–29.

Ordeshook, Peter. "Russia's Party System: Is Russian Federalism Viable?" *Post-Soviet Affairs* 12, no. 3 (1996): 195–217.

Powell, G. Bingham Jr. *Contemporary Democracies: Participation, Stability and Violence*. Cambridge, MA: Harvard University Press, 1982.

Remington, Thomas F., and Steven S. Smith. "The Development of Parliamentary Parties in Russia." *Legislative Studies Quarterly* 20, no. 4 (1995): 457–90.

——. "The Early Legislative Process in the Russian Federal Assembly." *Journal of Legislative Studies* 2, no. 1 (1996): 161–92.

Rose, Richard, William Mishler, and Christian Haerpfer. *Democracy and Its Alternative: Understanding Post-Communist Societies*. Baltimore: Johns Hopkins University Press, 1998.

Slider, Darrell. "Federalism, Discord, and Accommodation: Intergovernmental Relations in Post-Soviet Russia." In *Local Power and Post-Soviet Politics*. T.H. Friedgut and J. W. Hahn, eds., Armonk, NY: M. E. Sharpe, 1994, pp. 239–69.

Strom, Kaare. *Minority Government and Majority Rule*. Cambridge: Cambridge University Press, 1990.

Tsebelis, George, "Decision Making in Political Systems: Veto Players in Presidentialism, Parliamentarism, Multicameralism and Multipartyism." *British Journal of Political Science* 25, no. 3 (1995): 289–325.

Weingast, Barry R. "Constitutions as Governance Structures: The Political Foundations of Secure Markets." *Journal of Institutional and Theoretical Economics* 149, no 1 (1993): 286–311.

——."The Political Foundations of Democracy and the Rule of the Law." *American Political Science Review* 91, no. 2 (1997): 245–63.

White, Stephen, Richard Rose, and Ian McAllister. *How Russia Votes*. Chatham, NJ: Chatham House, 1996.

Wyman, Matthew. "Developments in Russian Voting Behaviour: 1993 and 1995 Compared." *Journal of Communist Studies and Transition Politics* 12, no. 3 (1996): 277–92.

Chapter 12

Aslund, Anders. *Gorbachev's Struggle for Economic Reform*. Ithaca, NY: Cornell University Press, 1989.

——. *How Russia Became a Market Economy*. Washington, DC: Brookings, 1995.

——. "Russia's Financial Crisis: Causes and Possible Remedies." *Post-Soviet Geography and Economics* 39. no. 6 (1998): 309–28.

Bergson, Abram. *Planning and Performance in Socialist Economies*. Winchester: Unwin Hyman, 1989.

——."Perestroika and the Chinese Model." In Robert W. Campbell, ed., *The Postcommunist Economic Transformation*. Boulder, CO: Westview Press, 1994.

Berliner, Joseph S. *The Innovation Decision in Soviet Industry*. Cambridge, MA: MIT Press, 1976.

Biggs, Barton M. "Russia: The Mother of All . . . ?" *Morgan Stanley Newsletter*, July 8, 1996, p. 3.

Blasi, Joseph R., Maya Kroumova, and Douglas Kruse. *Kremlin Capitalism*. Ithaca, NY: Cornell University Press, 1997.

Bond, Daniel L., and Herbert S. Levine. "An Overview." In Abram Bergson and Herbert S. Levine. *The Soviet Economy: Toward the Year 2000*, pp. 1–33. London: Allen & Unwin, 1983.

Easterly, William, and Stanley Fisher. "Living on Borrowed Time: Lessons of the Soviet Economy's Collapse." *Transition*, April 1994, pp. 1–3.

Financial Times, December 9, 1998, p. 3.

Garthoff, Raymond L. *The Great Transition: American-Soviet Relations and the End of the Cold War*. Washington, DC: Brookings Institution, 1994.

Gregory, Paul R., and Robert C. Stuart. *Soviet Economic Structure and Performance*. 3rd ed. New York: Harper & Row, 1986.

Hewett, Ed A. *Reforming the Soviet Economy: Equality versus Efficiency*. Washington, DC:

Brookings, 1988.

Kennan Institute. "Meeting Report," vol. XIV, no. 6, 1997.

Kim, Hae S. "Tradeoffs Between Military Spending, Quality of Life, and Economic Growth." *Comparative Economic Studies*, winter 1996, pp. 69–84.

Millar, James R. "From Utopian Socialism to Utopian Capitalism." *Problems of Post-Communism*, May/June 1995, pp. 7–14.

Nove, Alec. *An Economic History of the USSR*. London: Penguin Press, 1969.

OECD. *Economic Surveys: Russian Federation, 1997–1998*. September 30, 1997.

———. *Economic Outlook*. June 1998.

Schweitzer, Peter. *Victory: The Reagan Administration's Secret Strategy that Hastened the Collapse of the Soviet Union*. New York: Atlantic Monthly Press, 1994.

Soros, George. "The Capitalist Threat." *Atlantic Monthly*, February 1997.

Transition. The World Bank, Transition Economics Division. April and May 1996.

US Directorate of Intelligence. *Handbook of Economic Statistics*. Washington, DC, 1988.

World Bank. *From Plan to Market: World Development Report 1996*. New York: Oxford University Press, 1996.

Chapter 13

Brinkley, Douglas. "Democratic Enlargement: The Clinton Doctrine." *Foreign Policy* no. 106 (1997): 111–27.

Carothers, Thomas. "Democracy Promotion under Clinton." *Washington Quarterly* 18, no. 4 (995): 13–28.

———. *Assessing Democratic Assistance: The Case of Romania*. New York: Carnegie Endowment, 1996.

Csaba, László. *The Capitalist Revolution in Eastern Europe*. Hants, UK: Edward Elgar, 1995.

Dine, Thomas A. "US Aid for the Newly Independent States." *Problems of Post-Communism* 42, no. 3(1995): 27–31.

Economist. "Marshall Music," May 31, 1997, p. 47.

———."A Wider European Union," November 7, 1998, p. 17.

Elster, Jon, Claus Offe, and Ulrich K. Preuss. *Institutional Design in Post-Communist Societies: Rebuilding the Ship at Sea*. Cambridge: Cambridge University Press, 1998.

Ginsberg, Roy H. "Germany: Into the Stream of Democracy." In Mary Ellen Fischer, ed., *Establishing Democracies*, pp. 87–114. Boulder, CO: Westview Press, 1996

Goldgeier, James M. "NATO Expansion: Anatomy of a Decision." *Washington Quarterly* 21, no.1 (1998): 85–102.

Gower, Jackie. "EC Relations with Central and Eastern Europe." In Juliet Lodge, ed., *The European Community and the Challenge of the Future*, pp. 283–99. New York: St. Martin's Press, 1993.

Hoffmann, Steven A. "Japan: Foreign Occupation and Democratic Transition." In Mary Ellen Fischer, ed. *Establishing Democracies*, pp. 115–48 Boulder, CO: Westview Press, 1996.

Huntington, Samuel P. *The Third Wave: Democratization in the Late Twentieth Century*. Norman: University of Oklahoma Press, 1991.

Hutchings, Robert L. *American Diplomacy and the End of the Cold War*. Washington, DC: Woodrow Wilson Center Press, 1997.

Hyde-Price, Adrian G. V. "Democratization in Eastern Europe: The External Dimension." In Geoffrey Pridham and Tantu Vanhanen, eds., *Democratization in Eastern Europe: Domestic and International Perspectives*, pp. 220–54. London: Routledge, 1994,

Kanet, Roger E., and Julie A. Lund. "The Russian Federation and Central Europe's Integration into Europe." In Mike Bowker, ed., *Russia after the Cold War*. London: Addison Wesley Longman, in press.

Kozhemiakin, Alexander V. *Expanding the Zone of Peace? Democratization and International Security*. New York: St. Martin's Press, 1998.

Kürti, László, and Juliet Langman, eds. *Beyond Borders: Remaking Cultural Identities in the New*

East and Central Europe. Boulder, CO: Westview Press, 1997.

Lazar, Mark, *Fortifying the Foundations: US Support for Developing and Strengthening Democracy in East Central Europe.* New York: Institute of International Education, 1996.

Linz, Juan J., and Alfred Stepan, eds., *The Breakdown of Democratic Regimes.* Baltimore: Johns Hopkins University Press, 1978.

———. *Problems of Democratic Transition and Consolidation: Southern Europe, South America and Post-Communist Europe.* Baltimore: Johns Hopkins University Press, 1996.

Londregan, John B., and Keith T. Poole. "Does High Income Promote Democracy?" *World Politics* 49, no. (1996): 1–30.

Lynn-Jones, Sean M., et al. *Debating the Democratic Peace.* Cambridge: MIT University Press, 1995.

Mansfield, Edward, and Jack Snyder. "Democratization and War." *Foreign Affairs* 74, no. 3 (1995): 79–97.

Menges, Constantine C. "An Initial Assessment of US Aid to Russia, 1992–95: A Strategy for More Effective Assistance." *Demokratizatsiya* 43, no. 4: 538–60.

Morningstar, Richard L. Prepared Statement by Ambassador Richard L. Morningstar, Special Advisor to the President and the Secretary of State on Assistance to the New Independent States before the Senate Appropriations Committee on Foreign Operations. May 6, 1997. Included on Johnson's Russia List, 7 May 1997, djohnson@cdi.org.

Organisation for Economic Cooperation and Development. *Reforming the Economies of Central and Eastern Europe.* Paris: Organisation for Economic Cooperation and Development, 1992.

O'Donnell, Guillermo, and Philippe C. Schmitter. *Transitions from Authoritarian Rules: Tentative Conclusions about Uncertain Democracies.* Baltimore: Johns Hopkins University Press, 1986.

Pinder, John. "The European Community and Democracy in Central and Eastern Europe." In Geoffrey Pridham, Eric Herring, and George Sandford, eds., *Building Democracy? The International Dimension of Democratization in Eastern Europe.* New York: St. Martin's Press, 1994.

Plasser, Fritz, and Peter Ulram. "Measuring Political Culture in East Central Europe. Political Trust and System Support." In Fritz Plasser and Andreas Pribersky, eds., *Political Culture in East Central Europe*, pp. 3–34. Aldershot, UK, and Brookfield, VT: Avebury, 1996.

Pridham, Geoffrey. "The International Dimension of Democratisation: Theory, Practice, and International Regime Comparisons." In Geoffrey Pridham, Eric Herring, and George Sanford, eds., *Building Democracy? The International Dimension of Democratisation in Eastern Europe*, pp. 7–31. New York: St. Martin's Press, 1994.

Przeworski, Adam. *Democracy and the Market.* Cambridge: Cambridge University Press, 1991.

Przeworski, Adam, and Fernando Limongi. "Modernization: Theories and Facts." *World Politics* 49, no. 2: 155–83.

Quigley, Kevin F. F. *For Democracy's Sake: Foundations and Democracy Assistance in Central Europe.* Washington, D.C.: Woodrow Wilson Center Press, 1997.

Russett, Bruce. *Grasping the Democratic Peace.* Princeton, NJ: Princeton University Press, 1993.

Schedler, Andreas. "What Is Democratic Consolidation?" *Journal of Democracy* 9, no. 2 (1998): 91–107.

Shin, Doh Chull. "On the Third Wave of Democratization: A Synthesis and Evaluation of Recent Theory and Research." *World Politics* 47, no. 1 (1994,): 135–70.

Talbott, Strobe. "Spreading Democracy. "*Foreign Affairs* 75, no. 6 (1996): 47–63.

Ulrich, Marybeth Peterson. *Democratization and the Post-Communist Militaries: U.S. Support for Democratization in the Czech and Russian Militaries.* Unpublished Ph.D. dissertation, University of Illinois at Urbana-Champaign, 1996.

Wedel, Janine. "Clique-Run Organizations and U.S. Economic Aid." *Demokratizatsiya* 4, no. 4 (1996): 571–602.

Weiss, Charles. "Eurasia Letter: A Marshall Plan We Can Afford," *Foreign Policy*, no. 106 (1997): 94–110.

White, Stephen, Richard Rose, and Ian McAllister. *How Russia Votes.* Chatham, NJ: Chatham House, 1997.

Whitehead, Laurence. "International Aspects of Democratization." In Guillermo O'Donnell, Philippe Schmitter, and Laurence Whitehead, eds., *Transitions from Authoritarian Rule: Comparative Perspectives*, pp. 3–46. Baltimore: Johns Hopkins University Press, 1986.

———."The Imposition of Democracy." In Abraham Lowenthal, ed., *Exporting Democracy: the United States and Latin America*, pp. 357–74. Baltimore: Johns Hopkins University Press, 1991.

Chapter 14

Bienen, Henry, and Jeffrey Herbst. "The Relationship between Political and Economic Reform in Africa." *Comparative Politics* 29 (October 1996).

Boahen, A. Adu. *The Ghanaian Sphinx*. Accra: Ghana Academy of Arts and Sciences, 1989.

Bratton, Michael, and Nicolas van de Walle. "Toward Governance in Africa: Popular Demand and State Responses." In Goran Hyden and Michael Bratton, eds., *Governance and Politics in Africa*. Boulder: Lynne Rienner, 1992.

———. "Neopatrimonial Regimes and Political Transitions in Africa." *World Politics* 46 (July 1994).

Caruthers, Thomas. "Democracy without Illusions." *Foreign Affairs* 76 (January/February 1997).

Economist. "Polls to Nowhere." November 23, 1996.

———. "Democracy in Africa: Its Nuts and Bolts." March 1, 1997.

Freedom House, *Freedom in the World, 1995–6*. New York: Freedom House, 1996.

———. *Press Freedom World Wide: 1996*. Found at: ttp://www.freedomhouse.org/Press/TOC.HTM.

Herbst, Jeffrey. "The Dilemmas of Explaining Political Upheaval: Ghana in Comparative Perspective." In Jennifer Widner, ed., *Economic Change and Political Liberalization in Sub-Saharan Africa*. Baltimore: Johns Hopkins University Press, 1994.

Huntington, Samuel P. *The Third Wave*. Norman: University of Oklahoma Press, 1991.

Karl, Terry Lynn. "Dilemmas of Democratization in Latin America." *Comparative Politics* 23 (October 1990).

Kohli, Atul. *Democracy and Discontent: India's Growing Crisis of Governability*. Cambridge: Cambridge University Press, 1990.

Lijphart, Arend. *Democracies: Patterns of Majoritarian and Consensus Government in Twenty-One Countries*. New Haven, CT: Yale University Press, 1984.

Linz, Juan J. "Crisis, Breakdown, and Reequilibrium." In Juan J. Linz and Alfred Stepan, eds., *The Breakdown of Democratic Regimes*. Baltimore: Johns Hopkins University Press, 1978.

Morna, Collen Lowe. "Staying Ahead of the Opposition." *Africa Report*, July–August 1991.

Mutebi II. "Traditional Leaders and Democracy in Africa." *West Africa* 15 (April 1996).

Nzongola-Ntalaja, Georges. "Prospects for Democracy in Africa." *African Voices* 1 (summer 1992).

Przeworski, Adam, and Fernando Limongi. "Modernization: Theories and Facts." *World Politics* 49 (January 1997).

Stepan, Alfred. "Paths toward Redemocratization: Theoretical and Comparative Conclusions." In Guillermo O'Donnell, Philippe C. Schmitter, and Laurence Whitehead, eds., *Transition from Authoritarian Rule: Comparative Perspectives*. Baltimore: Johns Hopkins University Press, 1986.

van de Walle, Nicolas. "Neopatrimonialism and Democracy in Africa, with an Illustration from Cameroon." In Jennifer Widner, ed., *Economic Change and Political Liberalization in Sub-Saharan Africa*. Baltimore: Johns Hopkins University Press, 1994.

World Bank. *World Development Report 1996*. Washington, D.C.: World Bank, 1996.

Wright, Robin. "Hope Turns to Frustration as Wave of Freedom Ebbs." *Los Angeles Times*, February 16, 1997.

Young, Crawford. "Democratization in Africa: The Contradictions of a Political Imperative." In Jennifer Widner, ed., *Economic Change and Political Liberalization in Sub-Saharan Africa*.

Baltimore: Johns Hopkins University Press, 1994.

Chapter 15

Armijo, Leslie, Thomas Biersteker, and Abraham Lowenthal. "The Problems of Simultaneous Transitions." In Diamond and Plattner 1995.

Baregu, Mwesiga. "The Rise and Fall of the One-Party State in Tanzania." In Widner 1994.

Bates, Robert, "The Impulse to Reform in Africa." In Widner 1994.

Bienen, Henry, and Jeffrey Herbst. "The Relationship between Economic and Political Reform in Africa." *Comparative Politics* October 1996.

Bratton, Michael, and Nicolas van de Walle. "Popular Protest and Political Reform in Africa." *Comparative Politics* 24 (1992).

———. "Neopatrimonial Regimes and Political Transition in Africa." *World Politics* 46, (July 1994).

Callaghy, Thomas M. "Political Passions and Economic Interests: Economic Reform and Political Structure in Africa." In Callaghy and Ravenhill, 1993.

Callaghy, Thomas M., and John Ravenhill, eds. *Hemmed In: Responses to Africa's Economic Declin.* New York: Columbia University Press, 1993.

Clapham, Christopher, ed. *Patronage and Public Power.* London: Frances Pinter, 1982.

Deyo, Frederic C. *Political Economy of the New Urban Industrialism.* Ithaca,NY: Cornell University Press, 1987.

Diamond, Larry, Juan Linz, and Seymour Martin Lipset, eds. *Politics in Developing Countries.* 2d ed. Boulder, CO: Lynne Rienner, 1995.

Diamond, Larry, and Marc F. Plattner, eds. *Economic Reform and Democracy.* Baltimore: Johns Hopkins University Press, 1995.

Diamond, Larry. *The Democratic Revolution.* New York: Freedom House, 1992.

Duch, Raymond. "Economic Chaos and the Fragility of Democratic Transition in Former Communist Regimes." *Journal of Politics* 57, no. 1 (February 1995).

Encarnacion, Omar G. "The Politics of Dual Transitions." *Comparative Politics,* July 1996.

Haggard, Stephan. *Pathways from the Periphery.* Ithaca, NY: Cornell University Press, 1990.

Haggard, Stephan, and Robert Kaufman. *The Political Economy of Democratic Transitions.* Princeton, NJ: Princeton University Press, 1994.

Hart, Elizabeth, and E. Gyimah-Boadi. "Business Associations in Ghana's Economic and Political Transition." Presented at the Conference on State-Business Relations in Africa, American University, Washington, D.C., February 1997.

Huntington, Samuel. *The Third Wave: Democratization in the Late Twentieth Century.* Norman: University of Oklahoma Press, 1991.

Joseph, Richard. "Africa: The Rebirth of Political Freedom." *Journal of Democracy* 2, no. 4 (1991).

Lewis, Peter M. "Economic Statism, Private Capital, and the Dilemmas of Accumulation in Nigeria." *World Development* 22, no. 3 (March 1994).

———. "Economic Reform and Political Transition in Africa: The Quest for a Politics of Development." *World Politics* 48 (October 1996).

Lipset, Seymour Martin, *Political Man.* Garden City: Doubleday, 1959.

Olson, Mancur. *The Rise and Decline of Nations.* New Haven, CT: Yale University Press, 1982.

Remmer, Karen. "The Political Impact of Economic Crisis in Latin America in the 1980s." *American Political Science Review* 85, no. 3 (1991).

Rueschemeyer, Dietrich, John Stephens. and Evelyn Huber Stephens, *Capitalist Development and Democracy.* Chicago: University of Chicago Press, 1992.

Sandbrook, Richard. *The Politics of Africa's Economic Stagnation.* Cambridge: Cambridge University Press, 1985.

Uzodike, Ufo Okeke. "Democracy and Economic Reforms: Developing Underdeveloped Political Economies." *Journal of Asian and African Studies* 31, nos. 1–2 (June 1996).

Westebbe, Richard. "Structural Adjustment, Rent-Seeking and Liberalization in Benin." In Widner 1994.

Widner, Jennifer, ed. *Economic Change and Political Liberalization in Sub-Saharan Africa*. Baltimore: Johns Hopkins University Press, 1994.

World Bank. *Adjustment in Africa: Reforms, Results and the Road Ahead*. Washington, D.C.: World Bank, 1994.

———. *African Development Indicators*, Washington, D.C.: World Bank, 1996.

Young, Crawford. "Democratization in Africa: The Contradictions of a Political Imperative." In Widner 1994.

Chapter 16

Bueno de Mesquita, Bruce, and David Lalman. *War and Reason*. New Haven: Yale University Press, 1992.

Doyle, Michael W. "Liberalism and World Politics." *American Political Science Review 80* (1986):1151–70.

Farber, H. S. and Joanne Gowa. "Polities and Peace." *International Security* 20, no. 2 (1995): 123 –46.

Janis, Irving. *Groupthink: Psychological Studies of Policy Decisions and Fiascoes*. New York: Houghton Mifflin, 1982.

Jervis, Robert. *The Logic of Images in International Relations*. Princeton: Princeton University Press, 1970.

———. *Perception and Misperception in International Politics*. Princeton: Princeton University Press, 1976.

Layne, Christopher. "Kant or Cant: The Myth of the Democratic Peace." *International Security* 19, no. 2 (fall 1994): 5–49.

Levy, Jack. "Organizational Routines and the Causes of War." *International Studies Quarterly* 30 (June 1986): 193–222.

Mansfield, Edward, and Jack Snyder. "Democratization and War." *Foreign Affairs*, May/June 1995, pp. 79–97.

Maoz, Zeev, and Bruce Russett. "Normative and Structural Causes of Democratic Peace, 1946–1986." *American Political Science Review* 87, no.3 (September 1993): 624–38.

Morgan, T. Clifton, and Sally H. Campbell. "Domestic Structure, Decisional Constraints and War: So Why Kant Democracies Fight?" *Journal of Conflict Resolution* 35 (1991) 187–211.

Przeworski, Adam, and F. Limongi. "Modernization: Theories and Facts." *World Politics* 49, no. 2 (1997): 155–83.

Ruggie, John G. "International Regimes, Transactions, and Change: Embedded Liberalism in the Postwar Economic Order." *International Organization* 36, no. 2 (1982).

Russett, Bruce. *Grasping the Democratic Peace*. New Haven: Yale University Press, 1993.

Schelling, Thomas. *Strategy of Conflict*. Cambridge: Harvard University Press, 1960.

Sudweeks, B. L. *Equity Market Development in Developing Countries*. New York: Praeger Press, 1989.

Index

Abu Sayyak, as Filipino Muslim group, 158
Adenauer, Konrad, 39
Afghanistan, authoritarian regimes in, 148
Africa
    civil society in, 61
    colonial legacy and rule in, 12, 17, 25, 243-73
    democratization in, 4, 8, 9, 16, 22, 245-71
    dictatorships in, 22, 250
    economic crises in, 280
    economic reform in, 259-71
    elections in, 250
    European competition for territory and markets in, 8
    neopatrimonial regimes in, 263
    overthrow of autocrats in, 246
    partial democratization in, 252-5
    per capita income in, 245
    political and economic reform in, 16
    poverty in, 16, 61
    press-freedom rankings of, 256
    Soviet Union client states in, 8
    sponsored transitions in, 243-73
AFTA, 159
Agüero, Felipe, 13, 279, 290
Agrarian Party (Russia), 202
agrarian transition, role in democratization, 145
Albania, 227, 286
    PHARE program in, 234
Alfonsín, Raul, 47, 82, 85
Algeria, 282
    Islamic fundamentalists in, 180
Alien and Sedition Acts (U.S.), 143
Allende, Salvador, 42, 123
Alliance for Progress, 37, 38, 123
Allison, Graham, 186
Almond, Gabriel A., 23, 26, 66-7, 135-6, 138
American Institute for Free Labor Development, 38
American Revolution, 4, 22
The Americas
    European competition for territory and markets in, 8

Soviet Union client states in, 8
Angola, 250, 253, 254, 256
"anocracies", 188
APEC, 41, 159
APRA government, of Peru, 84
Aquino, Benigno, 300(n1;n2)
    assassination of, 151-2
Aquino, Corazon, 15, 148, 152, 153 154-9, 167, 174, 189
Arbenz, Jacobo, 123
Argentina
    democratization in, 10, 27, 47, 74, 79-80, 91-2, 118
    economy of, 43
    Falklands defeat of, 28, 82, 119, 301(n2)
    human rights problems in, 88
    military leadership in, 78, 89, 119, 121, 124
    military prerogatives in, 75, 82-3
    as oligarchial democracy, 116
    redemocratization in, 119
Arias, Oscar, 122, 124
Aristide, Jean-Bertrand, 126
Aristotle, 25, 54
Armed Forces of the Philippines (AFP), 153-4
Armenia, 233
    U.S. aid to, 236
ASEAN (Association of Southeasst Asian Nations), 41, 159, 160, 185
Asia
    colonial rule in, 25
    debt crisis in, 46
    democratization in, 3, 8, 9, 10, 11, 14, 15, 40, 60, 160-77
    developmental state of, 12, 131-91, 160-77
    dictatorships in, 22
    economic miracles in, 168-75, 182
    economic restructuring in, 40-1
    political regimes in (*table*), 164-5
    Soviet Union client states in, 8
"Asian democracies", 163, 178
Asian Development Bank, 29
"Asian flu" financial crisis of 1997 and 1998, 162, 169-71, 177, 222

Asian Tigers, average per capita income of, 46
Asian values
    in Singapore, 29, 35
    Western ideals at odds with, 60, 61
Association Agreements, of European Union, 235
Association of Major Religious Superiors in The Philippines (AMRSP), 150
associations
    in early China, 33
    role in democracies, 30, 31
Athens, democracy in, 22, 63
Atlantic Alliance, 232
Australia
    democracy in, 163, 176
    economic stagnation in, 169, 170, 174
    modernization in, 162
Austria, social democrats in, 44
authoritarianism
    after World War II, 8
    democratization and, 10, 187-8
    in South and Central America, end of, 71-129
Aviation Security Command (Avsecom), 152
The Awkward Embrace: One-Party Domination and Democracy (Giliomee & Simkins, eds.), 115
Aylwin, ___., 81
Azerbaijan, 233

"back-door" operations, in China, 34
BAIR (bureaucratic authoritarian industrializing regime), in Asia, 168
Baker, Pauline, 247-8
Balaguer, Joaquin, 126
Baltic states
    economy of, 223
    NATO and, 233
    PHARE program in, 234
Bangladesh
    democracy in, 163
    economy of, 171
    political regime in, 165, 166
Bashkir, 223
Belarus, 229
Belaunde, ___., 84
benevolent societies, in early China, 33-4
Benin, 22, 250, 254, 256, 265, 269, 270
Berliner, Joseph, 15, 46, 290
Boahen, A. Adu, 255
Bolivia
    democratization in, 46, 119
    military regime in, 119

Bolshevik Party, in Russia, 6
Booth, John, 124
Borges, Jorge Luis, 47
Bosnia-Herzegovinia, 233
Botswana, 250, 251, 254, 256
Brazil
    civilian-military relations in, 85, 90, 91, 92
    debt problems of, 187
    democratization in, 10, 74, 76, 79, 91, 116, 128
    economic growth in, 43
    institutionalization in, 78
    military regimes in, 119, 121, 124
    new constitution in, 77
    as oligarchial democray, 116
    redemocratization in, 119
    trade liberalization in, 47
Brezhnev, Leonid, 214, 220
Brezhnev Doctrine, abandonment of, 227
British Dominions, democratization in, 11
Brunei
    economy of, 171
    political regime in, 165, 167
Buchanan, Patrick, 134
Buganda, 257
Bulgaria, PHARE program in, 234
Bunyoro, 257
Burkina Faso, 250, 254, 256, 257, 258
Burma. *See* Myanmar
Burundi, 250, 251, 254, 256, 265
Bush, George, New World Order of, 288
Bush administration, Latin-American policy of, 124
Busoga, 257
Buyoya, Paul, 251

Cambodia
    democracy in, 163
    economy of, 171
    political regime in, 165, 166, 167
Cameroon, 250, 254, 256, 265
Canada
    asymmetric unions in, 208
    support of foundations for Latin America in, 125, 128
Cape Verde, 250, 254, 256
capitalism, in Europe and North America, 5
Capitalist Development and Democracy (Rueschemeyer et al.), 144
CAR (Central African Republic), 254, 256, 257
Cárdenas, Cuahtémoc, 96, 101, 102, 104
    Cárdenas, Lázaro, 95-6

Cardoso, ___., 87
Caribbean, average per capita income in, 46
Carothers, Thomas, 239, 240
Carter administration
    Asian policy of, 167
    Latin-American foreign policy of, 123
Casper, Gretchen, 14, 15, 290
Castro, Fidel, 190
Cato Institute, 136
Ceauçescu, Nicolae, 142, 240
Central African Republic, 250
Central America
    democratization in, 119-20
    postauthoritarianism in, 12, 13, 71-129
Central Asia, fundamentalist parties in, 282
Central Europe, democratization in, 59-60
Central European University, 239
Central Intelligence Agency (CIA), 140, 218
Chad, 22, 250, 254, 256
chaebôl (conglomerates), of Korea, 142, 169, 170
Chan, Steve, 14, 15, 41, 167, 177, 290
Chang regime, in Korea, 143
charrismo, in Mexico, 101
Chatichai, ___., 166
Chechnia, Russian campaign in, 210
Chernobyl disaster, 215
Chile
    authoritarianism in, 117
    civilian-military tensions in, 80-2, 88, 89, 90, 91
    democratization in, 10, 42, 46, 74, 79-80, 91-2, 116, 118
    economic restructuring in, 46, 47, 261
    institutionalization in, 78
    military prerogatives in, 75, 89
    military regimes in, 119, 120, 124
    new constitution in, 77
    as oligarchial democray, 116
    Pinochet's removal from, 28
    radical left in, 121
    redemocratization in, 119
    U.S. intervention in, 189
Chiluba, Frederick, 249, 251, 268
China. See also People's Republic of China
    "back-door" operations in, 34
    civil society in, 61
    class power in, 33
    communism in, 7, 173
    in cross-strait crisis, 190
    Cultural Revolution of, 217
    democratization in, 60, 178, 181
    developmental patterns in, 14
    economic liberalization in, 186
    economy of, 26, 27, 171, 176

export dynamism in, 168
Great Leap Forward of, 217
"guanxi capitalism" of, 174
guilds in, 33
liberalization in, 163
political regime in, 165
possible U.S. cold or hot war with, 287
post-Tiananmen era in, 61
reform in, 215
rising status of, 190
stock market of, 286
three-way division of state, public, and private spheres, 33
trade policies of, 280
Chinese, in non-China business communities, 175
Chôlla people, lack of Korean representation of, 142
chonin, in early Japan, 32
Chôn Tu-hwan, Korea coup of, 140-1, 143
Cho Pong-am, 139
Chubais, Anatoly, 237
Chun Doo Hwan, 148
Chun-Roh transition, in South Korea, 164
Churchill, Winston, on democracy, 25
"civic cost benefit analysis", 70
civic culture, key elements of, 24-5
The Civic Culture (Almond & Verba), 26, 135-6, 137
civic education, 62-3, 65
civic liberalism, 61-5
civic malaise, in Western societies, 54
civic spiritedness, in modern democracies, 64
"civilian corps", in Africa, 247
civil-liberties checklist, of Freedom House, 252-3
civil society
    articulation of interests and, 30-6
    associations in, 31
    cooperative virtues of, 68
    in early Europe, 32
    expansion of, 32
    in Korea, 133-46
    role in democratization, 4, 7, 10, 11, 18, 69
    strategy for, 69-70
Civil War, 4-5, 181
Clark, Cal, 14, 290
"The Clash of Civilizations" (Huntington), 134 class struggle theory, of Marx, 7
clinical depression, in United States, 54
Clinton, Bill
    on China's economic growth, 26
    on community spirit, 30
    on democratic transitions, 288
Clinton administration, foreign policy of, 227

Côte d'Ivoire, 250, 253, 254, 256
Cold War, 8, 21, 36, 122, 167, 181, 232, 263, 264
  NATO and, 233
  Russia and, 218-20
  U.S. foreign policy after, 125-9, 134, 216
  U.S. foreign policy during, 286
Collier, Ruth Berins, 13-14, 162, 291 Collor, Fernando, 86
Colombia
  avoidance of military rule in, 118
  debt crisis in, 46
  democratization in, 124
  as oligarchial democray, 116
Commission of the European Union, 234
Commission on Elections (Filipino Comelec), 152
Common Market, of Western European nations, 39
Commons, John R., "industrial goodwill" of, 49
communism, 6, 213
  after first wave of democracy, 22
  in Asia, 163, 165, 171
  collapse of, 3, 59, 196, 227, 258
  in Latin America, 122-3
  route to modernity of, 7
Communist Party, in Russia, 186
Communist Party of the Philippines (CPP), 150, 157, 158
Communist Party of the Russian Federation (CPRF), 200, 202
Communist Party of the Soviet Union (CPSU), 202, 207
communitarianism, in United States, 30, 35
Comoros, 250, 254, 256, 257
Comprehensive Agrarian Reform Program, of Corazon Aquino, 158
Confucian capitalism, 161, 162, 168
Confucianism, Asian values and, 143
Confucian world, democratic prerequisites of, 33, 34-5 Congo, 250, 254, 256, 257, 269, 282
Congreso de Trabajo (CT), as Mexican union, 112
Constant, Benjamin, 63
Constitutional Court, 81
Contradora countries, democratization in, 124
Contras, U.S. support of, 124
copper exports, of Chile, 81
Costa Rica
  democratization in, 118, 124
  military activity in, 122
  as oligarchial democracy, 116

Council of Europe, 238
Crédit Lyonnais, 39
crisis prevention, role in democratization, 128
Croatia, 233
"crony capitalism", of Marcos regime, 171, 173
"crosscutting", among societal groups, 66
cross-strait crisis of 1995, 190
CTM, as Mexican union confederation, 102, 112
Cuba
  economic embargo against, 190
  economic restructuring and democratization in, 46
Cuban Revolution, 117, 123
"cultural embeddedness", in East Asia, 176
cultural orientations, democratization and, 26
cultural progress, dependence on civil society of, 32
Cumings, Bruce, 14, 41, 60-61, 277, 291
CVC (Citizens Vetting Committee), 255
Czechoslovakia
  democratization and economic growth in, 27, 213
  "people power" revolutions in, 227
  PHARE program in, 234
  splitting of, 196
Czech Republic
  democratization in, 230
  NATO and, 233

Dahl, Robert, 12, 13, 135, 144, 277
  eight requirements for democracy of, 23-4
daimyos, in early Japan, 32
Das Kapital (Marx), 6
de Bari Hermoza, Nicolás, 84
debt crisis, in Latin America, 45
Decade of Development (1960s), 45
Declaration of Independence, 55
dedazo, as Mexican presidential choice, 109
Defense Law, of Argentina (1988), 82
De la Madrid, Miguel, as Mexican president, 48, 97
democracy
  Dahl's eight requirements for, 23-4
  definition of, 21-2, 143-6
  diversity in practice of, 36
  economic development and, 25
  enemies of, 21-36
  ideal and reality of, 36
  individual rights and collective responsibility in, 31
  liberal, 24
  markets and, 37-52

practical elements of, 23
Democracy in America (Toqueville), 135
democratic capitalism, in Asia, 160
democratic citizenship, social foundations of, 53-70
Democratic Liberal Party (DLP), of Korea, 141, 146
Democratic Party (U.S.), 145
democratic regimes, in Latin America, 73
"democratic republics, 21
democratization
    in Central America, 124
    economic restructuring as support for, 48-52
    effect on economic policy and performance, 174
    first wave of, 5, 6-7, 22, 250
    international influences on, 230-2
    international relations and, 12
    political economy of, 19-52
    in postcommunist Europe, 226-41
    regime changes and, 25-6
    second wave of, 7, 22
    U.S. foreign policy and, 275-89
Demosthenes Program, 238
Deng Xiaoping, economic growth under, 27, 176
Denmark, social democrats in, 44
dependencia/dependency, of democratizing states, 8, 9
de Schweinitz, Karl, 27
developing world, obstacles to democracy in, 25
Diamond, Larry, 177, 246
dictatorships
    after second wave of democracy, 22
    communism and, 123
    economic development fostered by, 58
    hallmarks of control by, 66
"distributional coalitions" theory, 174
diversity, in modern societies, 67
Dominican Republic
    elections in, 126
    U.S. military intervention in, 123
Dreyfus, Alfred, 5
Durkheim, Emile, on the state, 66
dysphoria, in Western societies, 54

East Asia
    democratization in, 22, 133-46, 178-91, 279-80
    economic reform in, 265
    industrialization in, 160
    modernization in, 162
    political economies of, 161

security environment of, 187-91
East Asian Dragons
    economies of, 170, 171
    industrial policies of, 169
    political regimes of, 164
"East Asian dynamism", modernization model of, 161
East Asian System, 134
East Central Europe
    democratization in, 3, 9, 10, 15
    Soviet Union client states in, 8
Eastern Europe
    consolidation in, 193-241
    definition of, 301(n3)
    democratization in, 9, 11, 16, 75, 143, 279
    former communist regimes in, 17
    political assitance to, 238-9
    postcommunist regimes in, 76
    private investment in, 15
East Germany, "people power" revolutions in, 227
Easton, David, 23
economic development
    dependence on civil society of, 32
    role in democratization, 26-9, 58
economic dislocation, effect on U.S. volunteerism, 69
economic liberalization, politics and, 37-40
"economic miracles", in Asia, 168
economic restructuring, as support for democratization, 48-52
Economist, 135, 246, 255
Ecuador
    constitutional crises in, 126
    democratization in, 119
    international missions to, 128
    restructuring in, 47
EDSA Revolution (Philippines), 151-4, 158, 159, 300(n2)
El Barzón, as Mexican debtors movement, 108, 109, 111
elections, in democracy, 23
embourgeoisement, in East Asia, 187
"the end of history" (Fukuyama), 5, 160, 296(n1)
Enigma of Japanese Power (van Wolferen), 134
The Enlightenment, 4, 116, 134
    Marx and, 6
Enrile, Juan Ponce, 151, 153, 154, 155
EPR, as Mexican guerilla movement, 108
Epstein, Leon, 117
equality, as U.S. principle of justice, 56
equal rights, in liberal tradition, 62
Equatorial Guinea, 250, 253, 254, 256
Eritrea, 250, 254, 256, 257

Esquipulas Accord, 124
Estonia, democratization in, 197
Ethiopia, 250, 254, 256
Etzioni, Amitai, 30
Eurocapitalism, 44
Europe
    democratic consolidation in, 228-232
    postcommunist, democratization in, 226-41
    regime transition in, 197
    regional integration in, 42
    state-society division in, 33, 34
    support of foundations for Latin America in, 125
    Western development assistance to, 234-8
European Bank for Reconstruction and Development (EBRD), 234, 236
European Coal and Steel Community, 38
European Commission of Democracy through Law, 238
European Community (EC), economic assistance from, 234
European Economic Community (EEC), 41
    Portugal's admission to, 40
European Monetary Union, 39
European Union (EU)
    Association Agreements of, 235-6
    communist trade in, 224, 227
Evans, Peter, 176, 177
expiry law (*ley de caducidad*), of Uruguay, 87, 90
EZLN, as Zapatista movement, 108, 111

Falklands, Argentinian defeat in, 28, 82, 119, 301(n2)
family breakup, in Western societies, 54
family instability, effect on U.S. volunteerism, 69
Far East, democratization in, 40-2
fascism
    after first wave of democracy, 22
    capitalism critique by, 117
    in Germany, 6
    in Italy, 6
Fay, Michael, 138
federalism, in Russia, 16, 195-212
Federalist Papers, 55, 56
feudalism, state-society division in, 32
fidelista position of fighting, in Mexico, 102
first wave of democracy, 6-7, 22
Foreign Affairs, 134
foreign aid
    to Latin America, 122
    by United States, 26
Foro, as Mexican union, 112

Four Little Dragons (Asia), 160, 185
    democracy in, 163, 186
Four Little Tigers, economic restructuring by, 41
France
    Dreyfus vindication in, 5
    indicative planning in, 38
Franco, Francisco, 45
Franco, Itamar, 85, 86
freedom
    in liberal democracy, 62
    "negative", 70
Freedom at Issue (Freedom House), 252-3
Freedom Constitution, of Corazon Aquino, 155
Freedom House, indices of, 252-3, 302(n1)
freedom of expression, in democracy, 23
free markets, role in democratization, 4, 11, 12, 14, 16
free societies, markets and foundations of, 54-5
French Revolution, 22, 139
Friedman, Milton, 43
Fuentes Irurozqui, Manuel, 42
Fujimori, Alberto, as Peruvian president, 84-5, 89, 126
Fukuyama, Francis, 5, 160, 296(n1;n2)
    "end of history" argument of, 5, 14, 22, 160, 296(n1)
fused-state conept, in Germany, 139

Gabon, 250, 254, 256
Gaidar, Egor, 208
Galenson, Walter, 27
Gambia, 250, 251, 254, 256
    dictatorship in, 247, 248
    free elections in, 22
Garcia, Alan, APRA government of, 84, 89
"Garrison Decree" of 1971, 140
GATT, 48, 297(n3)
gay rights referendum, in Colorado, 180
German Federal Republic, social market economy of, 38
German Miracle, 38
Germany, 138-9, 180, 181
    capitalist route to modernity in, 7
    fascism in, 6, 7
    fused-state conept in, 139
    postwar public policy of, 44
    Social Democrats in, 39
Gershenkron, Alexander, 27
Ghana, 250, 251, 254, 256, 257, 261, 265, 268, 270
    dictatorship in, 247, 249
    free elections in, 22

Giliomee, Hermann, 115
Gingrich, Newt, 134
Glade, William, 12, 13, 162, 284, 291
glasnost, in Russia, 186, 227
Golden Rule, in communitarianism, 30
Gonzalez, Felipe, Spanish socialist government of, 45
"good society", governmental promotion of, 57-58
Gorbachev, Mikhail, 15, 186, 208, 214-15, 218, 220, 237
Gramsci, Antonio, 143
Great Britain
    Crown and Parliament clashes in, 22
    Labor Party in, 38, 44
    women's suffrage in, 5
Great Depression, 97, 117, 118, 180
Great Reform Act of 1832 (Great Britain), 181
Great Society, freedom in, 64
Greece
    ancient, concept of democracy in, 22, 25
    democratization in, 10, 27
    military coups in, 22
    in NATO, 233
greed, perceived as social evil in China, 33
gross national product (GNP)
    role in self-governing society, 62
    role to democratization, 27, 283
"growth with equity" theme, 44-5
guanxi, role in Chinese "back-door" operations, 34
Guatemala
    constitutional crises in, 126
    international missions to, 128
    military regimes in, 122, 123, 124
    U.S. intervention in, 189
Guinea, 250, 254, 256
Guinea-Bissau, 250, 254, 256

Habermas, Jürgen, 143, 144
Habib, Philip, 153
Habyarimana, Juvenal, 251
Haiti
    overthrow of Aristide in, 126
    overthrow of dictators in, 120
Hamilton, Alexander, 55, 56
Haya de la Torre, military government of, 117
Hayek, Friedrich von, 43
Hegel, G. W. F., 5, 54, 138-9, 140, 145
Helms-Burton Act, 190
Herbst, Jeffrey, 16, 277-8, 280, 291
Hernándex Juárez, Francisco, as Mexican union leader, 107, 112
Herring, Pendleton, 23
Hitler, Adolf, 38, 57

Hobbes, John, 19, 58, 59, 296(n21)
    as progenitor of modern liberal democracy, 55
Hollifield, James F., 291
Holmes, Stephen, 58
Honasan, Gregorio, 157
Honduras
    military activity in, 122
    U.S. policy toward, 124
Hong Kong
    economic policies in, 41
    laissez-faire economy of, 169, 170, 173
    liberalization in, 163
    political regime in, 164, 185
Honnecker, Erich, 142
human capital
    in African countries, 266
    in Asian countries, 173
humanitarianism, 4
human rights
    in China, American trade and, 35, 41, 190
    Pinochet's alleged crimes of, 80, 82
    promotion in Eastern Europe, 238
    role in democratization, 4, 16
    Russian Commissioner for, 203
    Summit of the Americas section for, 128
    violations in Latin America, 123, 124
    violations in Philippines, 150
    violations in Uruguayan military, 87
Human Rights Committee, 84
Hungary
    authoritarianism in, 213
    democratization in, 230
    NATO and, 233
    PHARE program in, 234
Hunt, W. Ben, 17, 292
Huntington, Samuel, 134, 143, 186, 296(n21)
    first wave of democracy of, 5, 250
    political decay theory of, 167
    third wave of democracy of, 22, 77, 160, 163, 175, 178, 250
Hutu, in Burundi, 251

Ibero-America, constitutional government in, 116
Ignatieff, Michael, "civil society strategy" of, 69-70
India
    democracy in, 29, 163, 166, 176, 181, 287
    economy of, 171, 174
    low GNP in, 27, 28
    political regime in, 164
Indonesia
    Chinese communities in, 167
    corruption in, 175

economy of, 40, 171, 278
liberalization in, 163
political regime in, 165, 167
"industrial goodwill", 49
Institutional Act No. 5 (Brazil), 90-1
intellectual advancement, dependence on civil society of, 32
Inter-American Convention against Corruption, 129
Inter-American Development Bank, 45, 46, 128
Inter-American Foundation, 38
International Monetary Fund (IMF), 8, 9, 44, 97, 224, 228, 234, 236, 237, 259
Iran
    authoritarian regimes in, 148
    U.S. intervention in, 189
Iran-Contra scandal, 124
ISI model, 95, 97
Italy
    civil society in, 135, 136, 138
    fascism in, 6, 39
    postwar public policy of, 44

Japan
    capitalist route to modernity in, 7, 40
    colonialism of, 183, 191
    democratization in, 40, 139, 144, 163, 166, 176, 191, 239
    East Asian System and, 134-5
    economy of, 40, 170, 173, 174, 185, 217, 219
    feudalism in, 32
    foreign investment in, 40
    industrialization in, 160, 169
    Meiji reforms in, 5
    militaristic nationalism in, 7
    political regime in, 164, 190
    pre-war authoritarianism in, 145
    recession in, 168
    state-society division in, 33, 34
    zaibatsu structure of industry in, 40
Jay, John, 55
Jefferson, Thomas, 136, 137
Jillson, Calvin, 291
Johnson, Lyndon B., Latin-American policy of, 123
justice, basic concepts of, 21-36

Kanet, Roger, 16, 46, 162, 280, 282, 292
Kant, Immanuel, 180, 187
Kaunda, Kenneth, 251
Kazakhstan, authoritarianism in, 187
KBL, as Marcos party, 155
Kennedy administration
    foreign aid policy in, 26

Korean policy of, 140
    Latin-American foreign policy of, 123
Kenya, 250, 251, 253, 254, 256, 258, 265, 302(n1)
Keynesianism, 94, 95
Khasbulatov, Ruslan, 208-9
Khmer Rouge, U.S. opposition to, 167
Kim Young Sam, 141, 142, 175
King, Anthony, 29
KISS, 281-3
Konrad Adenauer Foundation, 238
Korea
    civil society in, 133-46
    democratization in, 60, 133-46, 277
    East Asian System and, 134-5
    economic policies in, 41, 261
    military dictatorships of, 142
    social movements in, 61
Kuomintang, in Taiwan, 185
Kwangju crisis (Korea), 140-1

LABAN, 152, 155
labor-based parties (LBPs)
    in Mexico, 93-4, 95-98
    in twentieth century, 94-5
labor unions, fiscal favors to, in Latin America, 50
Lacalle, ___., 87
laissez-faire doctine, 5
LAKAS/NUCD (National Union of Christian Democrats), 155
Länder governments, in post-war Germany, 38
Lane, Robert, 54
Laos
    economy of, 171
    political regime in, 165
Lasswell, Harold, 23
Latin America
    authoritarian and military regimes in, 13, 17
    average per capita income in, 46
    companies in, 39
    "constitution of tyranny" in, 75
    cost overburden of corruption in, 50-1
    debt crisis in, 45, 46
    delinking economic and political liberalization in, 42-4
    democratization in, 8, 9, 22, 27, 44-8, 118, 143, 226, 279
    economic restructuring in, 44-8, 265
    independent citizens groups in, 60
    military coups in, 22
    nondemocratic past in, 75
    principal/agent problem in, 49
    regime transition in, 197

regional integration in, 41-2
state-managed development in, 12
transitions to democracy in, external actors in, 116-29
U.S. promotion of democracy in, 239
Latin American Economic System, 42
Latin American Integration Association, 42
Latvia, democratization in, 197
Laurel, Salvador, 151, 152, 154, 156
leadership, role in good government, 28-9
Lee Kuan Yew, 163
Lee Kwan Yew, Asian values of, 35, 143
Lenin, V. I., 7, 75
    on imperialism, 6
Lesotho, 250, 254, 256, 257
Lewis, Peter M., 16, 162, 282, 292
liberal democracy, 55-7
Liberal Democratic Party (LDP)
    of Japan, 141, 146, 185
    of the Philippines, 157
Liberal-Democratic Party of Russia (LDPR), 202
liberal route, to modernity, 6
Liberia, 250, 254, 256
liberty
    definition of, 63
    threatening of, 63
    as U.S. principle of justice, 56
Lijphart, Arend, 248
Limann, Hilla, 249
Limongi, Fernando, 58
    economic growth and democracy studies of, 27
Linz, Juan, 229, 245
Lipset, Seymour Martin, 58, 135, 144-5, 186, 187, 260-1
    economic growth studies of, 25-6, 27
Lithuania, democratization in, 197, 230
Locke, John, 6, 10, 22, 55, 56, 58, 59, 135, 179, 182, 183, 296(n21)
"lost decade of development", 46
Low Countries, social democrats in, 44
Lugar, ___., 153, 154

Maastricht Treaty, 235
Macedo, Stephen, 12, 177, 292, 296(n22)
Machiavelli, Niccoló 136
"machine that would go of itself", United States government as, 56
MacIntyre, Alasdair, 139
Macpherson, C. B., 146
Madagascar, 250, 254, 256, 269
Madison, James, 55
el-Mahdi, Sadiq, 249
Making Democracy Work (Putnam), 135

Malawi, 250, 254, 256
    autocrat overthrow in, 247
Malaysia
    Asian democracy in, 163, 166, 176
    Asian values of, 35
    Chinese communities in, 167
    corruption in, 175
    democracy in, 163
    economic restructuring by, 41
    economy of, 171
    political regime in, 165
Mali, 250, 254, 256, 260
Malthus, Thomas R., 5
Maoz, Zeev, 287
Mao Zedong, 27, 217
Marcos, Ferdinand E., 15, 28, 149, 153, 156, 158, 165, 173
    overthrow of, 147, 148, 167
Marcos, Imelda, 151
Marcos, Subcomandante, as Zapatista leader, 108-9
"market democracies", 227, 231
markets
    democracy and, 37-52
    reforms of, 283-6
Marshall Plan, 37, 38, 223-4, 230, 301(n4)
Marx, Karl, 6, 7, 8, 138, 145, 180
Marxism, 47, 198
    capitalism critique by, 117
Marxist-Leninism
    in Russia, 197
    in South America, 121
Masan disorder, in Korea, 140
Mauritania, 250, 254, 256
Mauritius, 250, 254, 256
Medina, ___., 79, 87
Menem, Carlos, 28, 82, 83, 88
Mercosur, 42, 126, 279
Merriam, Charles, 23
"Mexican Miracle", 96
Mexican Revolution, 95, 99
Mexico
    authoritarianism in, 45
    debt crisis of, 9, 45
    democratization in, 46, 93-115, 119, 124
    economy of, 43, 47-8
    elections in, 102-8, 126-7
    labor-based one-partyism in, 93-115
    military regime in, 121
    multiple crises in, 108-12
    peso crisis in, 121
    PRI in, 13, 48, 96, 97, 98, 99, 100-15, 121, 298(n10)
    rounds of change in, 13
    social attitudes in, 138

Middle East, fundamentalist parties in, 282
Migdal, Joel, 177
military forces, role in democratization, 73-92
military regimes, in Latin America, 13, 120-1
Mill, John Stuart, 6, 136, 145
Ming dynasty (China), societies in, 34
minjung ideology, in Korea, 143
Miracle at EDSA, 153
Misuari, Nur, 157
MNLF, as Filipino Muslim group, 157, 158
mobility, effect on U.S. volunteerism, 69
modernity, Moore's three routes to, 6
modernization
    in Asia, 160-77
    contribution to democracy, 135
    first end of history and, 4-6
    first failure of, 6-7
    nationalism and, 6-7
    second failure of, 7-10
Mohamad, Mahathir bin, 35, 163
Mondale, Walter, 150
monetarism, Latin America and, 44
Mongolia
    democracy in, 163
    economy of, 171
    political regime in, 165
Monnet, Jean, 39
Moore, Barrington, routes to modernity of, 6-7
Morgenthau, Hans, 275
Morishima, Michio, 144
Moro Islamic Liberation Front (MILF), 158
Mosevani, ___., 257
Movement Toward Socialism, 47
Mozambique, 250, 256
multinational corporations
    in Asia, 185
    democratic rule and, 35
Muslim guerillas, in Philippines, 147, 155, 157, 158
Myanmar
    economy of, 171, 178
    political regime in, 165, 167
State Law and Order Restoration Council of,
    148

Namibia, 250, 254, 256
Nation, 135
National Democratic Congress (Ghana), 255
National Endowment for Democracy, 238
National Information Service (Brazil), 86
National Interest, 134
nationalism, modernization failure and, 6-7
National Movement for Free Elections
    (Namfrel), 152, 153
National Security Council (NSC), 81, 87, 90, 91

National Security Law (Korea), 142
national well-being, dependence on civil soci-
    ety of, 32 NATO, 190, 223, 233, 236
"democratic peace," European security, and,
    232-4
Nazis, economic planning by, 38
Ndadaye, Metchior, 251
"negative" freedom, from government inter-
    ference, 70
Nehru, Jawarhalal, 28
neodemocrats, 145
neopanistas, in Mexico, 99
Neves, Tancredo, 298(n5)
New Democratic Party (Korea), 141
"New Labor Culture" (Mexico), 110
New Left Review, 134
New People's Army (NPA; Philippines), 147,
    150, 151, 152, 155
New Society Movement (NBL), of Marcos,
    150
New Unionism (Mexico), 106, 107, 110, 112
New York Times, 134
New Zealand
    democracy in, 163, 176
    economy of, 162, 169, 170, 174
    modernization in, 162
    political regimes in, 164
Nicaragua
    democratization in, 46
    Sandinistas in, 122, 123
NIC (National Investigation Committee), 255
"NICS" (newly industrialized countries), 134
Niger, 256, 265, 269
elections in, 22, 247, 250, 251, 254
    military coup in, 251
Nigeria, 256, 269
    dictatorships in, 247, 249, 250, 254
NIS (Newly Independent States), as stable
    market democracies, 231
Nixon administration
    Korean policy of, 140
    Latin-American foreign policy of, 123
North Africa, fundamentalist parties in, 282
North American Free Trade Agreement
    (NAFTA), 279
North Korea
    communism in, 173
    economy of, 171, 173, 178
    political regime in, 165
Norway, social democrats in, 44
No Tlae-u, Korea coup of, 140, 141
Ntaryamira, Cyprien, 251
Ntigantunganya, Sylvestre, 251
Nzongola-Ntalaja, Georges, 246

Oceania
    economies of, 170
    modernization in, 162
    political regimes in, 164
O'Donnell, Guillermo, 76, 226
Odría, Manuel, 42, 43
Office for Free Elections, 238
office holding, eligibility for, in democracy, 23
oil shocks, 9, 46
oligarchial democracies, in Latin America, 116
Olson, Mancur, 174
"Open Society" projects, 239
Ordeshook, Peter, 210-11
Organization for Economic Cooperation and
    Development (OECD), 46, 234, 297(n1),
    300(n3)
Organization for Security and Cooperation in
    Europe (OSCE), 233, 238
Organization of American States (OAS), 85, 279
    programs adopted by, 126
    Unit for the Promotion of Democracy
    and, 128
organizations, freedom to join in democracy, 23
Our Home Is Russia, 202

Pakistan
    democracy in, 148, 163
    economy of, 171
    military coups in, 22, 167
    political regime in, 164, 166
PAN. See Partido Acción Nacional (PAN)
    Panama, democratization in, 124
Papua New Guinea
    democracy in, 163, 166
    economy of, 171
    political regime in, 165
Paraguay
    constitutional crises in, 126
    democratization in, 119
    military regime in, 124
    overthrow of dictators in, 120
Park Chung Hee, 140, 143
Parliament Act of 1911 (England), 5
Partido Acción Nacional (PAN), in Mexico,
    98-9, 100-15
Peace Corps, 38
peasant organizations, fiscal favors to, in Latin
    America, 50
People Power (Philippines), 147, 154, 155, 167
People's Action Party (Singapore), 185
people's representatives, government policy
    made by, in democracy, 23
People's Republic of China. See also China
    economic liberallization in, 41

    human rights in, 35, 41
perestroika, in Russia, 186, 227
Peron, Juan, military government of, 117
Peronists, role in Argentinian restructuring, 47
Perot, Ross, 134
personal responsibility, economic benefits of, 65
Peru
    civilian-military relations in, 83-85, 89, 91
    constitutional crises in, 126
    democratization in, 46, 74, 79, 92, 297(n9)
    economy of, 43
    international missions to, 128
    military leadership in, 42, 78, 79, 83-85,
    89, 117, 122
    as oligarchial democray, 116
PHARE program, for European economic
    assistance, 234-5
The Philippines
    Aquino's rule of, 154-9, 167, 174, 189
    authoritarianism in, 149, 150
    "booty capitalism" of, 174
    democratization in, 10, 14, 15, 143, 146,
    147-59, 163, 167, 183, 189
    economy of, 171, 173
    future of democracy in, 158-9
    Marcos's rule of, 28, 147, 148-51
    political regimes in, 165, 166, 282
Philosophy of History (Hegel), 54
Pinochet, Augusto, 28, 43, 47, 79, 80
    arrest of, 80, 81, 82
Plato, 21, 54, 62
pluralism
    fostering of, 67
    ideal of, 66
    lack in South America, 73
    role in democratization, 13, 37
PNDC (Provisional Defense Council), 255
Poland
    democratization and economic growth in,
    27, 76, 213, 221, 223, 230
    NATO and, 233
    PHARE program in, 234
Polanyi, Karl, 5
polis
    democracy in, 179
    slavery-provided leisure in, 63
political centralization, effect on U.S. volun-
    teerism, 69
political cultures, case studies on, 26
political leaders, competition for support of, in
    democracy, 23
Political Order in Changing Societies
    (Huntington), 296(n21)
polyarchy
    requirements for, 74

as theoretical essence of democracy, 23

The Pope, early European royal need for, 32

Portugal
democratization in, 10, 22, 27, 40, 226, 235
in NATO, 233

postauthoritarianism, in South and Central America, 71-129

postcommunist societies, in crises of governability, 58

PRD, as Mexican party, 102, 103, 109, 115

"predatory states", monopoly of force in, 174

Press Freedom World Wide (Freedom House), 253-5

PRI, effect on Mexican democratization, 13, 48, 96, 97, 98, 99, 100-15, 121

Primakov, ___., 223

privatism, in modern commercial democracy, 64

Problems of Democratic Transition and Consolidation (Linz & Stepan), 229

Pronasol, as Mexican community development program, 105

Przeworski, Adam, 27, 58, 77, 144, 229, 237

public safety, in democratizing states, 59

Puerto Rico, 239

Pusan disorder (Korea), 140

Putnam, Robert, 30, 64, 67, 133, 135, 136, 137, 138, 294(n3)

Pye, Lucian W., 12, 13, 177, 277, 293

pyramid investment schemes, 286

quadrant system, for market analysis, 278-9, 284

Ramos, Fidel, 148, 153, 154, 155, 156, 157, 158, 167

rationalism, 4

Rawlings, Jerry, 247, 255, 302(n2)

Rawls, John, theory of justice of, 67-8

Ray, James L., 182

Reagan, Ronald, Marcos regime and, 152, 153

Reagan administration
Asian policy of, 167
Latin-American foreign policy of, 123, 124
Sandinistas and, 122

"red-brown coalition", in Africa, 282

Reflections of a Radical Moderate (Richardson), 49

Reform Acts of 1832 and 1867 (England), 4

Reform the Armed Forces of the Philippines Movement (RAM), 151, 153, 155, 157, 158

"regime-change game", as Mexican political struggle, 113

regimes, effectiveness of, 182-4

religious sects, Smith's views of, 64-5

Remington, Thomas F., 15-16, 46, 280, 282, 293

Renewal of the Inter-American System, 126

Republic of Korea (ROK), democracy in, 142

The Republic (Plato), 21

Resolution 1080, 126, 128

Rhee, Syngman, 139, 143

Richardson, Elliot, 49

Rockefeller, Nelson, report on Latin America of, 123

Roh Tae Woo, 148

Romania
Ceauçescu dictatorship of, 142
NATO and, 233
PHARE program in, 234

Roosevelt, Franklin D., Latin-American relations of, 122

Rousseau, Jean-Jacques, 22, 62

royalty, early European need for Pope by, 32

Rueschmeyer, Dietrich, 144, 145

Ruggie, John, 284

Russell, Bertrand, on democracy, 24

Russet, Bruce, 287

Russia
antialcohol campaign in, 215
Cold War and, 218-20
Communist Party of the Russian Federation of, 200
communist route to modernity in, 7
consolidation in, 12, 193-241
democratization in, 3, 16, 279, 280-1, 282, 287
Duma of, 199, 200, 201, 203-5, 207, 210, 221, 223
economy of, 223-5, 231, 285, 286
Federal Assembly of, 199
federalism in, 16, 195-212
Federation Council of, 199, 200, 203, 204, 209
international role of, 223-5
"Land Code" of, 203
Law on the State Enterprise of, 215
longest transition in, 213-25
market reform in, 241
motivation for change in, 216-18
NATO and, 233-4
political dilemmas in, 198-210
private investment in, 15
proportional representation system in, 206
securities of, 224-5
U.S. aid to, 236
voter identification with parties in, 201

Rustow, Dankwart A., on leadership commit-

ment, 26
Rwanda, 250, 254, 256

Salazar, Antónion de Oliviera, 40
Salinas de Gortari, Carlos, as Mexican president, 13, 48, 105, 106, 107, 108, 121
Salvador, military regimes in, 122, 123
Sandel, Michael, 133, 136, 137
Sandinistas, 46
    victory in Nicaragua, 122, 123
Santiago Commitment to Democracy, 126
Sao Tomé and Principe, 250, 254, 256
Sarney, Jose, 79, 85-6, 298(n5)
Schattschneider, E. E., 23
Schmitter, Philippe, 226
Schumpeter, Joseph, democratic system of, 133, 141, 144, 179
Schweller, Randall L., 190
Scotland, asymmetric unions in, 208
Second Development Decade (1970s), 45
second wave of democracy, 7, 22
Secretariat for Strategic Affairs (Brazil), 86
self-interest, in modern commercial democracy, 64
selfishness, perceived as social evil in China, 33, 34
semidemocracies, in Asia, 162, 163, 164, 165, 167
Senegal, 250, 253, 254, 256
Serbia, 229
Serbia-Montenegro, 233
Seychelles, 250, 254, 256
Shagari, Shehu, 249
Sharman, Jason C., 16, 45-6, 162, 280, 282, 293
Shifter, Michael, 60
Shining Path, in Peru, 83
shogun, in early Japan, 32
Siberia, 223
Sierra Leone, 22, 250, 251, 254, 256
Simkins, Charles, 115
Sin, Cardinal, 152, 153, 154
Singapore
Asian democracy in, 163, 166, 176
    authoritarianism in, 134
    developmental patterns in, 14
    economic growth in, 27, 29, 34-5, 185
    economic policies in, 41, 169, 170, 173
    political regime in, 164, 185
Single European Act of 1986, 39
Skoepol, Theda, 7
slavery
    in ancient polis, 63
    in the South, 5, 137
Slovenia, NATO and, 233
Smith, Adam, 6, 67, 183, 238, 284
    on modern commercial society, 64

on religious sects, 64-5
on science, 65
socialism, European collapse of, 122
social networks, importance of, 67-8
Somalia, 250, 254, 256
Soros, George, on free market ideology, 54
Soros Foundation, contributions to Eastern Europe democratization, 239
South Africa, apartheid end in, 28
South America
    democratization in, 279
    institutional legacies in, 73-92
    leadership succession in, 77
    military and democracy in, 73-92
    postauthoritarianism in, 12, 71-129, 248
    transition pathways in, 73-92
South Asia
    economies of, 171, 176
    export dynamism in, 168
    fundamentalist parties in, 282
    modernization in, 162
Southeast Asia
    democracy in, 163
    economies of, 171, 176
    export dynamism in, 168
    political regimes in, 165
Southern Common Market, 42
Southern Cone, military regimes in, 124
Southern Europe, democratization in, 10, 27, 226
Southern Philippines Council for Peace and Development, 157
Southest Asia, modernization in, 162
South Korea
    authoritarianism in, 145, 178
    democratization in, 14, 27, 34, 133-46, 163, 167, 174-5, 178, 183, 191
    economic growth in, 27, 52, 170, 173, 174, 184, 185
    foreign trade in, 35
    industrial policy of, 169
    military coups in, 22
    as newly industrilized country, 134
    political regime in, 164, 167
    student dissident movements in, 60
Soviet Union
    client states of, 8, 9
    collapse of, 22, 24-5, 121, 124, 196, 216, 218, 227, 236, 258
    Cuban relations of, 117, 122
    democratization in, 10, 15, 75, 143
    economy of, 186, 218-23, 300(n4)
    lack of autonomous institutions in, 59
    as post-World War II superpower, 8
    waning support for Cuba, 122
    waning support for Nicaragua, 122

Spain
  asymmetric unions in, 208
  in Common Market, 40
  democratization in, 10, 22, 27, 226, 235
  socialist government of, 45
Sparta, democracy in, 63
Sri Lanka
  civil war in, 163
  democratization in, 176
  economy of, 171, 173
  political regime in, 165, 166
state, prevention of group oppression by, 66
State Law and Order Restoration Council (SLORC), 148
state-society division, in European feudalism, 32
Stepan, Alfred, 80, 229, 246
Stephens, Evelyne H., 144, 145
Stephens, John D., 144, 145
Stewart, Potter, 279
Strange, Susan, 175
Strategic Defense Initiative (SDI), 219, 220
student dissident movements, in South Korea, 60
Sub-Saharan Africa, democracy and economic change in, 16, 61, 266-9
Sudan, 250, 254, 256
  dictatorships in, 247, 249
suicides, attempted, 54
Sukarno, Achmed, 28, 165
Summit of the Americas
  human rights sections of, 128
Working Group on Honesty and Public Ethics of, 129
superpowers
  after World War II, 8
effect on Latin American democratization, 13
Suthorn, ___., 166
Swaziland, 250, 254, 256
Sweden, social democrats in, 44
Switzerlandd, party system in, 248

TACIS (Technical Assistance for the Commonwealth of Independent States), 234
Tadjikistan, 233
Taegu-Kyôngsang (T-K Group), in Republic of Korea, 141, 142 Taiwan
  authoritarianism in, 145, 178
  automobile industry failure in, 174
democratization in, 10, 27, 34, 146, 163, 167, 183, 191
  East Asian System and, 134-5
  economic growth in, 27, 41, 52, 169, 170,

173, 175, 184, 185
  foreign trade in, 35
  as newly industrilized country, 134
  political regime in, 164, 167
  UN and, 189
Tanzania, 250, 254, 256
teachers unions, fiscal favors to, in Latin America, 50
Telephone Workers' Union (STRM), in Mexico, 107
television, effect on U.S. social patterns, 30, 69
Thailand
  authoritarianism in, 178
  Chinese communities in, 167
  democracy in, 163, 175, 178
  economy of, 171
  political regimes in, 165, 167, 282
third wave of democracy, 10-11, 22, 77, 160, 163, 175, 178, 301(n1)
Third World, democratization in, 25
Thucydides, 54
Tiananmen Square Incident (1989), 36, 141, 165
Tocqueville, Alexis de, 30, 63, 64, 135, 137, 145
Togo, 250, 254, 256
tongshan bui, as Chinese benevolent societies, 33-4
trade associations, fiscal favors to, in Latin America, 50
transnational corporations (TNCs), 169, 175
  in Singapore, 169, 170
Treaty of Rome, 39
Truman, David, 23
Truth Commission, of Desmond Tutu, 28
Tupac Amaru revolutionary movement (MRTA), in Peru, 83
Turkey, 282
  military coups in, 22
  in NATO, 233
Tutsi, in Burundi, 251
Tutu, Desmond, Truth Commission of, 28

Uganda, 22, 250, 254, 256, 257, 258
Ukraine, 221, 231, 241
  U.S. aid to, 236
ul-Haq, Zia, 148
UN Economic Commission for Latin America, 44
United Democratic Organization (UNIDO), 152, 155
United Kingdom, party system in, 248
U.S. Constitution, 55, 56
United States
  aid to Eastern Europe, 236
  associations in, 30

democratization and foreign policy of, 11, 55, 275-89
diminishing volunteerism in, 69
effect on democratization in other countries, 13-14, 17, 44, 118, 122-6
Founding Fathers of, 22-3, 28
individualism in, 30
Latin-American foreign policy of, 123
liberalism in, 57
politician checking in, 29
as post-World War II superpower, 8
support of foundations for Latin America in, 125
women's suffrage in, 5
United States Agency for International Development (USAID), 237, 238
UNT, as Mexican union, 112
Uruguay
    authoritarianism in, 117
    civilian-military relations in, 87, 90
    democratization in, 27, 42-3, 74, 80, 92, 118
    economic stagnation in, 43, 47
    military leadership in, 78, 79, 119, 121
    military prerogatives in, 75
    as oligarchial democray, 116
    redemocratization in, 119

Valenzuela, Arturo, 13, 14, 279, 288, 293
van Wolferen, Karel, 134-5, 138, 143
Velázquez, Fidel, 101, 112
Venezuela
democratization in, 124
    liberalization in, 47
    military rule in, 118, 122
Venice Commission, 238
Verba, Sidney, 26, 66-7, 135-6, 138
Vietnam
    economy of, 171
    French colonialism in, 183
    liberalization in, 163
    political regime in, 165
voluntary organizations, Americans in, 137
voting rights, in democracy, 23

Wade, Robert, 41
war, in countries in transition, 36
Warsaw Pact, 285
Washington Protocol, 126
Wasmosy, ___., 126
The Wealth of Nations (Smith), 5
Weber, Max, 138
Weber/Parsonian pattern variables, 136
Weimar Republic, collapse of, 231
The West

democratization in, 32
    new democracies and, 16
Western Europe, democratization in, 11
West Germany
    Common Market and, 39
    democracy in, 239
    social attitudes in, 138
Westminster Foundation for Democracy, 238
Whitehead, Laurence, 239
Wilhelm II, King of Prussia, 180
Williams, Raymond, 136
Wilson, Woodrow, 7, 122, 180
women, as Asian governmental heads, 163
women's organizations, in Africa, 264
women workers, effect on U.S. volunteerism, 69
work hours, effect on U.S. volunteerism, 69
World Bank, 8, 44, 46, 224, 225, 234, 259
world systems theory, 9
World War I, 181
    economic crisis from, 117
World War II, 185, 216, 223, 287
effects on democratization, 6, 7, 22, 38, 117, 148, 183
    two superpowers after, 8

Yabloko, as Russian reformer party, 202
Yannomami Indians (Brazil), imperilment of, 86
Yavlinsky, Grigorii, 202
Yellow Revolution, 153
Yeltsin, Boris, 199, 201, 205-6, 208, 209-10, 220-1, 236, 237, 283
Young, Crawford, 247
Yugoslavia, 196, 227, 232
    PHARE program in, 234
Yusin system, in Korea, 140

zaibatsu structure, of prewar Japanese industry, 40
Zaire, 250, 254, 256, 282
Zambia, 250, 251, 254, 256, 257, 265, 268, 280
    autocrat overthrow in, 247
Zapatistas, in Mexico, 108, 109
Zedillo, Ernesto, as Mexican president, 13, 108, 109-10
Zhirinovsky, Vladimir, 202
Zimbabwe, 250, 251, 254, 256, 2